TERENCE CONRAN'S

DIY

BOOK

With more than 30 original projects

for improving your home

CONRAN OCTOPUS

First published in 1994 by
Conran Octopus Limited
37 Shelton Street
London WC2H 9HN
Reprinted in 1995

Copyright © Conran Octopus Limited 1989, 1991, 1992, 1994, 1995

ISBN 1 85029 572 7

All rights reserved. No part of this book may be reproduced, stored in a retrieval system, or transmitted in any form or by any means, electronic, electrostatic, magnetic tape, mechanical, photocopying, recording or otherwise, without the prior permission in writing of the publisher.

The designs for the projects in this book are copyright © Sir Terence Conran and may be built for personal use only.

The projects in this book were previously published in *Terence Conran's DIY By Design* (1989), *Terence Conran's Garden DIY* (1991) and *Toys and Children's Furniture* (1992).

Consultant Editors JOHN MCGOWAN
and ROGER DUBERN
Project Editors SIMON WILLIS
and JOANNA BRADSHAW

Art Editors HELEN LEWIS
and MERYL LLOYD
Assisted by ALISON BARCLAY
and ALISON SHACKLETON
Visualizer JEAN MORLEY
Illustrator PAUL BRYANT

Production Manager SONYA SIBBONS

Typeset by Servis Filmsetting, Manchester
Printed and bound in Hong Kong

DIMENSIONS
Exact dimensions are given in metric followed by an approximate conversion to imperial. Never mix metric and imperial dimensions when making a calculation or building a project.

SPECIAL NOTE
Before embarking on any of the projects in this book, you must check the law concerning building regulations and planning. It is also important that you obtain specialist advice on plumbing and electricity before attempting any alterations to these services yourself.

Whilst every effort has been made to ensure that the information contained in this book is correct, the publisher cannot be held responsible for any loss, damage or injury caused by reliance upon the accuracy of such information.

In Australia, it is illegal for electrical work to be undertaken by anyone other than a qualified electrician.

SAFETY
On page 254 there is a summary of the most important points relating to DIY safety and the design and construction of toys and children's furniture. It is strongly recommended that you read this summary before making any of the projects in this book.

CONTENTS

INTRODUCTION

There is a growing passion for improving houses and apartments as people young and old, rich and poor, take satisfaction in making their homes comfortable and stylish. People everywhere restore, revamp, repair and revitalize their homes, and in doing so many have discovered the pleasure of doing it themselves.

This book is intended to encouraged the DIY-er to extend his or her carpentry skills and to embrace the talents of the designer. I have selected the best projects from three DIY books I have written over the past few years, and have collected them in this new book. My aim has been to take the simple, practical, everyday things around the house and in the garden – the things for which we most often turn to DIY, such as a set of shelves or a compost bin – and to show how they can be designed and constructed to combine practicality and style. There are also more ambitious projects – such as the Summer House, the Japanese Wardrobe and the Garden Bench – which repay the time and skill invested with finished projects that are a pleasure to look at, will improve the quality of your life and will, provided that they are properly looked after, last you a good many years.

Achieving success in DIY is to do with confidence. Once you have completed a simple project, you will have the enthusiasm and the skills to attempt a more complicated piece. Many of the outdoor projects offer a good starting point, since precision and perfection are not really at home in the garden, where a weathered, rustic appearance can be a positive attribute. Many of the toys and pieces of children's furniture are also simply constructed, and there is no better way to demonstrate your love for your children than by making something especially for them.

I have started the book with a work-bench and tool cupboard. Get these right and they will provide the example and the temptation to encourage you to continue the good work elsewhere around your home. The greatest pleasure, for me, of DIY is the satisfaction of making something that has been tailored to suit your own needs and priorities. What you make will often be better designed and cheaper than the shop-bought equivalent; just as importantly, it will reflect your own taste and sense of style, and – with a little imagination and ingenuity – will respond exactly to your own requirements.

Terence Conran.

INDOORS

By designing and building your own fittings and fixtures, you will derive deeper satisfaction than any off-the-peg products can ever give. The final result will be tailored exactly to your own requirements in terms of style and practicality.

You can use your DIY skills to improve the character of any or all of the rooms in your home. In the kitchen – whether you are starting from scratch, improving an existing one or merely adding a wooden knife rack – building it yourself adds a personal quality and the sure knowledge that fittings are well designed and well built. In the bedroom, DIY allows you the opportunity to create clothes storage that exactly fits your space. You can make the room more comfortable and practical by making your own built-in wardrobe or by building the bed project, which itself incorporates ample storage space.

Home improvements can enhance the personality of a room dramatically by restoring existing features or introducing character by adding architraves, mouldings and other architectural devices. Shelves in living rooms are normally used for display and exert a strong influence on the overall look. Using DIY, shelves can be custom-built to suit the room and your possessions. While you're at it, wooden floors can be made good by stripping and waxing, staining or painting. With specially designed fittings and furniture a room can be transformed, so that it is in harmony with your own decoration and fulfills the functions you specifically require.

WORKBENCH AND TOOL CUPBOARD

This is the starting point for all serious DIY enthusiasts. If you make this well it will lead you to undertake many other projects around the home. You will also have a solid bench to work on and practical, safe storage for your tools – two ingredients that will make your DIY enjoyable, comfortable and efficient.

The workbench should be made first. For simplicity, I have used a ply-skinned fire door with a solid timber core; this is just as tough as the conventional solid beech top used for most professional benches, but is much cheaper. The frame is made from pine, and houses a plywood shelf for large pieces of equipment. A woodworker's vice and retractable stop for planing have been fitted to the bench.

The tool cupboard is fitted to the wall with bevelled battens and its two wings, which double as doors, are fitted with locks and fold back against the wall when the cupboard is in use. It is essential to incorporate lockable doors on a tool cupboard, especially in a household such as mine, where tools vanish with unfailing regularity. All your tools, fittings, nails and screws have their own storage area and are easily visible, so there is no excuse not to return them to their rightful place when your work is finished; searching around for missing tools never fails to upset the enjoyment of DIY work.

Work lamps are clamped to the top of the cupboard to provide sufficient light where it is most needed, and the gap behind the cupboard allows wiring to be installed for electrical sockets.

Several coats of clear, shiny varnish were applied to the cupboard to give it a thoroughly professional look. Enjoy it and use it well.

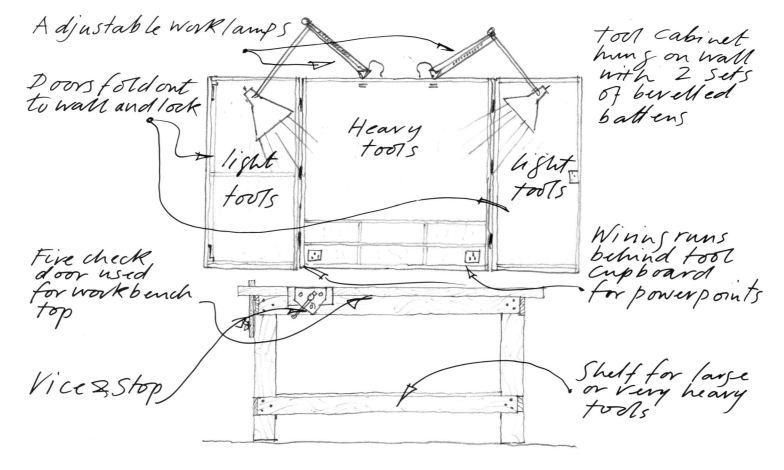

Adjustable work lamps

Doors fold out to wall and lock

light tools

Heavy tools

light tools

tool cabinet hung on wall with 2 sets of bevelled battens

Fire check door used for workbench top

Wiring runs behind tool cupboard for powerpoints

Vice & stop

Shelf for large or very heavy tools

WORKBENCH

A sturdy woodworking bench helps you to achieve good results, and constructing your own will provide valuable woodworking experience.

For neatness and a solid construction, the top and bottom rails are rebated into the bench legs. To speed up and simplify the job, you could omit the rebates and simply glue and screw the rails to the sides of the legs with a PVA adhesive.

The top of the workbench is a solid-core, fire-check flush door blank measuring 1980 × 610mm (6ft 6in × 24in). The top should overhang the frame – by 100mm (4in) at each end, by 12mm ($\frac{1}{2}$in) at the back and by at least 25mm (1in) at the front. The overhang allows enough space for G-cramps to hold items to the bench top. The overall height of the bench is 940mm (37in), which is a comfortable working height for a person about 1.8m (6ft) tall. Decide at an early stage what is a comfortable working height for you, and adjust the leg lengths accordingly.

The rail lengths are dependent on the size of the door blank used, to give the overhangs mentioned above. Whether or not you rebate the rails into the legs will also affect the length of the rails. The long rails fit inside the shorter end ones. If you rebate the rails, note that the top rails are thicker than the bottom ones. So the top rails will be shorter than the bottom rail lengths by the difference in thickness between the two rails.

MATERIALS

Part	Quantity	Material	Length
LEGS	4	150 × 150mm (6 × 6in) PAR softwood	902mm (35$\frac{1}{2}$in)
TOP RAILS	2 long 2 short	133 × 32mm (5$\frac{1}{4}$ × 1$\frac{1}{4}$in) PAR softwood	to suit door size
BOTTOM RAILS	2 long 2 short	150 × 25mm (6 × 1in) PAR softwood cut down to 133 mm (5$\frac{1}{4}$in) wide for neatness to match top rails	to suit door size
BENCH TOP	1	solid core, fire-check flush door blank	1980 × 610mm (6ft 6in × 24in)
BENCH TOP BATTENS	2	50 × 38mm (2 × 1$\frac{1}{2}$in) PAR softwood	length of the sides between the legs
SHELF	1	12mm ($\frac{1}{2}$in) plywood	as above
BENCH VICE	1		
HANGING BARS	2	25mm (1in) dowel	to suit bench width

TOOLS

FOLDING PORTABLE WORKBENCH/VICE

TRIMMING KNIFE

STEEL RULE

TRY SQUARE

PANEL SAW

TENON SAW

CHISEL about 19mm ($\frac{3}{4}$in) wide bevel-edge type

CHISEL about 25mm (1in) wide firmer type

MALLET

DRILL (hand or power)

TWIST DRILL BITS

COUNTERSINK BIT

MARKING GAUGE

WEBBING CRAMP (or rope and scrap of wood to make tourniquet)

SCREWDRIVER (cross-point or slotted, depending on screw type)

SMOOTHING PLANE

SANDING BLOCK and ABRASIVE PAPER

ROUTER (an alternative to a chisel for cutting rail rebates)

POWER JIGSAW (or padsaw or coping saw) – to make cut-out for vice

SPANNER to fit coach screws used to fix vice

FLAT DRILL BIT to make cut-out for bench stop, and holes for hanging bars

TWIST DRILL BIT to make holes for bench-stop bolt

MARKING OUT THE LEGS

Mark the legs to length, squaring the cutting line on all faces, and then cut the legs. Check they are of identical length by standing them together and comparing their height.

If the rails are to be rebated into the legs, mark out the rebates (see **Techniques, page 238**).

MARKING-UP FOR TOP RAIL

Line up one of the short rails flush with the top of the leg to mark off the depth of the rebate. Line up a try square underneath to mark off the line squarely. Score a line on to the leg with a trimming knife. Mark all four faces of the leg (see **Techniques, page 238**).

1 **Marking and Making the Leg Rebates for Rails**
Left **Mark rebates for the top and bottom rails.** *Centre* **Cut top rebates with a tenon saw; bottom rebates with a tenon saw and chisel.** *Right* **The leg rail after rebating has been done.**

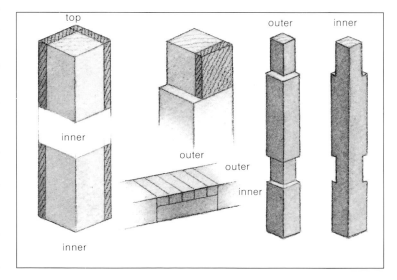

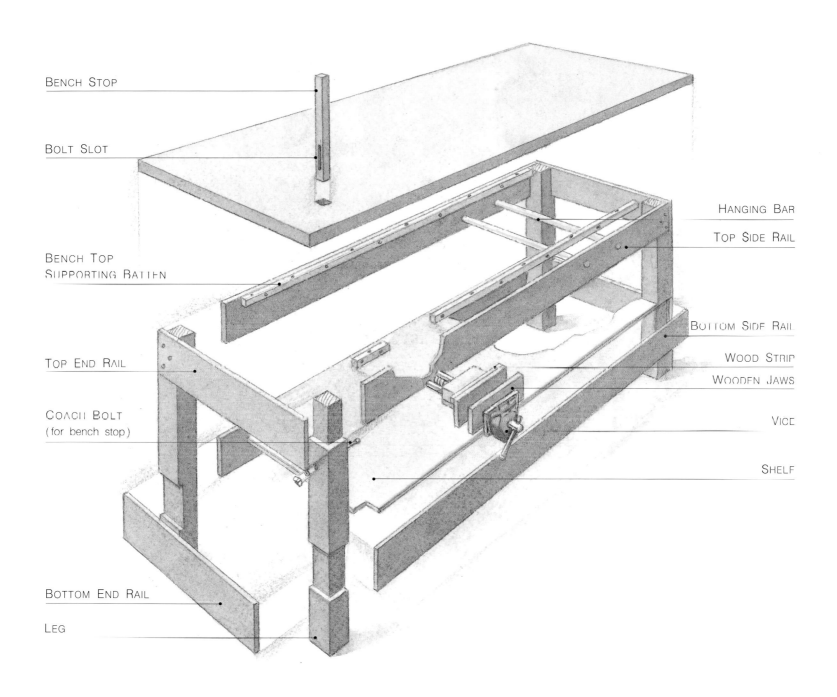

BENCH STOP

BOLT SLOT

BENCH TOP
SUPPORTING BATTEN

TOP END RAIL

COACH BOLT
(for bench stop)

BOTTOM END RAIL

LEG

HANGING BAR

TOP SIDE RAIL

BOTTOM SIDE RAIL

WOOD STRIP

WOODEN JAWS

VICE

SHELF

WORKBENCH

Set the marking gauge to the thickness of the top rail and mark this off on to the top, inner and outer faces of the leg, as shown (fig 1, page 12). Repeat the whole procedure for the other three legs.

MARKING-UP LEG FOR BOTTOM RAIL

For the top of this rail to finish 350mm (14in) from the ground, measure this distance up the leg and mark with a pencil. Put the rail in place underneath and line up your try square underneath. Remove the rail and score a line with a trimming knife for the position of the bottom of the rail. Replace the rail against the try square, then move the square to the top of the rail. Remove the rail again and score a line with a trimming knife for the position of the top of the rail. Lining up in this way ensures greater accuracy. Continue lines round to the other three faces.

Re-set the marking gauge to the thickness of the lower rail and mark this thickness off on to the inner and outer faces of the legs as shown (see fig 1, page 12).

CUTTING FOR TOP RAIL

Hold the leg in a portable workbench or cramp it to a solid table or trestle and, cutting on the waste side of the line, make the horizontal cuts first, using a tenon saw to the marked depths. Then make the vertical cuts, using a tenon or panel saw, on both the outer faces. Remove any waste with a chisel. Alternatively, use a router, with the depth set to the thickness of the rails.

Repeat this procedure for the other three legs.

CUTTING OUT FOR BOTTOM RAIL

Make horizontal cuts with a tenon saw on the outer faces of one leg at the top and bottom of the rail position, to your marked depths. To cut out the rebate, make a series of cuts with a tenon saw down to the marked depths, about 12mm ($\frac{1}{2}$in) apart; then pare out the waste with a bevel-edge chisel and a mallet *(see* **Techniques, page 238** *)*.

Repeat for the other three legs until the surface is flat.

END FRAME ASSEMBLY

The rails must fit tightly. If necessary, make the rebates so that they are fractionally undersize and plane down the rails slightly until they fit tightly in the rebates.

Apply glue to the leg rebates and position the bottom rail, so that it is flush with the sides. Drill and countersink through the rail into the legs and screw them together with 50mm (2in) No 10 screws – three on each leg. Repeat at the top for the top rail, gluing and screwing as before, using 65mm ($2\frac{1}{2}$in) No 10 screws.

Repeat the whole procedure for the second end frame. If you want to simplify construction by not using rebates, simply glue and screw the rails to the face of the legs. However, make sure that the frames are assembled square, and that the rails overhang the legs by the thickness of the rail.

Clean up, plane, and chamfer all the outer edges, then remove any excess glue and sand down all the surfaces for a smooth finish.

ADDING THE LONG RAILS

Stand the two end frames upright and fit the bottom long rails in place, gluing the leg rebates as before. Remember that the tighter the legs fit, the stronger the frame will be. For a sturdy frame, the shoulders must be pulled up tightly before screwing them together. To do this, use either a webbing cramp or a rope tourniquet around the frame at the joints. If using rope, loop a thin piece of wood in the rope each side and twist the wood round and round to make the frame secure.

Glue and fit the top rails and then tighten them together with a cramp or a rope tourniquet.

Pilot-drill and screw through the rails into the legs in three places, as for the end frames. Once the rails have been screwed, the cramp can be removed.

Clean up, and chamfer the top and bottom edges of the bottom rails and the bottom edges of the top rails. Sand down the framework and plane the top of the framework and the top rail flush.

1 Assembling the Workbench End Frame
Lay the legs on a flat surface and check that bottom rail fits tightly into the rebate. Glue and screw in place. Fit the top rail in a similar way then repeat for the legs at the other end.

2 Adding the Side Rails and Supporting Battens
Glue and nail the bottom side rails into the leg rebates first, then repeat for the top rails. In each case hold the frame tightly together with a rope tourniquet to keep it square. *Inset* Corner detail.

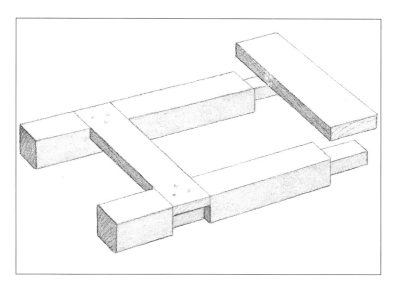

FITTING THE BENCH TOP

Take two battens of 50 × 38mm (2 × 1½in) PAR, cut to the length of the sides between the legs. Drill and countersink the battens on two adjacent faces for screws to fix to the side and top (ours had five along the side and six along the top). Choose the best side of the frame as the front. Then, at the back, cramp one of the battens in place to the inside of the frame, flush with the top of the top rail, and screw through the side into the rail. The front batten will be fixed after fitting the vice.

Put the top in place, equalizing the overhang each end and allowing 12mm (½in) overhang at the back, and the remainder at the front (enough to take a cramp). Do not screw the top down yet.

FITTING A VICE

You will need a vice that fits into the top rail. There is a wide range of woodworking vices to choose from. All have wide-opening jaws and are designed to fit to the underside of the bench top, on the front edge close to a leg, so that the top edge of the jaws (after the lining has been fitted – see below) is level with the bench top. Some smaller vices simply cramp on to the underside of the workbench, but it is best to use one that is designed to be bolted in place. A square body seating will ensure easy fitting to the bench top.

Choose the largest vice you can afford – a jaw opening of about 330m (13in) is ideal, but maximum openings range from 115mm (4½in) up to about 380mm (15in). The larger vices often have a useful quick-release mechanism which allows you to pull the jaw out and in without having to wind the handle as normal. Make sure that the body of the vice and the sliding jaw have holes to take the plywood liners which protect the work, the vice and the working tools.

The method of fitting varies slightly according to the make of vice chosen, but this is how we fitted ours. Remember that the top of the steel jaws must finish a little way down from the worktop, say 12mm (½in), to allow for a wooden strip, which is part of the jaw liners, to be fitted easily.

Measure the depth of the vice. Subtract from this the thickness of the worktop, minus 12mm (½in) (see fig 3). You will need a packing piece of the same thickness to go under the bench top and to fit between it and the vice.

MAKING THE CUT-OUT FOR THE VICE IN THE SIDE RAIL

You will first need to make a template of the vice. Put the vice on end with its packing piece in place, and draw round it on to a piece of thick paper or card. Simplify the lines to make cutting the side rail easier. Cut out the template and hold it to the underside of the bench top, about 300mm (12in) in from the front left hand for a right-handed person (or from the right for a left-handed

person), and draw round the cut-out on to the top rail.

To make the cut-out, remove the bench top, and cut round the line with a power jigsaw or by hand with a padsaw or coping saw.

Cramp the second bench-top supporting batten in place to the front top rail as before (see **Fitting the Bench Top, left**) and screw it in place, cutting out the section where the gap has been left for the vice with a padsaw or a coping saw. Glue and screw the bench top back in place through the battens.

Slide the vice into position, with the packing piece in place. Drill pilot holes up through the fixing holes in the bottom of the vice, through the packing piece, and into the worktop. Fix the vice securely in place using coach screws and washers.

MAKING THE WOODEN JAW LINERS

The liners are wooden pieces fitted inside the jaws of the vice so as to finish flush with the top of the bench. They serve to protect work while it is being held in the vice.

From 12mm (½in) plywood, cut two pieces slightly longer than the steel jaws of the vice. The width of the plywood should equal the distance between the top of the bench and the runner of the vice.

Cut a piece of scrap hardwood to the same thickness as the distance between the top of the steel jaws and the top of the worktop, and to the same length as that of the wooden jaw liners. Glue in place to the front edge of the bench, flush with the worktop, so that it rests on the vice.

FITTING THE REAR WOODEN JAW

Mark through the holes in the front of the vice on to one of the wooden jaw liners. Transfer the marks to the other liner. Drill and countersink the liners at these marks and screw through these holes and the holes in the back into the worktop.

FITTING THE FRONT WOODEN JAW

Close the vice with the front wooden jaw cramped in place, and screw through the front holes into the jaw.

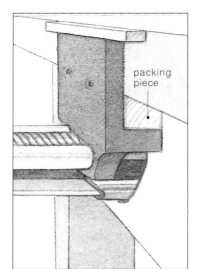

③ Fitting the Bench Vice
Thickness of packing piece is depth of vice, less thickness of worktop minus the wooden strip.

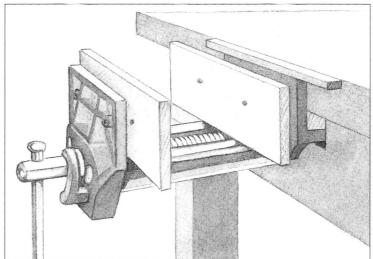

④ Fitting the Wooden Jaw Liners to the Vice
Jaw liners (made from 12mm [½in] plywood) finish flush with the bench top. The rear jaw liner is fixed by screwing it into worktop. Screw through the front of the vice to fix the front liner.

WORKBENCH

THE BENCH STOP

A bench stop which can be raised above the bench top when required is useful, for example, for pushing against while large pieces of work are planed or chiselled.

The bench stop fits just outside the front leg at the vice end. To mark the position of the bench stop on the bench top, square round from the outer edge of the leg using a pencil and try square. The line should be continued from the underneath, up the front edge, and on to the top of the workbench. Measure back from the front edge to coincide with the leg. Square off the line from the side.

Take a piece of hardwood batten about 25 × 38mm (1 × 1½in) and cut to about 250–300mm (10–12in) long. Mark round the end of the batten in position behind the pencil marks on the worktop as shown: that is, to the *outside* of them. Check that the lines will allow the bench stop to fit alongside the leg. Go over the pencil marks with a trimming knife.

Using a flat drill bit as near as possible in size to the bench-top cut-out, drill right through the worktop. Cramp a piece of packing underneath the hole, so that you can then pare out the edges down on to the packing, to avoid breaking the wood underneath. Take care to pare out fractionally *within* the line. Check occasionally with a try square that you are cutting down square. Keep paring out until the batten slots into the hole and can be moved up and down, but stop while the fit is still fairly tight.

TO FIX THE BENCH STOP

We used a 150mm (6in) long, 9.5mm (⅜in) diameter coach bolt with a washer and a butterfly nut. Mark where the bolt is to be on the leg. (This must be far enough down to clear the top rail.) Fit the stop in place flush with the top. Transfer the bolt mark on to the bench stop – this will be the top of the slot. Move the stop up to the highest position required, that is, about 75–100mm (3–4in), and mark off the bolt position for the bottom of the slot.

Take the bench stop out. Mark off the centre line and drill a line of holes 9.5mm (⅜in) in diameter along the length of the slot, with a packing piece held underneath. Pare out the slot with a chisel until the bolt slides freely inside. Alternatively, use a router to make the slot.

At the marked line on the leg, mark a vertical line in the exact centre of the bench-stop position, to make sure that the bolt fits in the middle of it. Use a 9.5mm (⅜in) drill bit to drill right through the leg at this point. Slide the stop into place and push the bolt through from the inside of the leg and through the slot. Fix the screw in place with a washer and a butterfly nut.

FITTING THE SHELF

Measure the outside dimensions of the frame and cut a piece of 12mm (½in) thick plywood to this size. Make notches in each corner for the legs by measuring and cutting with a power jigsaw or a panel saw. Clean up and chamfer the top edges of the shelf and then slot it in place on the bottom rails.

FITTING THE HANGING BARS

These hanging bars are fitted beween the long rails at the opposite end to the vice, and are very useful for hooking things on, such as G-cramps, a dustpan and brush, a paint kettle and other essential items that you may need to hand.

Cut two lengths of 25mm (1in) dowel to the width of the underframe, plus a little extra for planing off afterwards. Mark dowel positions about 300mm (12in) and 600mm (24in) in from each of the rail ends, in the centre of both the back and front top rails of the bench.

Using a flat drill bit of the same diameter as the dowel, drill holes at the marks, through the rails, back and front. Put dowels through the holes, hammering them in after smearing the ends with PVA glue. Plane off the ends flush with the rails for a smooth and neat finish.

THE VICE AND BENCH STOP
Often the vice can be used in conjunction with the stop to hold large items.

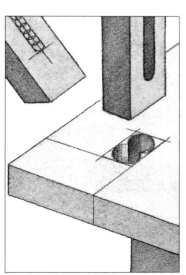

①　Fitting the Bench Stop
Enlarge the line of holes in the stop to form a slot. Slot in bench is formed in the same way.

Tool Cupboard

It is important to store tools in a safe and secure place where they are also readily accessible when required. Properly stored tools stay sharp and rust-free, and with each tool in its correct place you will not waste time looking for tools.

This cupboard provides an ideal place to store tools. It is fixed on to the wall of the workshop or garage where you would normally do DIY. When the cupboard is in use, the doors open out flat to the wall on each side for easy access to the tools. You can fit it out to suit your requirements and to leave space for new tools as you buy them.

The rack incorporates sockets for power tools, and adjustable lamps to give excellent illumination of the worksurface below. When not in use, the lamps can be pushed out of the way, and the doors closed. For safety, the cupboard is permanently screwed to the wall through bevelled battens and the doors have a lock for security and to keep the tools out of the way of children.

Main Cupboard Section

Cut the back panel by sawing the full sheet of 12mm ($\frac{1}{2}$in) plywood in half to form a 1220 × 1220mm (48 × 48in) sheet. Use a circular saw (or panel saw), running the sole plate of the saw against a straight batten cramped to the surface of the plywood sheet to ensure a straight cut (see **Techniques, page 237**).

Measure the exact length of the back panel and cut two pieces of 100 × 25mm (4 × 1in) timber to this length to form the side rails. Glue and screw these rails edge-on to the back panel with screws about every 230mm (9in), through from the back. Use 25mm (1in) No 8 screws.

Cut two pieces of 100 × 25mm (4 × 1in) timber about 1220mm (48in) long for the top and bottom rails. Offer up the pieces and mark off the internal lengths. Cut them squarely to fit between the side rails. Glue and screw these pieces in place on to the back panel, as for the side rails. Using 50mm (2in) No 8 screws, fix the sides to the top and bottom rails by inserting two screws into each corner joint.

Finish by removing excess glue and planing any protruding edges. Sand smooth.

Door Sections

The door front panels are formed by cutting the remaining 1220 × 1220mm (48in × 48in) wood panel in half in order to form two 610 × 1220mm (24 × 48in) panels.

Cut two pieces of 75 × 25mm (3 × 1in) timber to length for the side rails. Glue and screw these in place as for the main cupboard section.

Again using 75 × 25mm (3 × 1in) timber, measure for the top and bottom rails as above, and glue in place between the side rails, screwing through the door front. Insert two screws in each corner to secure the sides to the top and bottom.

Fitting Out the Inside

The inside of the tool cupboard can be fitted out to your individual requirements. However, for safety, heavy equipment *must* be in the main cupboard, while light things are best stored in the doors.

Materials

Part	Quantity	Material	Length*
SIDE RAILS	2	100 × 25mm (4 × 1in) PAR timber	1220mm (48in)
TOP & BOTTOM RAILS	2	100 × 25mm (4 × 1in) PAR timber	1220mm (48in)
CUPBOARD SHELVES	3	100 × 25mm (4 × 1in) PAR timber	1220mm (48in)
MOUNTING BATTENS	2	100 × 25mm (4 × 1in) PAR timber	1220mm (48in)
SHELF DIVIDERS	4	100 × 25mm (4 × 1in) PAR timber	100mm (4in)
DOOR SIDE RAILS	4	75 × 25mm (3 × 1in) PAR timber	1220mm (48in)
DOOR TOP & BOTTOM RAILS	4	75 × 25mm (3 × 1in) PAR timber	610mm (24in)
BOLT MOUNTING BATTEN	1	75 × 25mm (3 × 1in) PAR timber	1220mm (48in)
SLOTTED SHELVES	2	75 × 25mm (3 × 1in) PAR timber	610mm (24in)
SHELF EDGING STRIPS	3	12 × 12mm ($\frac{1}{2}$ × $\frac{1}{2}$in) PAR timber	1220mm (48in)
CHISEL MOUNTING SLOTS	1	50 × 50mm (2 × 2in) PAR timber	1220mm (48in)

From 1 sheet of 12mm ($\frac{1}{2}$in) plywood 2.44 × 1.22m (8 × 4ft)			
BACK PANEL	1		1220 × 1220mm (48 × 48in)
DOOR PANELS	2		610 × 1220mm (24 × 48in)

Also required: offcuts of planed timber and plywood to make tool-mounting blocks

*Approximate lengths only

Tools

STEEL RULE

TRIMMING KNIFE

TRY SQUARE

CIRCULAR SAW (or panel saw or power jigsaw)

TWO G-CRAMPS

SCREWDRIVER (cross point or slotted, depending on type of screws being used)

SMOOTHING PLANE

SANDING BLOCK and ABRASIVE PAPER

DRILL (hand or power)

TWIST DRILL BIT

MASONRY DRILL BIT

FLAT BIT

COUNTERSINK BIT

COPING SAW or POWER JIGSAW to cut blocks, to fit tool handles

TENON SAW

Tool Cupboard

The other safety note concerns electrical sockets. If you put these in as we have, they will be at a convenient working height and the cables serving them can be run neatly in conduit in the gap created behind the cupboard by the bevelled battens on which it is mounted. It is most important to ensure that the cupboard is screwed firmly to the wall, and to keep a note of the positions of the cable runs if you drill the back panel to mount tools in the future. The same caution must be applied to the wiring of lamps if these are fixed to the top of the cupboard.

Shelves for the Main Cupboard

Cut these from 100 × 25mm (4 × 1in) timber to the same length as the top and bottom rails. Work out the position of the shelves by laying the cupboard down and trying the equipment in place.

When the shelves are correctly positioned, mark the centre line on to the sides, and continue the line on to the back to give a line for the screw positions. Glue the shelves in place and screw through from the back and through the sides.

Decide, according to your requirements, how you want to partition the shelves. For the dividing pieces, measure up and cut them to size from the same size of timber as for the shelves. Put the dividers in place and mark round them on the inside of the cupboard. Take the dividers away, and drill through the back panel from the front so that you can see where to screw from the back. Replace the dividers, countersink the fixing holes in the back panel, and then screw through from the back.

Pin 12 × 12mm ($\frac{1}{2}$ × $\frac{1}{2}$in) battens in place at the front of the shelves to prevent things from falling off. Fit small strips across the shelves where planes will be positioned so that the plane blades do not rest on them and get damaged.

Mounting Tools

Some tools, such as power drills and mallets, can be mounted on solid blocks of wood.

Roughly draw round the shape of the handle on to a piece of thick paper, and cut wood to this shape with a jigsaw or coping saw.

To fit the handles in place, screw through from the back using the method for fitting shelf dividers.

For the chisel slots use a piece of 50 × 50mm (2 × 2in) timber with a row of holes drilled to a diameter smaller than the chisel handles.

Using a flat bit, drill a row of holes through the middle of the block. With a tenon saw, cut slots in the front as shown to allow the chisel blade to turn in through the slot.

Various spring clips and hooks can be used to hold other tools.

Shelves for the Doors

These shelves have slots cut in them to a variety of sizes, providing a useful way to store screwdrivers, marking gauges, and other tools that are longer than they are wide.

Drill holes in the middle of the shelves and cut through them from the front to form slots in the same way as for the chisels. Fit the shelves as for the main cupboard.

Try squares are held in place by pieces of 75 × 25mm (3 × 1in) timber rebated with a tenon saw.

Fitting the Tool Mounts

An advantage of this tool cupboard is its versatility. You can fit it out to suit your precise requirements, but leave enough space for more tools to be added later.

1 Forming the Chisel Slots
Holes are drilled in 50 × 50mm (2 × 2in) timber with chamfered edge, and slots are cut out.

2 Making a Saw Holder
A block of wood shaped to fit inside a saw handle is fitted with a turnbuckle made from plywood.

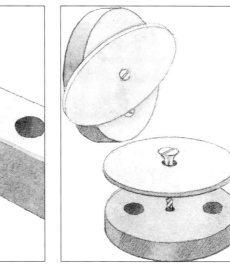

3 Fitting the Door Hinges
Doors carry a lot of weight so hinges must be substantial and secured with long screws.

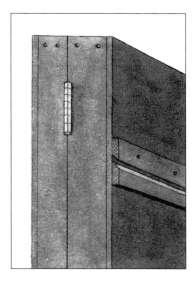

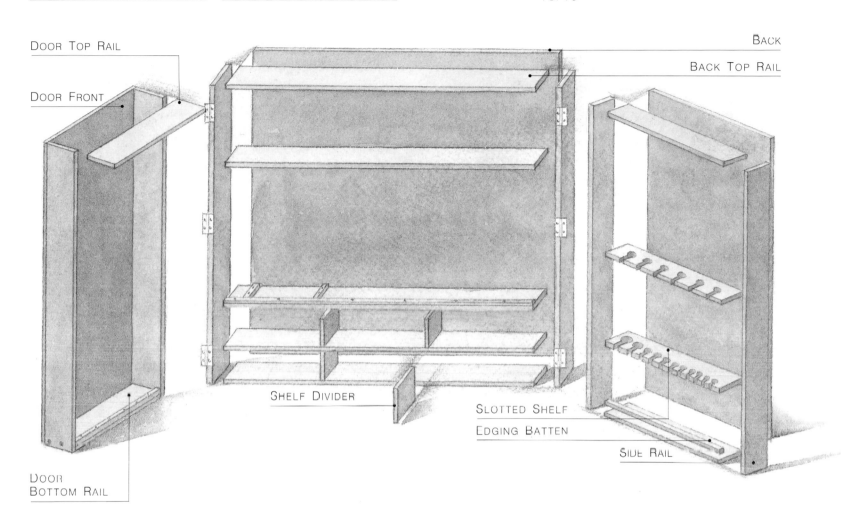

DOOR TOP RAIL

DOOR FRONT

DOOR BOTTOM RAIL

BACK

BACK TOP RAIL

SHELF DIVIDER

SLOTTED SHELF

EDGING BATTEN

SIDE RAIL

TOOL CUPBOARD ASSEMBLY

MOUNTING SAWS

Tools with open handles, such as saws, can be mounted on shaped blocks of wood fitted with turn-buckles that fit inside the handles.

Use a piece of wood slightly thicker than the handle and draw round the inner shape of the handle on to this wood. Cut out the wood to this shape with a jigsaw or coping saw and then cut a piece of 6mm ($\frac{1}{4}$ in) plywood or MDF.

Screw the block to the door with two screws. Screw the turn-buckle to the block with one central screw which is secure but will allow the turn-buckle to turn.

Screw hooks can be placed as necessary in the front doors.

HANGING THE DOORS

Hang the doors on the main cupboard using three butt hinges for each (see **Techniques, page 247**).

The left-hand door is secured with two swan-neck bolts which fit into catch plates fitted to the bottom rail and to the underside of the top shelf (the top rail is not easy to reach). To make it possible to fit the bolts, screw a strip of 75 × 25mm (3 × 1in) timber to the inside edge of the door's side rail. Fit a cupboard lock (see **Techniques, page 250**) and door handles as required.

FIXING TO THE WALL

For security, the cupboard is hung on bevelled battens (see **Techniques, page 241**). Cut two lengths of 100 × 25mm (4 × 1in) timber to the width of the cupboard. To bevel the battens, cut each piece lengthwise through half of its thickness with the saw blade angled at 45°. Screw the top batten to cupboard back; lower part to the wall.

Screw the top-section battens to the back of the cupboard about 180mm (7in) down from the top, and about 250mm (10in) up from the bottom, using about seven 38mm (1½in) No 10 screws in each.

Put the lower-section battens in place under the top-section battens and measure down from the top to the bottom edge of the lower batten. Decide where the cupboard is to sit on the wall, then measure this distance down and fix the lower batten to the wall at this height with 65mm (2½in) No 10 screws and wallplugs.

Measure down and fix the upper batten in the same way, or sit the cupboard on the first batten and mark the wall for the other batten.

Secure the cupboard firmly to the wall by screwing through the back into the lower-section battens. This is most important if electrical sockets are to be fitted inside the cupboard.

THE KITCHEN SYSTEM

The problem faced by many people when trying to install a fitted kitchen is that most walls are out of true and uneven, and are often not at right angles to the floor. The entire procedure of fitting your immaculate factory-made cupboards can easily become a nightmare, which is made worse when walls are covered with pipes and electrical wiring.

This system is designed to make the installation and scribing of kitchen fittings as simple as possible; it allows existing pipework to run behind the fittings and, most importantly, allows you to decide for yourself what sort of finish is most suited to your personal style.

This is a kitchen system that enables you to plan your space in the best possible way, allowing you to put all your cooking equipment on display or, if you prefer, shut away behind closed doors. You can fit in gleaming new modern equipment, or use existing cookers and fridges. The dimensions are flexible and the permutations are innumerable.

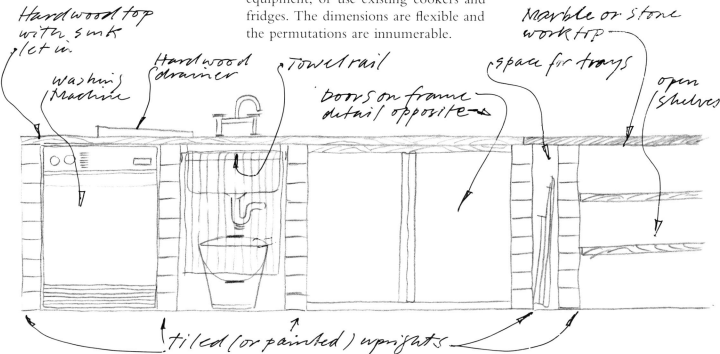

Hardwood top with sink let in.

washing machine

Hardwood drainer

Towel rail

Doors on frame detail opposite →

Marble or stone worktop

space for trays

open shelves

tiled (or painted) uprights

FRONT
ELEVATION

High level oven or Microwave with refrigerator below built into floor-to-ceiling partition

open shelves

open shelves

Cook top recessed into work surface

drawer

doors detail below

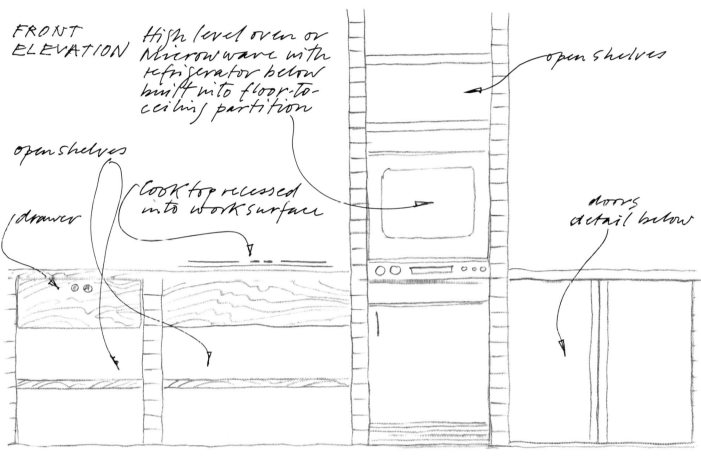

SECTION Thro'
Kitchen partition
Softwood frame
Skinned with plywood

and tiled

module of Tile

door frame fits tightly between floor & underside of work top, and between partitions

use Kitchen door hinges & magnetic catches.

door handles made from grooved hardwood dowels

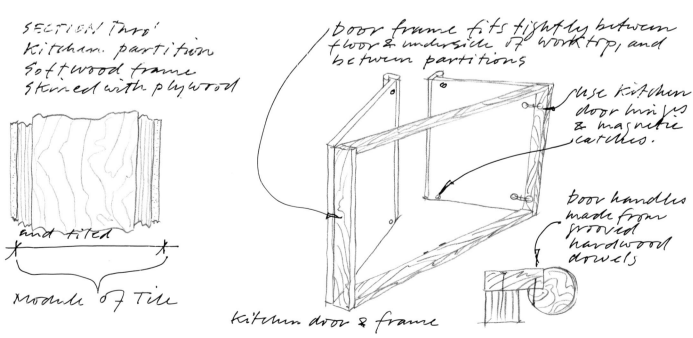

kitchen door & frame

PAINTED KITCHEN

THE KITCHEN SYSTEM: PAINTED KITCHEN

In this rustic kitchen, the basic partition units have been painted rather than tiled. Open shelves have been incorporated in between the partitions and a rail for storing hanging towels and tea-cloths has been built-in under the sink. A wood-lipped tiled worktop lies over the partition units and provides a workspace that is both practical and easy to clean.

To complete the country atmosphere, traditional slatted shelves, a hanging bar for kitchen utensils, and a knife rack have been mounted on the wall. These provide extra storage, are easy to construct, and make stylish additions to the basic kitchen system.

LAUNDRY ROOM

Using essentially the same basic system as the kitchen, the sturdy uprights of the laundry unit support a traditional deep-glazed ceramic Belfast sink which is set beneath a solid maple 'butcher block' worktop. A washing machine and tumble dryer can be placed on floor plinths and are housed on either side of the sink, underneath the worktop, to give a neat, symmetrical appearance.

A slatted shelf is built-in under the sink and between the two partition units to provide storage for washing powder and other essential cleaning materials. Below the shelf there is room for a large laundry basket to store dirty clothes.

A clothes horse on a pulley can be built and positioned over the unit for airing clothes, sheets and large items such as duvets. With a laundry like this, doing the washing could almost become a pleasure.

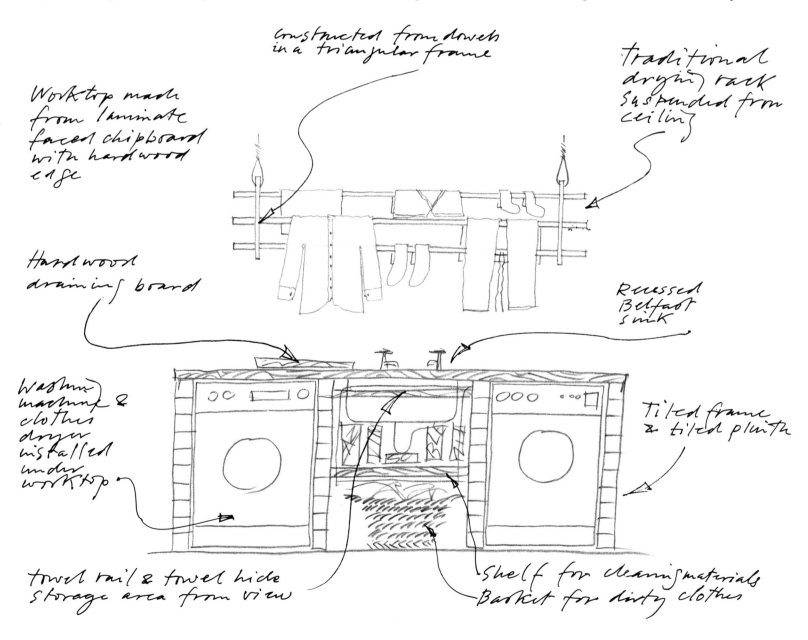

constructed from dowels in a triangular frame

traditional drying rack suspended from ceiling

Worktop made from laminate faced chipboard with hardwood edge

Hardwood draining board

Recessed Belfast sink

Washing machine & clothes dryer installed under worktop

Tiled frame & tiled plinth

towel rail & towel hide storage area from view

Shelf for cleaning materials
Basket for dirty clothes

The Kitchen System

The basic element of this kitchen is the upright partition, which is tiled. Alternatively, it could be painted, clad in tongued, grooved and V-jointed timber, or covered with melamine laminate.

The width of the partition units is adjusted to match the width of the tiles being used so that they exactly cover the edges of the tiles that are fixed to the side panels. The spacing between the partitions is adjusted to suit the width of the appliances, shelves and cupboards to be fitted. A worktop covers the tops of the panels, and overhangs them by 20mm ($\frac{3}{4}$in). As the overall width of the worktop affects the front-to-back depth of the partition panels, it is important to decide on the worktop depth right at the beginning (see **Worktops, page 36**).

The upright partition units are assembled, clad (skinned), tiled, grouted and battened ready for fixing the shelves, before the partitions are fitted in place.

Base Units

When building base units of a critical thickness, you may find it difficult to obtain wood of exactly the required thickness. In this case, buy wood that is slightly oversized and plane it to the correct thickness.

Height You may have to modify slightly the height of the panels to suit the tiles you are using and the equipment to be fitted into the kitchen. The working height used in this project is 930mm (36$\frac{1}{2}$in), which allows for a worktop thickness of 40mm (1$\frac{1}{2}$in), while the overall height of the basic element − the upright partition panel − is 890mm (35in). This height is based on using whole tiles to cover the partition panel (eight tiles high).

Depth The front-to-back depth of the partition panel is 630mm (24$\frac{3}{4}$in), which allows a worktop of 650mm

(25$\frac{1}{2}$in) in depth to overlap the panel by 20mm ($\frac{3}{4}$in). If you buy a standard 600mm (23$\frac{1}{2}$in) deep worktop you should reduce the partition panel depth to 580mm (22$\frac{3}{4}$in).

At the back of the panel, the rear stud is inset by 50mm (2in) to allow for scribing, if required, for pipe and conduit runs. This space can also be used to provide ventilation for cookers and refrigerators. Gas appliances must have a separate flue. Allowance has been made in the design for a back panel and/or a door to be fitted, if required.

Spacing You can adjust the spacing between partition panels to suit appliances, your preferences for cupboard widths, and so on. Our panels are 600mm (23$\frac{1}{2}$in) apart.

Shelves The design allows for the top shelf to rest one tile's depth down from the top of the partition panel to line up with the tiled fascias. When the hardwood lipping is added to the shelf, it finishes flush with the front edge of the partition.

Intermediate shelves also line up with the fascia tiles, but are set half-a-tile in from the front edge. This looks neat and allows doors to be fitted on the front if desired. (The top shelf is not fitted in this case.) All shelves rest on timber battens, which are then hidden by the front lipping on the shelves.

Floor Plinths These are optional, but they give a neat finishing touch, and are useful if the floor is very uneven. The underside of the plinths can be packed up as necessary if the floor is uneven, and the front edge scribed to the floor before tiling (see **Techniques, page 252**). The plinths are made one tile high.

The kitchen system has been designed to be adapted easily. Full instructions for building the kitchens illustrated on pages 22–3, 24–5 and 27 are given on the following pages.

If you decide to build the complete system, the order of work checklists (below), will help you to compile your own construction schedule.

The elements of each kitchen are listed below for ease of reference:

Tiled Kitchen

Basic Partition Units and Shelves
Worktop

Optional extras:
  Back panel
  Floor plinth
  Built-in slatted shelf
  Doors and door handles

Tall Partition Unit
Wall-Mounted Shelf Unit

Additional Projects:
  Built-in plate rack and drip tray
  Hanging bar for kitchen utensils
  Airing rack

Painted Kitchen

Basic Partition Units and Shelves
Knife Rack
Wall-Mounted Slatted Shelves
Removable Towel Rail

Order Of Work Checklist

Tiled Kitchen

Tiled base units incorporating shelves, back panels and floor plinths, and a worktop.

1 Decide depth of worktop.
2 Decide height of worktop (to match tile height and equipment).
3 Decide on thickness of partition units (thickness of the partition must match tile width).
4 Decide on spacing of units, and whether you will incorporate shelves or built-in appliances such as a dishwasher.
5 Construct the basic frame including tall partitions if required.

6 Decide on quantity and position of shelves.
7 Mark out position of shelf-support battens.
8 Attach intermediate cross rails.
9 Clad the frames in 12mm ($\frac{1}{2}$in) plywood, using round wire nails.
10 Fit the back panel support battens.
11 Tile the sides of the partition units except for the back and bottom rows of tiles (to allow room for scribing the partition unit to fit).
12 Make and fix the shelf-support battens.
13 Put partitions in place, adding any remaining tiles; scribe to fit if necessary, and fix to the wall battens and floor with angle brackets.
14 Cut the back panel and slot it into place.
15 Make up and fit the shelves.
16 Make, tile and fit the floor plinth.
17 Tile the front faces of the partition units.
18 Fit worktop and any lipping.
19 Fit door frame if required.
20 Construct wall-mounted shelf units (with shelves if required).

Painted Kitchen

Painted partition units with shelves, and a tiled worktop.

1 Decide depth of worktop.
2 Decide height of worktop.
3 Decide thickness of partition units.
4, 5, 6, 7, 8 as tiled kitchen.
9 Clad the frame in 12mm ($\frac{1}{2}$in) MDF, using oval nails punched in 2mm ($\frac{1}{16}$in) below the surface.
10 Make and fit the shelf-support battens.
11 Fit MDF fascia panel to front edge of each partition.
12 Fix the partition units in place. Attach to wall with angle brackets, and paint as required.
13 Make up and fit the shelves.
14 Fit and tile worktop.

TOOLS

TRIMMING KNIFE

STEEL RULE

TRY SQUARE

HAMMER

NAIL PUNCH

PANEL SAW (or circular power saw)

TENON SAW

SCREWDRIVER (cross-point or slotted, depending on type of screw used)

SANDING BLOCK and ABRASIVE PAPER (or power finishing sander)

DRILL (hand or power)

COUNTERSINK DRILL BIT

MASONRY DRILL BIT

PAINTBRUSH – 38mm ($1\frac{1}{2}$in)

TILING TOOLS

TILE-SCORING TOOL

TILE CUTTER

ADHESIVE SPREADER

TILE SPACERS

GROUT SPREADER

BUILDER'S SPIRIT LEVEL

TWO G-CRAMPS

ADDITIONAL TOOLS

POWER JIGSAW for cutting panels and fitting inset sinks and hobs

ROUTER (or circular power saw) for making cupboard handles

DOWELLING JIG for jointing worktops

V-BLOCK to hold dowelling for door handles

MATERIALS

Note: All dimensions are finished sizes – either sawn or planed.
Materials listed are for constructing one base unit with shelves, and a floor plinth.

BASE UNITS – BASIC FRAME

Part	Quantity	Material	Length
FRONT STUD	1	75 × 50mm (3 × 2in) sawn softwood	890mm (35in)
BACK STUD	1	As above	790mm (31in)
TOP RAIL	1	As above	575mm ($22\frac{3}{4}$in)
BOTTOM RAIL	1	As above	575mm ($22\frac{3}{4}$in)
INTERMEDIATE RAILS	As required	As above	480mm (19in)

CLADDING (covering for frame and floor)

SIDES	2	12mm ($\frac{1}{2}$in) shuttering grade plywood	890 × 630mm (35 × $24\frac{3}{4}$in)
FLOOR	1	12mm ($\frac{1}{2}$in) shuttering grade plywood	600 × 630mm ($23\frac{1}{2}$ × $24\frac{3}{4}$in)

SHELVES

TOP SHELF	1	15mm ($\frac{5}{8}$in) melamine-faced chipboard	600mm ($23\frac{1}{2}$in) wide × 618mm ($24\frac{1}{2}$in) deep
INTERMEDIATE SHELF	1	15mm ($\frac{5}{8}$in) melamine-faced chipboard	600mm ($23\frac{1}{2}$in) wide × 575mm ($22\frac{3}{4}$in) deep
TOP AND INTERMEDIATE SHELF LIPPING		38 × 12mm ($1\frac{1}{2}$ × $\frac{1}{2}$in) planed hardwood	600mm ($23\frac{1}{2}$in)

SHELF-SUPPORT BATTENS

TOP SHELF	1	19 × 19mm ($\frac{3}{4}$ × $\frac{3}{4}$in) planed softwood	618mm ($24\frac{1}{2}$in)
INTERMEDIATE SHELF	1	As above	575mm ($22\frac{3}{4}$in)

FLOOR PLINTH

FRONT SUPPORT JOIST	1	100 × 25mm (4 × 1in) sawn softwood	600mm ($23\frac{1}{2}$in)
MIDDLE SUPPORT JOIST	1	As above	As above
REAR SUPPORT JOIST	1	As above	As above

TILES

TILES	As required	108 × 108mm ($4\frac{1}{4}$ × $4\frac{1}{4}$in) white ceramic wall and floor tiles	

CONSTRUCTING THE BASIC PARTITION PANEL

BASIC FRAME

Nail the front stud to the top rail using 75mm (3in) round wire nails. Make the job easier by nailing against a spare batten cramped to a bench, nailed to the floor, or fixed to a wall, so that there is something solid to nail against. The parts should rest on a flat surface while being nailed; this will help to hold them flush and stable.

Turn the assembly over and nail the front stud to the bottom rail.

Fix the back stud between the top and bottom rails, 50mm (2in) in from the ends, and nail it in place. This will make it easier to fit the unit to the rear wall later on.

In the case of the partition panel of the laundry area, the back stud should be inset by 100mm (4in), which will allow for a ducting pipe from the tumble dryer.

POSITIONING INTERMEDIATE RAILS

Intermediate cross rails coincide with the centre line of the shelf support positions, so these must be decided upon at this stage. The finished project will look better if the shelves align with joins between whole tiles. In our basic unit, one shelf is positioned one tile down from the top, and the other is midway between this shelf and the surface of the floor plinth.

On the front and back studs, measure down and mark the shelf top at the required height. Next, mark off the shelf thickness of 15mm ($\frac{5}{8}$in) and then the thickness of the shelf support batten, 19mm ($\frac{3}{4}$in). The middle of the batten position will be the centre line of the internal cross rail. Repeat the procedure for the second shelf.

With the basic square frame resting on edge (support the back stud with an offcut of 50mm [2in] wood), nail all the intermediate rails, correctly positioned, firmly in place.

CLADDING THE FRAME

On the outside edges of the front and back studs, mark the centre lines of the cross rails. The sides (which will be nailed to these cross rails) will conceal these rail positions. It is best to mark the centre lines of the rails accurately, although the heads of the fixing nails give a rough guide to the positions of the cross rails. Also mark the centre line of the back stud on the faces of the top and bottom rails of the frame.

Lay the frame flat, place a side panel cut from 12mm ($\frac{1}{2}$in) shuttering plywood on top, and align the front edge of the panel with the front edge of the front stud. If you are going to tile the panel, nail it in place *along the front edge only* using 38mm (1$\frac{1}{2}$in) round wire nails, about 150mm (6in) apart. If you are going to paint the panel, then use MDF and oval nails.

You will have made sure that the side panels are cut square, so use these as a guide to getting the basic frame square. Having nailed the front only, pull the rest of the frame into square, if necessary, to align with the edges of the panel, then nail through the panel into the frame, spacing the nails 150mm (6in) apart. To ensure that the nails go into the frame, transfer the centre-line marks of the intermediate and back rails on to each side panel.

Turn the partition over and repeat for the other side panel.

TILING

It is best to tile the basic partition panels before they are fitted, unless you are fitting a back panel, (*see* **Fitting a Back Panel, page 32**). Lay the panel flat, mark guide lines to ensure accurate tile spacing, spread tile adhesive, and press the tiles in place, working on a small area at a time (*see* **Techniques, page 252**). Tile from front to back and top to bottom.

If the floor or wall is uneven where the units are to stand (or if there are pipe runs to cover), leave off the back and bottom rows of tiles and shelf-support battens until the units have been scribed to fit (*see* **Techniques, page 246**). Do not tile the front edge at this stage. When the tiles are dry, grout them. Turn over the units and repeat the process. Make up as many partition panels as are required to build your own kitchen system.

---

① The Basic Frame
The back stud is inset by 50mm (2in) between the top and bottom rails to make fitting to the wall easier.

② Intermediate Rail
Shelf batten position is one tile-space down from the top. Rail should coincide with shelf position.

③ Positioning Intermediate Rail for Lower Shelf
After the first intermediate rail has been nailed in place, the second one should be positioned accurately to coincide with the centre line of the shelf-support batten.

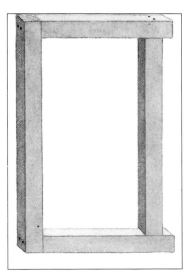

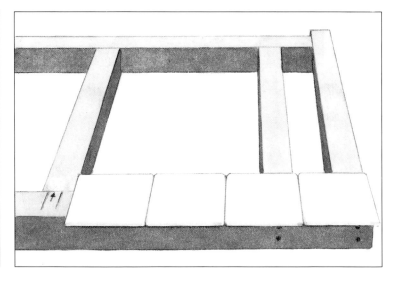

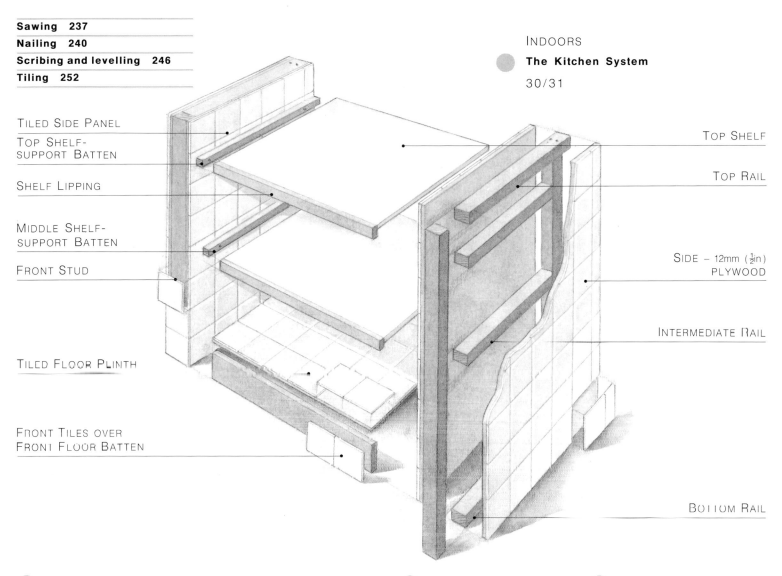

TILED SIDE PANEL

TOP SHELF-
SUPPORT BATTEN

SHELF LIPPING

MIDDLE SHELF-
SUPPORT BATTEN

FRONT STUD

TILED FLOOR PLINTH

FRONT TILES OVER
FRONT FLOOR BATTEN

TOP SHELF

TOP RAIL

SIDE – 12mm ($\frac{1}{2}$in)
PLYWOOD

INTERMEDIATE RAIL

BOTTOM RAIL

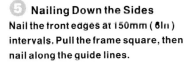

4 Cladding the Sides of the Basic Frame
Mark the centre lines of the cross rails on the outside of the frames and carefully join up these marks on the 12mm ($\frac{1}{2}$in) plywood as a guide for nailing the sides on to the frame.

5 Nailing Down the Sides
Nail the front edges at 150mm (6in) intervals. Pull the frame square, then nail along the guide lines.

6 Tiling the Basic Partition
Tile from front to back and from top to bottom to keep cut tiles out of sight at the back or at floor level.

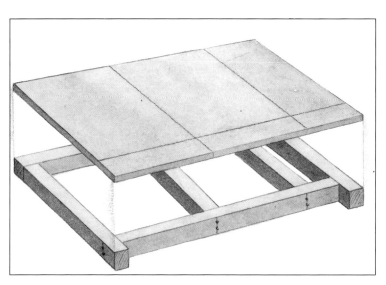

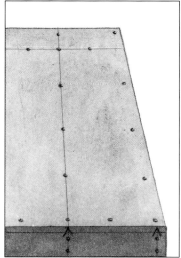

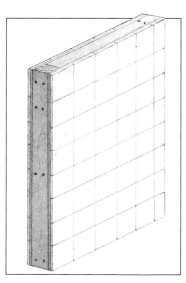

MAKING UP PARTITION UNITS

PAINTED PARTITION UNITS

Painted, as opposed to tiled partition units are shown in the photograph of the kitchen on page 24 and illustrate the versatility of the basic unit design.

The building techniques are the same as before, except that the frames are clad in 12mm ($\frac{1}{2}$in) MDF (medium-density fibreboard) instead of 12mm ($\frac{1}{2}$in) plywood. For a smooth finish, carefully punch the oval nail heads about 2mm ($\frac{1}{16}$in) below the surface of the board, then fill the holes with a proprietary wood filler. The frame should be sanded down once it is dry with a sanding block and abrasive paper.

Finish the front edge of each partition unit by applying a strip of MDF as a fascia panel, nailed in place and smoothed in the same way as the side panels. Chamfer the front edges of the fascia panels with a sanding block, then add the shelf battens. Fix the panels in place (see opposite page) and paint them.

TALL PARTITION UNITS

Tall partition units are required to house eye-level wall ovens, microwave ovens, refrigerators, and so on. Construction is as for low partition units, fixing all the cross rails at the levels required to coincide with the supports. Remember to fix a rail where the worktop meets the partition as this will take a lot of weight.

As the maximum standard length of plywood is 2440mm (8ft) there will be a join if the units are taller than this. The join must be at a cross rail so that the cut edges can be nailed down. If there is not a convenient cross rail, then put in an extra one for this purpose.

SHELVES SUPPORTING COOKERS

These shelves must be substantial to support the weight of the appliance. Use 50 × 25mm (2 × 1in) battens for the shelf supports and 25mm (1in) chipboard or MDF for the shelves. The front fascia is cut from the same material as the shelves, to the width of the shelf and to the depth required – in this case, one tile deep. Either screw or glue and nail the front piece to the front edge of the shelf, and tile the front face.

FITTING A BACK PANEL

If a back panel is to be fitted on a basic unit (perhaps to hide pipes where there is to be an open shelf), this must be done before fitting the shelves and floor plinth, and also before tiling the sides. The front-to-back measurements of the shelves and plinth should be reduced to make them fit. If the partition panel unit is to be fitted over pipes, scribe the partition around these now to ensure a good fit (see **Techniques, page 246**).

Once all the partitions are sitting in place, correctly scribed, take the first partition and mark a line 50mm (2in) in from the back. Cut two lengths of 19 × 19mm ($\frac{3}{4}$ × $\frac{3}{4}$in) batten to the height of the partition and fix a batten just in front of the marked line. Glue and nail it in position. Repeat for the second partition. Tile the surface (see **Techniques, page 252**), but only up to the batten. Repeat as necessary.

Make and fix the shelf-support battens (see opposite page) allowing a 6mm ($\frac{1}{4}$in) gap for the thickness of the back. Put partitions back in place and fix to the floor (see *opposite page*).

Cut the back panel from 6mm ($\frac{1}{4}$in) MDF or plywood. The height is the same as the partitions, and the width is as the floor and shelf widths. Slot the panel in place from the top and screw through to the battens, using four screws on each side. You may need to undo the shelf-support battens temporarily for an easy fit.

Make up the shelves (see opposite page) adjusting the front-to-back dimension accordingly. Replace the support battens and fit the shelves.

FLOOR PLINTHS

Each floor plinth is constructed from 12mm ($\frac{1}{2}$in) shuttering plywood with 100 × 25mm (4 × 1in) sawn timber battens supporting it, assuming you

① Cladding Painted Partition Units with MDF
Use 12mm ($\frac{1}{2}$in) MDF to clad units. Punch nail heads below surface.

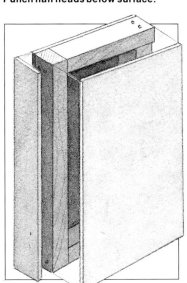

② Construction of Tall Partition Units
The basic construction method is the same as for the low partition units. Intermediate rails should be included wherever shelves are required or fixings are to be made.

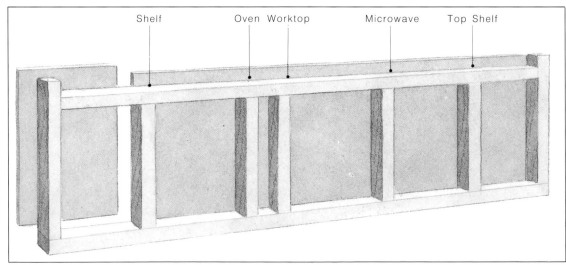

Shelf   Oven Worktop   Microwave   Top Shelf

are using 108×108mm ($4\frac{1}{4} \times 4\frac{1}{4}$in) tiles. The front-to-back dimensions are again adjusted accordingly.

Cut the 12mm ($\frac{1}{2}$in) plywood plinth panel to size and nail the battens to it at the front, back and middle. Inset the back one slightly to make scribing easier.

In a laundry room or kitchen it is normal to set the washing machine and tumble dryer on the floor, but 'built-in' models of washing machines are available also, and these look better set on tiled floor plinths as shown in the photograph. If you intend to do this, put in two extra support battens to take the weight of the machines. Pack glassfibre loft insulation between the battens to reduce noise.

Tile the top from front to back and from the middle outwards, so that any cut tiles are equal at either side (*see* **Tiling Techniques, page 252**). Grout the tiles to finish. If an appliance is to be placed on a floor plinth, make sure that tiles suitable for floors and walls are chosen as thin wall tiles will crack under the weight and vibration.

SHELVES

We chose easy-to-clean melamine-laminated chipboard for our shelves, but you may prefer to use another type of man-made board, such as blockboard or plywood (*see* **Materials, timber and boards, page 232**). All shelves are edged at the front with a wooden lip and this thickness has to be allowed for when fixing the shelf-support battens in position.

FIXING SHELF-SUPPORT BATTENS

The positions of the shelf supports are already marked on the front and back studs (*see* **Positioning Intermediate Rails, page 30**). With a pencil, link up the lines on the tiles.

Use 19×19mm ($\frac{3}{4} \times \frac{3}{4}$in) planed timber for the shelf supports, and cut them to the length required. The top one is the depth of the partition unit, minus the thickness of the lipping. The middle one is the depth of the partition, less half a tile width and the thickness of the lipping.

Hold each batten in position on the panel and mark two fixing-screw positions, approximately 50mm (2in) from the ends of each batten, but adjusted so that the screws will not be too near the edges of the tiles once in place.

Using a 4.5mm ($\frac{3}{16}$in) drill bit, drill two clearance holes in each batten (*see* **Techniques, page 23**). Hold each batten in place again and mark the screw positions on the tiles. Drill the tiles with a 7mm ($\frac{9}{32}$in) masonry drill bit to ensure that the batten-fixing screws will not crack the tiles when they are driven home.

Drill a 3mm ($\frac{1}{8}$in) hole through the centre of each clearance hole in the partition panel side. Countersink holes in the face of each batten and screw the battens into place using 50mm (2in) No 8 screws. I hide the battens by painting them with a suitable colour to blend with the tiles you have chosen.

MAKING THE SHELVES

Hold the shelf piece in a vice with the front edge, which is non-laminated, facing upwards.

Glue and nail 38×12mm ($1\frac{1}{2} \times \frac{1}{2}$in) planed wood lipping to this edge so that the top edge is flush. The lipping must underhang the shelf enough to hide the battens, that is by 19mm ($\frac{3}{4}$in). Use 25mm (1in) round wire nails, blunting the points first so as not to split the wood. Nail carefully, making sure that the lipping is flush with the surface as you proceed. Wipe off surplus glue. Punch the nail heads below the surface, then fill the holes and sand down.

Paint, or stain and varnish, the lipping. Ours is stained with white oil to match the worktop.

Where a shelf has to fit into a corner, cut off the underhang of the lipping where the front of the shelf meets a partition, and screw a batten to the wall, level with the side battens on the partition unit, to support the shelf at the back.

FIXING PARTITION UNITS IN PLACE

The partition units are neatly fixed to the rear wall with metal angle brackets at positions where they will be

③ Fitting a Back Panel
Scribe partition units around pipes and cut slots. Fit a panel-support batten to the face of the unit.

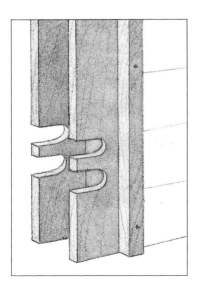

④ Construction of a Tiled Floor Plinth
Floor plinth comprises 12mm ($\frac{1}{2}$in) plywood on 100×25mm (4×1in) sawn timber battens. The back batten is inset by about 50mm (2in). Front tiles overlap the edges of the top tiles.

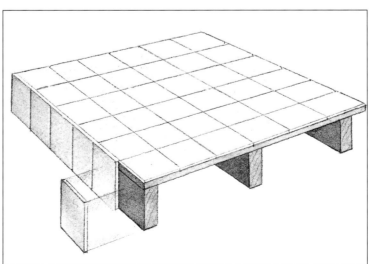

⑤ Fixing Shelves in Place
Hardwood lipping fixed to the front edge of a shelf (inset) hides support battens screwed to units.

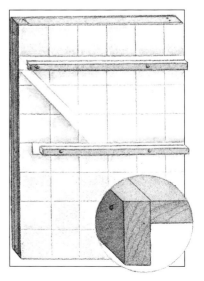

hidden at the very top and at shelf height. Brackets are also used to fix the units down into the floor where they will be hidden by the floor plinth units when in place.

Position the partition units according to the plans. It is important to have a partition unit where you have to turn a corner, to support the two edges of the worktop.

Do any scribing necessary to fit the partitions to the wall or floor (*see* **Techniques, page 246**).

Fix any remaining tiles that have been left off to allow for scribing. In order to do this you will have to unscrew the shelf-support batten and re-attach it after tiling. Fit in the shelves and then the floor plinth.

Fix the partition down to the floor using angle brackets (*see* **page 241**). Do this by removing the floor plinth and fitting the brackets where they will avoid the joists supporting the floor plinth. Slide the floor plinth back into position.

Fix high partitions to the wall batten, and also fix them to the floor and ceiling, if necessary, using angle brackets where they cannot be

seen, such as behind the cooker, just underneath the back shelf, or on top of the shelf above eye-level.

When all the partition units are fixed, tile and grout their front faces to finish the unit.

DOORS

The doors are hinged in pairs and inset within a timber frame as a neat addition to the basic unit.

MAKING THE FRAME

Measure the opening where the doors are to fit and make a frame to these external dimensions.

Dowel joint the horizontal rails between the uprights with two 12mm ($\frac{1}{2}$in) dowels at each frame corner (*see* **Techniques, page 245**). While the glue is setting, the frame should be held square on a flat surface with sash cramps. Alternatively, improvise by resting the frame against a batten temporarily nailed to the bench top. Another batten is nailed to the bench a short distance from the other side of the frame, and the cramp is tightened by driving two

folding wedges from opposing sides (*see* **Techniques, page 237**) between the edge of the second batten and the frame side.

From 12mm ($\frac{1}{2}$in) hardwood dowelling cut eight dowels, the length of which should be twice the thickness of the wood it is going through, plus 12mm ($\frac{1}{2}$in). Use a tenon saw to cut two grooves 1–2mm ($\frac{1}{32}$–$\frac{1}{16}$in) deep, along the dowel length. This will allow the glue and air to escape as the dowel is driven in. With abrasive paper, round off one end of each dowel.

With a 12mm ($\frac{1}{2}$in) drill bit, drill two holes through each corner joint to a depth of twice the thickness of the wood being fixed. Wrap a band of adhesive tape round the drill bit to indicate the correct depth.

Apply glue to each hole and wipe it around the inside with a small stick. Insert the dowels and hammer them almost home, leaving the ends protruding for the time being. Leave the frames cramped square.

When the glue has set, remove the cramps and saw off the dowel ends flush with the surface.

FIXING THE FRAME

Before fixing the frame, it must be held square by nailing a batten temporarily across the top and one side of the frame (*see* **Techniques, 3-4-5 method of bracing, page 237**, and fig 2 below). After fixing the bracing batten, saw off the ends of the batten flush with the frame to make a neat edge.

Drill and countersink the uprights of the frame and the bottom rails. Fit the frame in position and screw it to the partition units and to the floor. After fixing, remove the bracing batten from the frame.

MAKING THE DOORS

For a painted finish, cut the doors from 19mm ($\frac{3}{4}$in) MDF so that they fit the frame with a 2mm ($\frac{1}{16}$in) gap all round. There are many different types of door handles which can be fitted to finished doors. Opposite you will find instructions for making and fitting the handles shown in the illustration. Hinges and catches must also be fitted to the doors (*see* **Techniques, page 248**).

① Jointing of Frame Corners
Two 12mm ($\frac{1}{2}$in) dowel holes in the ends of the rails are the same length as the thickness of the uprights.

② Making the Door Frame Square
Before fitting the frame, hold it square temporarily by nailing a batten across the top and one side using the 3-4-5 method of ensuring a right-angled corner. See Techniques, page 237, for further details.

③ Fitting the Door Handles
A right-angled rebate is cut in 25mm (1in) dowel which is fitted to hardwood lipping on the door edge.

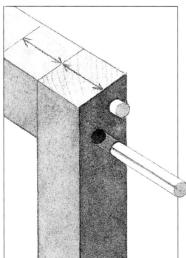

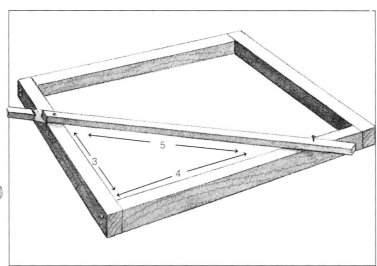

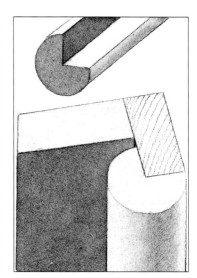

MAKING THE HANDLES

To make our handles, you will need a router, and a V-block to hold the dowelling from which the handles are made (see **Techniques, Making a V-block, page 239**). The dowelling is placed in the V-block and rebated with the router. (You can use a circular saw for this, but it is much more difficult to achieve a good finish.) Cut the doors so that they are narrower by the thickness of the lipping, that is, 12mm ($\frac{1}{2}$in).

Cut two lengths of 25mm (1in) diameter dowelling to the length of the door plus 50mm (2in) extra to allow the dowelling to be nailed in the V-block. The V-block should be a 1m (39in) length of 75 × 50mm (3 × 2in) timber with a 25mm (1in) deep V cut in one face. Nail each end of the dowel in the V-block and mark off the finished length. Hold the V-block firmly in a vice.

Working from one end to the other, rout to the depth of the lipping (12mm [$\frac{1}{2}$in]) between the marks. Cut the dowel to its final length. Cut two lengths of 32 × 12mm (1$\frac{1}{4}$ × $\frac{1}{2}$in) hardwood lipping to the length of the dowels. Glue and pin the lipping to the dowel, then sand smooth. Glue and pin the lipping on to the door edges and finish as required.

SLATTED SHELF

Slatted shelves are easy to build and are particularly useful in airing cupboards. In the laundry room (see **page 27**), a slatted shelf has been built-in under the Belfast sink. A number of cross slats are nailed to side rails which rest alongside the same type of shelf-support battens as those used in the basic partition unit in the main kitchens.

Cut two pieces of 50 × 25mm (2 × 1in) planed timber for the side rails to the required front-to-back depth of the shelf. Our shelf is set back about 100mm (4in). Cut the support battens to the same length

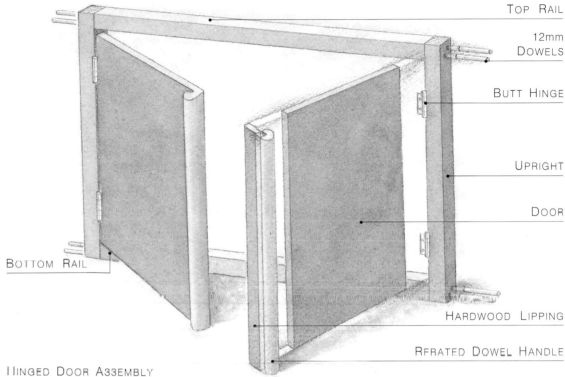

TOP RAIL

12mm DOWELS

BUTT HINGE

UPRIGHT

DOOR

BOTTOM RAIL

HARDWOOD LIPPING

REBATED DOWEL HANDLE

HINGED DOOR ASSEMBLY
Doors are hinged within a simple frame assembly which is screwed in place between partition units

and fix in place (see **Shelf-Support Battens, page 33**).

Cut the required number of slats (we used seven) from the 50 × 25mm (2 × 1in) planed timber. The length of these should be the width between partitions, less 2mm ($\frac{1}{16}$in) to fit exactly.

Set the side rails in from the ends of the slats by the thickness of the supporting battens. Use offcuts or scrap wood of the same thickness as the support battens. Lay them next to the side rails before laying the front slat across them, so that the battens are at the very ends. Nail the slats in place.

Cut a spacing batten (see **Techniques, page 236**) to ensure that the remaining slats are spaced evenly, then nail them in place. Finish off the shelf by painting, staining or varnishing it as required.

④ Making a Slatted Under-Sink Storage Shelf
A number of cross slats are nailed to side rails; these rails rest on 19 × 19mm ($\frac{3}{4}$ × $\frac{3}{4}$in) shelf-support battens which are then fixed at each side to the tiled partition units.

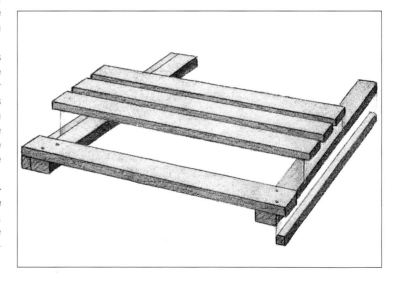

WORKTOPS

There is a wide range of worktops from which to choose. In the main kitchen we used a 38mm (1½in) solid wood top, finished with white oil. The worktop in the small kitchen is 25mm (1in) chipboard which is tiled, and lipped at the front with hardwood. A wide selection of melamine laminate worktops is available. The front edges are often rounded (post-formed), or they can be square-edged and lipped with hardwood. Most standard worktops are 32mm (1¼in) thick.

If a material like marble or granite is chosen, it will look better if it is made to look thicker at the front edge by bonding a strip of similar material under the front edge. At the back, the worktop's edge will probably be covered by the wall tiles.

Alternatively, the worktop can be fitted to the wall by scribing, or by cutting into the wall, although it is easier to cover the gap at the back with a narrow hardwood strip fixed to the wall. If the wall is very uneven, a hardwood strip can be fixed horizontally to the back of the worktop. This strip can be scribed to the wall.

JOINING WORKTOPS

You will probably not need to join worktops end-to-end unless you have a very long run, but you will almost certainly need to turn a corner. Remember that all joins must coincide with a partition for support.

Joins should be dowelled (*see* **Techniques, page 245**) using a dowelling jig to ensure that the surfaces are absolutely flush. You then rout out or drill the surfaces for jointing connector bolts on the underside; there are several types available and they all come with fitting instructions. Alternatively, for corner jointing post-formed worktops, specially shaped metal strips are available to cover the joints neatly.

FIXING DOWN WORKTOPS

Fix the worktop to the partitions with angle plates – two per side of each partition – and screw up through any door frames into the worktop. If you are fixing a solid-wood worktop, allow for expansion and shrinkage in the wood by using specially slotted angle plates. Where a worktop

meets a high partition, screw a 50 × 50mm (2 × 2in) batten to the partition for the worktop to rest on. Screw up into the worktop from the underside of the batten (if it is a solid wood worktop, use a screw slot). Angle the front edge of the support batten backwards so that it will not be seen and set it back from the front edge. Another method of fixing down a worktop is to use a flat metal plate screwed down into the pillar before the worktop is laid over it, and then up into the worktop, see fig 2.

If the worktop is to be tiled, do this after fitting, then add a hardwood lipping. Seal the gap at the back of the worktop to finish.

SINKS AND HOBS

These are supplied with templates for the required cut-outs. Hold the templates in position and draw round them. Drill 12mm (½in) diameter holes in each corner, inside the line. Put the blade of the jigsaw through one of the holes, and saw round the line (*see* **Techniques, Cutting a circle, page 238**).

FRONT CONTROL PANEL FOR HOB

Screw a small length of 19 × 19mm (¾ × ¾in) batten into the partitions at a depth and distance back to suit your control panel. Screw through into the battens following the appliance manufacturer's instructions.

BELFAST SINK

This type of sink sits on a support under a cut-out in the worktop. Make a template of the inside shape of the sink and use this to make the cut-out as for sinks and hobs (above). Because the worktop should overhang the sink, the cutout must therefore be smaller than the inside of the sink. With a router, form a shallow groove on the underside of the worktop, all round the cut-out, about 6mm (¼in) from the edge. This is a drip groove which will help to prevent water from running under the worktop. Seal round the rim of the sink and the underside of the worktop using a silicone-rubber sealant. Make a circular cut-out in the shelf support to allow the waste

❶ How to Join Worktops
When joining worktops, reinforce the under-surface by fitting jointing connector bolts.

❷ Fixing Down Worktops
Angle plates (brackets), top, and corner plates, bottom, are used for fixing worktops in place.

❸ Fitting an Inset Sink or Cooker Hob
Templates are supplied for marking the top so that a cut-out can be made with a jigsaw. Clips on the underside of the sink or cooker hob hold the appliance in place once a hole has been cut.

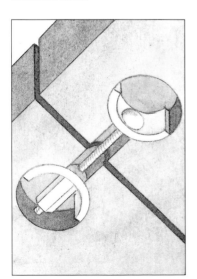

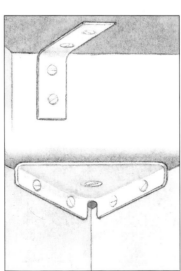

trap to be fitted into the sink. Stiffen the front edge of the shelf support with 50 × 25mm (2 × 1in) timber lipping. Cut a hole, or holes, in the worktop behind the sink to allow the taps to be fitted. Belfast sinks are generally very heavy, so it may be wise to consult a plumber before attempting to fit such a sink yourself.

TILING A WORKTOP

Tiling a worktop provides a very hard-wearing, hygienic surface which is easy to clean and therefore ideal for a kitchen. However, a tiled surface is not suitable for all purposes – for food preparation you need a smooth, wipe-clean surface, such as melamine laminate. For chopping vegetables and meat you need a surface of solid hardwood, such as maple, which is what butchers' blocks are made from. So in a kitchen there is a good case for having a choice of worksurfaces.

When buying tiles for a worktop, be sure to tell your supplier what you will be using them for. Some thin wall tiles crack when used to work on, so

thicker tiles suitable for both walls and floors are preferable. Some outdoor-type tiles, particularly those with a metallic glaze, are not suitable for preparing food on.

If possible, avoid white grout as it is very difficult to keep clean, although the latest two-part epoxy type is better in this respect. A good choice is a dark-coloured waterproof grout. A wide range of coloured grouts is available, and colouring powders can be mixed with white grout to your own requirements. If tiles without spacers are used, keep them close together to minimize the width of grouting.

It is essential that the worksurface to be tiled is stable and securely fixed before you begin tiling. We recommend 25mm (1in) chipboard. Plywood of the same thickness is also suitable, although more expensive. Try to avoid tiling over solid wood as the wood tends to expand and shrink too much, loosening the tiles.

Before starting to tile, tack a batten temporarily to the outer edge of the worktop to give a surface to

tile against. Then lay out the tiles in a dry run to see whether any cutting will be required. This will almost certainly be the case, so keep the cut tiles to the back. If the tiles have to be cut at each end of the worksurface, make sure that the cut ones will be at least half a tile's width. If the initial setting-out reveals only thin strips at each end, move all of the tiles sideways by half a tile's width so as to make the end tiles wider.

On the temporary edging batten, mark where the middle tile falls and start tiling from there. Spread tile adhesive over the worktop to cover about 1m square (1 yd square) using a notched tile adhesive spreader to ensure an even bed of adhesive. Press the middle tile into the adhesive with a slight twisting motion, then add other tiles to the front edge on each side of this tile. Make sure that they butt against the temporary edging batten. Next, fit whole tiles, working back from the front middle tile towards the back wall. Use a try square and a straight-edge to ensure that this row is straight. Now, working from front to

back again, fill in with tiles on each side of this row to complete the main area of tiling. (After this, cut and fit the edge tiles, see **Tiling Techniques, page 252**).

Complete the job by removing the temporary edging batten and replacing it with hardwood lipping, the top edge of which should be level with the surface of the tiles. The lipping should be deep enough to cover the entire thickness of the worktop. Grout the joints between the tiles and the space between the tiles and the lipping. Finally, seal the tile-to-wall joint with silicone-rubber sealant to make it waterproof.

④   Working out Tile Positions

Tack a batten temporarily to the front edge of the worktop. Set out tiles in a 'dummy run'.

⑤   Order for Laying Tiles

Lay front tiles from the middle, then work to the back and fill in at each side of the worktop.

⑥   Tiled Worktop

In the painted kitchen project shown on page 24, our tiled worktop is finished off with a neat wooden lipping to create a functional but attractive surface to work on when cooking.

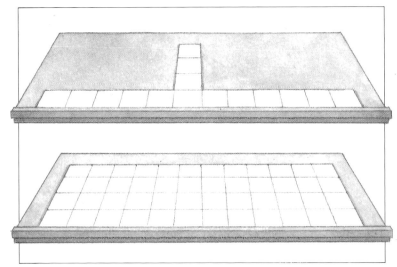

WALL-MOUNTED SHELF UNIT

The wall-mounted shelf units are built in a similar way to the floor units. They are neatly mounted to wall battens, so there is no visible means of support. When the units are mounted on a stud wall, extra support is required, so horizontal battens are fixed to the wall to support the vertical wall battens. Therefore, the top and bottom rails are thinner in these units, and the sides have cut-outs at the back to slot over the battens on the wall.

MAKING THE PARTITION

Remember that each shelf unit needs a partition panel at each end. Some partitions will support shelving at each side.

Mark out on the walls where you want the shelf runs to be. For the best visual effect, keep the wall shelf partitions above the centre lines of the base partitions. Work out what you want to incorporate within the shelves — for example, a cooker hood, a plate rack and a hanging bar for utensils. Decide on the overall height of the shelving. In our case, the partitions are 600mm ($23\frac{1}{2}$in) high by 350mm ($13\frac{3}{4}$in) deep.

The basic frame is made from 50 × 50mm (2 × 2in) PAR (planed all round) timber clad with 6mm ($\frac{1}{4}$in) MDF (medium-density fibreboard) panels. Two panels are required for each partition unit.

Cut two rails (for top and bottom) 350mm ($13\frac{3}{4}$in) long, and three uprights 510mm (20in) long. Note that for fixing to a stud (hollow) wall, the top and bottom rails will be 50 × 25mm (2 × 1in) and 325mm ($12\frac{3}{4}$in) long.

Nail together the basic frame so that the back stud is set one stud's thickness in. Glue and nail on the side panels, fixing one edge first, before pulling the frame into square so that the other sides line up with the panel. Check that the wall batten slides into the back space.

TOOLS

ADDITIONAL TOOLS

MATERIALS

Part	Quantity	Material	Length
PARTITION UNIT (two required per shelf unit)			
SIDE PANEL	2	6mm ($\frac{1}{4}$in) MDF	350 × 600mm ($13\frac{3}{4}$ × $23\frac{1}{2}$in)
FRONT FASCIA PANEL	1	6mm ($\frac{1}{4}$in) MDF	As above
TOP RAIL*	1	50 × 50mm (2 × 2in) PAR timber	350mm ($13\frac{3}{4}$in)
BOTTOM RAIL*	1	As above	As above
FRONT STUD	1	As above	510mm (20in)
BACK STUD	1	As above	As above
WALL BATTEN	1	As above	As above
SHELVES			
TOP SHELF	1	15mm ($\frac{5}{8}$in) melamine-faced chipboard	325 × 600mm ($12\frac{3}{4}$ × $23\frac{1}{2}$in), or as required
BOTTOM SHELF	1	As above	As above
MIDDLE SHELF	1	15mm ($\frac{5}{8}$in) melamine-faced chipboard	250 × 600mm (10 × $23\frac{1}{2}$in), or as required
SHELF LIPPING	3	12 × 38mm ($\frac{1}{2}$ × $1\frac{1}{2}$in) hardwood	As above
TOP AND BOTTOM SHELF-SUPPORT BATTENS	4	15 × 25mm ($\frac{5}{8}$ × 1in) PAR timber (Buy 19 × 25mm [$\frac{3}{4}$ × 1in] timber and plane down	325mm ($12\frac{3}{4}$in)
MIDDLE SHELF SUPPORTS	2	As above	250mm (10in)
*TOP RAIL (for stud wall fixing)	1	50 × 25mm (2 × 1in) PAR timber	325mm ($12\frac{3}{4}$in)
*BOTTOM RAIL (for stud wall)	1	As above	As above

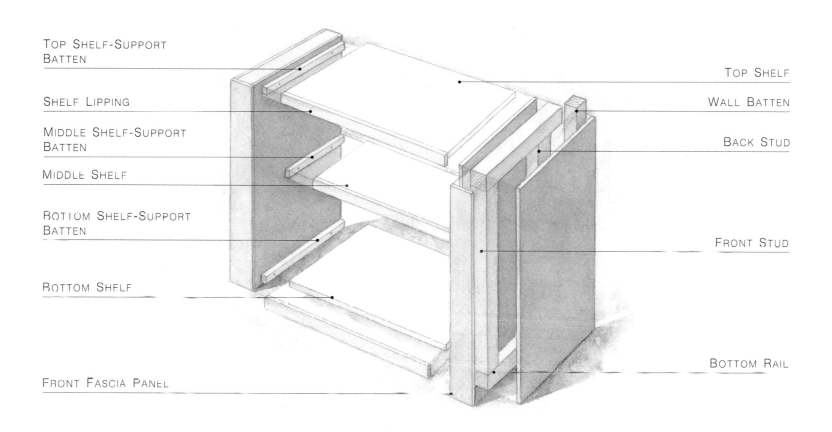

TOP SHELF-SUPPORT BATTEN

SHELF LIPPING

MIDDLE SHELF-SUPPORT BATTEN

MIDDLE SHELF

BOTTOM SHELF-SUPPORT BATTEN

BOTTOM SHELF

FRONT FASCIA PANEL

TOP SHELF

WALL BATTEN

BACK STUD

FRONT STUD

BOTTOM RAIL

① The Partition Basic Frame
Note that the back stud is inset by the thickness of the wall batten for a neat fit and to make scribing easier.

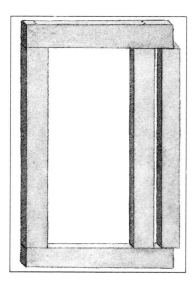

② Cladding the Frame Unit
6mm (¼in) MDF is nailed to the sides, and front fascia is nailed on to cover the edges of the frame unit.

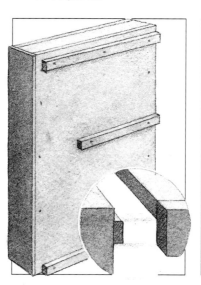

③ Fixing the Shelf Battens
Battens are fixed at the top, middle and bottom. *Inset* fixing a batten to make the top flush.

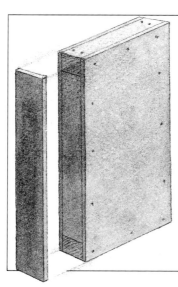

④ Solid Wall Fixing Method
Batten is securely plugged and screwed to the wall; the partition (cut-away) slots over the batten.

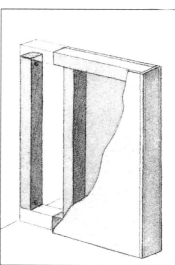

WALL-MOUNTED SHELF UNIT

Measure the total thickness of the partition and cut front fascia strips from 6mm ($\frac{1}{4}$in) MDF to that width and 600mm ($23\frac{1}{2}$in) high.

Nail on the front fascia and punch the nail heads below the surface (*see* **Techniques, Nailing, page 240**). Chamfer the edges with a plane and sand them down. If the panels are to be a different colour from the wall, it is a good idea to paint them before you fix them to the wall.

SHELF-SUPPORT BATTENS

Plane the timber down to 15 x 25mm ($\frac{5}{8}$ x 1in) to make shelf-support battens, and fit these to the partitions before fixing the partitions to the wall. The shelves will look better if they are set back slightly from the front of the partitions. The middle shelf has to be set back even farther – about 100mm (4in).

Decide how many shelves you need and where you want them according to your own storage requirements. Ours are flush with the top and bottom of the partitions, and a middle shelf is fixed midway between the top and bottom shelves.

① **Stud Wall Fixing Method**
The wall batten is screwed to horizontal battens that are nailed to wall studs.

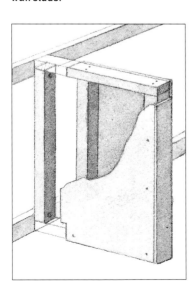

Cut the support battens to length, allowing for the lipping which is fixed to the front edge of the shelf (that is, the battens should be cut to the shelf's depth). Glue, then screw or nail the battens in place.

SHELVES

The shelves are made from 15mm ($\frac{5}{8}$in) melamine-faced chipboard with 12mm ($\frac{1}{2}$in) thick hardwood lipping. Glue and nail the lipping to the front edge. Fill the nail holes, sand smooth when dry, and finish as required, according to your chosen decorative scheme.

PLATE RACK

If you are incorporating a plate rack (see opposite and page 42 for assembly instructions), it is important to make this up before fixing in place the supporting partitions which sit on either side of it.

FIXING UP THE PARTITIONS

Solid walls In most cases the partitions will be fixed above a worktop. This should have been fitted level, so measure up from it when marking the positions of the wall battens. Use a spirit level to double check that these marks are level. Then, using masonry nails, temporarily fix a straight horizontal batten to the wall for the wall battens to rest on while they are fixed. Drill the wall for wallplugs and screw the wall battens securely to the wall.

Slot the partition unit over the wall battens and glue and screw through the sides into the wall battens with 25mm (1in) No 8 woodscrews, using four either side.

Stud walls Locate the wall studs (see **Techniques, Wall Fixings, page 240**) and nail a 50 x 50mm (2 x 2in) batten horizontally at the top and bottom of where the partition units will be placed. Screw the 50 x 50mm (2 x 2in) upright wall battens to the horizontal battens on the wall for support.

Nail up the frame as before, but use 50 x 25mm (2 x 1in) timber for the top and bottom rails which will be shorter by the thickness of the horizontal battens. Cut out 50 x 25mm (2 x 1in) slots on the back corners of the inside panels using a 50 x 25mm (2 x 1in) timber off-cut as a template. Nail the panels down, then slot the partitions over the wall battens, screwing through the sides into the wall battens as before. Do not include cut-outs at the ends of the shelf units.

COOKER HOOD

The hood can be a simple recirculating type, which needs only to be fixed between two partition panels and connected to a power supply, or it can be a more efficient extractor type. With the latter type,

USE SHELVES FOR DISPLAY

The wall-mounted shelf unit is ideal for display as well as for practical storage.

you will need to cut an outlet in a convenient external wall for fumes to escape through. The hood is then either connected directly to the outlet or linked to it with slot-together plastic ducting if they are some distance apart. The manufacturer's instructions will have full details.

It will probably be necessary to fit mounting battens to both the wall and the partition units. Fit a narrow shelf at the top to line up with the top of the partition units, but do not fit lipping at the front as the cooker hood's front panel will conceal this. Fit battens at an angle on each inside face of the partition units to hold the front panel. This can be a sheet of stainless steel or painted MDF. If you use MDF, secure the panel by screwing through into the battens. But if the panel is stainless steel, it is neater to glue it in place with epoxy resin.

You can adapt the fitting of the cooker hood according to its design and how it fits into the rest of your kitchen system.

HANGING BAR FOR UTENSILS

This is simply a chrome-steel or wooden rod which fits at each end into a wall partition panel. S-shaped meat hooks are hung on the bar to take utensils.

To fix the bar, drill holes of its diameter into the sides of the appropriate partition unit so that the bar will clear the bottom rail but rest on it. Use an off-cut of bottom rail as a spacer to mark off the lowest part of the hole on the bottom edge of the partition panel.

Cut the rod to a length equivalent to the distance between two partition panels, plus 100mm (4in).

2 Positioning the Hanging Bar
Use an offcut of the bottom rail to mark a position on the partition for the hanging bar.

BUILT-IN PLATE RACK AND DRIP TRAY

This is a simply designed storage unit which is intended to be built-in between two wall-mounted shelf units (see overleaf for instructions and page 22 for a photograph of the unit in position). For a perfect result, great accuracy and attention to detail as well as a helping pair of hands, is called for, but the finished unit is solid, secure and stylish. Wooden dowels are inserted at regular intervals into three wooden rails which are angled to suit the size of your crockery. Instructions for a drip tray made from melamine-faced chipboard are also included. The drip tray allows you to leave crockery on the plate rack to dry by itself.

SAVE TIME IN THE KITCHEN
Dishes can be neatly stacked and left to dry on this stylish plate rack.

TOOLS

TRIMMING KNIFE

STEEL MEASURING TAPE

TRY SQUARE

TENON SAW

HAMMER

MORTISE GAUGE

POWER DRILL

DRILL BITS

HOLE SAW 38–50mm ($1\frac{1}{2}$–2in) to suit frame diameter (or use a router)

POWER JIGSAW

MALLET

ADDITIONAL TOOLS

V-BLOCK

DRILL STAND (or home-made drill guide) – for accurate vertical drilling

MATERIALS

PLATE RACK

Part	Quantity	Material	Length
FRAME	3	38–50mm ($1\frac{1}{2}$in–2in) diameter softwood dowel	As required
RACK SPACERS	As required	12mm ($\frac{1}{2}$in) softwood dowel	137mm ($5\frac{1}{2}$in)
RACK SPACERS	As required	12mm ($\frac{1}{2}$in) softwood dowel	250mm (10in)

DRIP TRAY

Part	Quantity	Material	Length
TRAY BASE	1	15mm ($\frac{5}{8}$in) melamine-faced chipboard	As required
EDGE FRAME	4	38 × 12mm ($1\frac{1}{2}$ × $\frac{1}{2}$in) hardwood lipping	As required
SUPPORT BATTENS	2	10 × 6mm ($\frac{3}{8}$ × $\frac{1}{4}$in) softwood	As required

BUILT-IN PLATE RACK AND DRIP TRAY

Cut the three large frame dowels to length. To calculate the length of each dowel, add the distances between the partitions, plus 100mm (4in). The 100mm (4in) allows for 25mm (1in) at either end of the plate rack to slot into the partitions for fixing in position, and a further 25mm (1in) excess at either end. A nail can be driven in to this excess to secure the dowel to the V-block while the holes are being drilled in it (see **Techniques, Making a V-block, page 239**). The excess will be sawn off later.

Position one dowel in the V-block. Draw a straight line along its length using a steel straight-edge resting against one side of the block (fig 1). Starting 62mm (2½in) in from one end, mark off 35mm (1⅜in) centres along it. Use a pencil or mortise gauge to do this.

Using the first dowel as a guide, transfer the 35mm (1⅜in) centres to a second dowel. For the third dowel, mark a line down its length as described above, but this time continue the line across the end section to the centre. Draw a second line, at 96 degrees to the first. Continue the second line along the length of the dowel.

Use the first dowel to transfer the 35mm (1⅜in) centres to the third dowel, making the marks between the two lines. Put the first dowel in the V-block with the marked hole-centres vertical. Nail it down at either end to secure it.

DRILLING THE HOLES

Start to drill the vertical holes for the dowels at the marked centres (see **Techniques, page 239**).

Each hole should be drilled to a depth of 12mm (½in). Use a drill stand, a drill guide set at 90 degrees, or make your own drill guide.

MAKING A DRILL GUIDE

You will need a block of wood 100 × 50mm (4 × 2in). Make a V-shaped cut-out in it so that it will fit neatly over the dowel resting in the V-block. Drill a hole through it vertically (see above).

Thread the drill bit through the hole in the drill guide and place the tip of the bit on the first hole. Pull the guide into position, resting on the V-block, then drill a 12mm (½in) deep hole. Drill all the required holes in the same way.

ASSEMBLY

Cut 25mm (1in) from each end of each of the three frame dowels. (This is the excess used when nailing the dowel to the V-block to secure it in place.)

By tapping gently with a mallet, fit all the 137mm (5½in) dowels into one of the frame dowels (one with a single row of holes) and all the 250mm (10in) dowels into the other frame dowel.

Join the two sections together to complete the assembly. You will need help when aligning the dowels. If the fit is very tight, it will be easier to cramp it together in a woodworker's vice. An extra-tight fit may be achieved by cramping the rack in a vice. If the fit is loose, put a little waterproof glue in the holes to fill any gaps.

Look down the length of the rack to check that it is perfectly aligned. If it is not, twist the rack into alignment by getting one person at each end of the rack to adjust it.

FIXING IN POSITION

The plate rack must be fixed in position before the supporting partitions are finally fixed in place.

Offer up the rack to one partition. Tilt it back until an angle is found in which plates will sit comfortably. Mark the dowel positions on the partition sides.

Position the wall batten in its correct position at the back of the partition so that this can be drilled at the same time.

Cut out the holes to a depth of 25mm (1in) with a power drill and hole saw or with a router.

Fit one partition in place and carefully slot the rack into it. Meanwhile, ask someone to hold the partition against the other end of the rack for you so that the position for the three holes can be marked and the holes drilled. The partition can then be tapped into the rack to secure it in position. Finally, attach the second partition to the wall batten.

1 Marking-Up Plate Rack Dowel Hole Centres
Rest dowel in a V-block and mark off centres at 35mm (1⅜in) intervals. Transfer all the marks on to the second dowel. On the third dowel draw a second line at exactly 96 degrees to the first

2 Using a Drill Guide
With dowel nailed in to a V-block, line up on first hole. Use scrap wood as a drill guide.

3 Drilling the Dowel Holes
A drill guide, which you can make yourself, helps to keep the drill bit vertical. Drill 12mm (½in) holes.

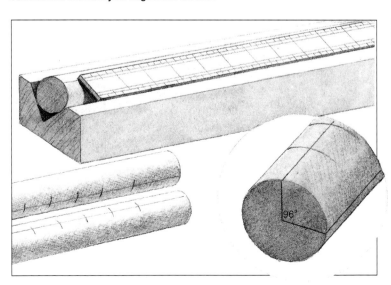

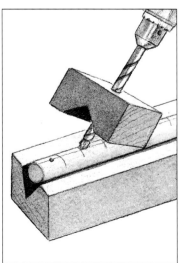

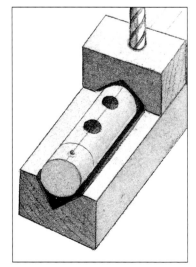

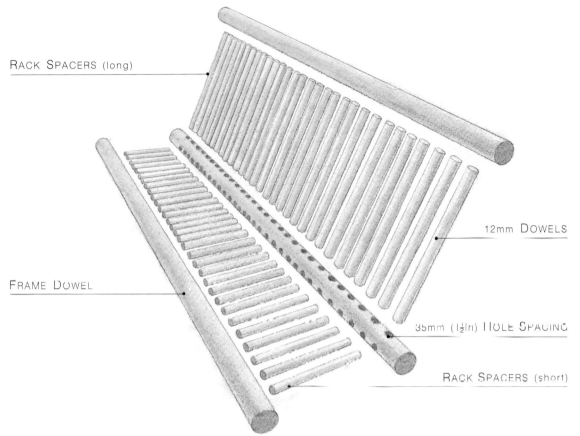

RACK SPACERS (long)

FRAME DOWEL

12mm DOWELS

35mm (1½in) HOLE SPACING

RACK SPACERS (short)

DRIP TRAY

This is removable for easy drying or cleaning. Cut the tray-support battens to the same length as the shelf-support battens, and pin and glue them to the bottom of the partitions.

Make a tray base from 15mm (⅜in) melamine-faced chipboard. Cut two pieces of lipping to the depth of the tray. Saw 10mm (⅜in) from each to leave them 25mm (1in) high. Glue and pin the pieces of lipping to the tray base ends so that they are flush with the underside (fig 5). Cut the front and back lippings to cover the length of the tray plus the end lippings. Pin and glue them in place, leaving a 10mm (⅜in) underhang at front and back. Make small cut-outs at the back to allow tray to slide over support battens.

Waterproof the interior edges of the tray with a silicone bath sealant. When using a mastic applicator gun, it is easier to push the nozzle away from you to provide an even flow of sealant rather than pulling the nozzle towards you.

4 Positioning the Plate Rack Between Partitions
The assembled plate rack is fitted between two wall-mounted shelf partition units and slips neatly into the three holes that are drilled into each partition side panel for a safe and secure fixing.

5 Making the Drip Tray
The melamine-faced chipboard tray, edged with hardboard lipping, rests on two support battens. End lipping strips are fixed first (top), then front and back lippings.

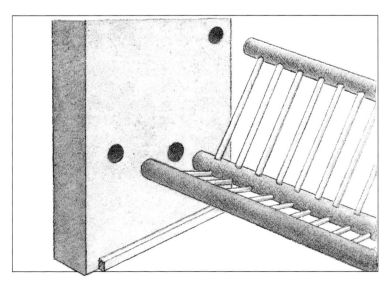

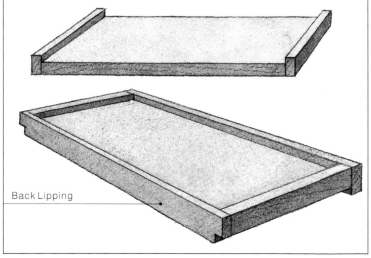

Back Lipping

WALL-MOUNTED SLATTED SHELVES

TOOLS

- STEEL MEASURING TAPE
- STEEL RULE
- TRIMMING KNIFE
- TRY SQUARE
- TENON SAW
- MITRE BOX
- SCREWDRIVER
- DRILL (hand or power)
- COUNTERSINK DRILL BIT
- MASONRY DRILL BIT
- FLAT DRILL BIT for hanging bar
- SPACING BATTEN (made from an offcut)

Cut a 45 degree mitre at each end of the 38mm ($1\frac{1}{2}$in) diagonal. Glue and screw together the two 75 × 25mm (3 × 1in) pieces. Use two 25mm (1in) No 8 screws.

Lay the L-shaped piece on the workbench and place the diagonal in position. Mark off the diagonal's internal shoulder on to the L-shape at both ends (fig 1). Continue the lines round edges and on to backs.

Mark the position for each screw hole, 19mm ($\frac{3}{4}$in) from the pencil line and centrally on the wood. Drill and countersink pilot holes. Lay the L-shaped section on the bench and place a 12mm ($\frac{1}{2}$in) thick offcut of wood in position (fig 2). This is so the diagonal lies centrally in the 75 × 25mm (3 × 1in) L bracket. The diagonal can now be repositioned, and glued and screwed in place.

Make up extra brackets as required. Allow one bracket for each 1200mm (48in) of shelf. If the shelves are likely to be heavily laden, fix brackets every 900mm (36in).

FIXING BRACKETS TO A WALL

The leg of the bracket that is overlapped by the other piece at the top is the one that is fixed to the wall (fig 3). Drill countersunk pilot holes and fix the brackets to the wall by means of a temporary batten, to ensure that they are level.

MATERIALS

Part	Quantity	Material	Length
L-SHAPE BRACKETS	2	75 × 25mm (3 × 1in) softwood	350mm (14in)
DIAGONAL BRACKET	1	50 × 38mm (2 × $1\frac{1}{2}$in) softwood	410mm ($16\frac{1}{2}$in)
SLATS	5	50 × 19mm (2 × $\frac{3}{4}$in) softwood	As required

Optional: hanging bar of 19mm ($\frac{3}{4}$in) wood dowel or metal rod

HANGING BAR

Drill holes for the bar in the brackets before fixing them to the wall. Decide the distance between the brackets and cut the bar to this length plus 38mm ($1\frac{1}{2}$in).

Mark on the diagonals the positions for the bar holes according to the size of the objects you intend to hang from it. Drill the holes to the same diameter as the bar and 19mm ($\frac{3}{4}$in) deep. Fix the first bracket to the wall, slot in the hanging bar, then fit the second bracket on the other end and fix it to the wall.

FIXING SLATS

Cut the slats to the required length, allowing an overlap of 75mm (3in) at each end. Fix the front slat flush with the front of the brackets. Use a single 12mm ($\frac{1}{2}$in) No 6 screw in each bracket. Space the remaining slats at equal centres, with the edge of the back slat butted up against the wall for a neat finish.

---

① Marking-Up Brackets for Positioning the Diagonals
Screw the flat pieces of wood together at right-angles. Temporarily fit the diagonal strut. Mark off the internal shoulders and continue the lines on to the back faces of the brackets.

② Fixing the Diagonal Strut
Use a suitable offcut of wood to give support to the diagonal strut when fixing it in place.

③ Finished Shelf Bracket
The top rail sits on top of the wall rail and the brackets are braced by the diagonal strut.

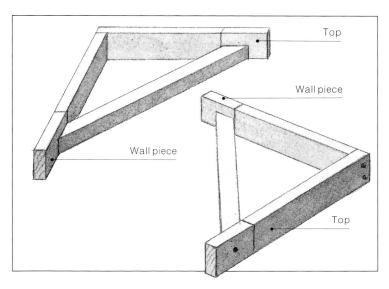

Top
Wall piece
Wall piece
Top

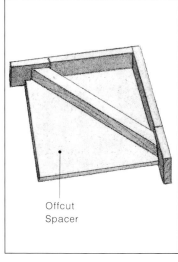

Offcut Spacer

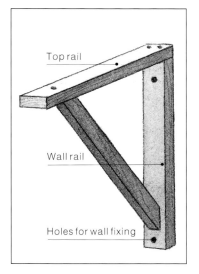

Top rail
Wall rail
Holes for wall fixing

REMOVABLE TOWEL RAIL

Made from 38–50mm (1½–2in) diameter dowel, available from timber and builders' merchants.

TOOLS

STEEL MEASURING TAPE
TRY SQUARE
TENON SAW
DRILL (hand or power)
DRILL BITS
HACKSAW
SCREWDRIVER
METAL FILE/EMERY CLOTH
PARING CHISEL OR ROUTER

Measure the distance between the base partitions. Cut the dowel to this length. Mark 25mm (1in) in from each end and cut off a disc from each end. Mark the centre of each disc and the dowel at either end.

Drill a pilot hole in one end of the dowel, then insert a 38mm (1½in) No 8 wood screw, leaving just the shank protruding by 12mm (½in). Repeat at other end. Use a hacksaw to cut off the screw heads. File off any burr from the shank ends so about 8–10mm ($\frac{5}{16}$ – $\frac{3}{8}$ in) of shank will be protruding. For the discs, drill a series of 4mm ($\frac{1}{8}$ in) diameter holes from the centre of each disc to the edge to form a slot. The holes should be drilled to the same depth as the protruding screw shanks. To ensure this, stick tape to the drill bit at the correct distance from the tip. Use a chisel to clean out the slot. A much easier method of forming a slot is to use a router with a 4mm ($\frac{1}{8}$ in) diameter cutter if you have one.

Drill 4mm ($\frac{1}{8}$ in) diameter screw holes through each disc on either side of the centre line. Hold the dowel horizontally in place and mark off the positions of the discs. Then hold each disc in position to mark off screw hole positions. They should be about 75mm (3in) below the work surface and set back about 50mm (2in) from the front. Screw to partition and slot rail in place.

---

4 Fixing Brackets to the Wall and Adding the Slats

Drill holes for hanging bar and slot it in place before fixing the second bracket to the wall. Nail a batten to the wall temporarily to keep the brackets level. Screw down slats.

5 Cutting and Shaping Ends

Use a screw shank to form the rail pivot. For the slot, drill a series of holes in an offcut.

6 Fixing the Rail in Place

Use a narrow chisel to form a slot in the disc for the rail pivot. Screw the disc to the partition sides.

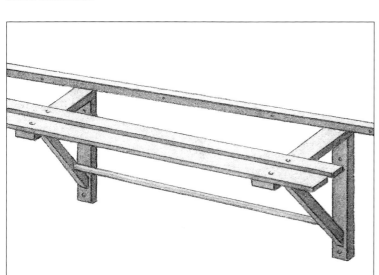

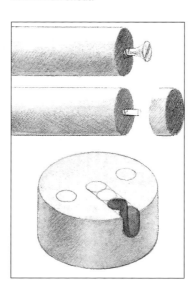

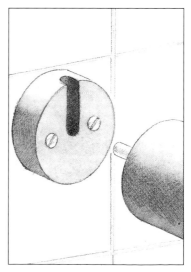

KNIFE RACK

TOOLS

STEEL MEASURING TAPE

TRY SQUARE

HAMMER

TENON SAW

TWO G-CRAMPS

DRILL (hand or power)

COUNTERSINK DRILL BIT

MASONRY DRILL BIT

SANDING BLOCK and
ABRASIVE PAPER

A knife rack is a useful addition to the kitchen system, and this is a quick and easy project to build.

Working from the back, glue and nail both verticals on to the first slat. Allow each end of the slat to protrude 75mm (3in) beyond the verticals (fig 1).

Fix the remaining slats at 38mm (1½in) centres. Use a spacing batten (*see* **Techniques, page 236**) to ensure accurate spacing between the slats. Leave a space for the knife slot. Glue the 25 × 6mm (1 × ¼in) spacers to the spare slat. There should be a spacer at each end and one in the middle of the slat (fig 2).

Glue the facing piece of the knife slot over the spacers. Secure with G-cramps, allow the glue to set and then sand it down.

Fix the knife-slot section to the verticals in the centre of the space left, again working from the back.

Drill countersunk holes through the front of the rails into the wall at the desired spot. As the load is light, it is not necessary to fix the rack to the studs in a lath-and-plaster wall or a hollow wall.

MATERIALS

Part	Quantity	Material	Length
SLATS	7	25 × 19mm (1 × ¾in) softwood	850mm (34in)
BACK OF KNIFE SLOT	1	25 × 25mm (1 × 1in) softwood	850mm (34in)
FRONT OF KNIFE SLOT	1	25 × 6mm (1 × ¼in) softwood	850mm (34in)
SPACERS	3	25 × 6mm (1 × ¼in) softwood	50mm (2in)
VERTICALS	2	25 × 19mm (1 × ¾in) softwood	450mm (18in)

① Nailing the Verticals to the Horizontal Slats
Work from the back and nail the vertical rails to the horizontal slats leaving a space for the knife slot to be fitted. Use a spacing batten to ensure that slats are evenly spaced.

② Forming the Knife Slot from Timber Battens
The knife slot batten is thicker than the others to accommodate knife handles. The slot is formed from a thin slat laid over three offcuts which act as spacers for the knives.

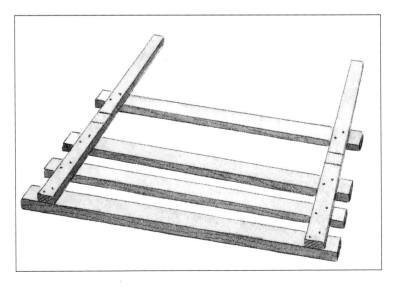

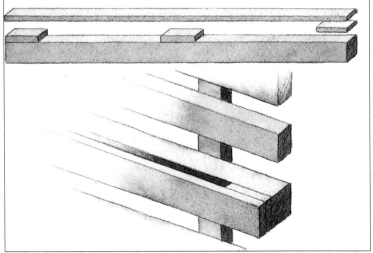

Airing Rack

TOOLS

STEEL MEASURING TAPE

STEEL RULE

TRY SQUARE

SANDING BLOCK coarse and fine abrasive paper

JIGSAW or PANEL SAW

POWER DRILL

FLAT BIT

TRIMMING KNIFE

Cut the square piece of wood in half diagonally. Round off all the corners with coarse, then fine abrasive paper. Paint the wood if required.

Mark the centres for the holes in one end piece. Mark the holes at 100mm (4in) centres and 45mm (1¾in) in from the edge. Drill the six (dowel) holes to 25mm (1in) diameter and the small (rope) holes to 6mm (¼in) diameter. Cramp both end pieces together, then use the first piece as a template to mark the hole positions on the second piece. Drill the holes in the second piece. Locate the dowels in the two end pieces, leaving about 75mm (3in) protruding either end.

Find the positions of the ceiling joists. If they run at right-angles to the rack, then, after fixing the pulleys, adjust the position of each end piece to align with the pulley above it. If the ceiling joists run parallel with the rack, choose the most convenient one to fix the pulleys to. Align the end pieces with pulleys. Fix double pulleys at the side from which you want to operate the rack.

Screw the cleat to a convenient place on the wall. Tie the rope to the rope hole in the end piece. Feed the rope through the single pulley, across to the double pulley, down to the cleat, up through the double pulley again, and then down to the other triangle. Tie this end in place to form a loop. Take up the slack rope and wind it round the cleat.

Check that the rack will move easily then apply wood glue into dowel holes to fix them.

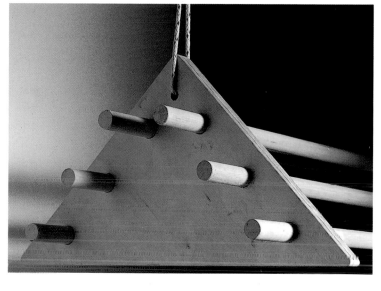

MATERIALS

Part	Quantity	Material	Length
ENDS	1	25mm (1in) plywood (or MDF)	400mm sq (16in sq)
RAILS	6	25mm (1in) diameter hardwood dowel	2m (6ft 6in) long

ONE SINGLE PULLEY, ONE DOUBLE PULLEY (screw-in or screw-on type)

A HANK OF SASH CORD AND ONE CLEAT

① Marking-Up Airing Rack End Pieces for Rails

Two triangular end pieces are cut from a 400mm (16in) square of 25mm (1in) plywood. Mark holes at 100mm (4in) intervals on a line 45mm (1¾in) in from the side edges.

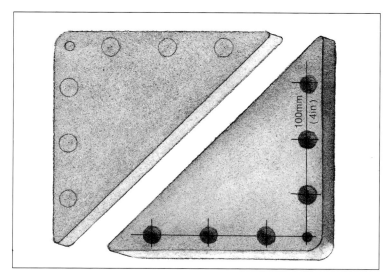

② Hanging the Airing Rack

A double and a single pulley should be securely fixed into ceiling joists. Fix a cleat firmly to a nearby wall and arrange cords as shown so that the airing rack can be raised and lowered easily.

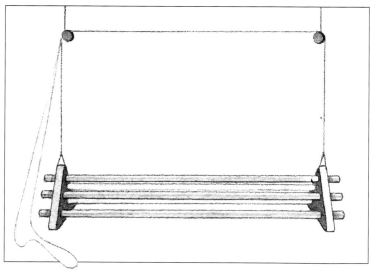

TILED BATHROOM

Traditionally, bathrooms tend to be rather badly organized rooms, in which a collection of pipework and bathroom equipment is arranged, so it seems, to suit the convenience of the plumber rather than the bather.

This design tries to organize the various elements of a bathroom so that plumbing work, which can often look rather brutal and unappealing, is hidden from view. The bathroom is uncluttered and easy to clean; requirements which I think are essential, given that the whole point of a bathroom is hygiene.

The bathroom system is remarkably easy to construct once you have mastered the simple art of cutting, laying and grouting wall tiles. The cavity behind the bath, shower and washbasin allows for pipework and drainage to be hidden from view. The large mirror behind the bath, whilst not essential, gives a sense of scale to a small space.

Tile colours and pattern can obviously be selected to suit your own particular preferences. I think that plain white tiles combined with white baths, basins, bidets and showers are particularly pleasant in bathrooms; they have light, reflective qualities, that induce an atmosphere of cleanliness and hygiene.

Tiled frame for a simple vanity unit

Mirror

light under tiled shelf

Recessed Basin in tiled top with wood shelf & towel rail

FRONT ELEVATION·

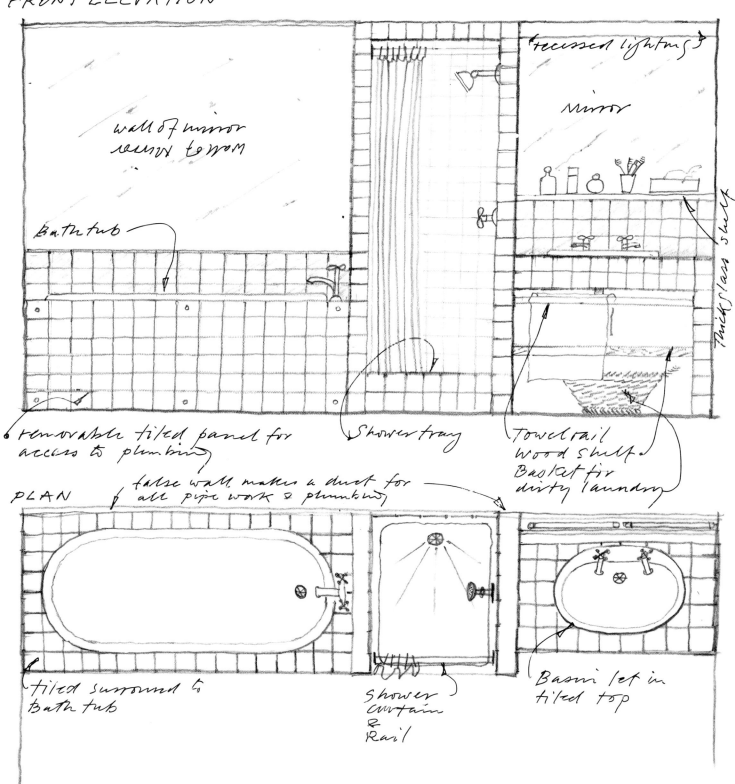

PLAN

TILED BATHROOM: BATH UNIT

This project shows how to make a tiled bathroom with the fitments set into hollow panel frames so that all the pipework is kept out of sight. The dimensions of the frames are based on those of your bathroom suite and your wall tiles. Obviously, the layout will have to be adapted to suit your particular bathroom.

It is strongly advised that you make a sketch of the proposed bathroom and discuss it with your plumber and electrician so that they can suggest the exact positioning of pipes and wiring, where access will be needed, and the sequence in which the work will be carried out. Coordinating your tasks with the installation of the plumbing and wiring will have to be carefully worked out between the three of you, since it is easier to put in the pipes and cables as the elements of the bathroom are built. Of course, this is not a problem if you are doing your own plumbing. This is now feasible, thanks to the availability of a wide range of easy-to-fit modern plumbing components, such as plastic supply and waste pipes, and push-fit joints. However, by building the frames and fitting some of the panels temporarily, it should be possible to do all the plumbing in one session.

Before starting, it is important to spend some time working out the dimensions carefully so that the minimum of tiles will need to be cut, and so that any cut tiles can be positioned where they will be least noticeable. Try to use only whole tiles. Where horizontal tiles meet vertical tiles at a corner, the horizontal ones should always overlap the vertical ones. This will occur at the top of the shower tray and where the bath and wall tiles come on to the bath. Always think about how water will run off the tiles. Wherever possible it should not run down into a joint, but off one tile and onto another to avoid unnecessary water penetration.

TOOLS

STEEL MEASURING TAPE

SPIRIT LEVEL

TRY SQUARE

METAL DETECTOR

TRIMMING KNIFE and MARKING GAUGE (useful but not essential)

CIRCULAR POWER SAW (or panel saw)

TENON SAW

POWER JIGSAW (or padsaw)

DRILL (hand or power)

TWIST DRILL BITS for pilot and clearance holes

MASONRY DRILL BIT to suit wallplugs being used

COUNTERSINK BIT

COLD CHISEL

SMOOTHING PLANE

ROUTER and ROUTER BIT

PLUMB BOB and CHALK

SCREWDRIVER

HAMMER

NAIL PUNCH

POWER FINISHING SANDER (or hand-sanding block)

TILING TOOLS

SILICONE-RUBBER SEALANT APPLICATOR (if required)

MATERIALS

Part	Quantity	Material	Length
BATH FRAME			
TOP AND BOTTOM RAILS	4	75 × 50mm (3 × 2in) PAR timber	Bath length, plus width of two tiles
UPRIGHT RAILS	8	75 × 50mm (3 × 2in) PAR timber	Height to bath rim, less 100mm (4in)*
END FRAME TOP AND BOTTOM RAILS	4	75 × 50mm (3 × 2in) PAR timber	Distance between inside faces of front and back panels
END FRAME UPRIGHT RAILS	4	75 × 50mm (3 × 2in) PAR timber	Height to bath rim, less 100mm (4in)*
END SHELVING STRIPS	2	12mm ($\frac{1}{2}$in) shuttering plywood; cut to tile width	Distance from back wall to front face of bath panel
BACK SHELVING STRIP	1	Plywood as above; width as above	Length of bath
FRONT SHELVING STRIP	1	Plywood as above; cut to tile width, less a tile thickness to allow shelf tiles to overlap edge of facing tiles on bath panel	Length of bath
BATH PANEL	1	Plywood as above; width as height of front frame	Length: as front frame and to overlap end panels (if fitted)

*Approximate lengths only – refer to copy for actual size

The entire framework is made from 75 × 50mm (3 × 2in) PAR softwood, skinned with 12mm ($\frac{1}{2}$in) shuttering plywood, which is strongly water-resistant. Our tiles are 108mm ($4\frac{1}{4}$in) square, a size which is readily available and works well with this framework.

BATH

Measure up for the frames to fit each side of the bath, allowing for 12mm ($\frac{1}{2}$in) plywood to be fixed on top. This will be exactly level with the rim of the bath and will allow the tiles to rest on the bath rim for an easily sealed joint.

Using 75 × 50mm (3 × 2in) timber, nail up the frames so that the top and bottom rails run the full length of the bath recess and the uprights fit between them – one at each end and two spaced inside them at equal distances.

The bath will either rest in a cradle or will be supplied with adjustable legs. The manufacturer's assembly instructions should be carefully followed. To spread the load across several floor joists, the bath feet should be rested on 75 × 50mm (3 × 2in) battens laid on their sides on the floor, and allowance should be made for these when measuring the height of bath. The bath should be carefully positioned lengthwise and widthwise to ensure that water drains properly to the waste outlet.

BATH FRAME ASSEMBLY

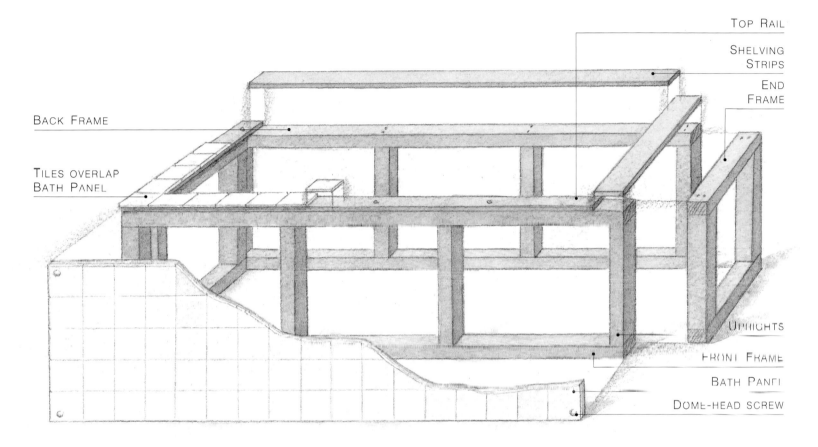

TOP RAIL

SHELVING STRIPS

END FRAME

BACK FRAME

TILES OVERLAP BATH PANEL

UPRIGHTS

FRONT FRAME

BATH PANEL

DOME-HEAD SCREW

End frames are made up in the same way as the front and back frames. They are fitted between them and allowance is made for the thickness of the front panel (12mm [$\frac{1}{2}$in] plywood). If you are fitting the bath tight to the wall or partitions at the foot or head, these end frames can be dispensed with, although you will need to cut top rails at the ends to support the shelving strips.

FIXING FRAMES

Screw the back frame to the wall, packing underneath it if necessary to ensure that it is level. Screw through the end frames into the back frame uprights and into the wall or partition at each end if there is one there. Put the bath in place and level it for correct drainage.

Position the front frame, screwing it into the end frames and the side walls or partitions where appropriate.

FITTING THE PLYWOOD SHELVING STRIPS

Measure up for these strips using 108mm (4$\frac{1}{4}$in) wide (or tile width if different) 12mm ($\frac{1}{2}$in) shuttering plywood to the width of the frame to the outer edges of the front frame, so that they fit across the bath at the head and foot, overhanging on the inside edges of the top rail.

Measure the spaces along the sides of the frame between the end shelves and cut two more lengths of plywood to fit between them. Note that the front shelf will be slightly narrower than the others as the tiles on this shelf will overlap the edges of the tiles used to cover the front panel of the bath unit.

Apply clear silicone-rubber sealant to the inside edges of all of the shelves and screw them down into the frame all round so that the plywood butts against the bath exactly level with the rim. The join between the bath and the shelves must be sealed with silicone-rubber to prevent water getting under the edging tiles. These strips make a good surface for tiling.

FITTING THE FRONT PANEL

Cut out the front panel from 12mm ($\frac{1}{2}$in) shuttering plywood and fit it over the frame and any end panels, if these are required. The front panel must be removable to make access easy in case you need to adjust or repair the internal plumbing. The panel is fixed with dome-head mirror screws inserted through the tiles once these have been fixed.

TILED BATHROOM: SHOWER UNIT

MATERIALS

SHOWER PARTITION

Part	Quantity	Material	Length
FRONT STUD	1	75 × 50mm (3 × 2in) PAR timber	Floor to ceiling height
TOP AND BOTTOM RAILS	2 per side	75 × 50mm (3 × 2in) PAR timber	Back of front stud to back wall
BACK STUD	1	75 × 50mm (3 × 2in) PAR timber	As front stud, less 100mm (4in)*
MIDDLE RAILS	As required	75 × 50mm (3 × 2in) PAR timber	Internal distance between front and back studs
SIDE PANELS	2 per side	12mm ($\frac{1}{2}$in) shuttering plywood	Length and width as overall dimensions of partition frame

SHOWER BASE

Part	Quantity	Material	Length
TOP AND BOTTOM RAILS	4	50 × 50mm (2 × 2in) PAR timber	Width between side partitions
SIDE STUDS	4	50 × 50mm (2 × 2in) PAR timber	Height of shower tray, less 112mm (4$\frac{1}{2}$in)*
FRONT PANEL	1	12mm ($\frac{1}{2}$in) shuttering plywood; width as distance between side panels	Height of base frame
TOP PANEL	1	As above; width as above	Distance from front of base panel to shower tray

SHOWER ROOF

Part	Quantity	Material	Length
ROOF PANEL	1	12mm ($\frac{1}{2}$in) shuttering plywood; width of recess	Depth of shower recess
FRONT PANEL	1	As above; width as shower base panel	Height of tiles, less 12mm ($\frac{1}{2}$in)
FRONT PANEL SUPPORT RAIL	1	50 × 50mm (2 × 2in) sawn timber	As width of roof panel
ROOF FIXING BATTENS	2	50 × 50mm (2 × 2in) PAR timber	As depth of roof panel, less 62mm (2$\frac{1}{2}$in)*

*Approximate lengths only – refer to copy for actual size

SHOWER PARTITIONS

Measure the floor-to-ceiling height for the front stud in exactly the place where it will be positioned. Then measure for the top and bottom rails to be positioned behind the front stud, having previously worked out the front-to-back depth of your shower recess. Cut them to length from the 75 × 50mm (3 × 2in) PAR timber. Next, cut the back stud to fit between the top and bottom rails, that is, the length of the front stud, less 100mm (4in) which is the thickness of the top and bottom rails (but measure these because 100mm [4in] is only their nominal rather than actual thickness).

BASIC FRAME

Nail the front stud to the top rail with 75mm (3in) round wire nails, driving them in with a support behind (see **Techniques, page 240**). Nail the bottom stud in place at the bottom, then insert the back stud 12mm ($\frac{1}{2}$in) in from the ends, to make scribing easier when the partitions are fitted to the wall. (If pipes have to be run along the back, this back stud can be positioned even farther in.) Nail the back stud in place. Repeat the process for a second side partition, if required.

MIDDLE RAILS

These brace the basic frame to make it sturdier, and are also used to make fixings from any adjacent support battens and fittings. They should therefore be placed at levels which coincide with the fixtures for these fittings.

In our case, a rail is needed where the basin and shelf supports meet the side. You may also need some additional support for the shower mixer or spray head, depending on the type of shower used (see fig 2, page 56). Another position for a cross rail would be where you have to make any joins in the plywood skin to make up the full height of your room. Space out other cross-rails at intervals of approximately 610–900mm (24–36in).

It is a good idea to fit a small removable access panel behind the shower fitments in case there is

1 **Assembly of the Shower Partition Basic Frame**
Assemble basic framework from PAR timber as shown, using round wire nails. Nail front stud on top rail, then bottom rail, and add the back stud, insetting it by 12mm ($\frac{1}{2}$in) to aid scribing.

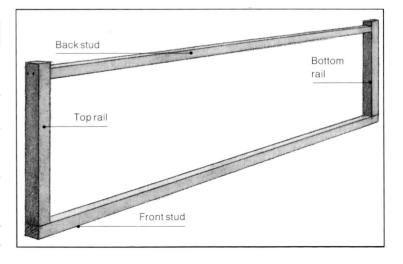

Back stud

Bottom rail

Top rail

Front stud

SHOWER UNIT ASSEMBLY

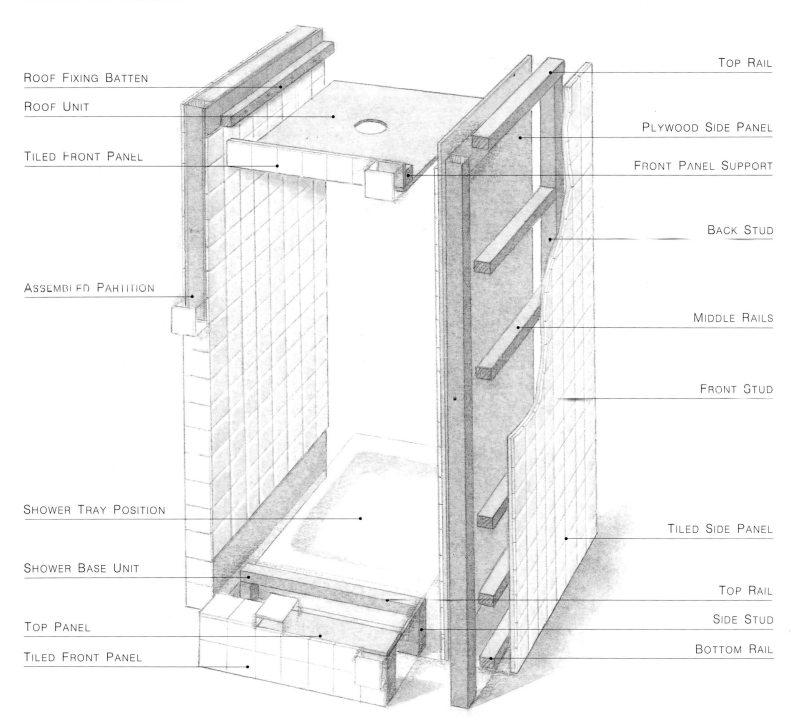

ROOF FIXING BATTEN

ROOF UNIT

TILED FRONT PANEL

ASSEMBLED PARTITION

SHOWER TRAY POSITION

SHOWER BASE UNIT

TOP PANEL

TILED FRONT PANEL

TOP RAIL

PLYWOOD SIDE PANEL

FRONT PANEL SUPPORT

BACK STUD

MIDDLE RAILS

FRONT STUD

TILED SIDE PANEL

TOP RAIL

SIDE STUD

BOTTOM RAIL

TILED BATHROOM: SHOWER UNIT

ever a problem with the plumbing. This is done by making a panel to coincide with whole tiles (fig 2). The panel is fixed into additional rails inside the frame. You may prefer to make one large panel to give access to the shower mixer control and the spray head. If you are using a plumber, ask his advice.

ADDING THE SIDES

When both frames are nailed up, measure for the side panels to finish flush with all the edges. Then cut out the required number of panels from 12mm ($\frac{1}{2}$in) shuttering plywood, making sure that you cut them all square. Mark the centre lines of all the studs on the edges of the frames as a guide for accurate nailing down of the side panels.

Lay the frame flat and lay the *inner* plywood panel on top. Line up the edge of the panel accurately with the *front* stud. Glue together, and then nail down into the stud about every 150mm (6in), using 38mm (1$\frac{1}{2}$in) round wire nails. Use the centre marks on the edges of the frame as a guide to the nail positions, to ensure that they are driven centrally into the rails.

Having nailed the front stud, pull the rest of the frame into square to align with the other edges of the plywood. Mark off on to the face of the plywood the centre lines of the rails and back stud so that you have guide lines for nailing.

Continue nailing down along the top and bottom rails, the back stud and the middle rails, checking as you do so that the frame is still square. Do not fix the other side panel at this stage.

Repeat for the other partition.

FIXING PARTITIONS

Put the partitions in place, spacing them by the width of the shower tray. Use a spirit level and plumb bob to check that the partitions are standing vertically. Do any scribing necessary to fit the partitions to the wall (*see* **Techniques, page 246**). This does not have to be very accurate as the finish to the wall will be achieved with the wall tiles. Fix the partitions in place by screwing through the back stud and packing any gaps be-

tween the back stud and the wall where the screws are positioned.

Screw through the top rail into the ceiling. If possible, screw into the ceiling joists. (You can find these by using a metal detector to locate the ceiling fixing nails *see* **Techniques, Wall fixings, page 240**). If the partitions fall between two joists (as is likely where the partitions run parallel with them), secure a length of 75 × 50mm (3 × 2in) timber between the joists and fix into this. Depending on the location of your bathroom, you may have to go into the loft to do this, or it may be necessary to lift a few floorboards in the room above the shower position. In this case, it is a good idea to get an electrician to install a ceiling light at the same time.

Finally, screw the bottom rail into the floor, packing under it if necessary to ensure that it sits square.

Temporarily fix the other plywood panel with a few nails only, not fully driven home. This will allow easy removal later, during plumbing, and will allow you to finish your framework first.

SHOWER BASE

Put the shower tray in place temporarily and adjust its legs so that the top of the tray is the height of the whole tiles. Make a frame from 50 × 50mm (2 × 2in) PAR timber to the width of the recess, by the height of the shower tray, but allowing for the thickness of the plywood panel which will rest on top. The rails should run to the full width between the partitions with the uprights between them. Butt the frame to the front of the shower tray and screw through the uprights into the plywood sides of the partitions.

Make up an identical frame to the front, to be positioned in from the front edge by the thickness of the plywood. Glue and screw through the upright into the side partitions as before. If, as in our case, the total width of the step is only one tile, the two frames will almost touch each other. Cut a piece of 12mm ($\frac{1}{2}$in) plywood to fit the front of this frame, flush with the top edge. Cut a top piece to rest on top of the frame, flush with the front of the frame and

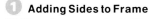

① Adding Sides to Frame
Middle rails are required at fixing positions for the bath or basin unit, possibly for the shower fixture, and also where it is necessary to join plywood panels. Nail down every 150mm (6in).

② Fitting an Access Panel
It is wise to fit an access panel behind shower fixtures. Panel should coincide with whole tiles.

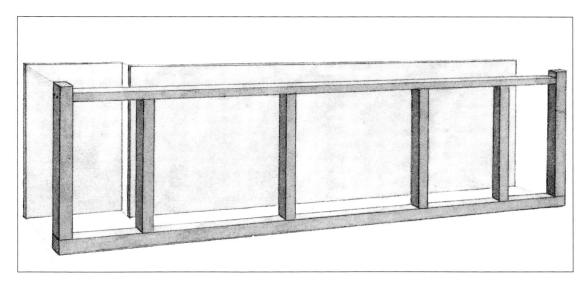

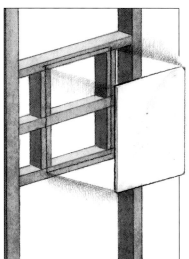

butting up to the shower tray. Do not fit these pieces yet: you will need access for fitting the shower tray and installing the waste trap and pipework (*see* **Plumbing and Wiring, page 60**).

Refer to the manufacturer's instructions on how to assemble and install the shower tray. Some trays have to be rested on sturdy timber battens to spread the weight of the tray when it is in use: if this is the case with yours, you may have to adjust the height of the support legs to accommodate the thickness of the support battens.

When fixing bathroom fittings into the timber frame, use an applicator to insert a generous line of clear silicone-rubber sealant between the fitting and the framework. This acts as a second line of defence should water get under the tiles owing to the breakdown of the sealant which will be used between the fitting and the tiles (*see* **Tiling, page 252**).

SHOWER ROOF

Measure the recess in the shower area and cut out a roof panel from 12mm ($\frac{1}{2}$in) shuttering plywood. Cut a front panel to rest on top of it, so that the total depth is sufficient to house a shower downlighter, while the panel lines up with a joint line in the tiled partitions and the wall. It is best to work out exactly where the tiles will fall. Alternatively, tile the partitions first only up to where you require the roof. Next, make up the roof unit and continue tiling.

Use a 50 × 50mm (2 × 2in) batten, glued and screwed in place, to join the roof panel and the front panel together at right angles. Assuming it is safe to do so, cut a hole in the middle of the roof panel, and fit the downlighter according to the manufacturer's instructions.

Cut two lengths of 50 × 50mm (2 × 2in) timber to be fixed horizontally on the inside faces of the partition panels, to allow the roof unit to be fixed to the sides. Cut these battens so that they will fit behind the front batten, but do not secure them, or the roof unit, at this stage as the plumbing must be completed first.

Buy a shower rail the width of the shower recess and fix in place.

③ Making Shower Base to Height of Shower Tray
The base comprises two frames, covered by a front panel and joined by a top panel which is cut to the width of one tile. If shower tray is only one tile high, top and bottom rails of frame will almost touch.

④ Shower Roof Assembly
Cut roof panel to fit between partitions. Front panel must be deep enough to hide shower downlighter.

GLASS SHELF
A sleek glass shelf sits above the basin unit, see page 61 for instructions.

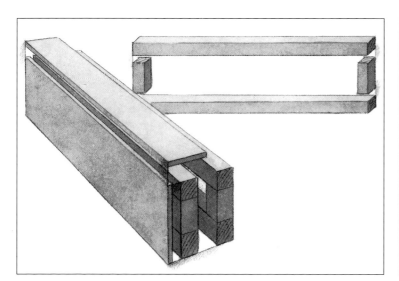

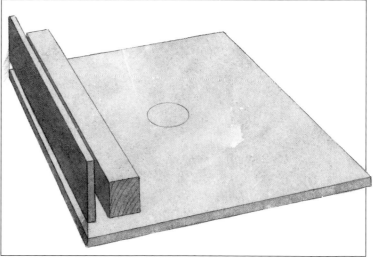

TILED BATHROOM: BASIN UNIT

MATERIALS

Part	Quantity	Material	Length
BASIN UNIT			
PARTITION FRAME FRONT STUD	1	75 × 50mm (3 × 2in) PAR timber	Height of basin, less 12mm ($\frac{1}{2}$in)
TOP AND BOTTOM RAILS	2	75 × 50mm (3 × 2in) PAR timber	Distance from inside face of front stud to back wall
BACK STUD	1	75 × 50mm (3 × 2in) PAR timber	Height of basin, less 12mm ($\frac{1}{2}$in) less 100m (4in)*
MIDDLE RAIL	1	75 × 50mm (3 × 2in) PAR timber	Distance between inside faces of front and back studs
SIDE PANELS	1 or 2	12mm ($\frac{1}{2}$in) shuttering plywood; width as overall width of frame	Height of frame
FRONT PANEL	1	Plywood as above; to give sufficient depth to hide underside of basin	Distance between partition panel and side of shower partition
TOP PANEL	1	19mm ($\frac{3}{4}$in) shuttering plywood; width as depth of recess	Width of alcove
FRONT PANEL SUPPORT RAIL	1	75 × 50mm (3 × 2in) or 50 × 50mm (2 × 2in) PAR timber, plus scrap pieces for securing	Width of alcove
BASIN SUPPORT BATTEN	1	50 × 50mm (2 × 2in) PAR timber	As top rail of basin partition frame
UNDER-BASIN SHELF PANEL	1	12mm ($\frac{1}{2}$in) melamine-faced chipboard or plywood (if to be tiled); width as depth of recess, less about 125mm (5in)	Distance between inside faces (after tiling) of shower and basin support partitions
SHELF LIPPING	1	50 × 25mm (2 × 1in) pine	As above
SHELF-SUPPORT BATTENS	2	25 × 25mm (1 × 1in) PAR timber	As width of under-basin shelf panel
GLASS SHELF	1	Toughened glass as recommended by supplier. Width as required, plus 12mm ($\frac{1}{2}$in) to be set in rear-wall plaster	Width of basin alcove, plus 25mm (1in)
REAR-WALL GLASS SHELF-SUPPORT BATTEN	1	12 × 12mm ($\frac{1}{2}$ × $\frac{1}{2}$in) hardwood (or as plaster thickness)	Width of basin alcove, plus 25mm (1in)
SIDE-WALL GLASS SHELF-SUPPORT BATTEN	1	12 × 12mm ($\frac{1}{2}$ × $\frac{1}{2}$in) hardwood (or as plaster thickness)	Width of glass shelf, less 12mm ($\frac{1}{2}$in), or batten thickness (if different)
PELMET PANEL	1	19mm ($\frac{3}{4}$in) plywood; width as tile depth	Width of basin alcove
PELMET SUPPORT BLOCKS	2	50 × 25mm (2 × 1in) PAR timber	As pelmet depth, less 25mm (1in)

*Approximate length only – refer to copy for actual size

BASIN

The basin is set into a tiled surface with a shelf underneath. The frame is fitted between the shower partition and another low-level partition. Alternatively, you can make the fixing between two low-level ones.

BASIN PARTITION

Decide how high you want your basin, and how far out from the wall you want it to extend. Allow a generous space around the basin.

Make up the partition frame in the same way as for the shower, but only one middle rail will be required. This will be at the level you want to fit the shelf supports. Note this level as you will need to know it once the sides are in place.

Mark the centre lines of the rails and studs on the edges of the frame as a guide for nailing on the side panels. Cut these out. If the partition is to be fitted against a wall, it will need only one side panel. Do not fix it at this stage. If it is not going against a wall, fix only the outer one (farthest from the basin) by following the procedure for the shower partition on page 54 (glue and nail the front stud first, and pull it into square to complete fixing). Fix the partition panel in place as described above.

If the partition is to be fitted to a wall, stand the framework 12mm ($\frac{1}{2}$in) away from the wall, checking that it is vertical and packing the bottom rail level if necessary. Use packing pieces between the frame and the wall at the point where the screws go in. If this distance varies because the wall is uneven, make the 12mm ($\frac{1}{2}$in) gap between the frame and the wall the maximum width. This will avoid any need for scribing to fit the frame to the wall, and will still allow for whole tiles to fit the front edge of the partition. Fit inner side panel in place and temporarily nail to frame.

BASIN UNIT ASSEMBLY

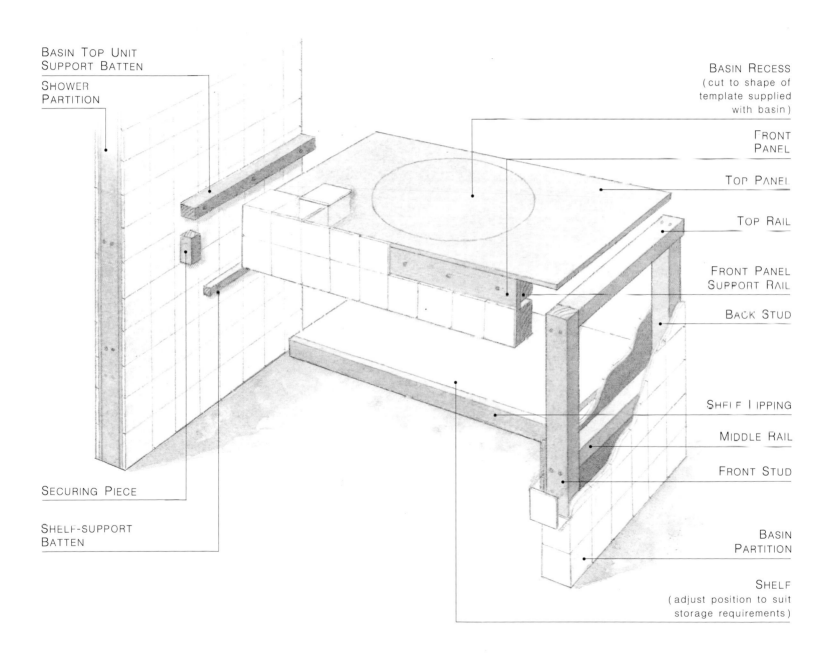

BASIN TOP UNIT
SUPPORT BATTEN

SHOWER
PARTITION

SECURING PIECE

SHELF-SUPPORT
BATTEN

BASIN RECESS
(cut to shape of
template supplied
with basin)

FRONT
PANEL

TOP PANEL

TOP RAIL

FRONT PANEL
SUPPORT RAIL

BACK STUD

SHELF LIPPING

MIDDLE RAIL

FRONT STUD

BASIN
PARTITION

SHELF
(adjust position to suit
storage requirements)

TILED BATHROOM

FRONT PANEL

Measure the width of the recess from inside the basin partition to the side of the shower partition and cut a piece of 12mm or 19mm ($\frac{1}{2}$in or $\frac{3}{4}$in) shuttering plywood to fit across this width. The depth of this piece should be enough to hide the underside of the basin. Work it out so that the total depth will coincide with whole tiles, after allowing for the thickness of the top panel.

TOP PANEL

Measure up for the top panel to fit the width and depth of the alcove, and to finish flush with the front of the low partition. Cut the panel from 19mm ($\frac{3}{4}$in) shuttering plywood. Use a 75×50mm (3×2in) or a 50×50mm (2×2in) batten cut to the length of the front panel to join the top and front panels together at right-angles. Make sure that the front panel rests under the top panel, and that there is a space at the end to slot over the end partition. Glue the batten in place and screw through the panels into it.

FIXING THE BASIN FRAME ASSEMBLY

To support the basin unit at the shower partition end, cut a 50×50mm (2×2in) batten to length and screw it to the side of the shower partition, fixing into the cross-rail inside the partition. It must be fixed exactly level with the top of the low partition. Rest the unit in place, but do not secure it yet as it will need to be removed for plumbing.

Cut the aperture for the inset basin by using the template supplied by the basin manufacturer. Use a power jigsaw to cut this hole, or do it by hand with a padsaw. Check that the basin fits in the hole, but do not fit it until you have tiled the top panel.

Screw scrap pieces of 50×50mm (2×2in) timber to the back of the front panel to secure it to the partitions at each side.

PLUMBING AND WIRING

At this stage the plumber can fit the basin, shower tray and bath, and install the supply and waste pipes.

Inset showers can be fitted now, and the pipework can be put in place for surface-mounted types, although the fittings themselves, for both types of showers, are installed after tiling.

Also, have the wiring put in at this stage, with tails left protruding for lights, shaver sockets, heaters or electrical showers and so on to be fitted later.

PERMANENT FIXING OF PARTITION SIDES, BASIN AND SHOWER UNITS

Fix all the second sides to the partitions by nailing into the studs and rails. Screw the basin unit in place down through the top panel into the partition and support batten and through the scrap pieces to secure to the partitions at each side.

For the shower base, screw the front panel in place on to the front frame, and fix the top piece down on to the front and back frame. Insert silicone-rubber sealant between the frame and bathroom fittings, where appropriate.

For the roof unit, screw the 50×50mm (2×2in) battens into the plywood sides for the roof to fit correctly, and screw through the roof panel into the battens. However, if you prefer to do most of the tiling on a flat surface, do not secure the roof panel until it has been tiled, leaving off the tiles at the edges, at the points where you will be screwing through into the battens. Fix the ceiling panel in place, then tile over the screws.

TILING

Protect the bathroom fittings while you are tiling, as they can be spoilt by adhesive and grout. If they are in wrappings, keep these on for as long as possible. Begin tiling (see **Techniques, page 252**); below are some tips relevant to this project.

Tile the sides of the partition first, but note the middle rail positions before, so you know where to fit the shelf supports. Work from the front edge to the back so that any cut tiles will be against the wall.

Apply the shower roof tiles before fixing the roof panel in place. Leave off the edging tiles so that you can screw the roof panel to its fixing

① Assembly of Basin Top Unit from 19mm ($\frac{3}{4}$in) plywood
Cut the top panel to the width and depth of the basin alcove. Glue and screw the top panel and front panel to a square batten so that they are at right-angles, the front panel resting beneath the top panel.

② Making up the Under-basin Shelf Assembly
The shelf is cut to inside width of recess and is set back slightly from front of the side partitions. Wooden lipping, glued and pinned to front edge of shelf, hides shelf-support battens which are screwed to partition units.

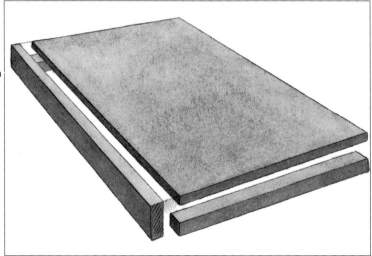

battens. If you have already fixed the shower roof, tile the partition walls up to it.

Tile the front surfaces next, that is, the front edges of the partitions, the front panels of the basin, shower tray and bath panel.

Tile the top surface, that is, around the bath, basin and shower. Around the bath, where a lot of water is likely to lie, put some extra adhesive around the outer sides of the tiles so that they slope very slightly towards the bath.

Tile the walls and remaining partitions next. If you are fitting a glass shelf, apply tiles up to one tile's width below the level of the shelf on those walls where the shelf will be fitted. Fit the glass shelf (see below) and complete the tiling afterwards.

Finally, if you previously tiled the shower roof whilst it was still flat, you can now fix the remaining tiles on the partition sides – these were initially left off in order to screw the roof unit to its fixing battens. These can be held in place with sticky tape while the tile adhesive sets. If the shower roof has already been fixed,

tile with the aid of a simple home-made timber T-support. This is lightly wedged in place between the roof and the floor to hold each row of tiles in place while the adhesive sets. The support will be needed for only about 15 minutes on each row.

After a minimum of 12 hours the joints between the tiles can be grouted with a waterproof grout, and the tiles can be polished clean.

Fix the bath panel, and any access panels, with dome-head mirror screws. You can drill clearance holes easily with a masonry drill bit. Do not press too hard, and make sure that your drill is *not* switched to hammer action. Put a piece of sticky tape on the tile where you want to drill the hole, to prevent the drill bit from skidding across the surface.

Finally, apply a silicone-rubber sealant to all joins between the bathroom fittings and the ceramic tiles and to all internal corners where partitions meet the original walls. Sealants are available in white, clear and a range of colours, and are supplied with full instructions. To eject a bead of sealant, you usually

press a plunger with your thumb, although trigger-operated aerosol packs are also becoming popular.

GLASS SHELF

Setting a glass shelf in a wall is an unorthodox method of fitting, but, if properly done, the effect of having no visible means of support is well worth the effort. However, for an easier solution, rest the glass on rubber door stops screwed into the wall – two stops at each end – after the wall or partition has been tiled.

For a concealed fixing, ask your supplier what thickness of toughened glass you need for your span. Ours is 12mm ($\frac{1}{2}$in) glass spanning 1100mm (43in). The glass must be cut to size and the edges polished.

Stop the tiles one tile's width below where you want the shelf. Cut a slot into the wall at the back and the end to the thickness of the plaster and about 25mm (1in) or so wide. Fix in place a thin batten to the thickness of the plaster, minus the thickness of the shelf.

Where the shelf meets the shower partition, you must cut a slot to the thickness of the glass in the facing panel. Do this either by drilling a row of overlapping holes with a bit the same diameter as the shelf's thickness, and chisel out the waste to make a straight-sided slot, or use a jigsaw or router to cut a neat slot.

Slot the shelf into place. This can be difficult and it may be necessary to cut away a little extra plaster above where the shelf has to go. Fill any gaps with wall filler or tile adhesive, then complete the tiling up to the shelf. Above the shelf you can add a mirror, or tile the wall.

UNDER-BASIN SHELF

This is made from 12mm ($\frac{1}{2}$in) melamine-faced chipboard, but you can use plywood if you are going to tile the shelf. Cut the shelf to the width of the recess and to the

required depth. It will look better if it is recessed back from the front edge a little way – 108mm ($4\frac{1}{4}$in), ie one tile's width, in our case.

Cut lipping from 50 × 25mm (2 × 1in) pine. Hold the shelf in a vice and glue and nail the lipping to the front edge of the shelf so that the top edge of the lipping is flush with the shelf surface and the bottom edge hides the support battens. Punch the nail heads below the surface, fill the holes, sand smooth and apply a finish.

SHELF-SUPPORT BATTENS

These support the shelf at each side from behind the lipping to the back wall. Cut two pieces to length from 25 × 25mm (1 × 1in) timber. Drill two clearance holes in each batten, then drill into the tiled sides at the marked levels. Countersink the holes and screw the battens in place.

MIRROR

Fit the mirror to the wall with dome-head mirror screws if it is already drilled for these. If it is not, use corner-fixing mirror plates. When using mirror screws, put a tap washer over each screw behind the mirror to keep it slightly away from the wall. Whichever type of mirror fixing you use, be careful not to over-tighten the fixing screws, as you may crack the glass; ask your glass supplier for advice.

PELMET

To conceal the overhead lighting, fix a pelmet above the mirror in the basin recess. Make the pelmet from 19mm ($\frac{3}{4}$in) plywood; cut it to the width of the recess and to the depth of one tile. Cut two support blocks from 50 × 25mm (2 × 1in) timber, about 25mm (1in) less than the pelmet depth, to fit behind the pelmet strip at each end. Screw these into the wall and the side partition in order to fit the pelmet in place securely.

③ Fitting a Glass Shelf Using Hidden Supports
The wall is channelled to the thickness of the plaster for a batten which is fixed at the back and sides of the alcove. The shelf is made of toughened glass and rests neatly on the batten. After fitting, fill any gaps then finish tiling.

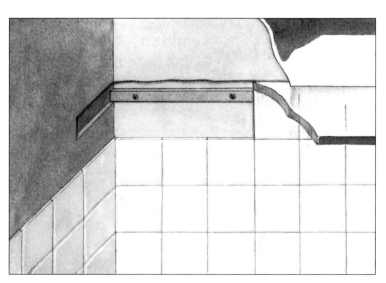

PANELLED BATHROOM

Often, the best ideas are the simple ones. Very few things in life are more unpleasant than trying to dry yourself with a damp towel, so if you install this room-width rail combined with a radiator you can remedy this forever. The rail here is made from chromed tube, but could be finished in coloured enamel or be made in timber like the spar of a yacht.

All of the pipework in this bathroom has been hidden neatly behind a false wall which is simply constructed from painted tongued-and-grooved pine boarding. This is a particularly good solution as a section of the panelling can be mounted on a batten frame to create an access panel which can be easily removed if you have any plumbing problems.

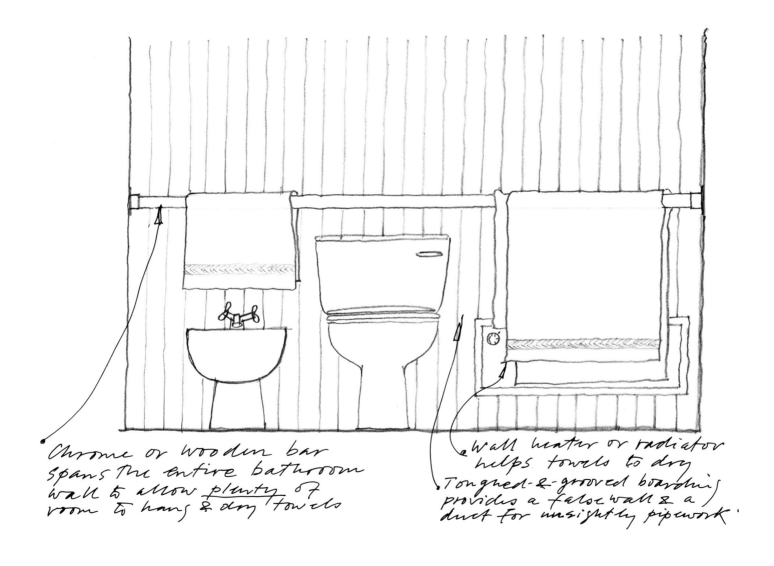

Chrome or wooden bar spans the entire bathroom wall to allow plenty of room to hang & dry towels

Wall heater or radiator helps towels to dry

Tongued-&-grooved boarding provides a false wall & a duct for unsightly pipework.

PANELLED BATHROOM

Building a false wall is a clever way of concealing ugly pipework in the bathroom. The job is relatively easy if you are fitting a new bathroom suite. However, if a suite is already installed, you may have to move one or more of the components to make space for the new wall. Check that this is possible, bearing in mind the position of waste pipes and drains.

The false wall is made by fixing battens to the existing wall and covering them with timber boards. These are normally tongued and grooved, and can range from plywood strips faced with an attractive veneer to solid timber such as pine. Normally, they are fitted vertically over horizontal battens.

The battens need only be of rough-sawn softwood, and should be at least 50 × 50mm (2 × 2in) if you intend to run pipes behind them. They should be fixed at centres of about 610mm (24in). There is no need to strip off any of the wall decoration before fixing the battens.

The spacing of the battens is determined largely by the thickness of the boards to be used, but also by the degree of rigidity required. It is important for the panelling to be more rigid in places where it may be leant against. As a general guide, 9mm ($\frac{3}{8}$in) boards would have battens at centres of 400–500mm (16–20in), while 12mm ($\frac{1}{2}$in) boards need battens set 500–610mm (20–24in) apart.

Always begin and end battens a short distance from corners or ceilings so that nails are not driven into the last few millimetres of the boards, as this can cause splitting.

In order to bring all the battens flush with each other, plywood or hardboard packing pieces may have to be used behind some of the screws. This will certainly be necessary with an undulating wall. Check the battens carefully with a long straight-edge, for unless they are completely flush, you will not be able to fix the boards on to them properly.

The 50mm (2in) battens should provide enough space to conceal most bathroom pipes. If not, use thicker battens. Screw the battens to the wall, cutting out sections to accommodate pipework where necessary. However, if the wall is perfectly flat, you can fix the battens with masonry nails, provided they are long enough to go at least 12mm ($\frac{1}{2}$in) into the masonry.

If you want to attach boards of random lengths, for effect, then additional horizontal battens will be needed, spaced to suit how you plan to cut the boards. Position the boards so that the cut ends meet in the centre of a batten and those at either end are both of a similar width.

You can fix the boards with nails or with special clips which slot on to the tongue and are then nailed to the battens. Nailing through the face of the boards is the simplest and quickest method of fixing, but the nail heads must be punched below the surface and the holes filled with a matching wood filler. It is not necessary to match the wood if the boards are to be painted.

TOOLS

STEEL MEASURING TAPE

SPIRIT LEVEL

SCREWDRIVER

NAIL PUNCH

HAMMER

PANEL SAW

TENON SAW (fine-toothed)

POWER JIGSAW (or padsaw)

TONGUE-AND-GROOVE CLIPS

MITRE BOX

POWER DRILL

DRILL BITS FLAT BIT (or
             expansive bit)
             COUNTERSINK BIT

MASONRY BIT

MATERIALS

Part	Quantity	Material	Length
WALL BATTENS	As required	50 × 50mm (2 × 2in) (minimum) sawn softwood	Width of wall
BOARDS	As required	9 or 12mm ($\frac{3}{8}$ or $\frac{1}{2}$in) thick boards	As required
ALUMINIUM POLE (or chrome or wood)	1	37mm (1$\frac{1}{2}$in) diameter aluminium, chrome or wooden pole	As required
SUPPORT DISCS	2	18mm ($\frac{3}{4}$in) thick MDF discs	

Nailing through the tongues with very thin 'lost head' pins provides an invisible fixing. These are driven at an angle into the tongue and are hidden by the groove of the next board. You may find that the wood splits in some cases, since dry pine is rather brittle. Do not worry if this should happen. Just break off any splinters; the splits will be covered by the groove of the next board, which is slotted over the tongue.

If the boards are to be pinned, fix the first with its groove in the corner, and check with a spirit level that it is standing vertically. Adjust the board as necessary before securing it by driving pins through the grooved edge. These are the only surface pins used and should be sunk below the surface with a nail punch. The holes should be filled with a matching wood filler.

Pin the other side of the board,

1 **Fixing Tongued, Grooved and V-Jointed Boards with Nails**
Left First board is scribed to a side wall, ensuring board is vertical. Pin to batten, driving nail through grooved edge. *Right* Tap next board over tongue and pin through tongue. Repeat for all succeeding boards.

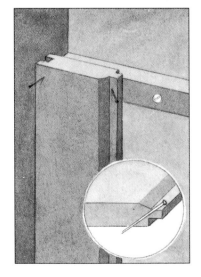
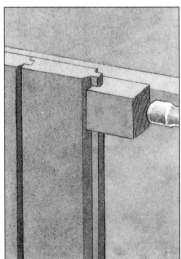

angling the pins through the tongue. Fit a pin into each wall batten.

Tap the next board over the tongue to hide the fixing nails. Protect the edge of the board from the hammer with a piece of scrap wood.

Clips are easy to use and provide a stronger fixing than pins, but are more expensive. They are designed to lock into the lower part of a groove.

The tongued edge of the first board goes into the corner you are starting from. Cut off the tongue with a fine-toothed tenon saw. Position the cut edge in the corner and pin it in place or use a special starter clip. Then secure the grooved edge with a clip. This is hidden by the next board inserted in the groove.

If boards of random length have to be butt-jointed at their ends, use a mitre box with a right-angle slot for very accurate saw cuts. Do not fill the gaps between the joints.

The boards used in our bathroom were stopped short of the floor, giving an attractive finish. The lower edge was decorated with beading. To do this, fit a temporary batten at the bottom at the required height above the floor, to serve as a finishing guide for the bottom edge of each board. When it is removed, the bottom edges of the boards will be flush with each other.

Glue and pin the beading in place along the lower edge of the boards. Also, fix the beading in the corners and along the ceiling line to hide gaps. It should be pinned to the walls or ceiling and not to the boards. Again, the heads of the pins should be sunk below the surface and the holes filled with a matching wood filler. If you prefer to avoid nail holes, fix the beading with a contact adhesive.

It is advisable to provide easy access to pipework and joints for maintenance or repair. Therefore, fix a few strategic boards with screws rather than pins, cutting off the tongues, so that the boards in question can be lifted out easily. Make a feature of the screws by using dome-head or brass screws.

Although timber boards provide an excellent way of covering up old or unsightly walls, they must never be used on damp walls. The cause of the dampness should be traced and eliminated. The only form of damp that they will cure is condensation, since the new wall surface will be warmer.

If an insulating blanket is to be applied between the battens to increase the heat retention of an outside wall, first cover the wall with vapour-check sheeting (either polythene or building paper) and fix the battens over it. Although this will ensure that no damp strikes through to the wall, it is not a cure for existing damp or the structural damage that it can cause.

Finally, remember that all timber can move with changes in moisture. Therefore, all boards should be conditioned before use by keeping them in the room in which they are to be used for about a week beforehand.

TOWEL RAIL

A feature is made here of the towel rail, which runs the width of the bathroom. A 37mm (1½in) diameter anodized aluminium pole was chosen, although chrome or wood can be used. If the pole is very long, a couple of intermediate supports will prevent it sagging.

If you have to make your own support discs, use 19mm (¾in) MDF. To mark out a circle for a disc, draw round an object of a suitable size. Cut out the circle (see **Techniques, page 238**) with a jigsaw or padsaw.

Mark off the diameter of the pole in the centre of each disc and cut it out with a flat bit or expansive bit, or a jigsaw or coping saw. Repeat for the other disc.

Countersink two drill holes in each disc, fit the discs on to the pole, and get a helper to hold the pole horizontally while you mark off the screw hole positions on the wall. Remove the pole and discs and drill and plug the holes in the wall.

Replace the discs on the pole and get a helper to hold the pole while the screws are fixed. Use 50mm (2in) No 8 screws.

Fill the screw holes, sand down when dry, and apply a finish to the discs to match the pole or the wall.

② **Fixing Boards with Clips**
Saw off tongue. Push the board over a starter clip and secure grooved edge with clips.

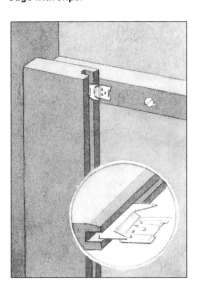

③ **Finishing the False Wall with Beading at the Bottom**
Boards are fixed to 50 × 50mm (2 × 2in) wall battens or whatever thickness necessary to hide pipes. For neatness stop the boards short of the floor and pin a beading here.

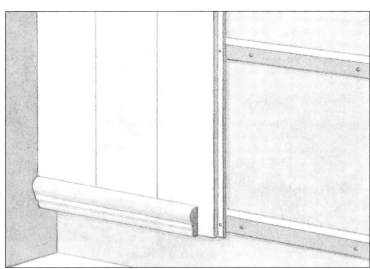

④ **Towel Rail Support Discs**
Make support discs from 19mm (¾in) MDF and cut hole in centre for rail using a jigsaw or a coping saw.

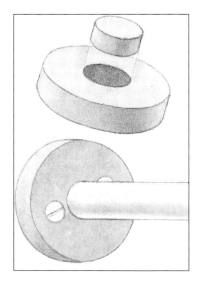

ALCOVE SHELVES AND CUPBOARDS

Many rooms have a chimney breast with an alcove on either side. This design allows you to integrate storage space into an alcove without disturbing the unity of the wall. This is achieved by repeating a triangular moulding from the face of the alcove cupboard doors on a decorative panel placed over the fireplace. Larger mouldings of the same shape also form the wall supports for the alcove shelves in the recesses, and for the angled pelmet which conceals the tungsten strip lights. The repetition of this decorative device provides a unifying element to the design and detailing of the whole wall.

How you decorate the shelves, doors and panels is dependent on your scheme for the rest of the room. This project is an example of my philosophy that tries to ensure that fittings which are built-in to the structure of a room blend into the existing architecture and features rather than argue with them.

SECTION OF CUPBOARD DOOR

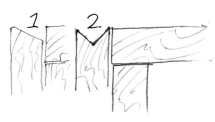

top edge of doors can be bevelled in 2 ways to provide a finger grip

PLAN OF CUPBOARD & WALL DECORATION

triangular slats glued & pinned to door panels — then filled & painted.

FRONT ELEVATION

Triangular shelf support battens echo the shape of the door & wall decoration

Wall decoration echos door panels

Concealed lighting at back of shelves.

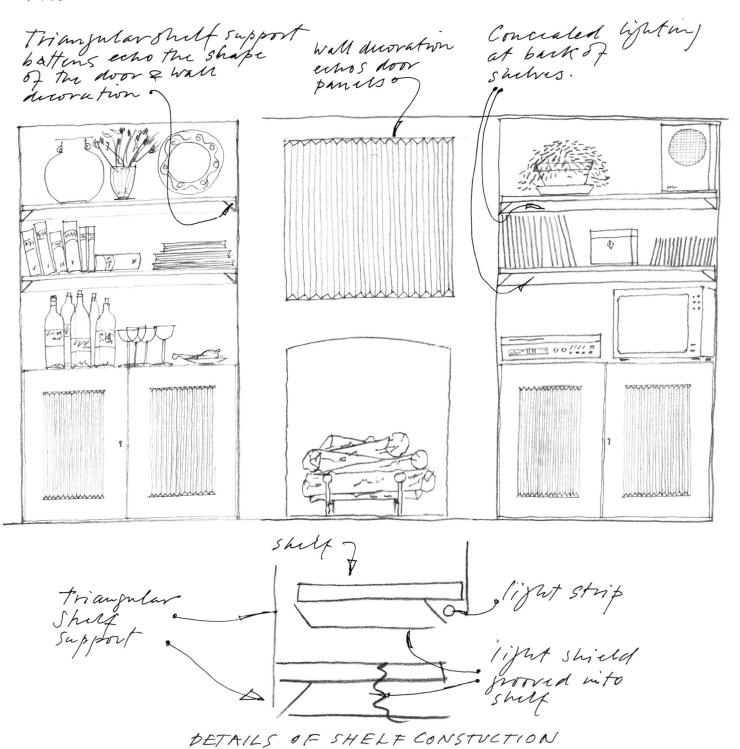

shelf

triangular shelf support

light strip

light shield grooved into shelf

DETAILS OF SHELF CONSTUCTION

ALCOVE SHELVES AND CUPBOARDS

Living rooms always call for a reasonable amount of storage and display space; one way of creating it is to make use of the wasted space on each side of a chimney breast, or in a corner, by fitting shelves and a cupboard. A basic design is described below, but the project is easy to adapt to suit your own requirements. You may want alcove cupboards and shelves to house a television, music equipment, books, drinks and glasses, or favourite ob-jects. The function will probably determine the height of your cupboards and shelves, so think about your specific storage needs before you start work. For example, you may want to construct just one cupboard for use as a drinks cabi-net. Alternatively, you may like to vary the number of shelves above a cupboard, according to the size and type of objects you wish to store or display on them.

The linenfold decoration which has been added to the cupboard doors here is echoed on the wall with a panel of the same design, adding an individual and interesting detailing. By varying the kind of moulding you use on the cupboards and on the wall, you will be able to adapt the overall design to suit your own decorative scheme. Another way of adding a personal touch to the design is to vary the cupboard door fittings, by using different door handles or knobs.

Whatever the design, it is most important to ensure that all gaps are filled and edges are smoothed so that the cupboards and shelves appear to be part of the structure of the room, even if they are not painted the same colour. The shelf battens should be disguised as much as possible to blend in with the wall. In this project we show how a shelf batten can incorporate a light above a shelf, lending muted tones to the colour scheme of the walls.

TOOLS

STEEL RULE

TRIMMING KNIFE

TRY SQUARE

PANEL SAW (or circular saw)

TENON SAW

HAMMER

SCRIBING BLOCK

CHISEL bevel-edge type

MALLET

DRILL (hand or power)

DRILL BIT

MASONRY DRILL BIT

COUNTERSINK BIT

END MILL for fitting concealed hinges

POWER JIGSAW

SANDING BLOCK and ABRASIVE PAPER (or power finishing sander)

HAND PLANE (or power plane)

SPIRIT LEVEL

NAIL PUNCH

MATERIALS For one alcove:

Part	Quantity	Material	Length*
UPRIGHTS	2	50 × 50mm (2 × 2in) PAR timber	As required – (ours 838mm (33in)
HORIZONTAL RAILS	2	50 × 50mm (2 × 2in) PAR timber	Width of alcove, less 100mm (4in)*
BACK SUPPORT BATTENS	2	50 × 25mm (2 × 1in) PAR timber	Width of alcove
SIDE SUPPORT BATTENS	4	50 × 25mm (2 × 1in) PAR timber	Depth of alcove, less 100mm (4in)*
BASE FRONT AND BACK SUPPORT BATTENS	2	25 × 25mm (1 × 1in) PAR timber	Width of alcove
BASE SIDE SUPPORT BATTENS	2	25 × 25mm (1 × 1in) PAR timber	Depth of alcove
ALCOVE SHELF-SUPPORT BACK BATTENS	2	38mm (1$\frac{1}{2}$in) triangular section	Width of alcove
ALCOVE SHELF-SUPPORT SIDE BATTENS	4	38mm (1$\frac{1}{2}$in) triangular section	Depth of alcove, less 38mm (1$\frac{1}{2}$in)
LINENFOLD-WALL PANEL DECORATION	As required	38mm (1$\frac{1}{2}$in) triangular section	Height of wall panel
LINENFOLD DOOR DECORATION	12 per door	25mm (1in) triangular section	Door height, less 200mm (8in)
DOWELS	1	Approximately 1.8m (6ft) hardwood dowelling	As required
BASE PANEL	1	4mm or 6mm ($\frac{1}{8}$in or $\frac{1}{4}$in) plywood	Alcove width × depth, less thickness of skirtings & front frame
TOP PANEL	1	25mm (1in) MDF, or blockboard	Alcove width × depth
CUPBOARD SHELF	1	19mm ($\frac{3}{4}$in) MDF, chipboard, or blockboard	Alcove width × depth of alcove, less 75mm (3in)*
DOORS	2	19mm ($\frac{3}{4}$in) MDF	$\frac{1}{2}$ alcove width, less 8mm ($\frac{3}{8}$in) × front frame height less 25mm (1in)
ALCOVE SHELVES	2	25mm (1in) MDF	Alcove width × alcove depth, less 25mm (1in)
CENTRE WALL PANEL	1	6mm ($\frac{1}{4}$in) MDF or plywood	Chimney breast width × height required

*Approximate lengths only – refer to copy for actual size

ALCOVE SHELVES AND
CUPBOARD ASSEMBLY

TOP SHELF

TRIANGULAR
BACK BATTEN

MIDDLE SHELF

CHAMFERED SHELF EDGE

LIGHTS BEHIND
BATTEN

TRIANGULAR
SIDE BATTEN

CUPBOARD TOP

SUPPORTING
BACK BATTEN

TOP RAIL

CUPBOARD
SHELF

SUPPORTING
SIDE BATTEN

DOOR

SKIRTING
(retained)

BASE SUPPORT
BATTENS

BOTTOM RAIL

TRIANGULAR-SECTION
DECORATION

25mm (1in) GAP

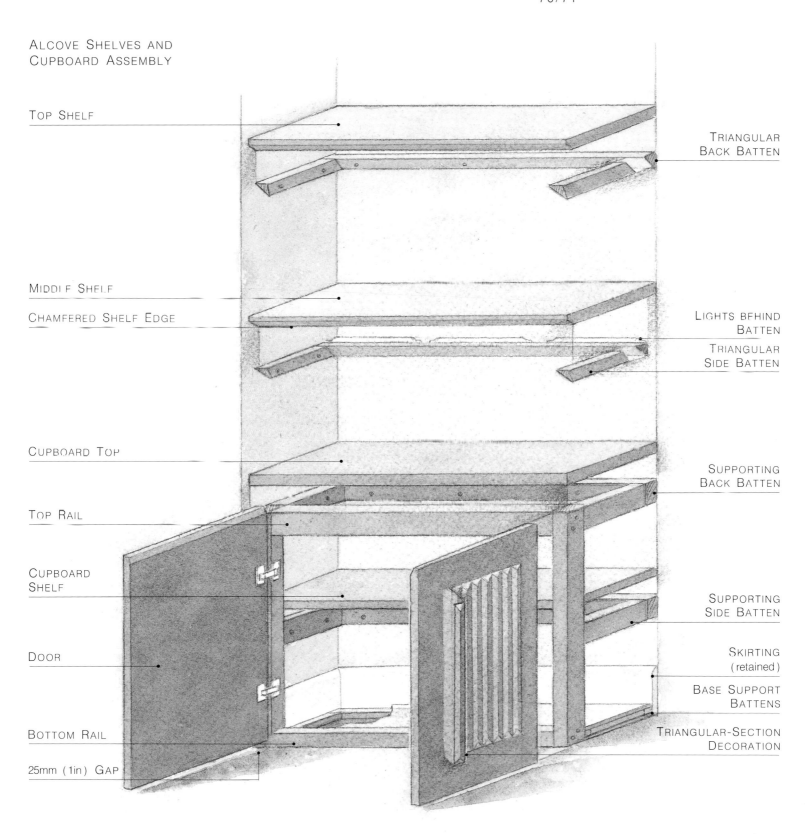

THE CUPBOARDS

MAKING THE FRAME

Using 50 x 50mm (2 x 2in) PAR (planed all round) timber, cut two uprights to the desired height, allowing for the thickness of the top. The height of our cupboards, including the top, is 865mm (34in).

Measure for two horizontal rails so that they fit inside the uprights, and cut these from the same size of timber as used for the uprights. Dowel joint the horizontal rails between the uprights with two 12mm ($\frac{1}{2}$in) dowels at each corner (see **Techniques, Dowel Joints, page 245**). Before fixing the frame it must be held square with a bracing batten (see **Techniques, page 236**). For a more detailed description and illustrations of making door frames, see The Kitchen System, Doors, page 34.

FITTING THE FRAME

To fit the frame into the alcove it will be necessary to scribe the uprights to the wall (see **Techniques, page 246**). If there is skirting around the walls of the alcove, the side rails should be scribed around it. Alternatively, remove small sections of skirting, using a tenon saw and a chisel, where the side rails will fit. Another option is to remove the skirting entirely, although this rarely looks satisfactory.

Set the frame about 25mm (1in) back into the alcove, fixing it in place with two screws and wallplugs on each side (see **Techniques, page 240**). Countersink the screwheads so that the holes can be filled and painted over.

FIXING THE SUPPORTING BATTENS

The supporting battens for the cupboard top and for the cupboard shelf are made from 50 x 25mm (2 x 1in) PAR timber.

Using a spirit level, mark a line all the way round the alcove from the top of the frame. Cut the back batten to the full width of the alcove and fix it to the wall, under the line at the back, using screws and wallplugs to secure it in position.

Cut two side battens to fit between the back batten and the front frame.

Fix the battens to the wall at the marked lines as before.

Decide on the height of the cupboard shelf or shelves, and cut and fit the supporting battens at the appropriate height, making sure that they are level.

FIXING THE BASE

The cupboard base panel is made from 4mm ($\frac{1}{8}$in) or 6mm ($\frac{1}{4}$in) plywood and is supported at the edges on 25 x 25mm (1 x 1in) battens.

At the front, glue and nail a supporting batten to the inner face of the bottom rail of the front frame. Fix it 4mm ($\frac{1}{8}$in) or 6mm ($\frac{1}{4}$in) down from the top (depending on the thickness of the plywood you are using), so that the base panel sits flush with the frame.

At the back, glue and pin a similar batten to the skirting. Use a spirit level resting on the bottom rail of the front frame to mark the height of the base panel at the back, and measure down 4mm ($\frac{1}{8}$in) or 6mm ($\frac{1}{4}$in) to mark the height of the rear base supporting batten so it can be fitted easily and accurately.

Using timber of the same size, cut side supporting battens to fit between the front and rear battens, and glue and pin these battens to the skirting at each side.

Cut the plywood base to size, and use panel pins to fix it to the supporting battens at the front, back and sides of the frame. Use a cellulose filler to fill the join between the base and the frame, and sand it smooth when dry.

FIXING THE TOP

Measure the width of the alcove and the depth from the back wall to the front edge of the frame. If the wall is very uneven, increase these measurements to allow the top to be scribed to the wall.

Cut out the top from 25mm (1in) medium-density fibreboard (MDF), blockboard or chipboard. If using blockboard or chipboard, it will need to have a lipped front edge for protection and neatness.

Scribe and fit the top in place and fix at the front by screwing up through the frame. At the back, screw down through the top, and do

1 Assembly of the Cupboard Framework Using Dowels
The cupboard frame is made simply by butt-jointing top and side rails. Joints are reinforced with dowels; two per joint. Protruding ends are cut off flush once glue has hardened.

2 Fitting the Cupboard Base
Battens are placed at the front, rear, and sides (not shown). The base is pinned to the top.

3 Fixing the Top Section
The frame is set back 25mm (1in) from front of alcove. Screw up into top panel.

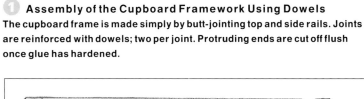

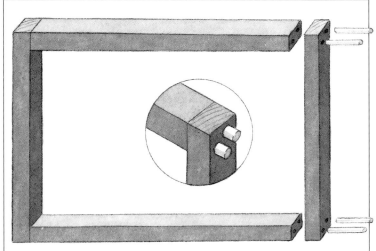

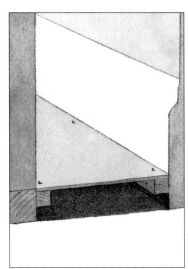

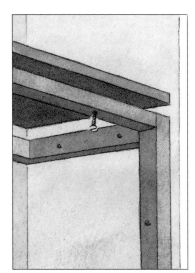

the same at each corner, countersinking the screwheads so that the holes can be filled and painted over afterwards.

Plane and sand the front edge flush with the frame if you have used MDF. Fill and sand this join flush.

FITTING THE CUPBOARD SHELF

Cut the cupboard shelf from 19mm ($\frac{3}{4}$in) MDF, blockboard or chipboard (with a lipped front edge). Check that it fits well and rest it on the supporting battens.

MAKING AND FITTING THE DOORS

Using 19mm ($\frac{3}{4}$in) MDF, cut two panels to fit the front, flush with the top, but leaving a 25mm (1in) gap at the bottom. The size of the gap at the sides of the doors is determined by the hinges used – consult the manufacturer's instructions. We have used concealed self-closing hinges, and the doors overhang the inner edges of the frame by an amount specified in the manufacturer's instructions, usually about

15mm ($\frac{5}{8}$in) so that the hinges will operate correctly (*see* **Techniques, page 247**).

For a finger-grip, chamfer the top edge of each door to 45 degrees through two-thirds of its thickness, leaving about 5mm ($\frac{3}{16}$in) flat on top.

The 'linenfold' front detail is created with 25mm (1in) triangular-section ramin or pine (fig 4). Measure and mark a square on each door for the 'linenfold', leaving a border around the edge (ours is 100mm (4in) at top and bottom, and about 90mm (3$\frac{1}{2}$in) at each side). Cut sections to length and chamfer the ends to 45 degrees (fig 4).

Mark a centre line vertically down the door, and working outwards from this, glue each length on to the surface, pinning through the side faces in about three places. Continue in each direction until the required number of triangular shaped sections are fixed with an equal border at each side.

Fit the doors using the concealed hinges according to the manufacturer's instructions (*see* **Techniques, page 248**).

DETAIL OF LINENFOLD DOORS
This photograph shows the full effect of the linenfold door decoration, together with the neatly chamfered fingergrip. You can vary the kind of decoration you use on the door front according to your personal taste.

4 Making and Decorating Cupboard Doors
Left Top edges of doors are chamfered to provide a fingergrip. *Inset* Fixing of linenfold. *Centre* First linenfold fitted. *Right* Cut a triangular section and chamfer the ends to 45 degrees.

ALCOVE SHELVES AND CUPBOARDS

THE SHELVES

The shelves are made from 25mm (1in) MDF boards that are supported by 38mm (1½in) triangular battens which are fixed to the walls of the alcoves.

CUTTING THE TRIANGULAR BATTENS

If you cannot find suitable triangular timber mouldings at your local timber suppliers, you can cut them yourself from 50 × 50mm (2 × 2in) PAR timber with a circular saw.

Tilt your circular saw blade to 45 degrees and cut the timber diagonally along its length so that it is split into two equal triangular sections. If your saw blade is not large enough to cut right through in one pass, cut partway through and complete the cut with a panel saw. Finally, clean up the sawn faces with a smoothing plane for a neat finish.

If you do not have a suitable circular saw, your timber supplier should easily be able to make this cut for you.

FIXING THE TOP SHELF

Decide on the height of the top shelf. From the triangular battening, cut a back batten to span the width of the alcove and fix to the wall.

Cut the side battens to length, which should be the distance from the back of the alcove to 38mm (1½in) in from the front edge. Use triangular battens, and cut a 45 degree chamfer on the front end so that the batten will tail away from the front edge of the shelf. Chamfer the back end of the batten in the same direction so that it fits snugly into the corner against the back batten. Fix side battens in place.

Cut out the shelf from 25mm (1in) MDF to the width of the alcove and to a depth whereby it is set back into the alcove by 25mm (1in). Chamfer the front edge of the shelf through half its thickness to allow the front edge of the bevelled side batten to run into the chamfer and create an unobtrusive support for the shelf. Screw shelf down on to back and side battens. Fill joins and gaps, and when the filler is hard, sand smooth.

① Cutting the Triangular Battens Yourself
Tilt your circular saw blade to 45 degrees and cut down length of timber.

② Fixing the Shelves
Top and middle shelves fix onto triangular battens that are screwed to the walls. One batten hides a light.

ALCOVE SHELVES IN PLACE
The shelves (above) are 25mm (1in) thick MDF boards which are screwed down on to the battens.

SHELVES AND BATTENS
The chamfered support battens blend neatly with the chamfered front alcove shelves (below).

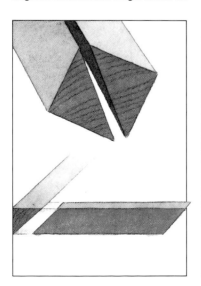

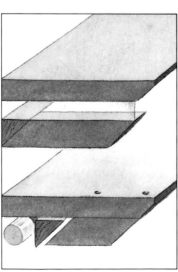

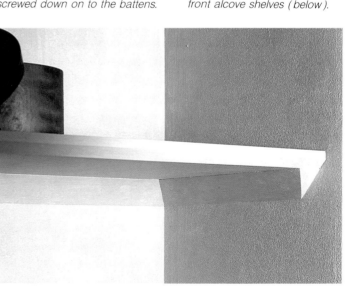

FIXING THE MIDDLE SHELF

Decide on the height of the shelf and cut the back batten to fit into the alcove. In this case the back batten is fixed about 75mm (3in) out from the wall so that a light can be fitted behind it. Do not fit the batten securely in place at this stage.

Cut the side battens so that when chamfered at front and rear they will be 75mm (3in) away from the wall at the back, and 38mm (1½in) in from the front. Fix the side battens in place, screwing and plugging them tightly to the alcove wall so that they are both level.

Cut the shelf to size from 25mm (1in) MDF and fit it on the side battens, chamfering the front as before. Screw it down on to the side battens, countersinking and refilling the screwheads.

The back batten, which is cut square at the ends, is positioned under the shelf behind the ends of the side battens. It is fixed in place by screwing down through the shelf. This provides a cover for the light fittings and also acts as a beam to support the shelf and prevent it from sagging. Countersink the screw holes and fill them after inserting the screws into the holes.

LIGHTING

For the concealed lighting under the middle shelf we used three 300mm (12in) long tungsten tube lamps secured behind the back batten.

THE CENTRE WALL PANEL

Although not essential to the project, we fitted a centre panel on the chimney breast to give a unified look by continuing the theme of the door decoration. The panel is 6mm (¼in) MDF or plywood on which 38mm (1½in) triangular-section timber is glued and pinned. The panel is simply screwed to the chimney-breast wall, filled, smoothed, and painted to match the walls, cupboards and shelving.

SOFT LIGHTING IN ALCOVES

When lighting is needed, built-in tungsten strips (above), offer a good alternative to a more commonly used fluorescent version.

CONCEALED LIGHTING

The concealed lighting under the middle shelf throws a muted shadow into the alcove and creates a softer atmosphere in the room. Taken from below, this photograph (left) shows the positioning of the concealed tungsten strip lighting. When viewed from straight on, the lighting is hidden behind the back shelf batten.

WALL OF DISPLAY SHELVING

The simplicity, style and sheer practicality of a whole wall of shelves without any visible means of support is what I wanted to achieve with this design.

I realized that if steel brackets were inserted into the wall and fixed firmly, I could then construct hollow-core shelves to slide over the brackets and hide them.

A great advantage of this construction method is that all of the wiring for audio-visual equipment, telephones and lighting can be contained in the cavity of the shelf rather than trailing around on the surface in an untidy, spaghetti-like mess.

They also give the room a horizontal emphasis as there are no uprights dividing the shelves, which are necessary with conventional shelving to stop the shelves sagging in their lengths.

To complete the shelves I painted them the same colour as the wall so that they had a sculptural quality and became part of the fabric of the room.

METAL SUPPORTS

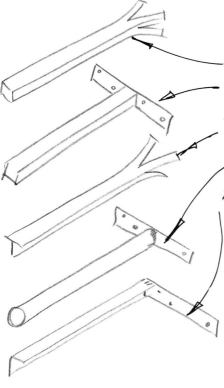

Various metal supports for shelves either grouted into a brick wall or screwed to the surface.

When you secure the metal supports to the wall, see that they are perfectly aligned to fit the shelf by tying them firmly to a pre-notched length of timber.

LONGITUDINAL SECTION

ply skin

metal support inserted into shelf frame

ALIGN YOUR SUPPORTS

metal support

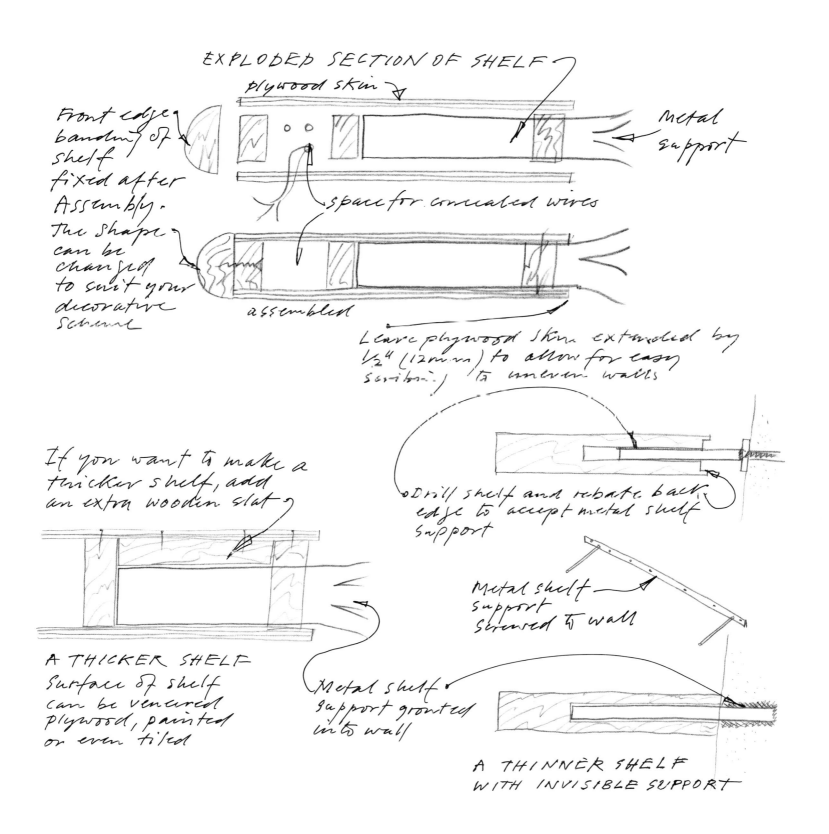

EXPLODED SECTION OF SHELF

plywood skin

Metal support

Front edge banding of shelf fixed after Assembly.

The shape can be changed to suit your decorative scheme

space for concealed wires

assembled

Leave plywood skin extended by 1/2" (12mm) to allow for easy scribing to uneven walls

If you want to make a thicker shelf, add an extra wooden slat

Drill shelf and rebate back edge to accept metal shelf support

A THICKER SHELF
Surface of shelf can be veneered plywood, painted or even tiled

Metal shelf support screwed to wall

Metal shelf support grouted into wall

A THINNER SHELF WITH INVISIBLE SUPPORT

WALL OF DISPLAY SHELVING

This project features shelving without any visible means of support, giving clean lines without any ugly brackets. It is all done by making a hollow box-section shelf unit comprising top and bottom plywood-skin panels over a sturdy timber framework, creating the appearance of a thick, solid shelf. For added strength on long shelf runs, protruding steel rods are fitted into drill holes in the rear wall. They slide into the box frame of the shelf. Battens-only fixing can be used for a run of shelving up to 2440mm (8ft) long and 450mm (18in) wide. It is important to note that steel rods should only be driven 75mm (3in) into walls, whether they are solid or hollow. For cavity walls, the rods should not bridge the cavity. If the walls are plasterboard or plywood, stud walls or lath and plaster, then the steel rods should be inserted directly into the main vertical timber studs within the wall.

CONSTRUCTION

Decide on the height of your shelves and, using a spirit level, mark their position on the wall; continue these lines on to the end walls. Measure up for length and the required depth and for each shelf cut two pieces of 9mm ($\frac{3}{8}$in) thick plywood, or 12mm ($\frac{1}{2}$in) MDF or chipboard. If the shelves are to be longer than 2440mm (8ft), you will have to butt-join the lengths. In this case there must be a batten positioned inside the shelving to support the cut ends.

From 50 × 25mm (2 × 1in) PAR battening, cut one piece to the length of the shelf for the front batten. Cut two end wall battens to the width of the shelf, less the thickness of the front batten. Cut two back battens to the length of the shelf less twice the thickness of the end battens so that they will fit between the latter. Cut further battens to the shelf width, less three batten thicknesses, to fit between the front and back shelf battens at each end and at about 610mm (24in) intervals along its length.

Lay out all the pieces in place on the top skin of the shelf to make sure that they fit together.

Fix some scrap pieces of wood to the underside of the top skin panel for the steel rods to rest on. These pieces should be of a suitable thickness (about 19mm [$\frac{3}{4}$in]) to allow the rods to fit roughly midway in the edges of the back battens. Cut the pieces, if necessary, to fit in between the cross battens inside the shelf, and use wood adhesive to glue them to the top skin. They will need to be at intervals of about 610mm (24in) to coincide with the steel rod positions.

Draw a guide line the thickness of the scrap wood on to the back batten to help positioning when you are drilling steel rod back battens.

The rods should be spaced about every 610mm (24in) roughly midway between the cross battens. They should run the width of the shelf from front to back, butting up against the inner side of the front batten and going into the wall about 75mm (3in), beyond the thickness of the plaster. Cut the required number of rods from 12mm ($\frac{1}{2}$in) steel rod.

Cramp the two back battens together, and using a drill bit which is slightly larger in diameter than the steel rod (a 13mm [approx. $\frac{1}{2}$in] drill bit and 12mm [$\frac{1}{2}$in] diameter steel rod), drill through the two battens together in the appropriate places. Use a pencil to number the battens.

Nail up the internal frame of the shelf, marking the side which is to be fixed to the upper skin. Spread glue on the top side of the frame and lay the top skin panel in place. Draw a line round the edges of the frame and the skin panel to mark a centre line of the inset battens to give you a

TOOLS

- STEEL MEASURING TAPE
- SPIRIT LEVEL
- TRY SQUARE
- PANEL SAW (or power circular saw or jigsaw)
- SCREWDRIVER (cross-point or slotted, according to screws used)
- HACKSAW
- TWO G-CRAMPS
- POWER DRILL or HAND BRACE
- TWIST DRILL BIT, FLAT BIT or AUGER BIT
- MASONRY DRILL BIT
- HAMMER
- NAIL PUNCH
- SMOOTHING PLANE
- POWER FINISHING SANDER (or hand-sanding block)
- METAL FILE

MATERIALS

Part	Quantity	Material	Length
SHELF PANEL	2	9mm ($\frac{3}{8}$in) plywood or 12mm ($\frac{1}{2}$in) MDF or chipboard – width as required	As required
FRONT BATTEN	1	50 × 25mm (2 × 1in) PAR timber	As shelf length
END WALL BATTENS	2	50 × 25mm (2 × 1in) PAR timber	As width of shelf, less thickness of front batten
BACK BATTENS	2	50 × 25mm (2 × 1in) PAR timber	Length of shelf, less twice thickness of end battens
INTERMEDIATE BATTENS	As required to fit at 610mm (24in) intervals along shelf length	50 × 25mm (2 × 1in) PAR timber	Shelf width, less three batten thicknesses
ROD SUPPORT BLOCKS	As above	50 × 25mm (2 × 1in) approximately PAR timber	About 300mm (12in)
STEEL ROD SHELF SUPPORTS	One per 610mm (24in) length of shelf run	12mm ($\frac{1}{2}$in) diameter mild steel rod	Distance from inner side of front batten to back of shelf, plus plaster thickness, plus 75mm (3in)
SHELF FRONT EDGE (rounded)	1	75 × 50mm (3 × 2in) PAR timber	As shelf length

BASIC ASSEMBLY

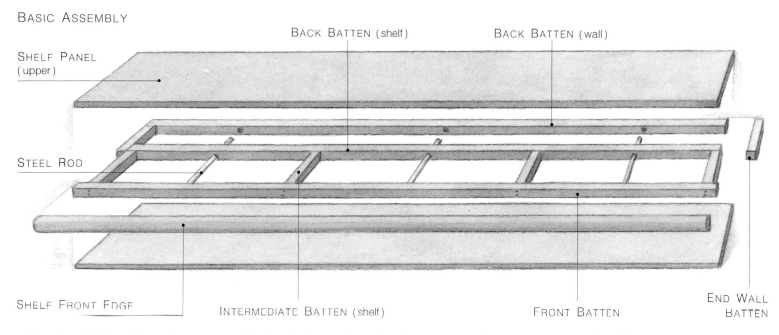

SHELF PANEL (upper)

BACK BATTEN (shelf)

BACK BATTEN (wall)

STEEL ROD

SHELF FRONT EDGE

INTERMEDIATE BATTEN (shelf)

FRONT BATTEN

END WALL BATTEN

nailing line Nail the skin in place, punch in nail heads and fill the indentations.

Repeat for the other skin panel.

To make a rounded edge at the front, cut a piece of 75 × 50mm (3 × 2in) timber to the length of the shelf. Glue and pin it (along the centre line) to the front edge and punch the nail heads well below the surface. Mark a half-round curve on the ends using a suitable plastic cup or carton. Continue rough guide lines on to the top face so that you can use a circular saw to take off the corner edges, before planing.

FIXING THE SHELF

Fix the rear-wall batten in place with screws and wallplugs. Then, using a 12mm (½in) masonry drill bit, drill through the pre-drilled holes in the wall batten, making the holes in the bricks or blocks about 75mm (3in) deep. Screw the end battens in place against the rear-wall batten.

Bevel both ends of the steel rods with a metal file, then push the rods into the holes in the wall. Slot the shelf on to the protruding rods and slide it over the end battens and on to the rear-wall batten

① Stages in Assembling the Box-section Shelf Unit
Basic framework nailed up; holes for steel rods between battens.

② The rear-wall and side battens fit neatly into the recess created by insetting the side and back shelf battens. Holes for rods match up.

③ The lower shelf panel is fixed and upper shelf panel exploded away to show how the softwood frame is neatly recessed.

④ Front edge is fixed to front batten and rounded off. Through-section (5) shows steel rod resting between support blocks.

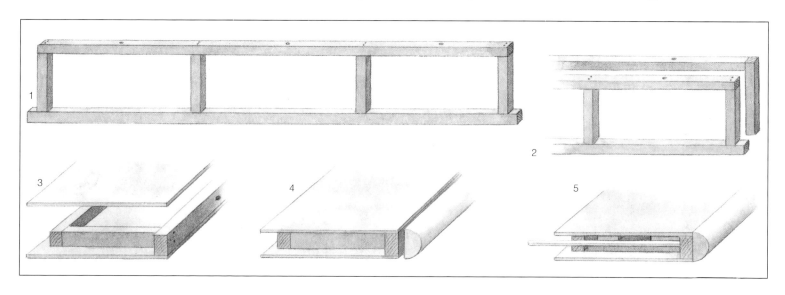

SERVING AND DISPLAY UNIT WITH MIRRORS

I built shelving similar to this a few years ago in my house in Provence; as it has been so successful there it seemed an ideal project for this book. It works on the principle that everybody likes to display their favourite china, bowls, platters and pans, as these objects create an appetizing backdrop for any kitchen or dining room. The shelving is based on an idea that I first saw in a restaurant in Positano, Italy. The most important aspect of the design is the panels of mirror that are slightly angled to reflect the components of the bowls and platters which sit on the shelf. In Positano, wonderful bowls of antipasto were displayed and the effect was mouthwatering and demonstrated that, with a little ingenuity, less can be more. The mirror provides an entrancing double vision of a rich arrangement of food and wine, to be enjoyed while sitting at the dining table or working in the kitchen.

The design also incorporates a waist-high wide shelf which can be used as a serving surface in a dining area. The finish you choose for the shelving unit can be varied to suit your particular decorative scheme. The wide shelf shown here is marble, which, while very effective as a display background for bowls of fruit, vegetables and seafood, may be substituted for a more economical material if your finances are limited. But don't dispense with the mirrors!

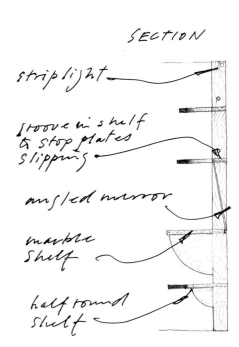

SECTION

striplight

groove in shelf to stop plates slipping

angled mirror

marble shelf

half round shelf

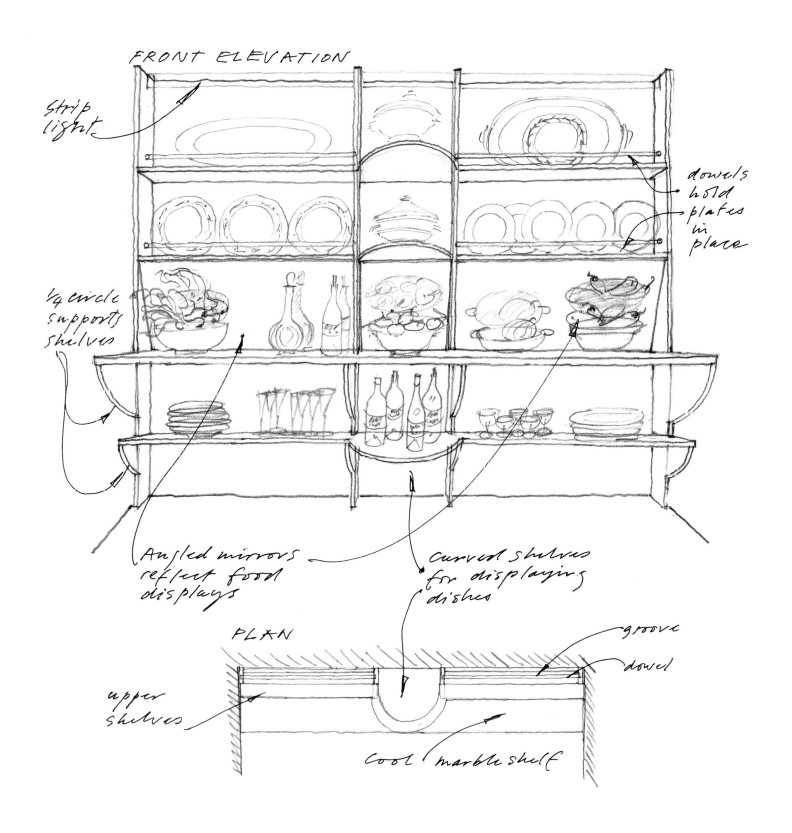

FRONT ELEVATION

Strip light

dowels hold plates in place

¼ circle supports shelves

Angled mirrors reflect food displays

Curved shelves for displaying dishes

PLAN

groove

dowel

upper shelves

cool marble shelf

Serving and Display Unit with Mirrors

This dining room shelf unit has been designed to be both decorative and practical. The wide serving shelf provides plenty of space from which food can be served and displayed, while the angled mirrors behind reflect the food and flowers, to create a pleasing interplay of colour and shape. Above, there are grooved shelves on which to display plates, and there is a shelf below the serving shelf for jugs, bowls, cutlery and so on. A concealed light behind the pelmet provides subtle mood lighting at meal times. To maximize impact and storage space, the unit reaches to the ceiling.

The unit can butt up against a wall at one end or fill an alcove, be free standing or run from wall to wall. The serving shelf can be marble (as here), slate, solid wood, or painted MDF or blockboard. If marble is used, any join *must* be made to lie over an upright so that it is fully supported.

For the main structure, the vertical partitions are 25mm (1in) MDF; the straight shelves are 19mm ($\frac{3}{4}$in) blockboard (for stiffness); and the curved shelves are 19mm ($\frac{3}{4}$in) MDF, which is easier to cut into curves than the thicker fibreboard.

The unit is built in two sections. The lower section up to the serving shelf is constructed and fixed in place, and then the top section, above the shelf, is added. The whole unit is fixed to the wall with angle brackets located in the shelf rebates, and the shelves are then slotted in to conceal the brackets.

The overall dimensions of the unit are based on the depth of the serving shelf. This one is 460mm (18in) deep, which is ideal. If you prefer a different size, you will have to adjust all the dimensions accordingly. Remember that the depth of the serving shelf should always be equal to the depth of the curved shelves for neatness.

Precise vertical dimensions up to the top of the mirror section are given, together with all the shelf depths, so that the angle of the mirror will be exact.

To allow the overall height and width to be varied, the top section above the mirror can be whatever height is required to reach your ceiling. The outer shelf sections can be whatever width is required, but for a balanced appearance make sure that they are of equal measurements either side of the central curved section.

If the unit does not have to fit into a specific width, then just make each outer section twice the width of the central section. This gives the unit attractive proportions.

Materials

Part	Quantity	Material	Length
UPPER VERTICAL PARTITIONS	4	25mm (1in) MDF	As required × 150mm (6in)
UPPER STRAIGHT SHELVES	4	19mm ($\frac{3}{4}$in) blockboard	As required × 150mm (6in)
HALF-ROUND SHELVES	2	19mm ($\frac{3}{4}$in) MDF	487 × 393.5mm ($19\frac{1}{4}$ × $15\frac{1}{2}$in)
PELMETS	3	19mm ($\frac{3}{4}$in) MDF	As required
PLATE-RETAINING RAILS	3	25mm (1in) diameter dowel	As required
SERVING SHELF	1	Optional thickness – minimum 25mm (1in) MDF	As required
SHELF SUPPORT BATTENS	3	50 × 25mm (2 × 1in) softwood	As required
LOWER VERTICAL PARTITIONS	4	25mm (1in) MDF	770 × 150mm (30 × 6in)
LOWER STRAIGHT SHELVES	2	19mm ($\frac{3}{4}$in) blockboard	As required × 280mm (11in)
CENTRE CURVED SHELF	1	19mm ($\frac{3}{4}$in) MDF	500 × 460mm ($19\frac{1}{2}$ × 18in)
LARGE QUADRANTS	4	25mm (1in) MDF	from 1250 × 300mm (49 × 12in)
SMALL QUADRANTS	4	25mm (1in) MDF	from 130 × 570mm (5 × $22\frac{1}{2}$in)

Also required: 3 mirrors; strip lights; 3mm ($\frac{1}{8}$in) lipping; 40 angle brackets, 65mm × 65mm × 16mm ($2\frac{1}{2}$in × $2\frac{1}{2}$in × $\frac{5}{8}$in)

Tools

PANEL SAW

POWER JIGSAW (or padsaw)

DOWELLING JIG

CRAMPS

STEEL MEASURING TAPE

TRY SQUARE

TRIMMING KNIFE

ROUTER

HAMMER

SPIRIT LEVEL

POWER DRILL

SCREWDRIVER

HACKSAW

PLANE

SANDING BLOCK and ABRASIVE PAPER

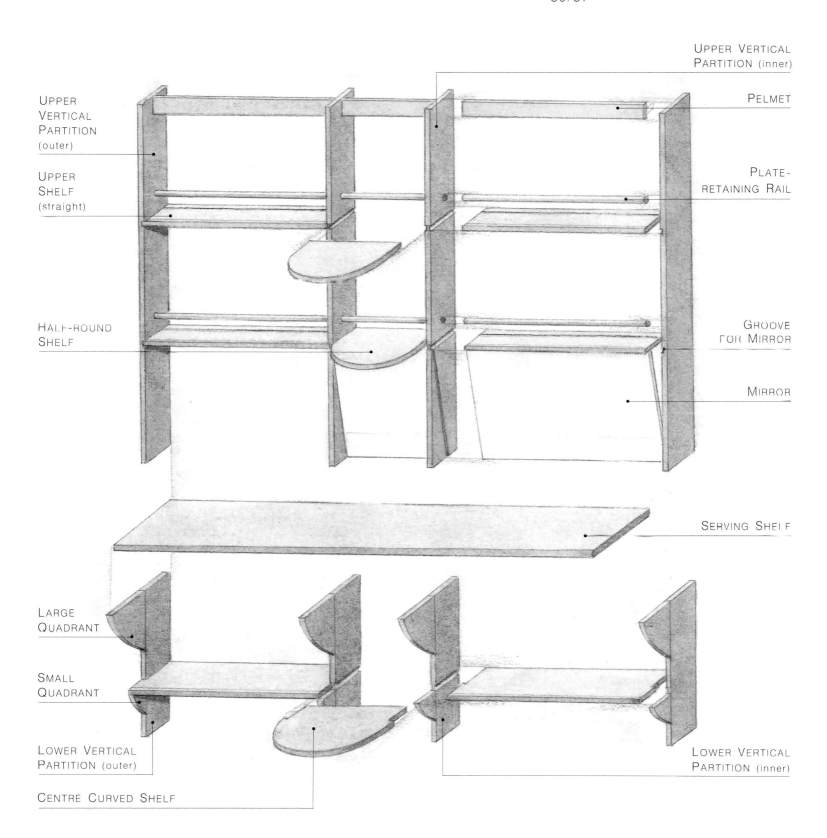

UPPER VERTICAL
PARTITION (inner)

PELMET

UPPER
VERTICAL
PARTITION
(outer)

PLATE-
RETAINING RAIL

UPPER SHELF
(straight)

HALF-ROUND
SHELF

GROOVE
FOR MIRROR

MIRROR

SERVING SHELF

LARGE
QUADRANT

SMALL
QUADRANT

LOWER VERTICAL
PARTITION (outer)

LOWER VERTICAL
PARTITION (inner)

CENTRE CURVED SHELF

SERVING AND DISPLAY UNIT WITH MIRRORS

LOWER SHELF SECTION

Using 25mm (1in) MDF, cut four verticals 770mm (30in) – the height of the underside of the serving shelf – by 150mm (6in). For the serving shelf supports, cut out four quadrants from a strip of MDF 300mm (12in) wide and at least 1250mm (49in) long, so that the radius of each can be 300mm (12in). Draw the shape of one quadrant before cutting it out with a jigsaw or padsaw and sanding this to a smooth curve. Use this quadrant as a pattern for marking out the remaining three quadrants. For the lower shelf supports, cut out four smaller quadrants from a strip 130mm (5in) wide by 570mm (22½in) long, so that the radius of each can be 130mm (5in). Again, cut out one quadrant and use this as a pattern for the remainder.

FIXING QUADRANTS

Using 10mm (⅜in) dowels, 50mm (2in) long, glue and fix the large quadrants to the front edges of the uprights. Use a dowelling jig or dowel points to align the holes, ensuring that the top edges of the quadrants and uprights are flush.

Cramp each assembly and allow sufficient time for the glue to set. This will be easier if you leave square notches on the quadrants to cramp against, sawing them off later to complete the curve.

Measure 300mm (12in) up from the bottom edge of each vertical for the position of the top of the smaller quadrants. Fix all four in place as for the large quadrants.

ROUTING FOR SHELVES

The top edge of each lower quadrant aligns with and supports the bottom of each lower shelf. Use a try square and a pencil or trimming knife to mark the top of the quadrant on to all vertical pieces where a shelf will be supported. Using a router with a 19mm (¾in) bit, cut out a housing to the top of the line at a depth of 6mm (¼in). Carry out this procedure on the inner faces of the end vertical pieces and then repeat the process on both faces of the inner vertical pieces.

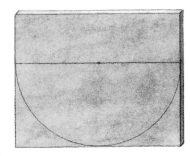

Upper Half-Round Shelf
Cut from a rectangle of 19mm (¾in) MDF measuring 487 × 393.5mm (19 × 15½in). Measure 150mm (5in) in from the back edge and draw a line across. At centre point of this line draw a semi-circle as indicated.

Centre Curved Shelf
Cut from a rectangle of 19mm (¾in) MDF measuring 460 × 500mm (18 × 19½in). Mark 280mm (11in) in from the back edge. From this line draw a curve to meet front edge in the centre. Saw rebates as shown.

Lower Straight Shelf
The span of the shelves is flexible, but they must be of equal length on each side. Shelf width is 280mm (11in). Both rebates are 150mm (6in) long. The outer rebate is 19mm (¾in) wide, the inner 6.5mm (¼in).

---

① Assembly of Lower Vertical Partition Panel
Cut lower vertical from 25mm (1in) thick MDF. Serving shelf support is quadrant of MDF with radius of 300mm (12in). Small quadrant has 130mm (5in) radius. Fix quadrants using dowels.

② Fitting a Lower Straight Shelf Between Partitions
Make sure that the shelves at each side are of equal length. The depth of each one should be 280mm (11¼in) including edge lipping. Shelf ends are rebated to cover the verticals.

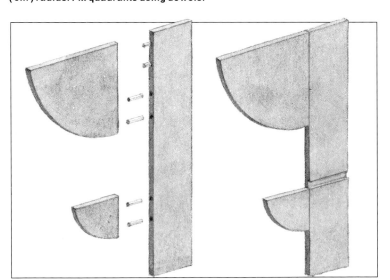

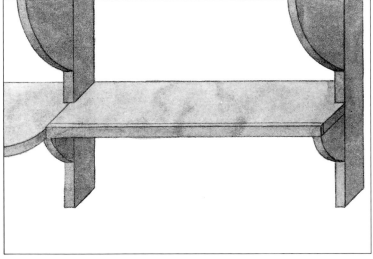

LOWER CENTRE CURVED SHELF

For the centre curved lower shelf, cut out a rectangle from 19mm ($\frac{3}{4}$in) MDF, 460 × 500mm (18 × 19$\frac{1}{2}$in). The 500mm (19$\frac{1}{2}$in) will be the width. Mark 280mm (11in) in from, and parallel to, the back edge – this will be the depth of the straight shelf. From this line, draw and cut a curve to meet the front edge in the centre. Mark 150mm (6in) in from and parallel to the back edge. Saw out rebates from both sides, 6.5mm ($\frac{1}{4}$in) wide and 150mm (6in) long; these locate in the housings cut in the vertical partitions.

LOWER STRAIGHT SHELVES

Calculate how long you want your 19mm ($\frac{3}{4}$in) blockboard shelves to be each side of the curved shelf, making sure that they are of equal length. The depth of each one should be 280mm (11in) including a 3mm ($\frac{1}{8}$in) lipping, glued and pinned to the front edge. Cut out the two shelves, then cut rebates from each end – 150mm (6in) long, and 6.5mm ($\frac{1}{4}$in) wide on the inner edge; 19mm ($\frac{3}{4}$in) wide on the outer edge. This will ensure that they meet at the centre line of the inner verticals with the curved centre shelf. The outer edges of the straight shelves should cross the outer verticals and finish flush with the outside of the unit.

FIXING IN PLACE

Position one of the uprights against the wall as a guide to marking on the wall the position of the serving shelf. Mark an accurate line for the underside of the shelf along the back wall and any side wall. Using a spirit level, ensure that the line is horizontal throughout its length.

Fix softwood battens measuring 50 × 25mm (2 × 1in) along the back wall on the underside of the line to give extra support to the serving shelf. Three battens are needed, cut to fit the distance between the verti-

cal sections. If an end vertical is being fixed directly into a return wall, screw directly through the upright and quadrant into the wall. Drill and generously countersink the holes – one near the top edge, one near the bottom of the vertical, and two in each quadrant. Put the upright in place and mark off the positions of the screws on the wall. Remove the vertical and drill holes for 50mm (2in) No 8 screws in the wall. Insert wallplugs, replace the vertical and screw into the wall.

If the end vertical is away from a return wall then it must be fixed to the back wall with 65mm × 65mm × 16mm (2$\frac{1}{2}$in × 2$\frac{1}{2}$in × $\frac{5}{8}$in) angle brackets – one at the top and one set into the shelf rebate.

The shelf rebate bracket will be concealed by the shelf when this is in position. The shelf will have to be trimmed to allow for this bracket. To conceal the top bracket, fix it vertically to the wall so that the top 'arm', which protrudes from the wall at a right-angle, will rest in a slot cut in the top edge of the vertical partition. The back arm of the bracket should be set into a slot chased into the wall so that it allows the rear edge of the vertical to be held firmly.

The bottom of the vertical can be fixed by using a 'dowel' of 3mm ($\frac{1}{8}$in) diameter steel rod or screw bolt cut to a length of 25mm (1in) with a hacksaw. Half of the 'dowel' should be sunk into the floor and the remainder into the underside of the vertical partition. The difficult part is locating the hole in the vertical partition directly over the 'dowel' protruding from the floor. To do this, first fix the 'dowel' in the vertical partition, then offer up the vertical in its exact position against, and at 90 degrees to, the wall. Tap the top edge sharply with a hammer so that an impression of the 'dowel' will be left in the floor. This indicates the drilling position. The 'dowel' can be an easy fit since its function is simply to hold the base of the partition in place.

Protect the top edge of the vertical partition with a block of scrap wood before striking it with a hammer.

Screw the protruding arm of the bracket to the top edge and fix the second bracket into the shelf rebate and the wall.

Fit the supporting batten in place against the underside of the line, fixing it to the wall with 50mm (2in) No 8 screws at 300mm (12in) centres. Offer up the next vertical and fix it to the wall using the same method as the first. Repeat this process for the remaining two verticals, gluing in the shelves as you work along the wall. The floor 'dowel' can be left out of the two middle vertical partitions.

SERVING SHELF

The serving shelf sits on the battens and verticals. If you are using marble or slate, no fixing will be necessary as its weight will be enough. For a timber shelf, use dowels to fix it to the top edges of the uprights and quadrants. If the shelf is to be painted, simply screw down into the uprights.

UPPER SHELF SECTION

Measure the distance from the top of the serving shelf to the ceiling. Measure it in three places – both ends and the middle. Take the smallest dimension, if they differ, and cut four verticals to this length from 25mm (1in) MDF. Each vertical must be 150mm (6in) wide. Measure up 655mm (25in) from the bottom

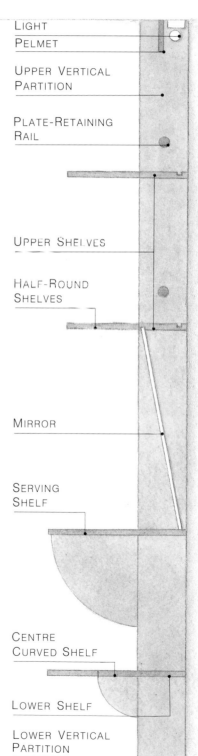

LIGHT

PELMET

UPPER VERTICAL PARTITION

PLATE-RETAINING RAIL

UPPER SHELVES

HALF-ROUND SHELVES

MIRROR

SERVING SHELF

CENTRE CURVED SHELF

LOWER SHELF

LOWER VERTICAL PARTITION

Side Section of Display Unit
This section shows how the shelves are spaced, and the positioning of the quadrant supports of the lower shelves. Note that the mirror slopes forwards to display items placed on the serving shelf.

Serving and Display Unit

Double the Impact with Angled Mirrors

The angled mirrors behind the serving shelf reflect its contents and create a lush and dramatic display of colour and shape. The curved shelves and quadrants add further interest to the composition.

edge. This gives a good size and enables the mirror to rest at a good angle. Divide the remainder of each vertical by the number of shelves required and space them equally.

Routing for Shelves

Using a 19mm ($\frac{3}{4}$in) cutter as before, rout out housings to a depth of 6mm ($\frac{1}{4}$in) for the shelves on all the inner faces. (Again, do not cut on the outside of the end sections.)

Mirror Section

Use the router with a 6mm ($\frac{1}{4}$in) cutter to make the grooves for the mirror. Cut 2mm ($\frac{1}{12}$in) in from the front and rear edges, to make a

6mm ($\frac{1}{4}$in) deep diagonal groove, as shown (far right). Do this on the inner faces of all four verticals.

Plate-Retaining Rails

Mark the centres of the holes to hold the rails, on the inner faces of the verticals, 100mm (4in) up from the shelf rebates and 75mm (3in) in from the front edges. Bore 25mm (1in) diameter holes, 12mm ($\frac{1}{2}$in) deep, using a router or a drill fitted with a flat bit.

Upper Straight Shelves

These are all lipped at the front in the same way as the lower shelves, to a total depth of 150mm (6in), includ-

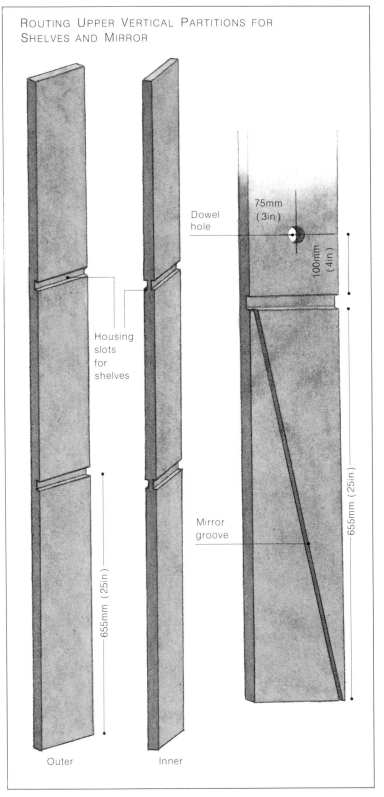

ROUTING UPPER VERTICAL PARTITIONS FOR SHELVES AND MIRROR

Dowel hole

75mm (3in)

100mm (4in)

Housing slots for shelves

Mirror groove

655mm (25in)

655mm (25in)

655mm (25in)

Outer

Inner

ing lipping. Cut the required number to length, then glue and pin lipping to the front edges.

HALF-ROUND SHELVES

Using 19mm ($\frac{3}{4}$in) MDF, cut out a rectangle for each shelf required, 487 × 393.5mm ($19\frac{1}{4}$ × $15\frac{1}{2}$in).

Draw a line across the sheet 150mm (6in) in from the back edge. The centre point of this line will be the centre point for the circle. Draw and cut out the half circle at the front on each shelf (see page 88).

CUTTING GROOVES

With a router, cut a groove for each mirror in the underside of two of the straight shelves; the groove should be 2mm ($\frac{1}{12}$in) back from the front edge. It should be 6mm ($\frac{1}{4}$in) deep and the same thickness as the mirror plus a little extra to allow the mirror to slot in. Cut a corresponding groove in the underside of one of the half-round shelves. Measure off from the grooves the exact dimensions for each mirror, making sure you allow for the amount slotted in the top and sides.

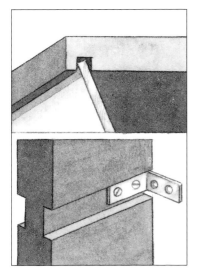

1 Mirror and Partition Fixing
Top edge of mirror is housed in a groove in the underside of the shelf. Angle brackets fix vertical panels.

The bottom edges of the mirror should be polished to avoid damage to the serving shelf.

Again with a router, cut plate grooves in the upper faces of all upper straight shelves, 6mm ($\frac{1}{4}$in) deep and wide, and forward from back edge to accommodate plates.

PLATE-RETAINING RAILS

Calculate the lengths for the plate-retaining rails to fit into the straight shelf sections, adding 10mm ($\frac{3}{8}$in) at each end so they slot into the uprights. Cut the required number from 25mm (1in) diameter dowel.

ASSEMBLY

Put one of the uprights in position (one against a wall first if you have one) resting on the serving shelf, directly above the lower vertical. This upright is fixed either to a side wall with screws or fixed to the back wall with angle brackets set into the shelf rebates as for the lower section. Fix an additional bracket in the mirror section, as low as possible behind the groove. This will then be hidden when the mirror is in place.

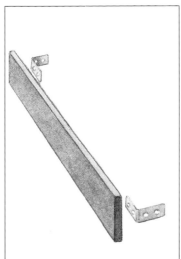

2 Fixing of Pelmets
Pelmets are cut from 19mm ($\frac{3}{4}$in) MDF. They shield strip lights and are fixed with angle brackets.

USING THE UPPER DISPLAY SHELVES TO BEST ADVANTAGE
The upper shelves reach to the ceiling for maximum visual impact and to give plenty of storage space. The half-round shelves bring objects on view forwards in a dramatic way.

For the next part of the assembly you will need an extra pair of hands. Slot the mirror and rails into place, gluing as you go. You will need to sand the ends of the dowels to fit.

Offer up the next upright in position. Secure it with angle brackets fitted in the shelf rebates and at the very top, on both sides. You can fix an extra bracket on one side, before the mirror is installed.

Plane or sand the shelves, slot over the brackets, then glue the edges and slot into place.

Offer up the central mirror, rails and the next upright, and secure as before. Fit the shelves, then repeat the procedure for the last section.

PELMET

Measure the internal dimensions between the verticals for the three pelmets. Cut the three pieces to length from 19mm ($\frac{3}{4}$in) MDF. These must be deep enough to shield the strip lights. Fix angle brackets to each end of each pelmet section, then screw them into the uprights.

Before securing the pelmet in place, you can fit extra brackets from the back of the wall to the top of the verticals to give extra rigidity, but ensure that the pelmet will conceal these. Fit the tungsten strip lights. Finally, fill over all of the screw heads prior to decoration.

JAPANESE WARDROBE

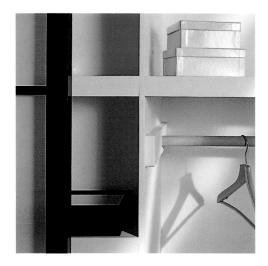

Although this particular sliding screen has been designed as a wardrobe in a bedroom, the same construction would look equally stylish in a living room. To me, there is nothing more serene than a traditional Japanese room and I have tried to echo this serenity in this project.

It is essential that the frame that holds the screens forms a rectangle, with every corner an exact right-angle. For this reason you will notice that there is a scribing fillet around the edge of the screen's frame to take up the inaccuracies of your floor, walls and ceiling.

The screens are simply constructed to a rectangular module which will vary according to the exact size of the wall you wish to screen. I have used a tough, natural, creamy cotton rather than traditional Japanese paper to back the screen, but you could alter the material to suit your own decorative scheme.

One of the great bonuses of this screen wall, apart from the benefit of hiding away clutter, is that a light inside the wardrobe will be gently diffused by the fabric and provide an elegant backdrop to your bedroom or living space.

PLAN OF WALL FIXING-

Block to take up unevenes between wall-ceiling & frame

WALL

wallplug

sliding door track

sliding Door

cloth backing held in place by fillet

scribing fillet painted the same colour as Wall and Ceiling

SIDE ELEVATION OF CEILING FIXING

CEILING

scribing fillet

fabric covering

sliding door track

Tungsten strip light mounted on back of frame produces diffused LIGHT

FRONT ELEVATION OF JAPANESE WARDROBE

Gap between wall
and wardrobe frame
filled with scribing
fillet.

PLAN

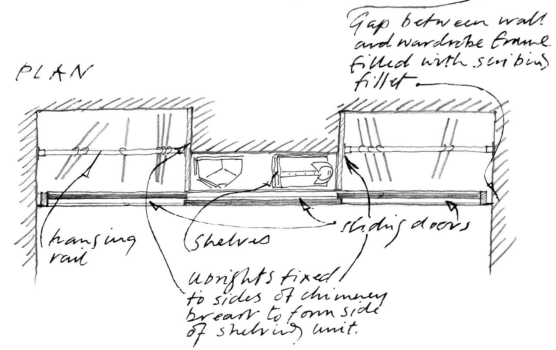

hanging
rail

shelves

sliding doors

uprights fixed
to sides of chimney
breast to form side
of shelving unit.

JAPANESE WARDROBE

The lightweight sliding doors of this fitted wardrobe are divided with a narrow, trellis-like framework and backed with fabric to produce a Japanese-style 'wall'. The doors are designed to fit wall-to-wall across a room with (or without) a chimney breast and alcoves. Lights are fitted behind the doors to light the inside of the wardrobe and to throw a diffused light into the room when the doors are closed – an excellent way to create a restful atmosphere in a bedroom.

In our design, the doors slide in front of the chimney breast, completely hiding it. Vertical partition panels are fitted to each side of the chimney breast, protruding a short distance in front of it and allowing narrow shelves to the width of the chimney breast to be incorporated.

If you are building this wardrobe on a flat wall, you will still need to fit two internal partition panels to support the hanging rails and the deep shelves. However, in this case all the shelves will be deep, and there will be room for three hanging rails instead of two.

For neatness, where there is no chimney breast, make the vertical partition panels as two narrow plywood-covered box sections.

MATERIALS

Part	Quantity	Material	Length
PARTITIONS	2	19mm ($\frac{3}{4}$in) plywood, blockboard or chipboard. Width as inside depth of cupboard (530mm [21in] in our case)	Room height
DEEP SHELVES	4	As above; 518mm (20$\frac{1}{2}$in) wide to allow for thickness of shelf lipping	Distance between partition panels and side walls
SHALLOW SHELVES	6	19mm ($\frac{3}{4}$in) plywood, blockboard or chipboard. Width as distance from chimney breast to front of partition panels, less 12mm ($\frac{1}{2}$in)	Distance between partition panels
SHELF LIPPING	10	38 × 12mm (1$\frac{1}{2}$ × $\frac{1}{2}$in) PAR pine or hardwood	As shelf lengths
DEEP SHELF REAR SUPPORT BATTENS	4	25 × 25mm (1 × 1in) PAR softwood	As shelf length
DEEP SHELF SIDE SUPPORT BATTENS	8	25 × 25mm (1 × 1in) PAR softwood	Shelf depth, less 38mm (1$\frac{1}{2}$in)
SHALLOW SHELF REAR SUPPORT BATTENS	6	25 × 25mm (1 × 1in) PAR softwood	As shelf length
SHALLOW SHELF SIDE SUPPORT BATTENS	12	25 × 25mm (1 × 1in) PAR softwood	Shelf depth, less 38mm (1$\frac{1}{2}$in)
HANGING RAIL	2	Chrome rail or 25mm (1in) diameter dowel	Alcove width
RAIL SUPPORT BATTENS	4	75 × 25mm (3 × 1in) PAR softwood	2 at 530mm (21in) 2 at 610mm (24in)

DOOR FRAMES

Part	Quantity	Material	Length
TOP AND BOTTOM RAILS	2	100 × 50mm (4 × 2in) PAR softwood	Room width, plus 150mm (6in)*
UPRIGHTS	2	As above	Room height*
TOP SCRIBING FILLET	1	25 × 30mm (1 × 1$\frac{1}{4}$in) PAR softwood	Room width*
SIDE SCRIBING FILLET	2	As above	Room height*

DOORS (quantities are for one door. Our project uses three doors)

Part	Quantity	Material	Length
STILES (side rails)	2	50 × 50mm (2 × 2in) PAR softwood	Internal height of door frame, less clearance for door gear
TOP RAIL	1	50 × 50mm (2 × 2in) PAR softwood	One-third of internal width of frame
BOTTOM RAIL	1	100 × 50mm (4 × 2in) PAR softwood	As above
HORIZONTAL TRANSOMS (central bars)	3	25 × 25mm (1 × 1in) PAR softwood	Internal width of door frame, plus 25mm (1in)
VERTICAL MULLIONS (central bars)	2	25 × 25mm (1 × 1in) PAR softwood	Internal height of door frame, plus 25mm (1in)
SIDE FABRIC FASTENING BATTENS	2	9 × 9mm ($\frac{3}{8}$ × $\frac{3}{8}$in) PAR softwood	Internal height of door frame, plus 100mm (4in)
TOP AND BOTTOM FABRIC FASTENING BATTENS	2	9 × 9mm ($\frac{3}{8}$ × $\frac{3}{8}$in) PAR softwood	Internal width of door frame, plus 100mm (4in)

*Dimensions are oversize to allow for trimming later

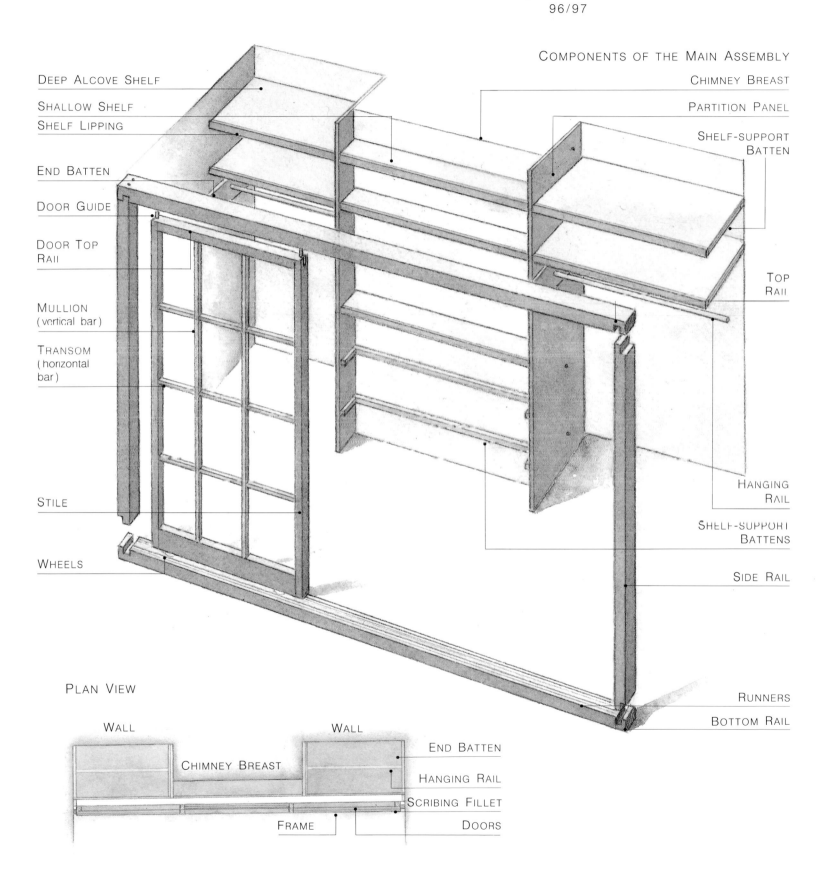

COMPONENTS OF THE MAIN ASSEMBLY

DEEP ALCOVE SHELF

SHALLOW SHELF

SHELF LIPPING

END BATTEN

DOOR GUIDE

DOOR TOP RAIL

MULLION (vertical bar)

TRANSOM (horizontal bar)

STILE

WHEELS

CHIMNEY BREAST

PARTITION PANEL

SHELF-SUPPORT BATTEN

TOP RAIL

HANGING RAIL

SHELF-SUPPORT BATTENS

SIDE RAIL

RUNNERS

BOTTOM RAIL

PLAN VIEW

WALL

WALL

CHIMNEY BREAST

END BATTEN

HANGING RAIL

SCRIBING FILLET

FRAME

DOORS

Japanese Wardrobe

Setting out

Decide on the internal layout of the wardrobe: the height of the hanging rails, the position of the shelves, etc. Our shelves are spaced at 350mm (14in) centres down the chimney breast, with hanging rails in the alcoves at either side and two deep shelves above the main hanging rail.

Mark the internal depth of the wardrobe (ours is 610mm [24in], a good width for hanging clothes). Mark all the way round: on walls, floor and ceiling. Start by marking a point 610mm (24in) out from the rear wall at each end and mark on to the side walls just above the skirting. Hang a chalked plumb line on each wall to align with these marks and snap the line to mark a vertical line. Snap a chalked line on to the ceiling to join these two lines. Repeat for the floor. This line will be the inside of the door frame.

If you are working in an old house where the room is not square, you may not be able to measure out from the end wall to fix the position of the door frame. Instead, you may have to use the 3-4-5 method (see **Techniques, page 236**) to get the frame at right-angles to one, or both, of the side walls. Mark the frame position on the floor, then snap vertical lines on the side walls and finally snap a line on the ceiling. Also, in an old house the floor, walls and ceiling may slope a lot. If this is the case, you may have to use packing pieces under the floor rail and scribe wide packing pieces between the sides and top of the door frame to fill odd-shaped gaps. It is vital that the door frame is square, regardless of how much the walls, floor and ceiling are out of true.

After marking the inside of the door frame line, measure back 75mm (3in) and snap another line round the walls, floor and ceiling parallel with the first line. This inside line marks the front edge of the shelves and partition panels.

Partitions

Cut partition panels to the height of the room from 19mm ($\frac{3}{4}$in) plywood, blockboard or chipboard. These are fixed on each side of the chimney breast and their width is the distance from the rear wall to the inside line (530mm [21in] in our case).

Position the panels, check that they are upright by packing them out if necessary, and screw and wallplug them to each side of the chimney breast.

If there is no chimney breast, make and fix two twin-skinned hollow partition panels as follows:

Each partition is made from two panels of 9mm ($\frac{3}{8}$in) plywood on a 50 × 25mm (2 × 1in) PAR timber framework. The panels should be slotted over 50 × 25mm (2 × 1in) battens fixed to the rear of the wall, floor and ceiling to give a strong, invisible fixing. Within the panels, fit cross battens to provide a strong fixing to coincide with the positions of the shelves and hanging rails.

Shelves

On the back and side walls mark the positions of the undersides of the shelves, using a pencil, spirit level and straight-edge (a straight length of planed timber batten will do).

Cut shelf-support battens from planed pine to run along the back and side walls, allowing for the thickness of the lipping on the front of the shelves. The battens are 25 × 25mm (1 × 1in) (see **Materials list, page 96**).

Drill and screw the battens to the rear walls, side walls and partition panels, ensuring that they are level with one another, and on each side of the partition panels. Wallplugs will be required where the battens are fixed to masonry walls.

Fill over the screwheads and paint the battens so that they match the wall colour.

Cut the shelves to fit from 19mm ($\frac{3}{4}$in) plywood, blockboard or chipboard, and lip the front edges with 38 × 12mm (1$\frac{1}{2}$ × $\frac{1}{2}$in) pine or hardwood so that the top edge is flush and the lipping overhangs to hide the support battens.

Hanging Rails

Use proprietary chrome rails and end supports, or 25mm (1in) diameter wooden dowels, cut to fit the widths of the alcoves. The dowels are fitted in 75 × 25mm (3 × 1in) end battens cut to fit the width of the cupboard from the frame to the back wall in the case of the end battens, and from the front edge of the partition panels to the back wall for the inside battens. To form the hanging rail, the inside battens are drilled centrally to hold the dowels and the end battens drilled to correspond. To fit the rail, screw the end batten to the wall, slot the inside batten on to the dowel, then fit the dowel in the fixed batten, and finally screw the other batten in place, checking with a spirit level that the rail is level. Make sure that the rails on each side are level with one another, and are at the desired height.

Sliding Door Frame

The frame is built to give a 30mm (1$\frac{1}{4}$in) gap at the top of the frame and at each side, to allow for scribing for a neat finish while coping with skirting and irregularities in the wall and ceiling surfaces. When you measure up, allow for these spaces and make the frame to these external dimensions.

The frame is made from 100 × 50mm (4 × 2in) PAR (planed all round) timber and is constructed with bare-faced housing joints (see **Techniques, page 243**) at the corners. This type of joint is very strong, but the short grain on the outside of the grooves is a weakness and therefore the top and bottom rails are left about 150mm (6in) overlength to form 'horns' which are trimmed off after the joint is made.

Put the top and bottom rails side by side and cramp them together. Mark off the external width of the frame on to them. Rest a frame upright across the top and bottom rails to mark off the internal dimensions and then mark this line square on the top and bottom rails using a try square and a trimming knife. Set a marking gauge to half the thickness of the uprights and mark off from the internal face, squaring across as you go with a try square and a trimming knife.

Use a router to cut out the housing (or groove) as marked, or saw along the inside (waste side) of the housing lines using a fine-toothed tenon saw and then chisel out the waste wood.

Cut the frame uprights to length. (Note that these fit into the bottom of the housings.) Using the marking gauge as set for marking out the housing, mark off for the tongues at the ends of the rails which will fit into the housings.

Cut out the waste with a tenon saw so that the tongues fit securely in the housings.

Dry assemble the frame to check that the external dimensions are accurate enough to fit the room size with approximately 30mm ($1\frac{1}{4}$in) spaces at the top and at each side of the frame. These will be filled using the scribing fillets which will ensure a neat fit.

Take the frame apart and fit the sliding door gear. The method of fitting depends on the type and you must follow the manufacturer's instructions. It is very important to choose a door gear in which the wheels run along a bottom track, rather than hang from a top track, otherwise our frame will not be suitable. It is much easier to fit this bottom-running track and the guide track at the top before the frame is finally assembled.

Assemble the frame, gluing the joints and screwing through the top and bottom rails into the uprights. At this point the frame must be braced square before the glue sets. This is done by nailing two diagonal braces on opposing corners of the frame following the 3-4-5 method of bracing (see **Techniques, page 236**).

FIXING THE FRAME

Lift the frame into position, ensuring that the upright rails are centralized between the side walls, with a 30mm ($1\frac{1}{4}$in) gap at each side. Use a spirit level to check that the bottom rail is absolutely level, and if necessary adjust it with packing pieces. With the diagonal braces still in position, screw the bottom rail to the floor after scanning the floor with a metal detector to ensure that the screws will not puncture pipes or wiring just beneath the floorboards. Use 75mm (3in) No 10 woodscrews, and, if possible, try to coincide the screws with the positions of the floor joists (floorboard fixing nails will indicate their location).

Check that the frame is vertical, then drill the side rails and wall at about 610mm (24in) intervals so that the frame-fixing screws complete with wallplugs (ie, Fischer Frame Fixings or equivalent) can be inserted. Before tightening the screws, insert packing pieces between the uprights and the wall at the fixing points, keeping the pack-

ing pieces 25mm (1in) back from the front edge of the frame so that the scribing fillets can later be fitted between the frame and the wall. Check that the frame is still square by measuring across the diagonals, to ensure that they are of an equal length. If necessary, adjust the packing on either side.

Drill and screw the top rail to the ceiling, using 100mm (4in) No 12 screws, and fixing into the ceiling joists where possible. As with the uprights, at the screw position insert packing pieces between the top of the rail and the ceiling before finally tightening the screws.

Check again that the frame is square, and then remove the bracing battens.

Between each side and the walls, and between the top rail and the ceiling, scribe a fillet, made from 6mm ($\frac{1}{4}$in) plywood, to the wall and ceiling to fill the space. Fix the fillet by screwing into packing pieces.

Fill over the screwheads and, when dry, paint the frame the same colour as the wall so that it blends in with the rest of the room.

① Shelf Construction and Fitting of Shelf-support Battens
Shelves have lipping on front edges to hide the support battens and to stiffen the shelves to help prevent them from sagging. Remember to allow for the thickness of the lipping by setting back the side battens.

② Shelf Lipping
Plywood, blockboard or chipboard shelves have hardwood lipping glued and pinned to the front edge.

③ Housing Joints in Frame
Housing joints are used at the corners of the frame. Note the horns which are cut off later.

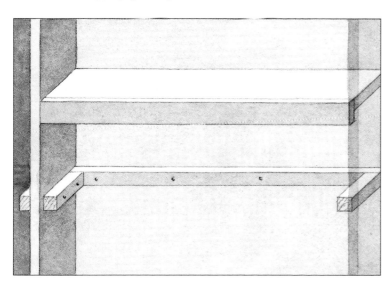

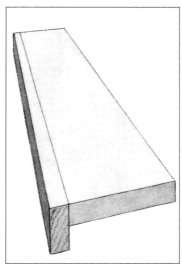

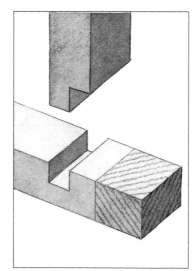

Japanese Wardrobe

Sliding Doors

Work out the external dimensions of the doors. For the door height, measure the height of the internal frame, allowing for the clearance specified in the instructions supplied with the sliding door gear. For the door width, divide the internal width of the frame by the number of doors required (we use three), allowing for the doors to overlap each other by the thickness of the door stiles.

Using timber as specified in the Materials list (page 96), cut the door stiles (side rails) slightly overlength and mark off on them the positions of the top and bottom rails. Haunched mortise and tenon joints are used to join the door components at the corners (see **Techniques, page 244**).

Cut the top and bottom rails to length and chop out the mortises in the stiles, then cut the tenons on the rails. The stiles are left overlength at this stage to avoid breaking out the end of the mortise while cutting it.

Dry assemble the door frame and check that the joints fit well.

Repeat the procedure for the other doors.

To make the transoms (horizontal internal bars) on each door, measure the internal width between the stiles, and cut three transoms to this length, plus 25mm (1in). (The number of bars can be varied according to the size of the doors you are making.) Measure the distance between the top and bottom rails and cut two mullions (vertical bars) to this length, plus 25mm (1in). (Again, the number of bars can be varied to suit the door size.) The bars are joined to the frame with bare-faced tenon joints and where they overlap they are joined with cross halvings.

Take the frame apart and cut the mortises for the sliding door wheels in the bottom edge of the bottom rails (see the manufacturer's instructions).

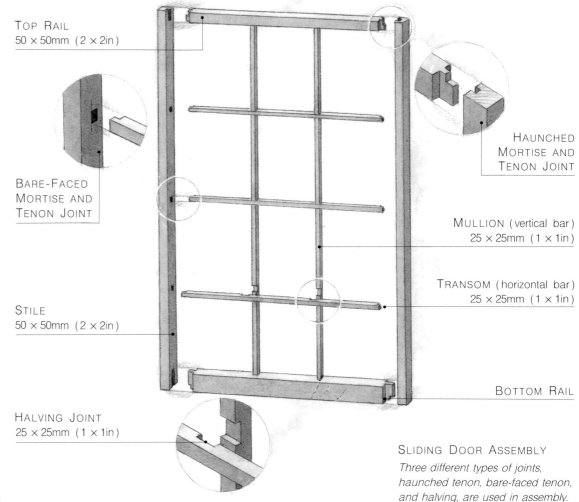

TOP RAIL 50 × 50mm (2 × 2in)

BARE-FACED MORTISE AND TENON JOINT

STILE 50 × 50mm (2 × 2in)

HALVING JOINT 25 × 25mm (1 × 1in)

HAUNCHED MORTISE AND TENON JOINT

MULLION (vertical bar) 25 × 25mm (1 × 1in)

TRANSOM (horizontal bar) 25 × 25mm (1 × 1in)

BOTTOM RAIL

SLIDING DOOR ASSEMBLY
Three different types of joints, haunched tenon, bare-faced tenon, and halving, are used in assembly.

Work out the spacing for all the internal bars and mark them on the inside faces of the frame. Set the mortise gauge to the full thickness of the 25 × 25mm (1 × 1in) bars, and gauge a line from the back of the door frame to mark the front positions of the bars.

Using a square-edge chisel (a mortise chisel is ideal, although an ordinary firmer chisel will do), or a router cutter, chop out, or rout, mortise slots to 12mm ($\frac{1}{2}$in) depth, and to half the thickness of the square bars, by their full width.

Set the marking gauge to the width of the chisel or router cutter that you have used for cutting the mortises, and using this setting, mark off the thickness of the tenon on the ends of the internal bars. Reset the gauge to 12mm ($\frac{1}{2}$in) and mark off the lengths of the tenons on both ends of each bar. Cut the (bare-faced) tenons. When fitted, the back of each bar should lie flush with the back of the door frame.

Cut halving joints at the intersections of all of the bars (see **Techniques, page 242**).

Start assembly by gluing the cross halving joints and assembling the bars carefully, as they are easy to break. Assemble the top and bottom rails into the mullions, gluing all the joints beforehand.

Apply glue to the mortises and shoulders on one side of the doors and assemble the stile on to this side of the tenons of the top and bottom rails and transoms simultaneously.

Repeat the procedure to fit the second stile.

Put sash cramps across the doors in line with the transoms, or put a web cramp right round the door. Check that the door is flat and square (the diagonals should be equal).

When the glue has set, remove the cramps and cut the excess timber off the door stiles. Use a sharp plane to skim the faces of the door to ensure that all the joints are flush.

JAPANESE WARDROBE

With the lights switched on, this wardrobe becomes an interesting trellis-like framework. The diffused light behind the fabric panels creates a restful backdrop in any room.

Repeat for the other doors. If you find these joints too hard to make, or too time-consuming, the door could be dowelled together *(see* **Techniques, page 245** *)*. Dowel joints are perfectly secure when glued with PVA adhesive.

To fit the fabric behind the door, a groove is formed in the back of the door frame, and the fabric is laid in the groove, where it is then held in place with a batten pressed into the groove. Use a router to make the groove, which should be 9mm ($\frac{3}{8}$in) wide and the same depth. The groove is cut in the back of the door frame with its outer edge 25mm (1in) in from the inside of the frame.

Cut a 9mm ($\frac{3}{8}$in) square batten and check that it is a tight fit when slid into the groove. If necessary, plane it to fit. Cut lengths of batten to fit the groove, mitring the corners.

Following the door gear manufacturer's instructions, fit the wheel into the mortises previously cut in the bottom of the doors, and fit the guides to the tops of the doors.

Try the doors in place and check that they run correctly. If necessary, adjust the door gear according to the manufacturer's instructions. Paint or finish the doors as required.

For the fabric we used 50% polyester/50% cotton sheeting. Cut and fit the fabric by laying the door

① Fitting the Fabric Behind the Door Using Battens

To fit the fabric neatly, it is held in a groove in the back of the door by a batten which fits into the groove, holding the fabric taut. Mitre the corners of the battens for a neat effect.

frame down and draping the fabric over it. You will need a helper to keep the fabric taut. Fit one long edge, screwing the batten in place to hold the fabric down. Pull the fabric taut to fit the opposite edge in the same way. Fit one end like this, and finally fit the opposite end in the same way. Screw the battens in place rather than pin them, as this allows them to be removed neatly when the fabric is to be cleaned.

Fit the doors in place *(see* **Techniques, page 247** *)*.

Wire in the internal lights. We used tungsten-tube strip lights fitted to the back of the door frame at the top and sides, to give an even light.

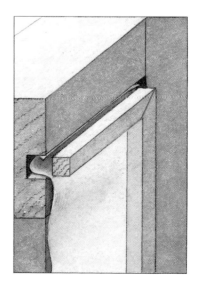

STORAGE HOUSE

Play and practicality come together in this witty 'doll's house' storage structure, designed to encourage children to participate in tidying up and taking care of their own things, whilst helping to make a game of it. Attractive, interesting and amusing storage like this not only enlivens a bedroom but is fun to use, and this house, with its opening windows and doors, helps to teach children to put back their toys and other belongings literally 'where they live'.

The construction demands only the most basic DIY skills. There are only a few angles or curves, and the main framework consists of straight panels made of MDF, a good surface on which to decorate. The house here fits into a recess but it could equally be free-standing or set against a wall without being retained on either side. Down the centre of the house, the arches over the windows are cut out to make handles to open either doors or drawers, whichever you choose.

The house can be decorated entirely to your own architectural preferences. If you are not confident about your painting skills, you can make a window stencil and a door stencil and use these as templates to ensure uniformity of design, or you could cut out squares of paper and glue these on top to make window panes or door shapes, varnishing over the top so they do not peel away. Inside, storage spaces can be left plain or painted or papered to take the doll's house illusion a stage further.

Storage House

Here is a free-standing storage unit with a difference – it is built in the shape of a town house. The storage is divided into compartments which have either conventional side-hinged doors, bottom-hinged flap-down doors, toy boxes to slide in and out, or they can be left as open shelves. For safety's sake, you should only fit toy boxes along the bottom row because these can be heavy when full.

The dimensions given are easily modified if you want a larger or smaller unit, or if it is to fit into an alcove. If it is free-standing, the storage house must be screwed to the wall through the back panel to ensure it is absolutely secure.

The cupboard is made from four 2440 × 1220mm (8 × 4ft) sheets of 15mm ($\frac{5}{8}$in) MDF (medium density fibreboard); alternatively, 15mm ($\frac{5}{8}$in) blockboard can be used.

Materials

Part	Quantity	Material	Length
SIDE PANEL	2	15mm ($\frac{5}{8}$in) MDF	1460 × 380mm ($57\frac{1}{2}$ × 15in)
TOP PANEL	1	As above	1200 × 380mm ($47\frac{1}{4}$ × 15in)
BOTTOM PANEL	1	As above	As above
CENTRAL DIVIDER	2	As above	1438 × 365mm ($56\frac{5}{8}$ × $14\frac{3}{8}$in)
OUTER SHELF	4	As above	428 × 365mm ($16\frac{3}{4}$ × $14\frac{3}{8}$in)
INNER SHELF	2	As above	326 × 365mm ($12\frac{7}{8}$ × $14\frac{3}{8}$in)
BACK PANEL	1	As above	1440 × 1200mm ($56\frac{3}{4}$ × $47\frac{1}{4}$in)
ROOF PANEL	2	As above	780 × 380mm ($30\frac{3}{4}$ × 15in)
ROOF DIVIDER	2	As above	Cut from 365 × 310mm ($14\frac{3}{8}$ × $12\frac{1}{4}$in)
ROOF BACK PANEL	1	As above	Cut from 1200 × 300mm ($47\frac{1}{4}$ × $11\frac{7}{8}$in)
ROOF FIXING BLOCK	1	Softwood offcut	380 × 50mm (15 × 2in)
PLINTH FRONT	1	15mm ($\frac{5}{8}$in) MDF	1220 × 40mm (48 × $1\frac{9}{16}$in)
PLINTH BACK	1	As above	As above
PLINTH SIDE	2	As above	350 × 40mm ($13\frac{3}{4}$ × $1\frac{9}{16}$in)
OUTER DOOR	As required	As above	470 × 420mm ($18\frac{1}{2}$ × $16\frac{1}{2}$in)*
INNER DOOR	As required	As above	470 × 320mm ($18\frac{1}{2}$ × $12\frac{5}{8}$in)*
TOY BOX FRONT	1 per box	As above	470 × 320mm ($18\frac{1}{2}$ × $12\frac{5}{8}$in)*
TOY BOX BACK	1 per box	As above	As above
TOY BOX SIDE	2 per box	As above	470 × 345mm ($18\frac{1}{2}$ × $13\frac{5}{8}$in)*
TOY BOX BASE	1 per box	As above	335 × 310mm ($13\frac{1}{4}$ × $12\frac{1}{4}$in)*

* Door and toy box sizes are approximate; pieces should be cut to fit as required to give a 1.5mm ($\frac{1}{16}$in) clearance all round; the topmost inner door will need to be shaped to follow apex of roof

Tools

- WORKBENCH (fixed or portable)
- STEEL MEASURING TAPE
- STEEL RULE
- TRY SQUARE or COMBINATION SQUARE
- SLIDING BEVEL
- JIGSAW or CIRCULAR POWER SAW – for cutting out panels
- POWER DRILL
- DRILL BIT – 3mm ($\frac{1}{8}$in)
- COUNTERSINK BIT
- HOLE SAW – 50mm (2in) diameter
- SCREWDRIVER
- CLAW HAMMER
- SMOOTHING PLANE
- ROUTER
- STRAIGHT BIT – 15mm ($\frac{5}{8}$in)
- G-CRAMPS
- POWER SANDER (or hand-sanding block)

Carcass

Mark and cut out all of the components for the carcass – that is, the top, bottom, two sides and two central dividers.

Side Panels

Mark and cut a 15mm ($\frac{5}{8}$in) deep rebate into the top and bottom edges of each side panel (fig 1, page 106), using a router fitted with a 15mm ($\frac{5}{8}$in) straight cutter bit.

Divide each side panel into three equal sections, then mark 15mm ($\frac{5}{8}$in) wide housings centrally at these heights, across the inside face of each panel. Rout the housings to a depth of 5mm ($\frac{1}{4}$in).

Top and Bottom Panels

Mark off positions for the 15mm ($\frac{5}{8}$in) wide housings on the inside faces of the top and bottom panels so that there is a central section with an internal dimension of 320mm ($12\frac{5}{8}$in) wide. This leaves an internal dimension of 420mm ($16\frac{1}{2}$in) for the two outer sections.

Cut the two housings 15mm ($\frac{5}{8}$in) wide and 5mm ($\frac{1}{4}$in) deep across the inside face of the bottom panel (fig 2, page 106). The top panel will be housed on both sides, so mark round for the upper housing, but this time cut the housings to a depth of 3mm ($\frac{1}{8}$in) only, so the panel will not be too thin at the point where the housings have been cut.

Central Dividers

These are 22mm ($\frac{7}{8}$in) shorter than the side panels. Offer one of the central dividers up to the side panel so the side panel overlaps by 10mm ($\frac{3}{8}$in) at the bottom and by 12mm ($\frac{1}{2}$in) at the top, and mark off the housings for the shelves (fig 3, page 106). Square round to the sides. Mark off on to the other central divider. Cut the housings on the central dividers 15mm ($\frac{5}{8}$in) wide and 3mm ($\frac{1}{8}$in) deep.

Back Panel Rebating

Cut a rebate 15mm ($\frac{5}{8}$in) wide and 5mm ($\frac{1}{4}$in) deep round the back inside faces of both side panels and the top and bottom panels.

STORAGE HOUSE ASSEMBLY

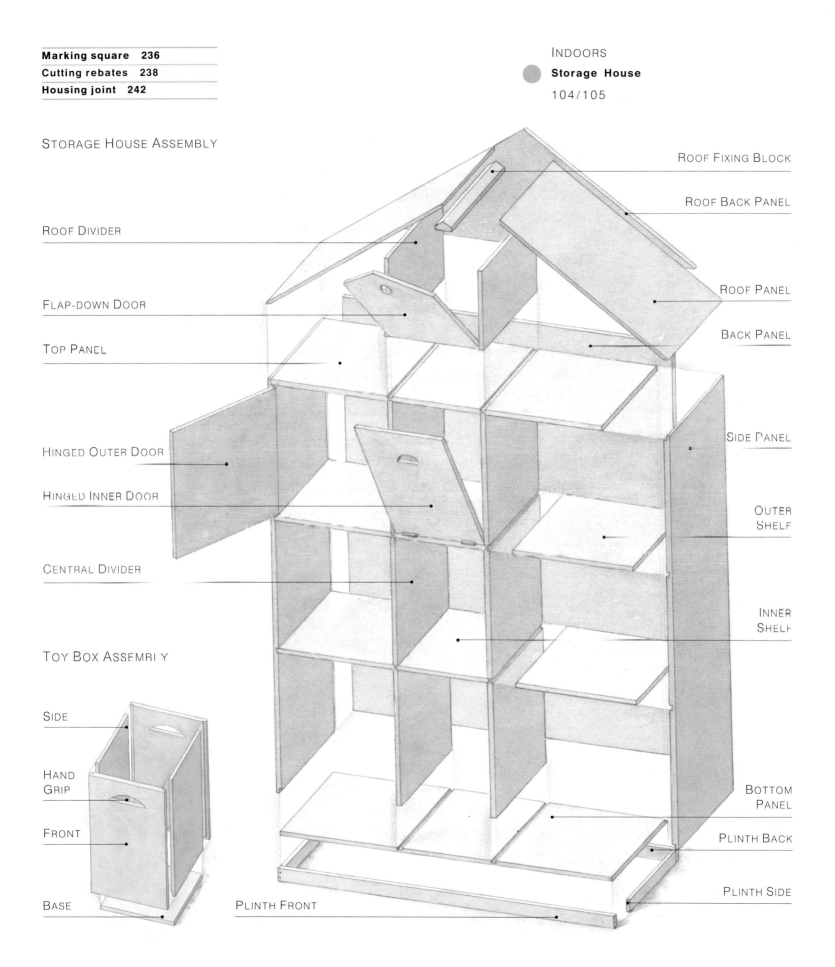

ROOF DIVIDER

FLAP-DOWN DOOR

TOP PANEL

HINGED OUTER DOOR

HINGED INNER DOOR

CENTRAL DIVIDER

TOY BOX ASSEMBLY

SIDE

HAND GRIP

FRONT

BASE

PLINTH FRONT

ROOF FIXING BLOCK

ROOF BACK PANEL

ROOF PANEL

BACK PANEL

SIDE PANEL

OUTER SHELF

INNER SHELF

BOTTOM PANEL

PLINTH BACK

PLINTH SIDE

Storage House

Assembly

Drill and countersink 3mm ($\frac{1}{8}$in) holes in three places through the centre line of all the rebates on the top, bottom and side panels. Make sure the central dividers are flush at the front. Glue and screw the carcass together – top, bottom, sides and central dividers – using 32mm (1$\frac{1}{4}$in) No 8 woodscrews.

Check that the diagonals are equal to ensure that the carcass is absolutely square. Nail temporary battens diagonally across the front and back, to hold the carcass square while the adhesive dries.

Back Panel

Check the dimensions of the back panel from the assembled carcass, then cut out the back panel ensuring it is square.

Offer the back panel in place and mark off the positions of the central dividers from the inside to give the fixing line. Drill through the back panel from the inside, down the centre of these lines in about six places spaced equally. Countersink the holes from the outside.

Drill and countersink from the outside of the back panel into the top, bottom and sides along the centre line of the back panel rebate width in six places to fix the back panel to the carcass.

Glue and screw the back panel in place through the top, bottom and side panels into the back, and through the back panel into the central dividers.

Shelves

Check the internal dimensions of the assembled carcass and cut out the inner and outer shelves. Check the fit, then apply adhesive to the rebates, and slide the shelves into position to line up flush with the front. Drill, countersink and screw through the side panels into the outer shelves (fig 4).

Plinth

Cut out the plinth components and glue and screw the side pieces between the front and back pieces with the corners flush (see **Storage House Assembly, page 105**).

Lay the assembled carcass on its back and fit the plinth using glue blocks (offcuts) glued and screwed in several places all round.

Roof

Roof Panels

Cut out the two roof panels to the correct width, but leave them slightly overlength for the time being. Set a sliding bevel to 63 degrees and chamfer the apex ends of the panels to this angle, either with a circular saw or a jigsaw set to this angle, or plane the bevel by hand (fig 5).

At the eaves level, set the bevel to 27 degrees and mark off and cut the angles of the two panels.

Temporarily pin the eaves edges down into the top panel and check that the apex comes together neatly.

Rebating the Side Panels
Cut 15 × 5mm ($\frac{5}{8}$ × $\frac{1}{4}$in) rebates across the top and bottom inside edges of the side panels.

Roof Dividers

Take the roof dividers and offer them up to the rebates in the top panel, holding them at right angles to the top panel. Mark off the required length and the angle at which to cut each roof divider at the top using a sliding bevel (fig 6). Cut both dividers to length and carefully angle the top edges.

Remove the roof panels and drill and countersink at the eaves in three places at an angle (fig 5). Next, drill and countersink vertically through the roof into the roof dividers in three places, making sure the dividers are flush at the front (fig 6). Dry assemble the roof structure to the main carcass.

Fixing Block

Cut the roof fixing block to length, offer it up to the apex of the roof, and mark and plane off the angles of the top surfaces so the block fits neatly against the underside of the apex. Dry assemble, screwing the block up so that it is square to the roof panels (fig 5 bottom left).

Top and Bottom Housings
Top Rout 3mm ($\frac{1}{8}$in) housings in both faces of top panel. _Bottom_ Rout 5mm ($\frac{1}{4}$in) housings for bottom panel.

Roof Back Panel

Take the roof back panel and offer it up to the roof section, lining up the bottom edge with the top of the main back panel. Mark off the roof angles from the inside. Remove the roof back panel and cut to the marked lines so that it fits inside the roof with the back flush (see **Storage House Assembly, page 105**).

With the roof back panel in position, mark off the positions of the roof dividers from the inside to give a fixing line. Remove the panel, drill through from the inside in two places on each of the centre lines of the dividers' positions. Countersink these holes from the back. Dry assemble the dividers.

Drill and countersink down square to the roof through the centre line of the back panel thickness in four places in the top of each roof panel.

Dismantle the roof structure, glue up all the joints and reassemble, gluing, screwing and countersinking the back panel in place. Leave the roof structure to dry.

Cutting the Central Dividers
Hold central divider 12mm ($\frac{1}{2}$in) short of top of side panel; transfer shelf housing positions to divider.

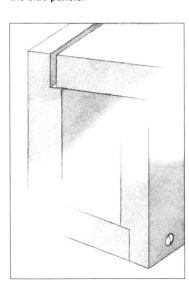

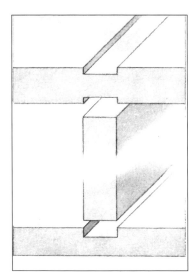

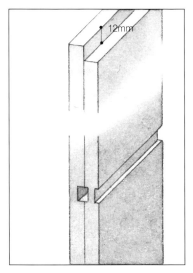

DOORS

SIDE DOORS

Measure the aperture and reduce the size by 3mm ($\frac{1}{8}$in) each way to give a gap of 1.5mm ($\frac{1}{16}$in) all round. Cut out a door, wedge it in place so that it is perfectly square in the opening and hinge it in position with two flush hinges so it is flush with the front. Fix a magnetic touch-latch so the door will not need a handle.

Make and fix as many side-hinged doors as required.

FLAP-DOWN DOORS

Cut out and install the flap-down doors in the same way as the side-hinged doors, but fit the hinges on the bottom edge. Make cut-outs as handholds using a jigsaw.

SHAPED FLAP DOWN

This is shaped to fit the apex of the roof. Fit flush hinges along the bottom edge and a magnetic touch-latch to the underside of the roof fixing block. For a handhold, cut a 50mm (2in) diameter circle.

TOY BOX

The toy box simply slides in and out of the central lower or outer lower compartments. Measure the aperture, and reduce the size by 3mm ($\frac{1}{8}$in) each way. Cut out the front and back panels to these dimensions. Cut 15 × 5mm ($\frac{5}{8} × \frac{1}{4}$in) rebates down the long inside edges of the front and back panels (*see* **Toy Box Assembly, page 105**). Cut out the sides to the internal depth of the compartments, less 20mm ($\frac{3}{4}$in).

Cut 15 × 5mm ($\frac{5}{8} × \frac{1}{4}$in) rebates along the bottom inner edges of the front, back and side panels. Drill and countersink through the front and back panels in four places on the centre line of the side panel thickness. Glue and screw the box carcass together.

Cut the base to fit in the rebates of the bottom of the box. Drill and countersink in three places through the side, front and back panels to the centre line of the base thickness. Glue and screw together.

Cut out the handholds in the front and back panels using a jigsaw.

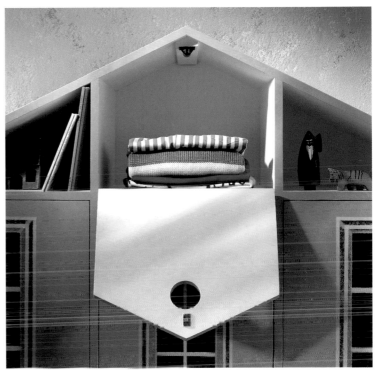

FLAP-DOWN DOORS

The flap-down door at the apex of the storage house is shaped to fit the apex of the roof. A circular cut-out provides a finger grip opening, while the magnetic latch 'invisibly' holds the door shut when it is closed.

---

④ **Fitting the Shelves**
Top Glue shelves into housings in central dividers. *Bottom* Screw shelves into side panel housings.

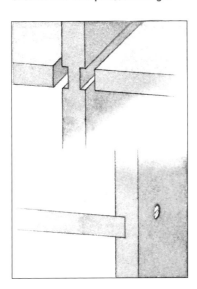

⑤ **Adding the Roof**
Top left Angle apex end of roof panel at 63 degrees and other end at 27 degrees. *Right* Pin roof in place to check the fit. *Bottom left* Angle roof fixing block to fit flush with apex; screw up through block into roof panels.

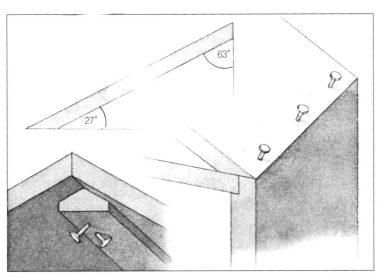

⑥ **Roof Dividers**
Angle top edges of roof dividers to sit flush with roof panel and screw in place, flush with front of house.

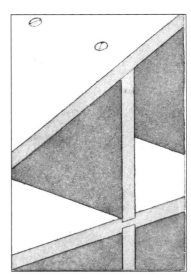

BED WITH TRUCKLE DRAWER

A lack of adequate storage space for blankets, duvets and unseasonal clothing is a perennial problem in bedrooms.

This generous bed provides storage space under the mattress, in a pull-out truckle drawer, and beneath the headboard, which is padded to make sitting up in bed and reading a book a real pleasure. The bed is designed so that it is easy to dismantle should you wish to move house, something that is quite often a problem with conventional double and king-size beds.

The loose covers of the headboard and footboard are easily removable for cleaning and can be made from fabric to coordinate with the other soft furnishings in your bedroom.

Generous storage space at the head and in the foot of the bed

pull on loose covers fit over 1" (25mm) foam glued to the foot & head-boards

Angled back provides comfortable support for reading in bed.

Velcro fastening

pullout drawer on castors slides underneath foot of bed.

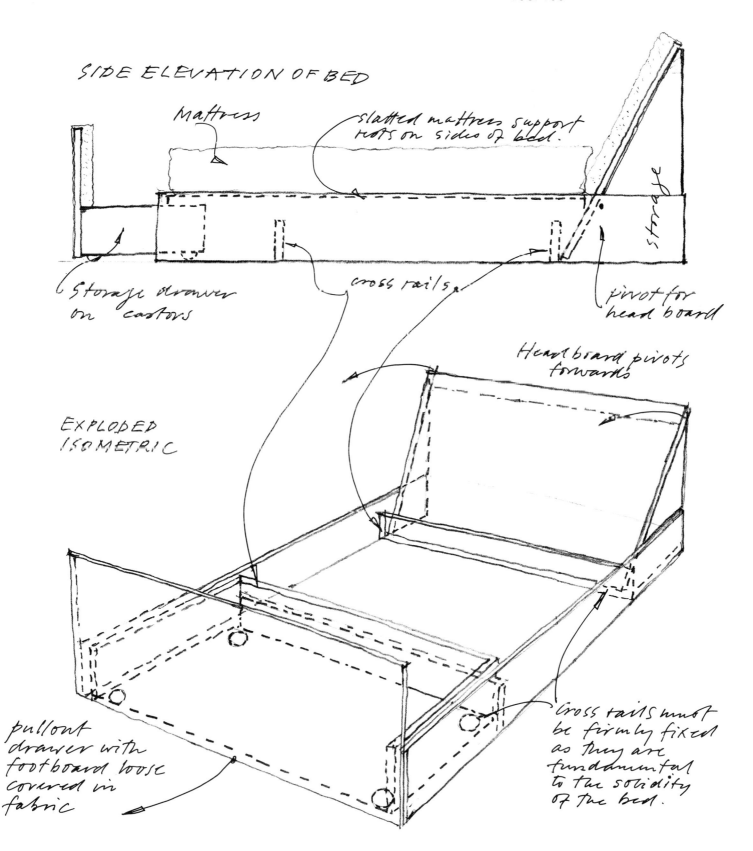

SIDE ELEVATION OF BED

Mattress

slatted mattress support
rests on sides of bed.

storage

Storage drawer
on castors

cross rails

pivot for
head board

Headboard pivots
forwards

EXPLODED
ISOMETRIC

pullout
drawer with
footboard loose
covered in
fabric

Cross rails must
be firmly fixed
as they are
fundamental
to the solidity
of the bed.

BED WITH TRUCKLE DRAWER

The bed should be assembled in the room for which it is intended. However, it is designed to be taken apart and reassembled if necessary – when moving house, for example.

Firstly, decide how large the bed is to be. The length will be determined by that of the mattress – 2m (6ft 6in) is standard – plus 350mm (14in) for the headrest section. When the bed is positioned in the room, there must be sufficient space between its end and a wall or furniture for the truckle drawer to be pulled out fully by means of the footboard. The drawer shown is 610mm (24in) long.

The width of the bed is again determined by the size of the mattress. The 'king size' mattress here is 1.8m (6ft) wide, but the bed can be made for one of 1.5m (5ft) or 1.35m (4ft 6in). It can also be adapted for a single-width mattress. The bed's height is also optional. Ours is 450mm (18in), offering plenty of storage space below.

The angled headboard provides comfortable support when you are sitting up in bed, and the upholstered top panel is readily removable to give access to ample storage space in the headrest section.

Further 'long-term' storage space – for duvets and other bedding, for example – is available below the bed. This is reached by removing the mattress and the central slatted section of the mattress support.

The main components of the bed are constructed from 19mm ($\frac{3}{4}$in) plywood, MDF or chipboard. The edges of the latter will have to be lipped with hardwood, which must be allowed for when you are calculating the dimensions.

The Shaker-style pegboard shown in the photograph on page 110 is simple to construct. It consists of a timber batten fixed around the room at picture-rail height which is then fitted with wooden hanging pegs at regular intervals. The pegs are used for storage, to hang curtains or even pictures.

MATERIALS

Part	Quantity	Material	Length
THE BASE			
SIDE PANELS	2	19mm ($\frac{3}{4}$in) plywood, MDF or chipboard	Length of mattress plus 350mm (14in) × required height
CROSS DIVIDERS	2	As above	Width of mattress × height of sides less 100mm (4in)
CORNER BATTENS	4	50 × 50mm (2 × 2in) softwood	Height of cross dividers
HEADBOARD			
TRIANGULAR HEADBOARD SUPPORTS	2	19mm ($\frac{3}{4}$in) plywood, MDF or chipboard	1125 × 575mm (45 × 23in) divided diagonally
TRIANGULAR FILLERS	2	As above	As required to fit
CROSS RAIL	1	75 × 25mm (3 × 1in) softwood	Width of mattress
HEADBOARD SECTIONS	2	19mm ($\frac{3}{4}$) plywood, MDF or chipboard	Width of mattress (see text for height)
STRENGTHENING BATTEN	1	50 × 50mm (2 × 2in) softwood	Width of mattress less 37mm (1$\frac{1}{2}$in)
MATTRESS SUPPORT SECTION			
SIDE RAILS	2	75 × 50mm (3 × 2in) softwood	Length of mattress plus approximately 75mm (3in)
END RAIL	1	As above	Width of mattress
CENTRE RAIL	1	As above	Length of mattress plus approximately 75mm (3in)
SLATS	As required	75 × 25mm (3 × 1in) softwood	Width of mattress
CROSS BATTENS	4	75 × 25mm (3 × 1in) softwood	Internal distance between cross dividers
TRUCKLE DRAWER			
FOOTBOARD	1	12mm ($\frac{1}{2}$in) MDF	Width of bed less 12mm ($\frac{1}{2}$in) × height as required
DRAWER SIDES	2	As above	Height of sides of bed less 150mm (6in)
BACK	1	As above	Height of drawer sides × width of mattress less 50mm (2in)
BASE	1	As above	Internal dimensions of truckle drawer

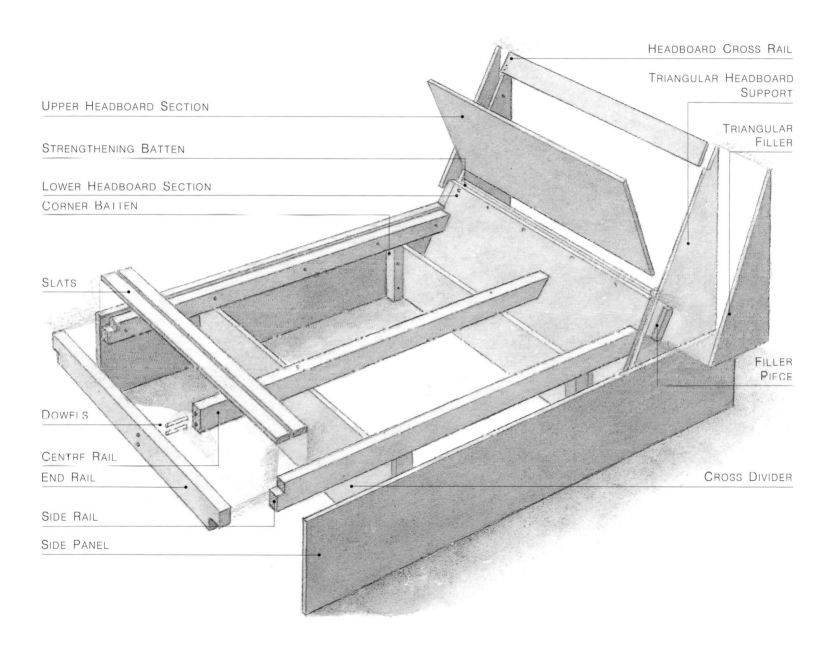

HEADBOARD CROSS RAIL

TRIANGULAR HEADBOARD SUPPORT

TRIANGULAR FILLER

UPPER HEADBOARD SECTION

STRENGTHENING BATTEN

LOWER HEADBOARD SECTION

CORNER BATTEN

SLATS

DOWELS

CENTRE RAIL

END RAIL

SIDE RAIL

SIDE PANEL

FILLER PIECE

CROSS DIVIDER

THE BASIC CONSTRUCTION OF THE BED
All the main components of the bed are shown here, except for the cross battens which fit under the slats, and the truckle drawer which fits under the bed end.

Bed with Truckle Drawer

Tools

- STEEL MEASURING TAPE
- ADHESIVE
- TRY SQUARE
- SPACING BATTEN
- PANEL SAW
- POWER DRILL
- TENON SAW
- ROUTER
- SCREWDRIVER
- CRAMPS
- HAMMER
- FILLING KNIFE
- SMOOTHING PLANE (hand or power)
- SANDING BLOCK and ABRASIVE PAPER (or power finishing sander)

The Base

Cut two side panels from 19mm (¾in) plywood, MDF or chipboard to the mattress length plus 350mm (14in) × required height. This one is 2.35mm × 450mm (7ft 8in × 18in).

You will also need two cross dividers and four corner battens. Measure 610mm (24in) in from each end of the side panels and mark the positions of the cross dividers. Drill and countersink the corner battens on one face. Check that they are square with a try square. Then, glue and screw them to the sides, inside the positions for the cross dividers and flush with the bottom edge.

Put the cross dividers in position against one of the sides, flush with the bottom edge (and outside the four corner battens), then drill, countersink and screw through the dividers into the corner battens (fig 1). Do not glue this fixing, as it can then be taken apart easily if the need arises, when moving house for example.

Put the other side panel in place and fix in the same way.

Headboard

By dividing diagonally, cut two triangular headboard supports from one rectangle measuring 1125 × 575mm (45 × 23in).

Headboard Cross Rail

A headboard cross rail supports the headrest at the top. Cut one length from 75 × 25mm (3 × 1in) timber, to the width of the mattress.

Making the Frame

Lay down one of the triangles and stand the cross rail on end, flush with the front edge of the triangle at the top, and as far to the point as it will go without overhanging the back. Mark its outline on to the end of the triangle. Repeat on the other triangle (fig 2).

Using a tenon saw or a jigsaw, cut inside the marked lines to remove the waste. This creates a notch for the headboard cross rail to sit on.

Fit the two triangular supports inside the sides, at the head end, flush with the ends of the sides. Drill and countersink the inside of the triangles in at least four places on each side, and screw one to each of the side panels (fig 3).

Put the cross rail in place. Drill and countersink the cross rail and screw it into the triangle's notches, keeping the screws low in the cross rail. Make sure that the ends of the cross rails are flush with the outside of the triangles (fig 4).

For the triangular fillers (fig 5), position a piece of MDF on the side panel. Line it up with the back edge of the triangular support and mark off the triangle on to it. Cut out this triangle and repeat for the other side. Fix the fillers in place by drilling, countersinking and screwing from the inside of the triangular supports. Use three screws each side.

The headboard consists of two pieces, one above the other, cut to the width of the mattress. For the height of the lower piece, measure up the triangular support from the floor to about three-quarters of the way up the thickness of the mattress,

---

① Fixing the Cross Dividers to the Side Panels
Glue and screw the corner battens to the side panels, then position the cross dividers against the battens, flush with the bottom edge, and screw in place through the dividers and into the battens.

② Headboard Cross-Rail
Hold the cross rail on end at the top of the triangular support and mark out the notch.

③ Fixing the Triangular Headboard Support
Screw headboard supports to insides of the side panels.

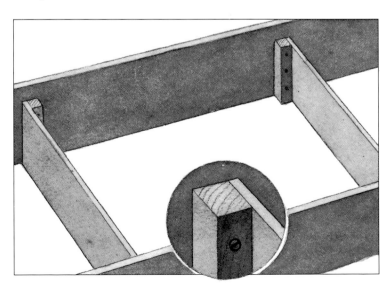

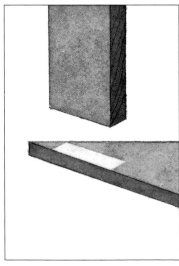

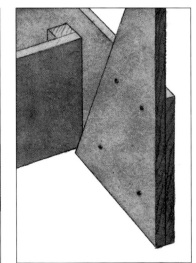

with the mattress in place. The higher piece measures the distance from that point to the top of the triangle plus 12mm ($\frac{1}{2}$in). The extra portion is a fingergrip for removing the panel when necessary for access to the space below.

STRENGTHENING BATTEN

The strengthening batten is cut from 50 × 50mm (2 × 2in) softwood to the width of the mattress minus 38mm (1$\frac{1}{2}$in), which is the thickness of the two triangular supports. Glue and screw the lower headboard section to the front edges of the triangular supports. Put the strengthening batten at the top of the lower headboard section on the underside, and cramp it in place half way up its thickness, thereby creating a 25mm (1in) rebate for the top part of the headboard to be located in. Drill, countersink and screw through the lower headboard section into the batten. Try the top headboard piece in place, then remove it for covering. The upholstery will bring it flush with the sides of the triangular fillers for a tidy finish.

Hold a piece of 25 × 25mm (1 × 1in) softwood batten against the gap between the top of the lower headboard section and the side panel. Mark off the top and bottom and cut with a tenon saw. The bottom will be at an angle to fit the side of the bed. Glue and nail or screw the batten in place to each side (fig 1, page 116). Plane, then sand off completely flush. The batten acts as a filler to give a clean line, and will be filled and painted in with the rest of the bed.

The top edge of the side panels should be rounded over either with a router and a rounding-over cutter, or by planing and sanding. Alternatively, glue and pin a half-round moulding to the top edges for a professional-looking finish.

PADDED HEADBOARD

The padded and upholstered headboard pulls forward to reveal additional storage space at the bed head.

4 Fixing Headboard Cross Rail in Place
Headboard cross rail is fixed with two screws kept low in the cross rail.

5 Fixing the Triangular Fillers at each Side
Triangular fillers made from the same material as the side panels give a flush finish at each side. Cut the fillers to fit exactly and screw through from the inside of the triangular supports.

6 Headboard and Batten
Screw lower headboard section in place. Cramp the strengthening batten to top edge and screw down.

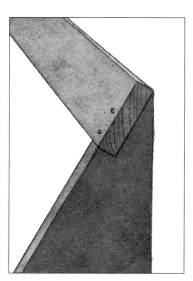

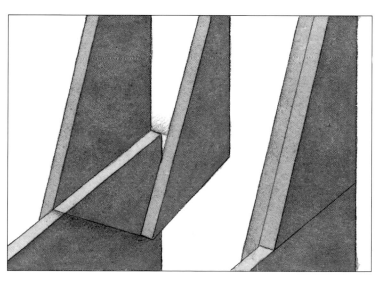

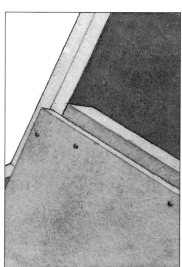

BED WITH TRUCKLE DRAWER

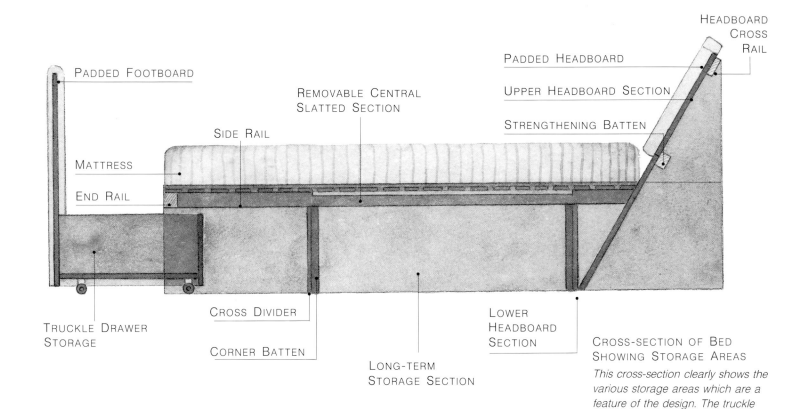

HEADBOARD CROSS RAIL

PADDED FOOTBOARD

PADDED HEADBOARD

UPPER HEADBOARD SECTION

REMOVABLE CENTRAL SLATTED SECTION

STRENGTHENING BATTEN

SIDE RAIL

MATTRESS

END RAIL

TRUCKLE DRAWER STORAGE

CROSS DIVIDER

CORNER BATTEN

LONG-TERM STORAGE SECTION

LOWER HEADBOARD SECTION

CROSS-SECTION OF BED SHOWING STORAGE AREAS
This cross-section clearly shows the various storage areas which are a feature of the design. The truckle drawer is particularly accessible.

1 Adding the Filler Piece
Use a piece of softwood to fill the gap between the side and lower headboard section.

2 Fixing the Mattress-support Side Rails in Place
Cut the headboard ends of the mattress-support side rails at an angle to fit neatly against the lower section. Note that the top edge of the side panel is rounded over to give a neat finish.

3 Joining the End Rail
End rail is joined to side rails using corner halving joints; end rail laps on top and is screwed to side rails.

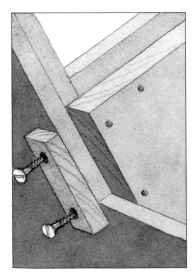

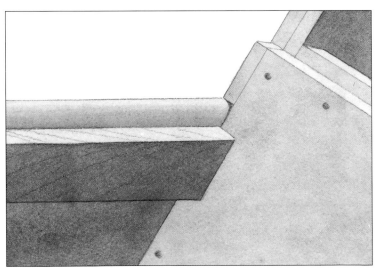

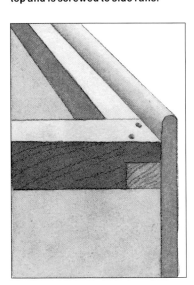

MATTRESS SUPPORT SECTION

The side rails are cut to the length of the mattress, plus a little overlength so that the angle can be cut into the headboard. Place their 50mm (2in) faces on the cross dividers alongside the sides, and scribe one end of each rail to the headboard. Cut this angle and push them up against the headboard, then mark them off flush with the ends of the side panels and cut them square.

The end rail is cut to the width of the mattress. Cut corner halving joints (see **Techniques, page 242**) to join the side and end rails (fig 3)

Glue and screw the side rails in place, screwing through the rails and into the side panels. Fix the end rail in place by inserting small screws through the halving joints.

The centre rail is cut from 75 × 50mm (3 × 2in) softwood to the length of the mattress plus a little overlength. Rest it on the cross dividers, and scribe to the angle of the headrest, as before. Cut the centre rail to length to butt tightly

A unit of the mattress support section (above) lifts out for access to ample but unobtrusive storage space under the bed.

against the inner face of the end rail. Screw it down into the cross dividers.

Drill through the end rail into the end of the centre rail in two places, to a depth of between 75mm and 100mm (3–4in) and dry-dowel the joint using 12mm (½in) dowelling (see **Techniques, page 245**).

Work out how many slats you need by dividing the length of the mattress by 100mm (4in) – the total of one slat plus a gap. Cut all the slats to the width of the mattress. The area between the cross dividers is a slatted unit which can be lifted out to give access to storage below.

The softwood cross battens hold the slats together on the slatted unit. Measure the internal distance between the cross dividers and cut four lengths of 75 × 25mm (3 × 1in) to this dimension.

Using a spacing batten (see **Techniques, page 236**), space the slats equally and mark the position of the cross battens on to the first slat. The two outermost slats should be positioned in from the ends by the thickness of the side rails – that is, at least 50mm (2in). Screw the ends of the outer cross battens in place to the first slat. Continue along the cross battens, spacing and screwing down the rest of the slats. Then space the innermost two cross battens equally in between and screw them in place (fig 5).

Place this panel on the centre section and screw the remaining slats into the side rails, spacing them equally. Make sure that there is a slat flush with each end.

④ **Joining End and Centre Rail**
Centre rail butts against end rail. Drill through end rail and hammer dowels in place.

⑤ **Making the Under-Mattress Lift-Out Slatted Unit**
The slatted unit between the cross-dividers can be lifted out. Slats are screwed to four cross battens. The outer two cross battens are inset so that they clear the side rails.

⑥ **Spacing the Fixed Slats**
Place lift-out unit over the centre section and screw remaining slats, equally spaced, to side rails.

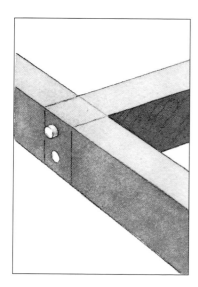

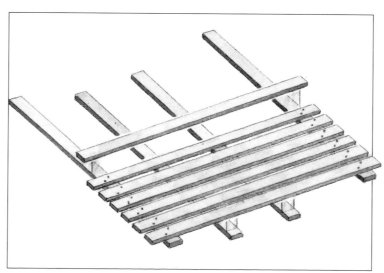

Bed with Truckle Drawer

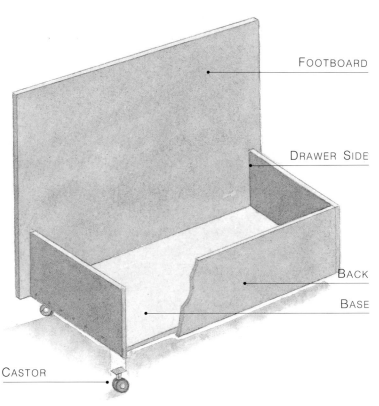

FOOTBOARD

DRAWER SIDE

BACK

BASE

CASTOR

① Truckle Drawer Assembly
Note that sides are set in from the footboard and that the back sits within the sides.

The Truckle Drawer

The bed should be finished before you make the drawer. The footboard is cut from one piece of MDF to 12mm (½in) less than the overall width of the bed. Its height is as required – ours is 890mm (35in).

Preferably, the height of the two MDF drawer sides should be at least 150mm (6in) lower than the sides of the bed. This allows the drawers to run underneath the end rail and accommodates castors. Our sides are therefore 300mm (12in). The length is 610mm (24in).

For the back, cut one piece of MDF to the height of the drawer sides. Its width should be that of the mattress minus 50mm (2in). Glue and screw through the sides into the back edges, then glue and screw through the footboard into the sides, ensuring that the footboard overlaps the sides equally.

Measure the internal dimensions of the rectangle for the size of the base, and cut it to size from MDF. The base should be spaced 25mm (1in) up from the bottom edges of the sides. To fix it firmly in place for screwing, lay the base on scrap battens 25mm (1in) thick, then place the carcass over the base. This will ensure an even 25mm (1in) spacing up from the bottom edges of the carcass.

Screw through into the edges of the base on all four sides, having marked the height of the centre line

of the base round the outside of the carcass. Finally, screw 50mm (2in) castors to the four corners of the base to allow easy movement.

Upholstery for the Bed

The Padding

The padding is expanded-polystyrene foam of three different thicknesses, covered with Dacron. The best way to cut the foam is to use an electric carving knife. Alternatively, use a bread knife, a hacksaw blade, or any blade with a serrated edge.

Headboard

Cut a piece of 50mm (2in) foam to the size of the headboard's upper section. Spray one face of the headboard with latex spray adhesive and stick the foam to it, smoothing it down carefully.

Cut a piece of 50mm (2in) foam to the length of the top edge and, positioning it carefully, stick it in place with spray adhesive.

② Padding the Headboard
Stick 50mm (2in) thick foam to upper headboard section and top edge; 25mm (1in) foam at sides.

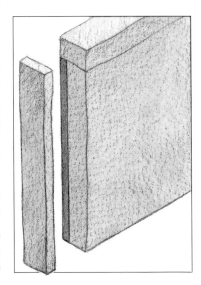

Use 25mm (1in) foam for the sides. Cut two pieces, each to the length of the headboard's side, plus the thickness of the foam covering the top, and stick one on each side.

Stick a thin layer of Dacron over all the foam with the spray adhesive and leave to dry.

Footboard

Cut one piece of 25mm (1in) foam to the width of the footboard, to run from the top of the drawer sides up and over the top of the footboard and down to the bottom edge.

Draw a line on the inside face of the footboard in line with the top of the drawer sides and spray adhesive on the wood down to this line, and on to the outside face.

Stick down the foam, starting at the line and smoothing it on to the wood. Ease it over the top and down the other side of the footboard.

Cut two pieces of 25mm (1in) foam to fit the small sections either side of the drawer, on the inside face of the footboard, and stick in place.

Cut two pieces of 12mm (½in)

③ Padding the Footboard
One piece of 25mm (1in) foam covers front/back of footboard, plus 12mm (½in) foam at sides.

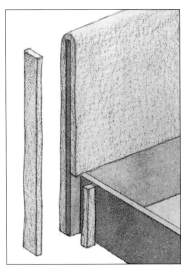

foam to the size of the side edges and stick one to each edge.

Put a layer of Dacron over the foam, stick in place and leave to dry.

THE COVERS

These are welted covers with loose flaps folded under the bottom edge and joined by Velcro.

You will probably need to join widths of fabric. Joins should be made in two equally spaced seams. If you use a patterned fabric, you will also have to match from width to width, which can be quite difficult. Plain fabrics are therefore the easiest to work with. If you want to avoid joining widths, you could use a plain fabric and work with it sideways instead of lengthways.

If you do not feel capable of making a panelled border on the covers, you can achieve equally good results by using a single seam to join the front and back sections of the cover together.

HEADBOARD

Cut two panels – one for the front and one for the back of the padded headboard, allowing additional fabric all round for seams, and for joining any widths. If you have to make joins, do so first, cutting the fabric oversize and matching the seam positions of the front and back panels.

Fold the panels in half across their width and make a nip at the centre of the top edge, to match up the panels when sewing.

Next, measure for the long border to go round the top and sides and under the bottom edge by 75mm (3in) at each end. Cut out the border panel, allowing extra each side for the seams. Fold in half widthways and make nips in the centre and where the corners will be, on both edges.

Place the front section to the border panel, edge to edge and right sides together, matching the nips and corners. Pin, tack and then machine-stitch the seam, working from the centre nip outwards, first in one direction and then the other, along the top and down the other two sides as far as the corners. Machine-stitching in both directions

ensures that the two pieces of fabric are sewn evenly.

Attach the back panel to the other edge of the border, right sides together and with nips and corners matching exactly. Pin, tack and machine-stitch as before, down to each corner.

Neaten all the edges of the flaps by turning under the hems to the wrong side and machine-stitching. Cut a strip of Velcro to the length of the long flaps and machine-stitch it in place to the edges of the fabric so that one overlaps the other. Fold in the two end pieces first, and join the long flaps together with the Velcro for a neat finish.

FOOTBOARD

Measure the padded footboard from edge to edge and cut one panel for the inside face, allowing extra all round for the seams, plus about 75mm (3in) to enclose the padding at the bottom (be sure to account for joining any widths and make the joins first). Cut the panel for the outside face, allowing extra all round, plus enough to flap under

the bottom edge. Cut out material for the long panel, allowing enough extra fabric for the seams and for folding under the bottom edge.

Make up the cover as for the headboard, equalizing the seams and attaching the outside face first. On the inside face, sew down as far as the drawer sides, then attach a small piece of fabric each side to cover the narrow border either side of the drawer. Machine-stitch them on to the cover with the right sides together. Carefully cut and fit round each drawer side turning the edges under and then machine-stitching. Neaten all the bottom edges by turning under a flap and machine stitching.

On the outside, fold in the ends and fold the long edge under. Fit to the bottom edge with Velcro, using the soft part on the fabric and the hard part on the wood. To attach Velcro to the wood, glue, tack, or staple it in place, or use self-adhesive Velcro.

On the inside face, secure the bottom edge and side flaps with Velcro as before.

④ Making the Cover for the Headboard
Cut the front and back panels allowing extra fabric all round for seams and joining widths, plus about 75mm (3in) to flap under the bottom edge. Pin, tack, then machine sew seams.

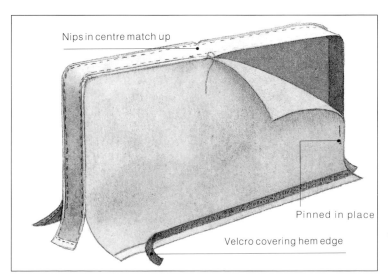

Nips in centre match up

Pinned in place

Velcro covering hem edge

⑤ Making the Cover for the Footboard
Make up as for the headboard, carefully cutting and fitting round drawer sides. At the narrow sides of the drawer, attach thin strips of fabric. Fix down with Velcro along the bottom edge and along side flaps.

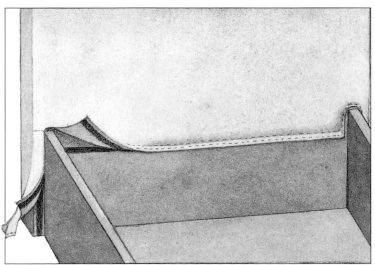

CRIB

A baby's crib has great sentimental value. Before the baby is born, making or trimming a crib or basket is often a way for parents to express all their hopes and feelings for the future. Fathers, in particular, may take pride in fashioning their child's first bed, making their own contribution at a time when they can otherwise feel somewhat left out. And the significance of the crib will outlast its usefulness. Later in life, the child will see the crib as proof of the parents' concern and love and it may become a family heirloom.

A rocking cradle or crib is a traditional bed for a newborn baby, the gentle lulling motion soothing and reassuring a baby unaccustomed to perfect stillness. The rockers are the most complicated part of the construction, albeit an interesting woodworking exercise. They are fashioned by gluing and cramping strips of plywood together around a former to build up into curves. Holes drilled in the end panels are primarily decorative, but could also be used for suspending a soft toy or rattle.

The basic design of the crib shown here consists of a simple pine frame, with dowels at the sides. A little care is needed to ensure that the angles are correct for insetting the plywood end panels.

The crib is very much scaled to the first few months of a baby's life – a sense of enclosure seems to be important to a baby in its early days. But although the crib is soon outgrown, it will find a new use when the next baby comes along. The dimensions of the crib accommodate a standard-sized baby's mattress.

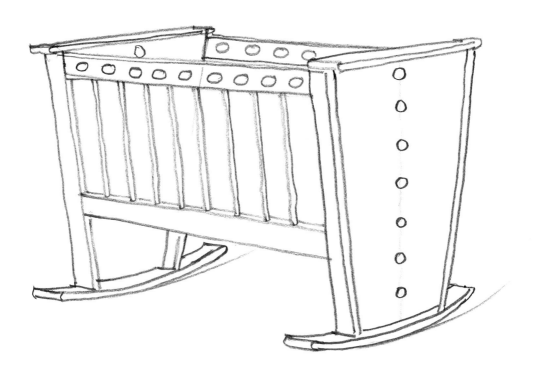

CRIB

A new baby can easily get 'lost' in a cot, and for those important first few months a crib is a must. Our crib is equipped with curved rockers that allow it to be rocked from side to side to lull a baby to sleep. Proprietary crib mattresses are available from baby shops, and our design is based around a mattress measuring 730 × 350mm (28¾ × 13¾in).

For safety's sake, do not attempt to modify or alter the design. The size of the rockers, and the height of the mattress base from the ground,

MATERIALS

Part	Quantity	Material	Length
UPRIGHT	4	75 × 25mm (3 × 1in) PAR softwood, reduced to 55mm (2³⁄₁₆in) wide	625mm (24⅝in)
RAIL	4	As above	700mm (27½in)
CAPPING BOARD	2	As above	580mm (about 23in)
SLAT	18	12mm (½in) hardwood dowel	300mm (12in)
END PANEL	2	6mm (¼in) plywood	640mm (25¼in) high × 512mm (20³⁄₁₆in) wide at the top × 312mm (12¼in) wide at the bottom
ROCKER	2	Each formed from 4 pieces of 6mm (¼in) laminated plywood	Cut from a sheet approx. 650 × 58mm (25⅝ × 2¼in)
BASE	1	6mm (¼in) plywood	Cut to fit (approx. 750 × 385mm [29½ × 15¼in])
BASE-SUPPORT BATTEN	2	25 × 25mm (1 × 1in) PAR softwood	Cut to fit (approx. 750mm [29½in])
DOWEL (for joints)	24	10mm (⅜in) diameter	

Also required: 18mm (¾in) chipboard, to make former for rockers

have been carefully worked out to ensure stability. And the spacing between the dowels which form the sides of the crib ensures that a baby's head, hands and feet cannot become trapped. Similarly, the holes in the end panels and along the top side rails must be 25mm (1in) in diameter to ensure that little fingers cannot become caught in them.

The main frame of the crib is made from 55 × 25mm (2³⁄₁₆ × 1in) PAR (planed all round) softwood. You will not be able to buy this size 'off the shelf', so buy 75 × 25mm (3 × 1in) softwood and cut this stock down to size using a circular saw, or ask the supplier to do this for you. The newly sawn edge will need to be planed smooth.

The sides are formed using 12mm (½in) hardwood dowels, and the end panels and crib base are cut from 6mm (¼in) plywood. Choose the plywood carefully, especially if the crib is to be given a clear finish (for this you will need a 'faced' or veneered plywood). Stops could be fitted beneath the rockers to prevent any risk of tipping.

CONSTRUCTION

Cut down the softwood framing timbers and plane to finish 55mm (2³⁄₁₆in) wide. Then cut all the main components (that is, the uprights, rails and slats) to length.

SIDE FRAMES

Each side of the crib is constructed from nine slats of dowelling fixed vertically between two horizontal rails (fig 1). Along the centre line of a narrow edge of one rail mark positions for nine holes, spaced equally at 70mm (2¾in) centres. Cramp all four rails together side by side and transfer the marks from the first rail to the other three rails.

Fit a 12mm (½in) dowel bit in an electric drill, and drill a hole at each mark on the rails to a depth of 10mm (⅜in). This is best done with the drill held upright in a drill stand. Alternatively, you can cramp the four rails firmly to a workbench.

Apply a little adhesive to each hole and assemble the two sides. Fit the dowels between two rails and

tap them together with a mallet, using scrap wood to protect the surface of the rails from the mallet blows. Lay the side frames on a flat surface for about six hours until the adhesive has firmly set.

1 Making the Side Frames
Nine holes spaced at 70mm (2¾in) centres are drilled along top and bottom rails to take dowel 'slats'.

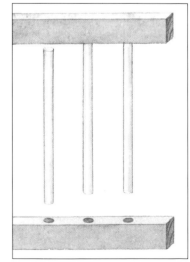

CRIB ASSEMBLY

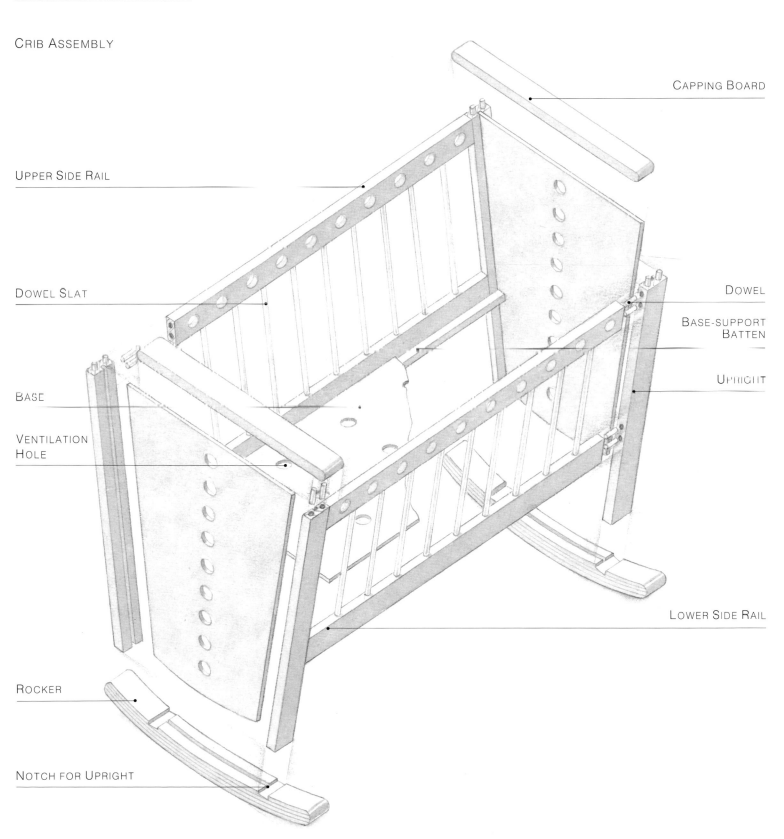

CAPPING BOARD

UPPER SIDE RAIL

DOWEL SLAT

DOWEL

BASE-SUPPORT BATTEN

UPRIGHT

BASE

VENTILATION HOLE

LOWER SIDE RAIL

ROCKER

NOTCH FOR UPRIGHT

CRIB

UPRIGHTS

Down the length of the centre of the inside face of each upright rout a 6×6mm ($\frac{1}{4} \times \frac{1}{4}$in) groove.

The four uprights are joined to the rails of the assembled side frames using two dowels at each joint (fig 1). Lay the side panels flat on the bench with an upright at each end and mark the four joint positions for each panel – the tops of the uprights must be flush with the tops of the upper side rails. Using a dowelling jig, drill out two holes for 10mm ($\frac{3}{8}$in) dowels in the end of each rail and in matching positions in the uprights. Dry assemble to test the fit. Then apply a little adhesive to the holes of the joints, insert the dowels and tap the uprights in place with a mallet, using a piece of scrap wood to protect the surfaces (fig 2).

MAKING THE ROCKERS

The rockers are each made by laminating four strips of plywood bent round a chipboard former – offcuts of any 18mm ($\frac{3}{4}$in) board will do – to make the curve (fig 3).

The radius for the arc of the rocker former is 960mm (approximately 38in). The best way to mark this curve is to use a pencil tied to a suitable length of string attached to a nail at a central point. Mark the arc on to a piece of 18mm ($\frac{3}{4}$in) chipboard measuring approximately 700×300mm (28×12in), and cut round this curve using a jigsaw.

Build up the thickness of the former at the curved edge using two extra pieces of board (about 700×150mm [28×6in]) to bring the thickness of the curve to 54mm ($2\frac{1}{8}$in). Screw the three pieces together (fig 3, bottom).

From the 6mm ($\frac{1}{4}$in) plywood cut the eight strips, each 650mm ($25\frac{5}{8}$in) long, to form the rockers. Cutting these to 58mm ($2\frac{5}{16}$in) wide allows a little extra for finishing to 55mm ($2\frac{3}{16}$in) which is the width of the stock used for the uprights.

Glue together the four strips to form each rocker using a non-flexible powdered resin wood glue such as Cascamite (*not* the ready-to-use PVA type). This gives a rigid setting. Form one rocker at a time,

cramping one set around the former (fig 3) and holding with G-cramps or a webbing cramp until the adhesive sets (about 8 hours). Then repeat for the second rocker.

END PANELS

Mark out end panels on 6mm ($\frac{1}{4}$in) plywood so they are 640mm ($25\frac{1}{4}$in) high, 512mm ($20\frac{3}{16}$in) wide at the top and 312mm ($12\frac{1}{4}$in) wide at the bottom. Check that they taper equally each side of the centre line. Cut out the panels.

Line up a rocker to the bottom edge of an end panel, align the centres and mark round the curve on to the bottom edge of the panel. Trim the panel to shape using a jigsaw. Transfer the curve on to the other panel and cut this one out.

Dry assemble the end panels on to the side frames and turn the whole unit upside down.

Place one of the rockers in position alongside the end panel. Make sure the centre line of the rocker lines up with the centre line of the end panel. Mark on the rockers where the uprights will sit.

Using a try square, extend the marks of the upright positions across the rockers. Saw down these lines with a tenon saw, and chop out the notches with a chisel (*see* **Crib Assembly, page 123**).

Using a router, rout a 6mm ($\frac{1}{4}$in) wide groove, 10mm (about $\frac{3}{8}$in) deep, centrally on each rocker between the notches to accept the bottom edge of the end panel.

From the underside, drill and countersink through the rockers at an angle into the uprights (fig 4) and fix with 64mm ($2\frac{1}{2}$in) No 10 woodscrews, two to each upright. Dry assemble to check the fit.

ASSEMBLING THE BASE

Cut two base-support battens from 25×25mm (1×1in) PAR softwood, to the internal length between the end panels at the height of the lower side rail.

Plane a bevel along one length of each batten so the top edge will be horizontal to the base (fig 5). Glue and screw the battens flush with the bottom of the lower side rail. Use $1\frac{1}{2}$in (38mm) No 8 woodscrews.

---

1 Joining Sides to Uprights
Mark the side rail positions on the sides of the uprights. Drill and dowel ends of rails to uprights.

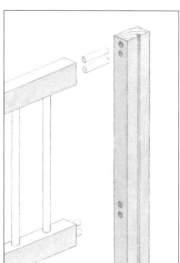

2 Finished Side Assembly
Note 6×6mm ($\frac{1}{4} \times \frac{1}{4}$in) groove down centre line of inside face of each upright to accept end panel.

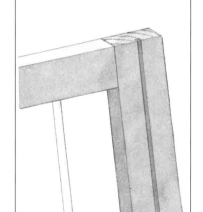

3 Forming the Crib Rockers
Each rocker is made from four strips of 6mm ($\frac{1}{4}$in) plywood, which are bent round a purpose-made chipboard former with a radius of 960mm (38in). The plywood strips are then glued and cramped together until the adhesive sets.

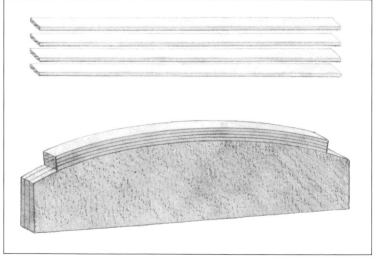

Check that the diagonals are equal to ensure the crib is square, pulling it to adjust if necessary. Then take the internal measurements of the crib, and cut the plywood base panel to fit. Once in place, the base will hold the crib square.

CAPPING BOARDS

Remove the end panels and plane the top edges of the side frames so they are horizontal. Plane from the ends towards the middle to avoid splintering the outside edges of the uprights. Replace the end panels.

Cut the two capping boards to length. At the ends these will be dowel jointed to the uprights (fig 6), but between these dowel positions a 6 × 6mm ($\frac{1}{4} \times \frac{1}{4}$in) groove, 512mm ($20\frac{3}{16}$in) long, will be required centrally along the underside of each capping board to take the top edge of the end panel.

Drill down into the uprights and up into the underside of the capping boards to take the dowels and dry assemble with 10mm ($\frac{3}{8}$in) dowels, two to each upright. A dowelling jig may make drilling more accurate.

DECORATIVE HOLES

Take the crib apart, and with the relevant parts held on scrap wood, drill 25mm (1in) diameter holes centrally down the end panels at 70mm ($2\frac{3}{4}$in) centres.

Drill 25mm (1in) holes through the top rails, spacing these centrally between the dowel slats *(see* **Crib Assembly, page 123** *)*. Do not hang toys etc between the holes as there is a risk of strangulation.

In the base panel drill 12 ventilation holes (four rows of three holes), again to a diameter of 25mm (1in).

FINAL ASSEMBLY

With a sanding block or finishing sander, round off the ends of the rockers and capping boards.

Glue up the crib in the following order: (i) end panels to side frames; (ii) rockers to base of end panels; (iii) capping boards to top of end panels. Finally, simply drop the base panel into place.

Before applying your finish, make sure all edges and holes are rounded and sanded smooth.

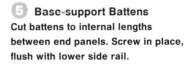

4 Fitting the Rockers to the Uprights and End Panels
Locate the end panels in the uprights and turn the crib upside down. Cut notches in the rockers to accept the ends of the uprights and rout grooves to accept the end panels. Screw through underside of rockers into each upright.

5 Base-support Battens
Cut battens to internal lengths between end panels. Screw in place, flush with lower side rail.

6 Fitting the Capping Board
Rout underside of capping board to accept top of end panel. Dowel capping board ends to uprights.

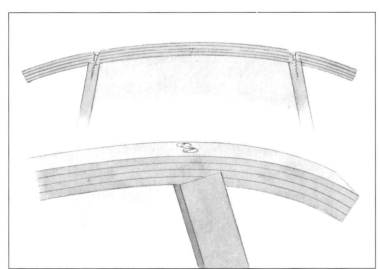

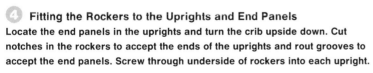

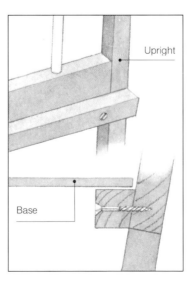

Upright

Base

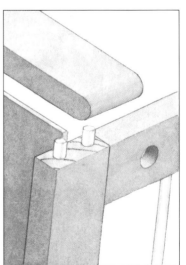

ROCKING CHAIR

A rocking chair is a classic item of nursery furniture. An adult-sized rocker is an ideal place for reading a bedtime story to a sleepy child. But a small, specially made rocking chair, such as the one shown here, has much more personal meaning and appeal for the child itself. Having a chair of one's own is something to be proud of, a symbol of childhood that is accorded special significance and often cherished for many years to come.

The design and construction of this rocking chair are fairly straightforward. The most complicated part of making it consists of shaping the rockers which are built up from strips of plywood. The rest of the chair is also made of plywood, jigsawed into the appropriate shapes. The plywood provides an easy surface to decorate. The chair could be painted a colour to complement the room, and you might add a cushion for extra comfort.

Wit and humour are important elements that should not be overlooked in designs for children's furniture. The rounded wings of the rocker, which resemble great Mickey Mouse ears, are vaguely anthropomorphic, a quality accentuated further by the two 'eyeholes' drilled through the back. Chairs which wrap around and encircle a child in this way make a cosy place to sit and offer a pleasing sense of security.

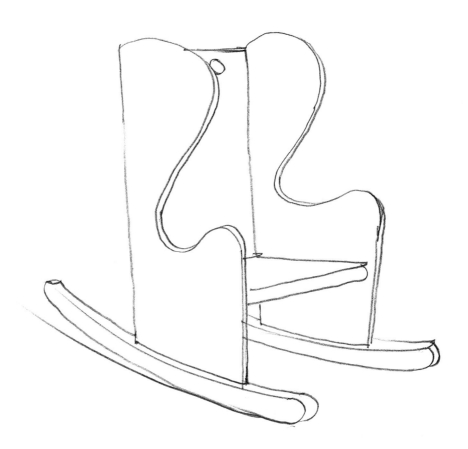

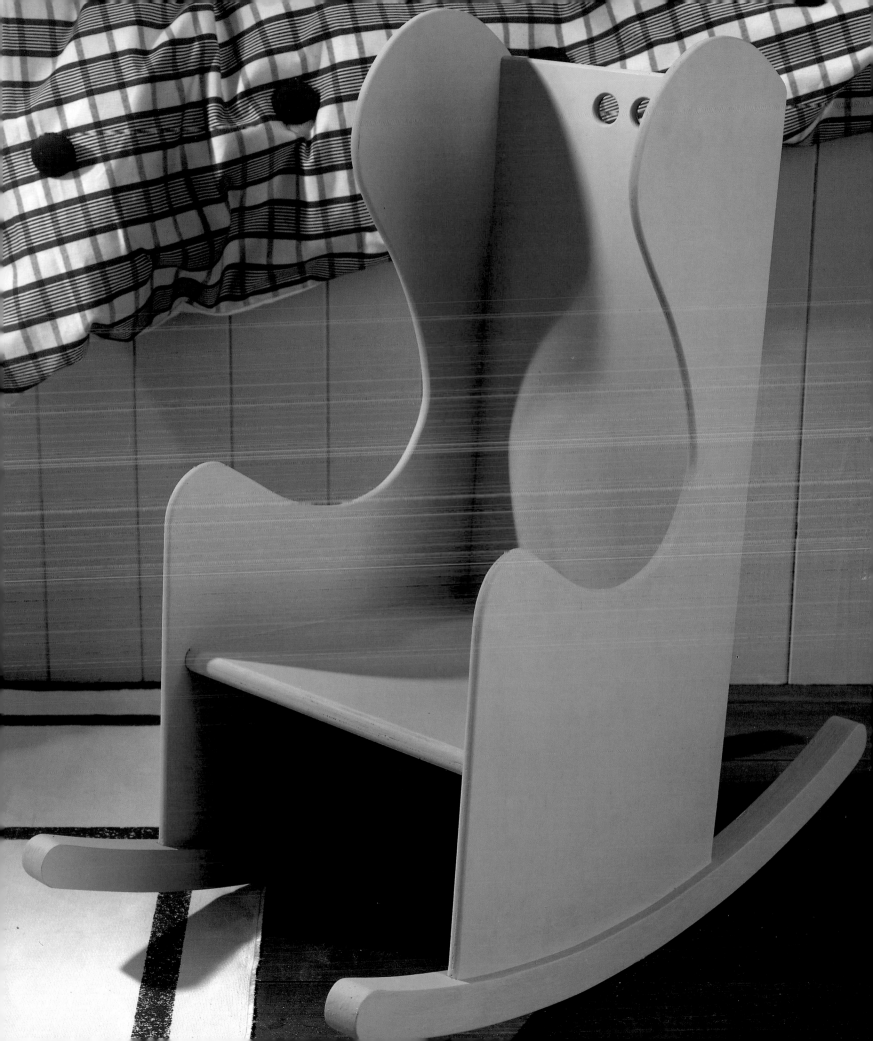

ROCKING CHAIR

Even small children eventually stop running around to take a breather and when they do it is a good idea for them to have their own comfortable chair where they can rest and relax, read, or watch television. The child's rocking chair made here is ideal. The chair is about 700mm ($27\frac{1}{2}$in) high overall, and it is perfect for children aged about four years old. The entire chair is made from 9mm ($\frac{3}{8}$in) plywood. You only need a sheet measuring 1400 × 910mm (about 5 × 3ft), but you will probably end up having to buy a sheet measuring 1800 × 910mm (6 × 3ft), which is a stock size. This will result in some waste but the offcuts may be useful for some other project.

TOOLS

WORKBENCH (fixed or portable)

TRIMMING KNIFE

STEEL MEASURING TAPE

STEEL RULE

TRY SQUARE

MARKING GAUGE

PANEL SAW or CIRCULAR POWER SAW

POWER DRILL

FLAT BIT – 25mm (1in), to cut holes in back panel

2 G-CRAMPS

2 SASH CRAMPS or WEBBING CRAMP

SMOOTHING PLANE

POWER ROUTER and 6mm ($\frac{1}{4}$in) STRAIGHT-CUTTING BIT

ROUNDING-OVER CUTTER for router (or plane, Surform tool or sanding block)

POWER FINISHING SANDER (or hand-sanding block)

POWER JIGSAW

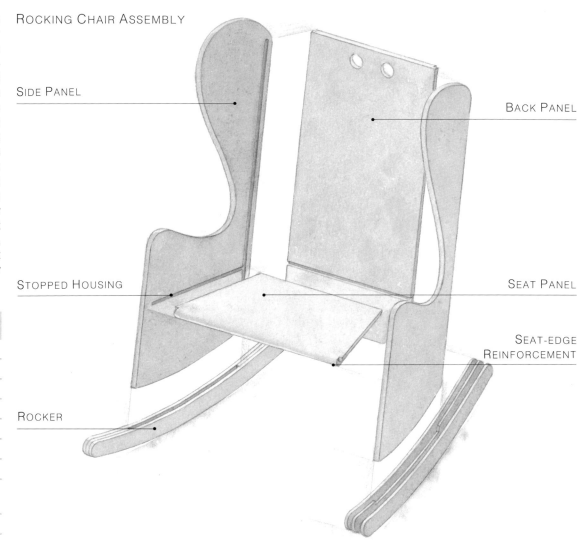

ROCKING CHAIR ASSEMBLY

SIDE PANEL

BACK PANEL

STOPPED HOUSING

SEAT PANEL

SEAT-EDGE REINFORCEMENT

ROCKER

MATERIALS

Part	Quantity	Material	Length
SIDE PANEL	2	9mm ($\frac{3}{8}$in) plywood	Cut from 700 × 320mm ($27\frac{1}{2}$ × 13in)*
BACK PANEL	1	As above	600 × 260mm ($23\frac{5}{8}$ × $10\frac{1}{4}$in)
SEAT PANEL	1	As above	296mm ($11\frac{5}{8}$in) deep × 310mm ($12\frac{1}{4}$in) wide (tapering to 260mm [$10\frac{1}{4}$in] at the back)
SEAT-EDGE REINFORCEMENT	1	As above	310 × 50mm ($12\frac{1}{4}$ × 2in)
ROCKER	2	Each formed from 3 pieces of 9mm ($\frac{3}{8}$in) plywood	Cut from 660 × 400mm (26 × $15\frac{3}{4}$in)*

* Cut from grid pattern provided on page 129

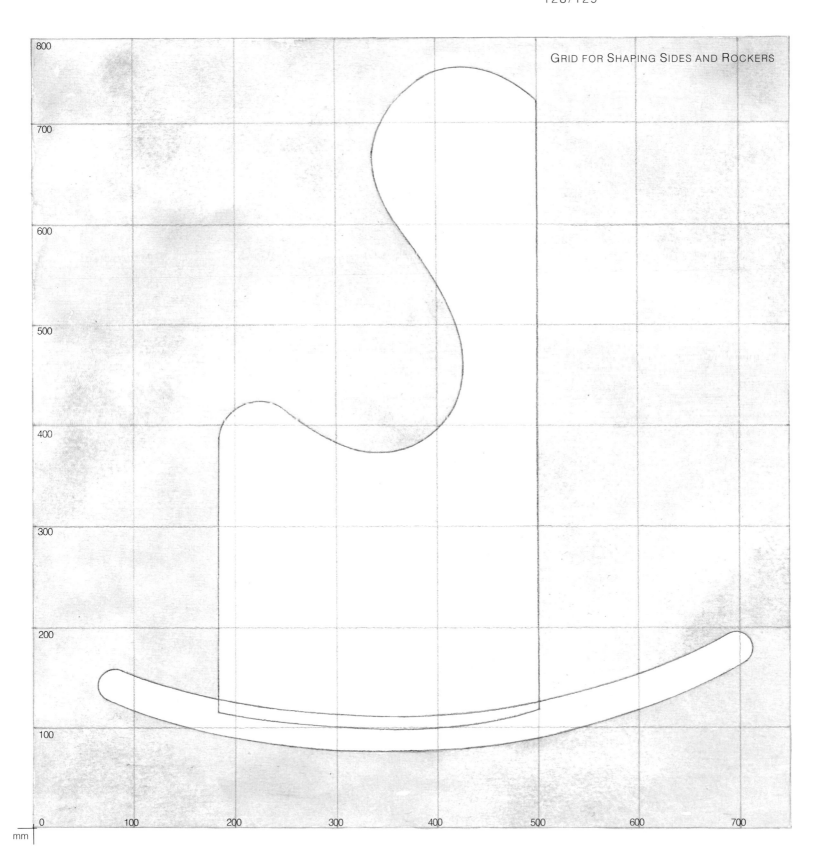

GRID FOR SHAPING SIDES AND ROCKERS

ROCKING CHAIR

CONSTRUCTION

Mark out the main pieces for the sides, back and seat on the 9mm ($\frac{3}{8}$ in) plywood sheet. Double check the measurements are accurate, then cut out the pieces using a jigsaw or a circular power saw.

SHAPING THE SEAT

Mark out the front of the seat so that it measures 310mm (12$\frac{1}{4}$in) wide at the front, narrowing evenly at each side to 260mm (10$\frac{1}{4}$in) wide at the back. The front-to-back measurement is 296mm (11$\frac{5}{8}$in). When you are sure that the seat is a regular shape, cut it out using a jigsaw or a circular power saw.

SHAPING THE SIDES

Using the grid (page 129), transfer the shape of the side panel and rocker on to a large sheet of paper. Brown paper is ideal for the pattern, but newspaper will do.

Once you are satisfied with the shape of the side (it does not have to be *exactly* as shown here), trans-fer the outline to one of the plywood side panels. The easiest way to do this is first to trace over the drawn outline on the *reverse* side of the paper using a soft pencil, then lay the paper pattern on to the plywood panel the right way up and secure it down at the sides and corners with adhesive tape. Now go over the outline again, pressing hard with the pencil. The outline will be transferred on to the wood.

Cut out the shape using a jigsaw, and sand the edges smooth. Lay this shaped piece on top of the plywood for the second side panel, draw round it and cut out and smooth as before.

SHAPING THE ROCKERS

Each rocker is made from three thicknesses of plywood, so you have to cut out six shapes in total. Following the method described above for the side panel, transfer the pattern of the rocker on to the plywood sheet set aside for the rockers and cut out the first rocker piece using a jigsaw. Sand or plane this accurately to shape as shown on the grid (page 129). The concave (upper) edge of the rocker can be shaped using either a jigsaw or a Surform tool.

Use this first rocker section as a template to mark out the other five pieces on the plywood panel. Cut all of these out with a jigsaw and sand all the edges smooth.

MAKING THE ROCKERS

The rockers are made by laminating three shaped pieces of plywood together. Before this is done, the two central pieces are notched to create slots to take the side panels (fig 1). To mark out on the central pieces, hold one of the shaped pieces against a side panel, referring to the grid to position it correctly. The rocker should protrude about 120mm (4$\frac{3}{4}$in) in front of the panel and 220mm (8$\frac{5}{8}$in) behind it.

Mark off the width of the side panel on to the concave edge of a rocker strip. Cut out a 12mm ($\frac{1}{2}$in) deep section across the full thickness between these marks, following the curve of the bottom edge of the side panel. Repeat the process on another rocker strip.

Glue up each set of three strips, with one whole rocker on each side of the slotted rocker (fig 1, below). Cramp together and, when the adhesive has set, round off the ends and sand the surfaces flush. Stops could be added to prevent tipping.

MAKING THE HOUSINGS FOR THE BACK PANEL

The back and seat panels fit into housings (slots) which must be cut in the inside faces of the side panels. A typical section of this, with dimensions marked, is shown (fig 2). Both the back panel and the seat panel are rebated along their sides to fit snugly into the housings.

To mark out the back housing on the side panel, measure and draw a line 15mm ($\frac{5}{8}$in) in from the back edge of the panel (fig 3). This marks the front edge of the housing. Mark a parallel line 6mm ($\frac{1}{4}$in) towards the back edge using a marking gauge. This second line marks the width of the housing for the back panel.

To determine the length of the housing, place a side panel into a rocker and offer up the back panel

---

① Forming the Rockers
Each rocker is made from three pieces of plywood; notch central piece to accept chair side panel.

② Housing and Rebate Detail
The main chair parts are joined using 6 × 5mm ($\frac{1}{4}$ × $\frac{3}{16}$in) housings and matching rebates as shown.

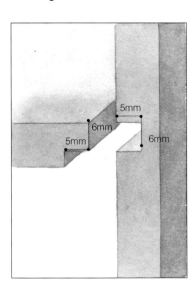

5mm
6mm
5mm
6mm

③ Back and Side Panels
Rout housing to accept back panel rebate 15mm ($\frac{5}{8}$in) from and parallel with back of side panel.

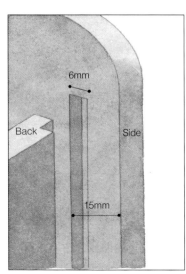

6mm
Back
Side
15mm

④ Seat and Back Panels
Rout a housing 150mm (6in) up from bottom of back panel to accept rebate in back edge of seat panel.

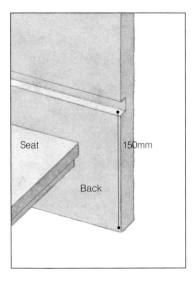

Seat
150mm
Back

so that it comes just above the rocker. Mark off the top and bottom of the back panel across the marked lines to indicate the length of the housing.

Make corresponding marks for the housing on the other side panel. (Remember they are 'handed' left to right, so will be mirror images.)

CUTTING THE HOUSINGS FOR THE SEAT

Measure 150mm (6in) up from the bottom edge of the back panel and, using a marking gauge, mark off a 6mm (¼in) wide housing for where the seat panel will be rebated to join the back panel (fig 4).

Offer up the back panel to each of the side panels and transfer marks for the height of the seat panel on to the side panels. Offer up the seat panel to each side panel at this height, positioned at 90 degrees to the housing marks for the back panel (fig 5), and measure for the length of the seat housing on the side panel so that, when it is cut, a 6mm (¼in) stopped shoulder will be left at the front of the seat (fig 6).

Mark the housing for the seat on the inside face of the other side panel in the same way.

Cut out all the housings using a router fitted with a 6mm (¼in) wide straight-cutter bit set to cut to a depth of 5mm (3⁄16in).

CUTTING THE REBATES IN THE SEAT AND BACK PANELS

To fit into the housings, the tongues in the seat and back panels must be 6mm (¼in) wide and 5mm (3⁄16in) deep. To ensure the panels are a tight fit you will need to rout rebates 5mm (3⁄16in) wide and to a depth so that they leave 6mm (¼in) of fixed tongue to fit into the housing. Practise the routing technique first on plywood offcuts to get the fit right, then rout round the back and sides of the seat panel underside remembering to leave the 6mm (¼in) stopped shoulder at the front of the seat (fig 6). Also rout a rebate down the reverse side of the long edges of the back panel (that is, the side that does not have any seat housing cut into it) (fig 3).

FINISHING OFF

Drill two 25mm (1in) diameter holes through the back panel, about 35mm (1⅜in) down from the top edge to the centres of the holes and about 35mm (1⅜in) apart, centre to centre. These holes are decorative and are useful for lifting the chair.

Rub down all the panels with abrasive paper until smooth. Dry assemble them to check the fit.

For aesthetic reasons, glue and pin a strip of 50mm (2in) wide plywood offcut to the underside of the front of the seat panel (fig 7).

Using a rounding-over cutter fitted in a router, or Surform tool or sanding block, round off the front edge of the seat, the edges of the seat-reinforcing strip, the top and bottom edges of the back panel, all round the shaped side panels and the inside of the holes, so that all exposed edges are smooth.

Apply adhesive to the housings and assemble all the components, holding the seat together with sash cramps or a webbing cramp.

Finish the chair as required.

---

⑤ **Seat and Side Panels**
Mark back panel housing position on side panels. Rout housings for seat at right angles to marked points.

⑥ **Seat Panel Rebates**
Rout 6 × 5mm (¼ × 3⁄16in) rebates along back and side edges. Rebates at sides are stopped 6mm (¼in) short.

⑦ **Seat-edge reinforcement**
Glue and pin an offcut to underside of seat panel, flush with front edge. Round over front edge to finish off.

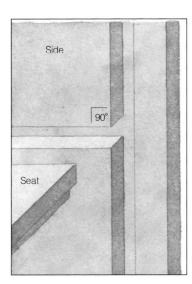

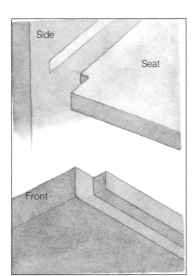

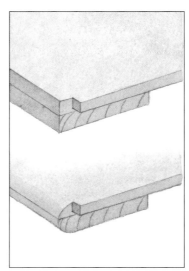

DOLL'S HOUSE

The doll's house has always been a popular toy, and it is easy to understand why. The first dolls' houses were elaborate curios, intricate architectural models with highly detailed interiors. But, ever since the eighteenth century, there have also been dolls' houses for children to play with and exercise their own creativity. A house in miniature gives children the opportunity to invent a whole world, and there is the added fascination of making or collecting pieces to furnish the rooms.

Rather reminiscent of a Scottish house, with its pedimented roof and blockwork framing the door, this design is a very simple box construction, with a hinged front panel. The four rooms inside are visible through cut-out windows. A strip of moulding and pediment shape elegantly trim the top; thin plywood scored to resemble large blocks is stuck around the door. The basic material is MDF, which is easy to cut and provides the best surface for decorating.

If you already have a collection of doll's house furniture, the dimensions of the house could be altered to make rooms of suitable proportions. And decoration, inside and out, can be as elaborate as you like. The paint finish for the outside of the house in this example consists of a sandy base colour with boot polish wiped over the top to give a textured look.

The finished house is handsome enough to sit in the living room. Every child should have one!

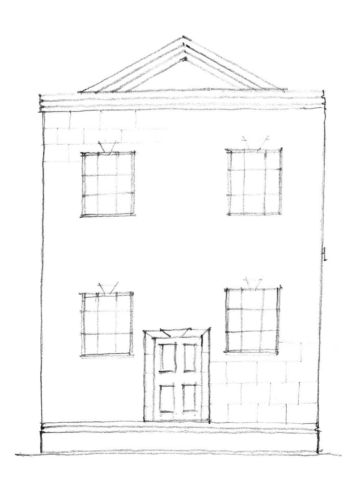

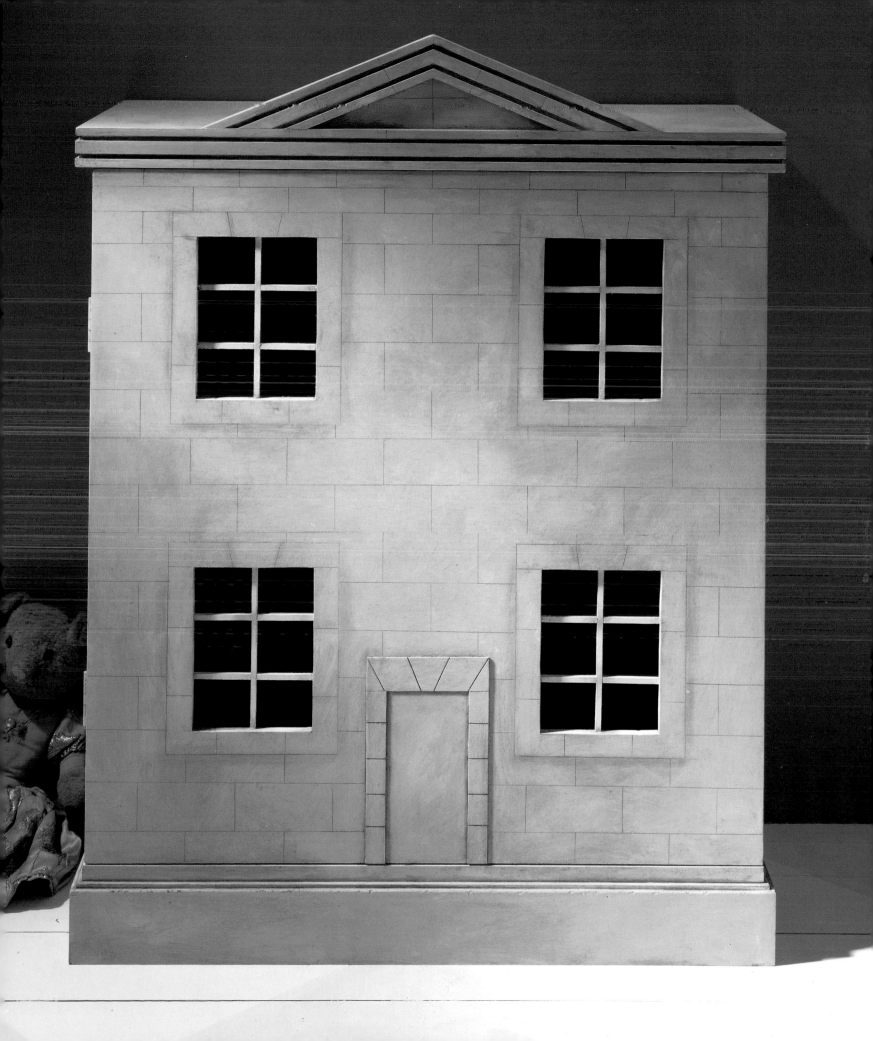

DOLL'S HOUSE

MATERIALS

Part	Quantity	Material	Length
CARCASS			
TOP	1	15mm ($\frac{5}{8}$in) MDF	650 × 321mm ($25\frac{1}{2}$ × $12\frac{5}{8}$in)
BASE	1	As above	650 × 335mm ($25\frac{1}{2}$ × $13\frac{1}{8}$in)
SIDE	2	As above	705 × 321mm ($27\frac{3}{4}$ × $12\frac{5}{8}$in)
CENTRAL PARTITION	1	As above	695 × 316mm ($27\frac{3}{8}$ × $12\frac{1}{2}$in)
SHELF	2	As above	312 × 316mm ($12\frac{1}{4}$ × $12\frac{1}{2}$in)
BACK	1	4mm ($\frac{1}{8}$in) MDF or plywood or hardboard	705 × 640mm ($27\frac{3}{4}$ × $25\frac{1}{4}$in)
DOOR PANEL	1	12mm ($\frac{1}{2}$in) MDF	660 × 650mm (26 × $25\frac{1}{2}$in)
PLINTH			
PLINTH FRONT	1	18mm ($\frac{3}{4}$in) MDF	670 × 75mm ($26\frac{3}{8}$ × 3in)
PLINTH BACK	1	As above	634 × 75mm (25 × 3in)
PLINTH SIDE	2	As above	345 × 75mm ($13\frac{1}{2}$ × 3in)
DETAILING			
FRONT MOULDING	1	15mm ($\frac{5}{8}$in) MDF	680 × 40mm ($26\frac{3}{4}$ × $1\frac{1}{2}$in)
SIDE MOULDING	2	As above	Cut 2 from 680 × 40mm ($26\frac{3}{4}$ × $1\frac{1}{2}$in)
TOP MOULDING	2	As above	500 × 40mm ($19\frac{5}{8}$ × $1\frac{1}{2}$in)
TOP TRIANGLE	1	4mm ($\frac{1}{8}$in) MDF	445 × 90mm ($17\frac{1}{2}$ × $3\frac{5}{8}$in)
DOOR STOP	2	15mm ($\frac{5}{8}$in) MDF	650 × 35mm ($25\frac{1}{2}$ × $1\frac{3}{8}$in)
DOOR (imitation)	1	2mm ($\frac{1}{16}$in) MDF	200 × 75mm (8 × 3in)
GLAZING BAR (vertical)	4	6 × 6mm ($\frac{1}{4}$ × $\frac{1}{4}$in) balsa-wood	165mm ($6\frac{1}{2}$in)
GLAZING BAR (horizontal)	8	As above	125mm (5in)

TOOLS

- ROUTER
- SET OF CHISELS
- TENON SAW
- PIN HAMMER
- NAIL PUNCH
- FILLING KNIFE
- SCREWDRIVER
- SLIDING BEVEL
- DRILL (hand or power)
- JIGSAW or PADSAW
- DRILL BIT – approximately 3mm ($\frac{1}{8}$in) to drill pilot holes

A traditional doll's house is a wonderful toy that any child lucky enough to own will treasure and enjoy for endless hours of make-believe. This simple yet classic model is easy to construct with the help of a router. The advantage of its design is its adaptability – you can scale its dimensions up or down to tailor them to specific requirements. When constructing a doll's house it is important to base the scale on what is to be placed inside it, so that the rooms are built in correct proportion to furniture, furnishings or figures of a specific size.

The house is built almost completely of medium-density fibreboard (MDF). A small amount of balsawood provides the glazing bars, and plywood or hardboard may be used instead of MDF for the back.

Paper or paint the walls as you wish. You can either improvise or visit specialist shops for ready-made furniture and accessories.

MAIN CARCASS

Cut out all the components of the main carcass – the top, base, sides, central partition, shelves and back.

Rout a rebate 15mm ($\frac{5}{8}$in) wide and 10mm ($\frac{3}{8}$in) deep along the two side edges of the top panel from front to back (fig 1, top).

Cut rebates of the same dimensions in the two side edges of the base, but stop 15mm ($\frac{5}{8}$in) from the front to allow the base to protrude (fig 1, bottom). Chisel the corners of the rebates square.

① Rebating the Main Carcass
Top Rout 15 × 10mm ($\frac{5}{8}$ × $\frac{3}{8}$in) rebates along top panel. *Bottom* Rebates along base stop short.

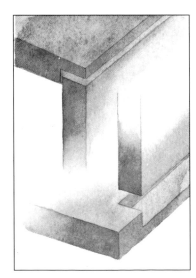

② Top and Base Housings
Cut 15 × 5mm ($\frac{5}{8}$ × $\frac{1}{4}$in) housings across centre of top and base panels, stopping short in base.

DOLL'S HOUSE ASSEMBLY

FRONT MOULDING

SIDE PANEL

DOOR STOP

DOOR PANEL

GLAZING BAR

BASE PANEL

TOP MOULDING

TOP PANEL

SIDE MOULDING

BACK PANEL

SHELF

CENTRAL PARTITION

BACK PLINTH

SIDE PLINTH

FRONT PLINTH

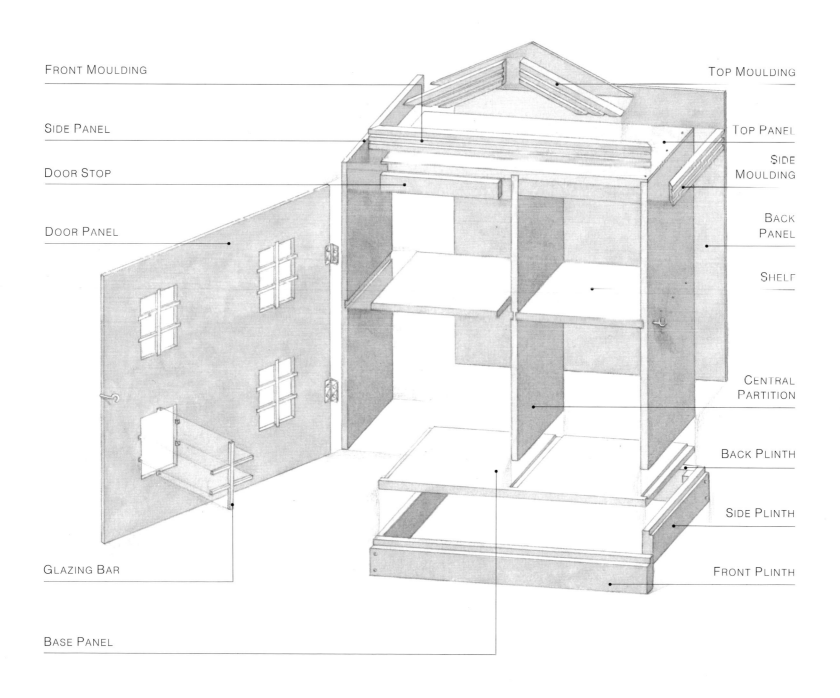

DOLL'S HOUSE

CUTTING THE HOUSINGS

Across the centre of the top and the sides and across the centre of both sides of the central partition, cut 15 × 5mm ($\frac{5}{8} \times \frac{1}{4}$in) housings to accept the interior partitions. Cut a housing across the base but stop 15mm ($\frac{5}{8}$in) short of the front, in line with the side edges (fig 2, page 134 and fig 1, this page).

REBATING BACK PANEL

Cut a rebate into the back edges of the top, sides and base for the back panel. This rebate should be 10mm ($\frac{3}{8}$in) wide and the thickness of the back panel – 4mm ($\frac{1}{8}$in).

ASSEMBLING THE CARCASS

Glue and pin the top to the sides and then the base. Ensure all edges are flush and square. Slide the central partition in from the back and glue and pin it in place. Next, slide in the two shelves from the back of the carcass and glue and pin them through the sides of the main carcass. Finally, glue and pin the back panel in place (fig 2). All

the pin heads should be driven below the surface with a punch, covered with filler and smoothed flush with the surface when dry.

PLINTH

Cut out the four sides of the plinth and glue and screw them together using two 38mm (1$\frac{1}{2}$in) No 6 screws at each joint. The sides fit behind the front and on either side of the back. Glue an 18mm ($\frac{3}{4}$in) offcut of MDF into each corner to strengthen the joints. The offcuts should be flush with, or slightly below, the top of the plinth (fig 3). Cut a decorative rebate 6 × 6mm ($\frac{1}{4} \times \frac{1}{4}$in) into the top outside edge of the plinth front.

Screw the plinth to the base using 50mm (2in) angle brackets – two at the front and two at the back.

FITTING THE DOOR STOPS

Cut two lengths of 15mm ($\frac{5}{8}$in) MDF for the door stops. Fix these in position to the underside of the top panel on either side of the central partition using glue and 25mm (1in) No 6 screws (see **Doll's House Assembly, page 135**).

MOULDINGS

Cut all the mouldings (front, side and top) roughly to length, then use the router to cut two decorative 6 × 6mm ($\frac{1}{4} \times \frac{1}{4}$in) grooves along their length (fig 4). Cut mitres for the corners of the front and side mouldings, then glue and pin them in place, flush with the top (fig 5).

Cut out the triangle for the top decoration from a piece of 4mm ($\frac{1}{8}$in) MDF. The two top mouldings must be angled at their base (where they meet the top of the house) and mitred to meet each other at the apex. Use a sliding bevel to mark the angles, then glue and pin them on to the triangular piece of MDF, flush with the edges and so that the grooves meet exactly.

Using a small drill bit, drill pilot holes into the front triangular moulding and pin in position through the moulding and into the roof. Glue an offcut of MDF to the back of the triangle and the top of the house to hold the triangle in place. Punch all the pin heads below the surface and fill.

WINDOWS

Cut out the door panel and mark the outlines of the windows on it: ours measure 150 × 110mm (6 × 4$\frac{1}{2}$in). Cut out the window openings using a jigsaw, a padsaw (drill a starter hole in the corner of each window first) or a router.

GLAZING BARS

Balsa-wood, obtainable from model shops, is ideal for the glazing bars. For each window, cut one vertical and two horizontal bars. Each should be 15mm ($\frac{1}{2}$in) longer than the length and width of the window opening – in this case, 165mm (6$\frac{1}{2}$in) and 125mm (5in). Use a fine saw and a tiny chisel to cut halving joints half way across the horizontal bars and one third and two thirds of the way down the vertical bars (fig 6). Glue the pieces together. Mark off the positions of the glazing bars around the inside faces and inside edges of the window openings. Use a tiny chisel to cut out the 6 × 6mm ($\frac{1}{4} \times \frac{1}{4}$in) notches and glue all the assembled bars in position.

---

1 Central Partition Housings
Cut 15 × 5mm ($\frac{5}{8} \times \frac{1}{4}$in) housings for interior partitions across centre of both sides of central panel.

2 Adding the Back Panel
The back panel fits into 10 × 4mm ($\frac{3}{8} \times \frac{1}{8}$in) rebates cut in the back edges of the top, sides and base.

3 Assembling the Base Plinth
Top Glue and screw plinth together, strengthening corners with MDF offcuts. *Bottom left* Cut a 6 × 6mm ($\frac{1}{4} \times \frac{1}{4}$in) rebate in top edge of plinth front. *Bottom right* Use angle brackets to screw plinth up into base.

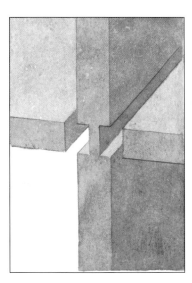

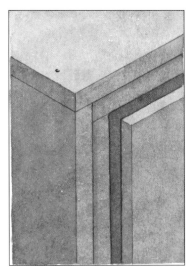

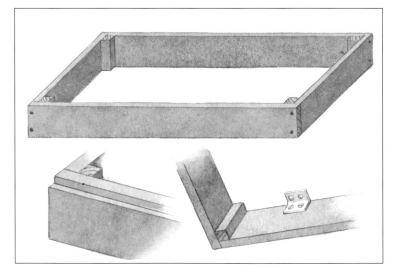

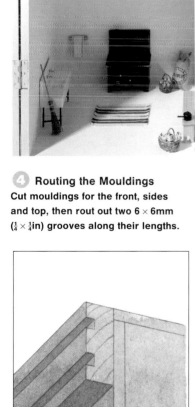

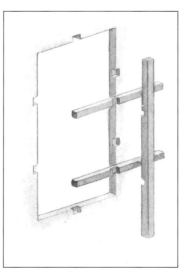

④ Routing the Mouldings
Cut mouldings for the front, sides and top, then rout out two 6 × 6mm (¼ × ¼in) grooves along their lengths.

⑤ Adding the Mouldings
Cut mitres in the ends where front and side mouldings meet. Glue and pin them flush with top of carcass.

⑥ Fitting the Glazing Bars
Cut halving joints to join horizontal and vertical bars. Glue the bars into notches around window edges.

Door stop

FINISHING OFF

Make a false front door from an offcut of MDF and glue it in place on the front of the door panel. Hang the door panel using two butt hinges and fit a hook-and-eye catch on the other side of the house.

You can paint the house in various ways: for example, emulsion for the walls, and undercoat and gloss to pick out the door, windows and mouldings. The exterior finish shown here is achieved by painting the carcass with a base colour of sandy emulsion. When this has dried, roughly pencil in the brick-work. Finally, rub a small amount of boot polish gently over the surface. Use an artist's paintbrush around delicate areas such as the window frames. Protect the paint effect with a top coat of clear varnish.

PUPPET THEATRE

Giving hours of amusement as the focus of children's theatrical interest and skills, this grand and exciting puppet theatre would make a superb Christmas present. It has been designed for use with marionettes, and is tall and deep enough for productions to be easily staged. The theatre can be easily dismantled and packed entirely flat when not in use, or it could provide a focal point in a child's bedroom or playroom, or even in the corner of the sitting room. Although it looks imposing, it takes time rather than money to make, and it is not demanding in terms of woodworking skills.

Based on a traditional design, the theatre consists of a front 'proscenium' arch whose sides curve round to support a backdrop flat, a middle section with a staircase at one side going up to a balcony, and a rear section comprising two L-shaped portions which frame another flat. Below the balcony, doors open to reveal another view. The entire effect is very theatrical, with a sense of different spaces opening up, false perspectives and light filtering in from the sides. The three flats can be painted on both sides to provide twice as many scenes, and extra ones can be made later on for new shows.

The theatre is constructed from thin plywood and battens. Although construction is very simple and no joinery is required, the stairs are rather fiddly to make and the middle section would be simpler if you omitted them. The main skill required is the ability to cut out each section accurately so that the individual parts slot correctly on to the locating pieces screwed to the base.

Undecorated, the theatre has a strong architectural character. For decoration, copy details from cut-out paper theatres or adopt a simpler style if you are not confident about your painting skills.

PUPPET THEATRE

Youngsters will keep themselves amused for hours with this traditional puppet theatre, making up and performing their own plays.

The theatre is made entirely from 4mm ($\frac{3}{16}$in) plywood – the cheap interior-quality redwood type is fine – and 25 × 25mm (1 × 1in) PAR (planed all round) softwood battens to strengthen the frame. The base section which forms the stage is supported by a framework of 50 × 25mm (2 × 1in) PAR softwood.

The theatre is made up in four parts – the front section, the central section, the back section and the base – and has three different flats for changes of scenery which can be painted on both sides for twice as many backdrops. The sides are kept open to allow the puppets to be brought on and off the stage.

TOOLS

WORKBENCH (fixed or portable)

STEEL MEASURING TAPE

TRY SQUARE

POWER JIGSAW

POWER DRILL

DRILL BIT – 4mm ($\frac{3}{16}$in)

PAIR OF G-CRAMPS

SMOOTHING PLANE (hand or power)

POWER FINISHING SANDER (or hand-sanding block)

LIGHTWEIGHT HAMMER

COPING SAW – for cutting stairway tread slots

MATERIALS

Part	Quantity	Material	Length
FRONT SECTION			
FRONT ARCH SECTION	2	4mm ($\frac{3}{16}$in) redwood plywood	1000 × 800mm (39 × 31$\frac{1}{2}$in)
SIDE WING	2	As above	800 × 270mm (31$\frac{1}{2}$ × 10$\frac{3}{4}$in)
FRONT FLAT SUPPORT	4	As above	800 × 150mm (31$\frac{1}{2}$ × 6in)
FRONT FLAT	1	As above	800 × 740mm (31$\frac{1}{2}$ × 29$\frac{1}{8}$in)
SPACING BATTEN	2	25 × 25mm (1 × 1in) PAR softwood	780mm (30$\frac{3}{4}$in)
SPACING BATTEN	4	As above	800mm (31$\frac{1}{2}$in)
CURTAIN POLE	1	12mm ($\frac{1}{2}$in) dowel	1000mm (39in)
CENTRAL SECTION			
CENTRAL ARCH SECTION	2	4mm ($\frac{3}{16}$in) redwood plywood	800 × 600mm (31$\frac{1}{2}$ × 24in)
BALCONY SUPPORT	4	As above	400 × 173mm (15$\frac{3}{4}$ × 6$\frac{3}{4}$in)
BALCONY	1	As above	990 × 350mm (38$\frac{1}{2}$ × 13$\frac{3}{4}$in)
CENTRAL FLAT	1	As above	800 × 290mm (31$\frac{1}{2}$ × 11$\frac{1}{2}$in)
STAIRCASE SIDE	2	As above	400 × 250mm (15$\frac{3}{4}$ × 10in)
STAIRCASE BACK PANEL	1	As above	400 × 145mm (15$\frac{3}{4}$ × 5$\frac{3}{4}$in)
STAIR TREAD	12	As above	155 × 30mm (6$\frac{1}{8}$ × 1$\frac{3}{16}$in)
SPACING BATTEN	4	25 × 25mm (1 × 1in) PAR softwood	800mm (31$\frac{1}{2}$in)
SPACING BATTEN	4	As above	400mm (15$\frac{3}{4}$in)
LOCATING PIECE	2	As above	Approx. 130mm (5$\frac{1}{8}$in)
BALCONY STIFFENING PIECE	As required	As above	Cut to fit from approx. 3.5m (11$\frac{1}{2}$ft)
BACK SECTION			
BACK FLAT SUPPORT	4	4mm ($\frac{3}{16}$in) redwood plywood	800 × 300mm (31$\frac{1}{2}$ × 12in)
BACK WING	2	As above	800 × 475mm (31$\frac{1}{2}$ × 18$\frac{3}{4}$in)
BACK FLAT	1	As above	800 × 440mm (31$\frac{1}{2}$ × 17$\frac{1}{4}$in)
SPACING BATTEN	4	25 × 25mm (1 × 1in) PAR softwood	800mm (31$\frac{1}{2}$in)
BASE SECTION			
STAGE	1	4mm ($\frac{3}{16}$in) redwood plywood	1040 × 1040mm (41 × 41in)
STAGE PLINTH	2	50 × 25mm (2 × 1in) PAR softwood	1040mm (41in)
STAGE PLINTH	7	As above	Cut to fit
LOCATING PIECE	9	25 × 25mm (1 × 1in) PAR softwood	Cut to fit

Also required: canvas and fabric adhesive for hinges; approx. 1.5m (5ft) of fabric for curtains

PUPPET THEATRE ASSEMBLY

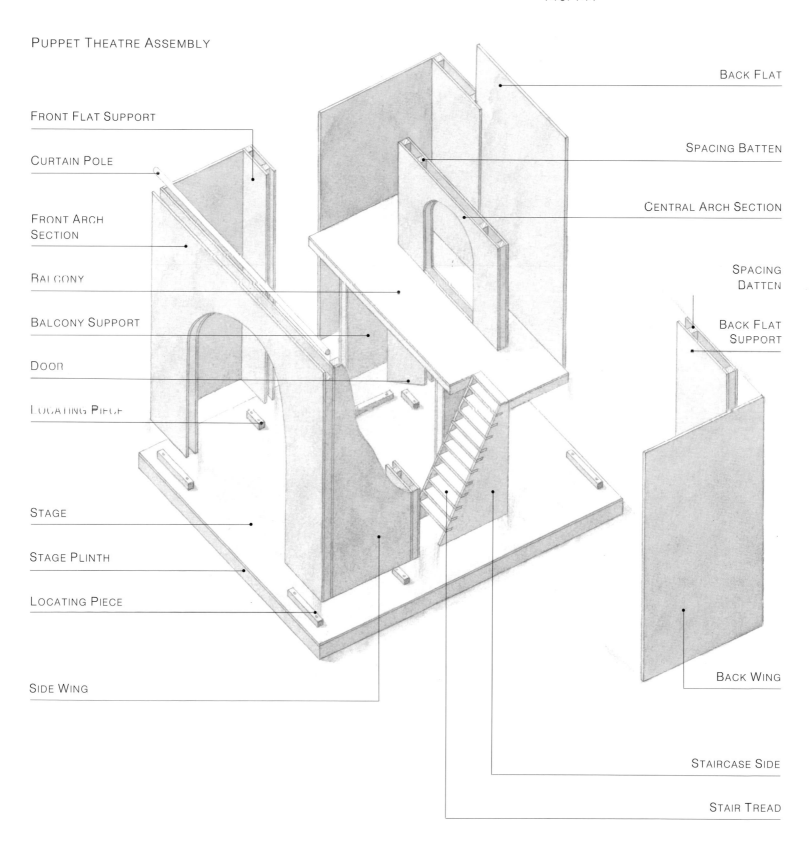

FRONT FLAT SUPPORT

CURTAIN POLE

FRONT ARCH
SECTION

BALCONY

BALCONY SUPPORT

DOOR

LOCATING PIECE

STAGE

STAGE PLINTH

LOCATING PIECE

SIDE WING

BACK FLAT

SPACING BATTEN

CENTRAL ARCH SECTION

SPACING
BATTEN

BACK FLAT
SUPPORT

BACK WING

STAIRCASE SIDE

STAIR TREAD

Puppet Theatre

Front Section Assembly

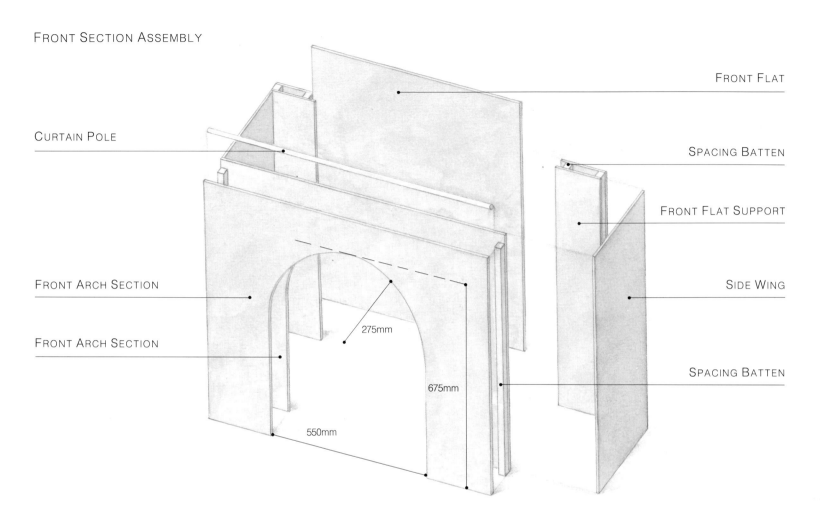

FRONT FLAT

CURTAIN POLE

SPACING BATTEN

FRONT FLAT SUPPORT

FRONT ARCH SECTION

SIDE WING

FRONT ARCH SECTION

SPACING BATTEN

275mm

675mm

550mm

Front Section

Cut out all of the plywood pieces required for the front section.

On one of the plywood panels for the front arch section, mark out the arch centrally so that it is 550mm (21¾in) wide and 675mm (26½in) high, leaving 125mm (5in) of plywood above the top of the curve. Mark out the curve so that it has a radius of 275mm (10⅞in).

Cut out the arch using a jigsaw. Transfer the outline to the other front panel and cut it out; alternatively, cramp the two panels together and cut both pieces simultaneously.

Cut two spacing battens 780mm (30¾in) long, then glue and pin them between the two arch panels, flush with the side and bottom edges (see **Front Section Assembly**). This leaves space for the curtain pole to sit on top of the battens and the curtains to be drawn back.

Cut four spacing battens 800mm (31½in) long, and glue and pin two between each pair of front flat support panels. One batten is flush with the edges of the plywood, the other is 20mm (about ¾in) in from the opposite edges to allow the front flat to slot in place (fig 1). The flat can be painted both sides to allow different scene changes.

Side Wings

The two side wings are attached to the front arch section and the two front flat supports with long canvas hinges (fig 2). This allows the side wings and front flat supports to be folded flat against the front arch section for packing away. Cut four strips of canvas 800mm (31½in) long. Using fabric adhesive, glue two of these to the insides of the front arch section and the side wings so that the sides are flush with the edges of the front section. Glue the other two strips to the outside of the side wings at the back to join them to the front flat supports.

Curtain Pole

The curtain pole is a 1000mm (39in) long piece of dowelling that rests on top of the spacing battens in the front section (see **Front Section Assembly**). Once the curtains have been made and threaded on to it, the dowel can be pinned in place down into the batten at both ends.

Central Section

Cut out all the plywood pieces for the central arch section, including the central flat, the balcony and the balcony supports.

On the central arch section, two cut-outs are required for doorways (fig 3). On one of the arch section plywood panels mark out the lower doorway and top arch centrally, 250mm (10in) wide. Mark the lower doorway 300mm (12in) high. For the top arch mark the base line 405mm (16in) up from the bottom and 355mm (14in) high. The radius of the top curve is 125mm (5in), leaving 40mm (about 1½in) of plywood above the arch (fig 3).

Cut out the doorway and arch using a jigsaw, then use the cut out panel as a template to transfer the marks to the other panel; alternatively, cramp the panels together and cut out both pieces simultaneously. Keep one of the lower door cut-outs to make into a pair of doors for the lower doorway later on.

From 25 × 25mm (1 × 1in) PAR softwood, cut four lengths of spacing batten, each 800mm (31½in) long. Glue and pin these between the two plywood arch panels, one down each long edge, and one 20mm (about ¾in) in from each edge of the doorway cut-outs (fig 3).

CENTRAL SECTION ASSEMBLY

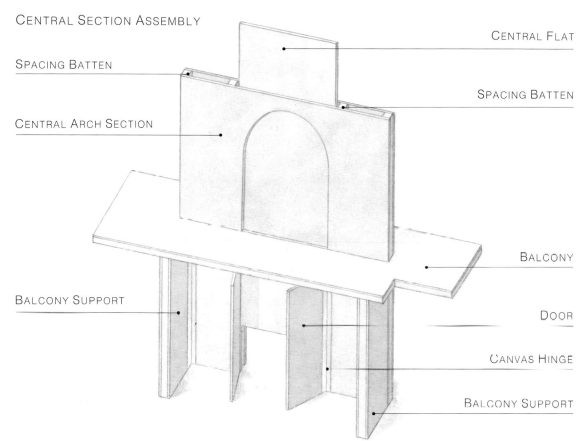

CENTRAL FLAT

SPACING BATTEN

SPACING BATTEN

CENTRAL ARCH SECTION

BALCONY

BALCONY SUPPORT

DOOR

CANVAS HINGE

BALCONY SUPPORT

1 Front Flat Supports
Position spacing battens; one flush with panel edges, the other inset 18mm (¾in) from opposite edges.

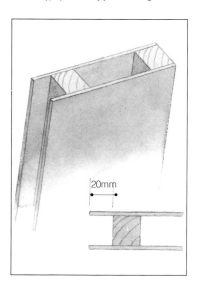

20mm

2 Hinging the Front Section
Top left Fabric-hinge inside face of side wings to back of front arch section.
Top right Fabric-hinge outside face of side wings to outside edges of front flat supports. *Bottom* Plan view shows how front section folds flat for storage.

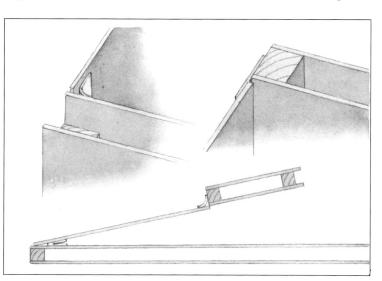

3 Central Arch Section
Make cut-outs for two doorways; cut both central arch panels and join using four spacing battens.

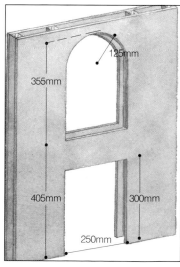

125mm

355mm

405mm

300mm

250mm

Puppet Theatre

Balcony Supports

Cut four spacing battens, 400mm (15¾in) long. Glue and pin these between the balcony support pieces, flush with both edges (fig 1).

Make hinges for the supports by cutting two lengths of canvas, 400mm (15¾in) long. Fabric-hinge the supports to the front of the bottom half of the central section so that each support is flush with an outside edge (fig 1).

Double Doors

Saw one of the lower door cut-outs in two lengthways to make a pair of doors. Make hinges for the doors by cutting two lengths of canvas 300mm (12in) long. Fabric-hinge the doors to the front of the central section on either side of the lower opening (fig 2).

Balcony

The balcony needs a cut-out on the front right-hand corner to take the staircase. This cut-out should be 155mm (6⅛in) wide and 100mm (4in) deep (fig 3, top).

① Balcony Supports
The balcony support pieces are fabric-hinged to central arch section flush with outside edges.

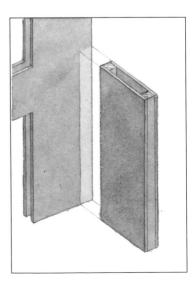

The central arch section fits into a slot cut into the balcony. This slot measures 602mm (24$\frac{1}{8}$in) long and 30mm (1$\frac{3}{16}$in) wide, and is situated centrally on the length of the balcony panel and 193mm (7$\frac{1}{2}$in) back from the front edge (fig 3, top). It is important that the slot is precisely positioned, so double check your markings before cutting out. Cut out the slot using a jigsaw after first drilling a couple of holes for the blade to go through.

Turn the balcony upside down. Cut lengths of 25 × 25mm (1 × 1in) PAR softwood to go all the way round the edges of the balcony on the underside and across it, then glue and pin these in place (fig 3, bottom). These balcony stiffening pieces strengthen the floor.

Cut two locating pieces from the 25 × 25mm (1 × 1in) PAR softwood, about 130mm (5$\frac{1}{8}$in) long; these will fit into the cavities at the top of the two balcony supports (fig 1). To position these pieces, slot the balcony over the central arch section, turn the assembly upside down, and draw round the

balcony supports to mark their positions on the underside of the balcony. Remove the balcony and position the locating pieces centrally in the marked positions. Glue and pin them in place.

CENTRAL FLAT

Cut an 800 × 290mm (31$\frac{1}{2}$ × 11$\frac{1}{2}$in) plywood flat to fit into the central arch section. This can be painted to depict views through the doorway and arch – again, paint both sides of the flat to give a different change of scenery on each side.

STAIRCASE

Cut out the back panel, the two sides and 12 stair treads following the dimensions given in the Materials chart (page 140). The height of the staircase should be to the balcony level, allowing for a 4mm ($\frac{3}{16}$in) thick tread which sits on the top of the staircase sides.

Cramp the staircase side pieces together and cut them diagonally through their length so that they are 25mm (1in) wide at the top and 250mm (10in) wide at the bottom.

Mark out 11 equally spaced slots for the treads along the diagonal edge. These should be parallel with the base of the side section and should measure 30mm (1$\frac{3}{16}$in) long and 4mm ($\frac{3}{16}$in) wide to take the stair treads. The top tread simply sits on top of the staircase (fig 4).

To make it easier to cut out the slots, drill a 4mm ($\frac{3}{16}$in) diameter hole at the end of each slot, then cut down each side of the slot using a tenon saw if working by hand, or using a power jigsaw. To cut exactly matching slots, which is important if the stair treads are to be level, cramp both side panels together, one on top of the other and cut out the slots at the same time.

Glue and pin the back panel in place between the two sides, flush at the back. Glue and pin the top tread in place, then glue and slide in the bottom one, using PVA (polyvinyl acetate) adhesive. Allow the glue to set, then glue and slot in all the other treads, keeping a tight fit for maximum strength. When dry, sand down the ends of the stair treads flush with the side panels.

BACK SECTION

Cut out from the plywood the back flat, the four back flat support panels and the two back wings following the Materials chart (page 140).

Cut four lengths of spacing batten 800mm (31$\frac{1}{2}$in) long and make up the two back flat supports in the same way as the front flat supports, with the battens sandwiched between the panels. Two battens should be glued and pinned flush with the outer edges of the panels, and the other two should be set 20mm (about $\frac{3}{4}$in) in from the inner edges to form a slot into which the back flat will slide.

Fabric-hinge the two back wings on to the back flat supports (fig 1, page 146) so that they can be folded either way to allow use of both sides for scene changes, and to allow the section to fold flat for storage.

Cut the back flat 800mm (31$\frac{1}{2}$in) high and 440mm (17$\frac{1}{4}$in) wide to fit between the flat supports. Again, this flat can be painted on both sides with different scenes.

---

② **Adding the Doors**
Make a pair of doors from one of the lower cut-outs; fabric-hinge them to the central arch section.

③ **Making the Balcony**
Top Measure accurately for cut-outs in middle to take central arch section and in right-hand corner for staircase. *Bottom* Add battens to underside of balcony for strength, plus two locating pieces to fit in balcony supports.

④ **Making the Staircase**
Glue and pin the back between the sides. The top stair tread sits on top, the others slot in place.

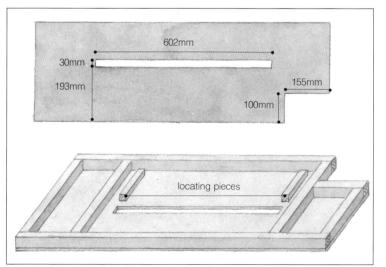

602mm

30mm

193mm

155mm

100mm

locating pieces

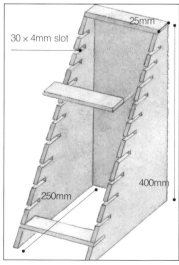

25mm

30 × 4mm slot

250mm

400mm

PUPPET THEATRE

BASE SECTION

Cut out this section to form a stage 1040mm (41in) square. This will be large enough to allow about 20mm (¾in) all around the theatre when all the pieces are in place.

For the stage plinth, we used 50 × 25mm (2 × 1in) PAR softwood. This is fixed to the underside of the stage, flush with the edges all the way round and across the middle to act as strengthening (fig 2). Cut two battens to the full length of the stage to fit flush along the front and back edges. Cut three more battens to fit exactly between these first two lengths – two to fit flush along the sides, and the third to sit mid-way between them. Finally, cut four lengths of batten to fit flush between the battens at the sides and the batten half way across.

Glue and nail up the strengthening framework of battens, then glue and pin the stage panel on top, securing through the plywood into the timber framework.

Sand all of the edges flush.

LOCATING PIECES

These lengths of 25 × 25mm (1 × 1in) battens are positioned on the base section to hold the front, central and back sections in place (see **Puppet Theatre Assembly, page 141**). Cut the battens to lengths that will allow them to fit *loosely* inside all of the box sections that will be standing on the base.

To position the locating pieces, stand the three sections in place on the base with roughly 20mm (¾in) lip all round. Make sure that the stage plinths that run to the full length are positioned at the front and the back, since the front plinth will be visible to the audience. Either mark round the box section on to the base using a pencil, or measure in for their positions. Remove the sections, and mark the positions for the locating pieces, allowing for the width of the plywood of the box sections and for the spacing battens. Then glue and screw the locating pieces in place, and check that they are correctly positioned by repositioning the front, back and central sections.

FINISHING OFF

For a really splendid, theatrical look, it is worth spending that extra bit of time making sure that you get the details just right.

CURTAINS

For curtains that pull across, allow one and a half to twice the width of the arch, divided into two to make two curtains. The width for the curtains depends on how thick the fabric is as you will probably want the curtains to pull back completely into the sides of the arch section. Allow extra fabric on the sides for turning and neatening the edges, and about 75mm (3in) on the length to allow for a hem at the bottom and turning over at the top to take the curtain pole (fig 3).

Cut out the fabric and hand- or machine-stitch the sides and hem. Turn over the top edge to make a casing, and thread the curtain pole through. Place the pole across the front arch section and pin it down on to the battens at both ends.

For decorative effect, you could tie the curtains back, leaving them in full view as shown in the photographs (opposite). We have also glued a remnant of fabric at the top of the arch for a pelmet.

PAINT EFFECTS

We painted the flat supports and wings of the theatre in bold, contrasting colours. The front of the theatre, however, shows just how spectacular the finished effect can be. The paint is applied in quite an impressionistic fashion, and the details then inked in with a black marker pen. This is undeniably ambitious, and you may not think your own skills can match those shown here. You can still attempt a fair imitation, however: the design consists of a series of boxes and panels, and it would be relatively straightforward to paint these in over a background colour, and then to add a few details.

On the flats, a field of grass, a beach or a sky at night can all be depicted with as much or as little detail as you choose.

---

① Hinging the Back Section
Top Fabric-hinge back wings to back flat supports on the outside. *Bottom* Plan shows back folded flat.

② Making the Base Section
Glue and nail 50 × 25mm (2 × 1in) strengthening battens around the perimeter of the underside of the stage, another across the middle, and four more to fit between the side and middle battens.

③ Adding the Curtains
Turn over the top edge of the curtains to make a casing through which to thread the curtain pole.

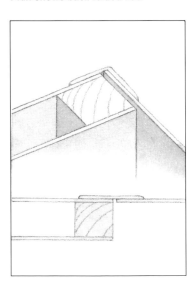

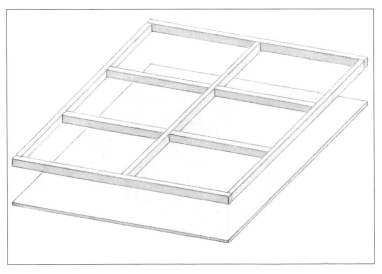

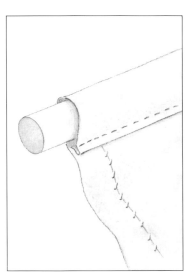

PAINTING TABLE

Although the kitchen table may be a practical place for children to draw and paint, it is much better if they have a table scaled to their own size, where they can also keep crayons, brushes and a supply of paper permanently to hand. From a surprisingly early age children enjoy making pictures, even if at the beginning these are no more than the briefest of scribbles. A painting table will encourage them to explore their creative instincts.

No more than about half a day's work, this simple pine table consists of a framework that is glued and screwed or dowelled together. It is topped with a hinged lid made of melamine-faced board to enable splashes and spills to be wiped away easily. The lid covers a storage space deep enough to take boxes of crayons and other drawing and painting materials. Alternatively, the top can be screwed down and the base omitted.

Children can get through a great deal of paper. At one side of the table, a dowel drops in place and can be used to hold a roll of lining paper, a versatile and cheap way of meeting children's paper needs; you can tear off individual sheets or unroll a long length for murals or banners. At the other side of the table, there is a place to keep plastic beakers filled with poster paints or water, which helps to reduce mess and accidental spills.

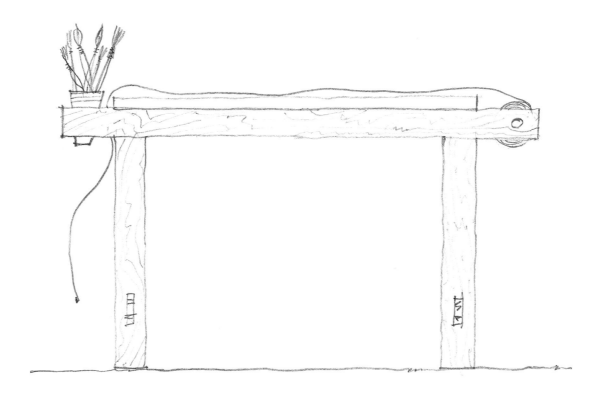

PAINTING TABLE

MATERIALS

Part	Quantity	Material	Length
LONG RAIL	2	75 × 25mm (3 × 1in) PAR softwood	1000mm (39in)
LEG	4	As above	610mm (24in)
TOP CROSS RAIL	2	As above	570mm (22½in)
BEAKER-HOLDER SHELF	2	As above	As above
BOTTOM CROSS RAIL	2	As above	528mm (20¾in)*
PAPER RAIL	1	12mm (½in) dowel	610mm (24in)*
DOWEL	8	As above	80mm (3¼in)
TOP	1	15mm (⅝in) melamine-faced chipboard	765 × 610mm (30 × 24in)*
BASE (optional)	1	4mm (⅛in) plywood or hardboard	725 × 570mm (28½ × 22½in)*
BASE-SUPPORT BATTEN	4	9 × 9mm (⅜ × ⅜in) hardwood	2.5m (8ft) cut to fit

Also required: iron-on edging strip; stay for hinged top; two 75mm (3in) flush hinges for hinged top *or* four 50mm (2in) angle brackets for permanently fixed-down top

* Approximate dimension – measure exactly and cut to fit

PRIDE OF PLACE

When they have finished painting, children need a means to display their work. We painted a board with a church and some houses, cut it out and stuck a magnetic strip across the bottom to hold the paintings.

TOOLS

STEEL MEASURING TAPE
TRY SQUARE
TENON SAW
DRILL (hand or power)
FLAT BIT – 12mm (½in)
SCREWDRIVER
COUNTERSINK BIT
ONE PAIR OF G-CRAMPS
HAMMER
EXPANSIVE BIT or HOLE SAW or JIGSAW or PADSAW
CHISEL
MALLET or HAMMER

Every child loves to paint. It is the perfect outlet for fun, imagination, education and creativity. When a child has a paintbrush, lovely colours and water with which to experiment, it is clearly time to leave self-expression free to develop. But this cannot be achieved in a restrictive atmosphere, and finding that ideal somewhere for such a messy activity is not always easy.

The understandable and necessary concern for the protection of furniture and furnishings can be obviated, however, with this simple, functional painting table. It provides an activity centre combined with storage for materials so that setting up and clearing away takes only a minute or two.

The design of this table is based on a standard roll of wall lining-paper which can be obtained at any decorating shop. It is a cheap, white paper normally pasted on to walls but which provides a large amount of paper ideal for painting on. The roll is stored on a dowel at one end of the table and can be pulled across the top to provide a continuous clean painting surface as required. The used paper is fed through a small gap at the other end of the table. Circular holes are cut in a shelf at one end of the table to provide safe storage for paint and water containers.

The table top is made from melamine-faced chipboard, so it has a wipe-clean surface. Although the top could be permanently fixed down, with a little more effort a base can be added and the top fixed with hinges so that it can be raised to give access to a convenient storage area for materials beneath it.

PAINTING TABLE ASSEMBLY

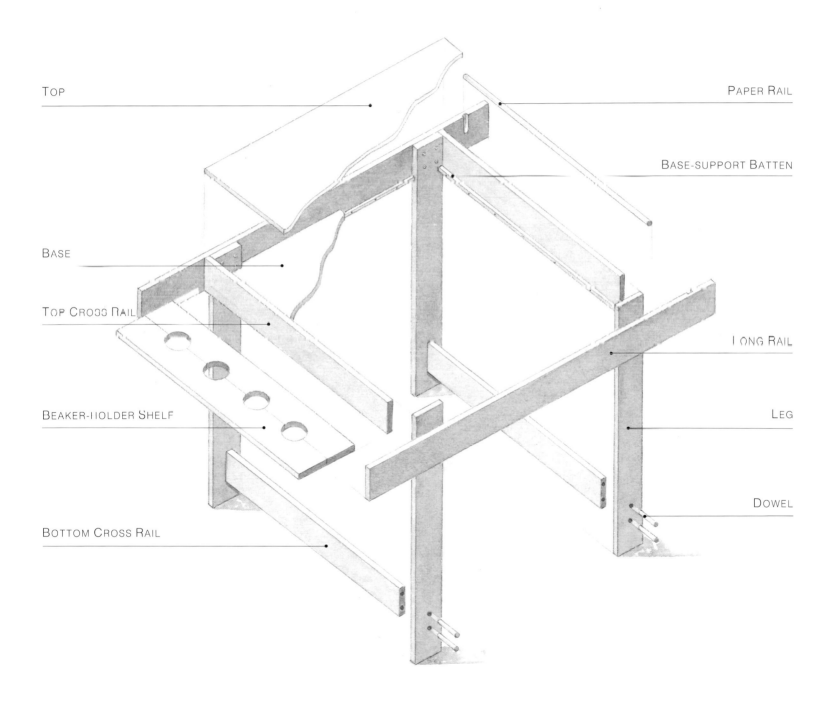

TOP

PAPER RAIL

BASE-SUPPORT BATTEN

BASE

TOP CROSS RAIL

LONG RAIL

BEAKER-HOLDER SHELF

LEG

DOWEL

BOTTOM CROSS RAIL

PAINTING TABLE

CONSTRUCTION

Cut the top rails and legs to length. Round over the ends of the long rails to reduce impact injuries. Cut the beaker-holder rails and join them with PVA (polyvinyl acetate) adhesive; cramp and leave to dry.

TOP FRAME

On the two long rails, mark the positions of the centre lines of the top cross rails. These will be 150mm (6in) in from the beaker-holder end and 110mm ($4\frac{1}{2}$in) in from the other end. Square the marks round on to the opposite faces of the long rails.

Into each of the four marked centre lines, drill three equally spaced holes to accept 50mm (2in) No 8 screws. Countersink each hole so that the screw heads will be flush with the surface (*see* **Techniques, page 239**). Glue and screw the long rails to the ends of the top cross rails ensuring that the rails are exactly square at the points where they join (fig 1). Cramp the joints together while the glue dries.

LEGS

The legs should be fitted tight into the inside corners of the frame to ensure rigidity. Each leg is glued and screwed from inside the frame using four 38mm ($1\frac{1}{2}$in) No 8 screws (fig 2). Drill and countersink the holes through the legs and into the long rails, ensuring that their top edges are flush with the top of the frame.

BOTTOM CROSS RAILS

Measure for and cut the bottom cross rails to length. The top edge of each rail should be 150mm (6in) up from the bottom of each leg. Mark a line and square round on to the opposite face and mark off two equally spaced dowel positions. Cramp one rail accurately centred in position between two legs, then drill 12mm ($\frac{1}{2}$in) diameter, 75mm (3in) deep holes through the legs and into the rail. Repeat for the other bottom cross rail.

Cut and prepare eight 12mm ($\frac{1}{2}$in) diameter dowels, 80mm ($3\frac{1}{4}$in) long. Score thin grooves along the length of each dowel. Apply PVA

HINGED TABLE TOP

The simple addition of hinges to the table top and a base beneath creates a space in which paints, pencils and crayons can be stored. The beaker-holder shelf prevents pots of paints from tipping over.

1 Constructing the Top Frame
Mark on the long rails the positions of the top cross rails so they are 150mm (6in) in from one end and 110mm (4½in) from the other. Glue and screw through the long rails into the ends of the top cross rails.

2 Fitting the Legs
The legs are glued and screwed tightly and squarely into the inside corners of the top frame.

3 Bottom Cross Rails
Position the cross rails between the legs, 150mm (6in) up from the bottom. Drill and dowel in place.

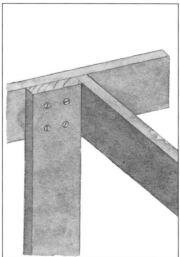

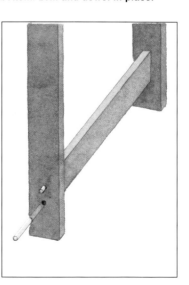

adhesive to each hole, then hammer home the dowels leaving the ends protruding (fig 3). Leave the cramps in place until the adhesive has set, then saw off the protruding dowel to leave a flush finish.

BEAKER-HOLDER SHELF

The number and diameter of holes is optional and will be determined by the size of the beakers or other containers used. Here we used four equally spaced 50mm (2in) diameter holes (fig 4). They can be cut using an expansive bit, a hole saw, a jigsaw or a padsaw (see **Techniques, page 238**).

Position the shelf between the long rails, flush with their undersides and ends. You should leave a small gap between the innermost edge of the beaker-holder shelf and the outside face of the top cross rail for the paper to feed through – if the gap is not wide enough, plane a little off the edge of the shelf.

Drill four countersunk holes in the edge of each long rail and fix the shelf in place using 50mm (2in) No 8 screws (fig 5).

PAPER RAIL

At the opposite end of the table, fix the dowel that holds the roll of paper. This simply rests in slots cut centrally into the protruding ends of the long rails (fig 6). The slots are 12mm ($\frac{1}{2}$in) wide and 25mm (1in) deep. Ensure the two slots are aligned with careful marking before drilling. Drill a hole at the base of the slot, then saw down the sides with a tenon saw. Pare out the waste of each slot with a chisel. Cut the dowel long enough to fit snugly in position, without it being too tight.

TABLE TOP

The top should be cut to fit flush with the outside edges of the long rails and cross rails. Measure the exact dimensions before cutting. It is a good idea to ask the supplier to cut this to size for you, since melamine-faced board sometimes splinters along the cut. The exposed, sawn edges of the top should be covered with iron-on edging strip which is readily available where you buy your melamine-faced chipboard.

If you want a fixed top, secure it to the cross rail using 50mm (2in) angle brackets screwed to the inside of the top frame and the underside of the table top – two on each side will give a secure fixing.

For a hinged top, use two 75mm (3in) hinges – flush hinges are easiest to fix (see **Techniques, page 247**). For safety, fit a support stay to hold the top firmly in position when it is raised up.

BASE

Fit this only if you hinge the top. Cut four lengths of 9 × 9mm ($\frac{3}{8}$ × $\frac{3}{8}$in) ramin for the base supports, and glue and pin them flush with the bottom edges of the rails (fig 7).

The base should be cut to fit the inside dimensions of the long rails and cross rails, so measure before cutting. Use an offcut from one of the 75 × 25mm (3 × 1in) legs as a template for the corner notches. Dab adhesive on to the supports to hold the base in position.

Make sure the wood is free from splinters, then paint, stain or varnish according to the finish you want.

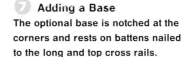

④ Beaker-holder Shelf
Join two lengths of 75 × 25mm (3 × 1in) PAR edge-on. Cut holes to fit the beaker size.

⑤ Fitting Beaker-holder Shelf
Position the shelf between the long rails, flush with the undersides and ends. Screw in place.

⑥ Fitting the Paper Rail
Cut slots on the inside faces of the long rails and rest a length of 12mm ($\frac{1}{2}$in) dowel in place.

⑦ Adding a Base
The optional base is notched at the corners and rests on battens nailed to the long and top cross rails.

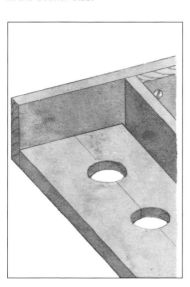

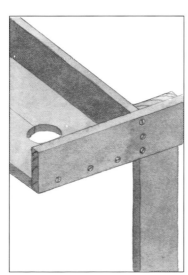

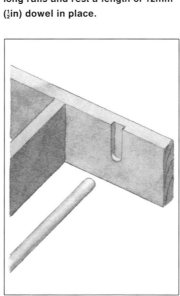

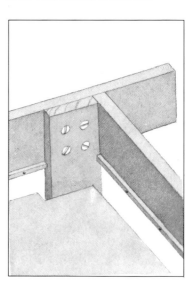

OUTDOORS

Your ideas about comfort, elegance, style and decoration should not be restricted to the inside of your home. DIY can be and is practised outside as well as inside. If you have a garden, the chances are that you already do it yourself anyway: planting, seeding, mowing, turfing, fencing and paving are all DIY activities for the majority of gardeners.

The range of projects in this section varies from the simple to the sophisticated, and covers garden structures from essential containers and seats to the luxury of a summer house. All of these are important, classic garden accessories, the design of which is too often overlooked. Materials need not be expensive, and what you make will usually have cost less than the equivalent in your local garden centre, though you need to examine carefully what is available commercially. Ready-made trellising, for example, costs less than the wood you would need to buy in order to make it yourself.

One advantage of DIY in the garden is that if your house has distinctive architectural features – such as bay windows or decorative bargeboarding – it is easy to incorporate these elements into the design of your garden structures. Something as simple as picking out a colour from a door to use on seating or containers can unify the overall design, visually linking the house to the garden. Whether a roof garden, a balcony or a large, landscaped plot, your outdoor space can and should reflect your personality as closely as the rooms indoors.

GARDEN BENCH

When it comes to garden furniture, people tend to have rather conservative taste. Although they might tolerate modern and even occasionally avant-garde pieces in the home, these are less welcome for outdoor living, where the emphasis has generally been on the traditional. Wrought-iron seating typically has a Victorian flavour, and, in recent years, the designs of Sir Edwin Lutyens have been enormously influential, with their classically inspired curves.

This garden bench with its upright railed back and plain, flat seat and legs owes something to the strict functional beauty of nineteenth-century Shaker furniture. Extremely simple by comparison with much of what is commercially available for the garden, the bench is nevertheless one of the more demanding projects to make. This is partly because garden furniture must be finished to a higher standard than other garden structures, as it will receive closer inspection.

Even if you move your garden furniture indoors for the winter it will have to take some degree of weathering. Allowing water to collect on a surface is the quickest way of causing deterioration and decay. Here the seat slopes slightly so that water drains off and, similarly, where the back joins the seat a narrow gap has been left to allow water to flow down. The straight edges of the legs are bevelled so that accidental knocks by the lawnmower do not cause too much damage.

The height of the back is a critical factor in the design. Equally distinctive is the back's reeded quality. This is, perhaps, not a bench for lounging, although, supplied with a long cushion, it would work very well indoors.

Do not be afraid to let colour make a positive statement in the garden. Yellow and various tones of blue look as good in winter as they do in summer and are more eye-catching than the more sedate shades of dark green or white.

GARDEN BENCH

The garden bench is perhaps the most familiar piece of garden furniture. Building one yourself will almost certainly be cheaper than buying one, and will give you a real sense of satisfaction. If needs be, you can adapt the design shown here to suit the size and proportions of your garden and your individual requirements. Choose the site for your bench with care, positioning it to serve as a focal point that draws the eye in a certain direction; alternatively, you could place it to provide sanctuary in a tranquil, shady corner of the garden where you can retreat to sit in peace, quiet and comfort.

This garden bench could be made from hardwood, but it will be considerably cheaper and more environmentally acceptable if you make it from good-quality softwood. In the latter case, it is important that you treat the timber with good-quality wood preservative at all stages of construction to ensure that it will give you many years of service. A clear wood preservative should be applied to the timber after the component pieces have been cut, but before the joints are assembled; the strength of the joint will not be affected if you allow about 24 hours for the preservative to dry thoroughly before applying the glue.

A second coat of preservative should be applied after construction, before the application of the final finish.

Using clear preservative will allow you to keep your options open regarding whether you finish the bench by painting or by applying a water-repellent wood stain of the type used widely on timber window frames. If you finish the bench by painting it, it is a good idea to use an exterior gloss paint or microporous (satin sheen) system. Such paint often contains a penetrating preservative wood primer, and this should be used in preference to a second coat of clear wood preservative.

The ideal way to construct the bench to ensure many years of service is to use traditional mortise and tenon joints for the main frame and dowel joints for the back rest slats and the seat boards. However, if you feel that you do not possess the necessary skills to cut accurate mortise and tenon joints, then the entire bench could be made using dowel joints throughout. If you do only use dowel joints, however, it will be more important than ever to apply a good-quality waterproof woodworking adhesive to each joint before assembly, and to keep each joint firmly cramped until the adhesive is thoroughly set.

MATERIALS

Part	Quantity	Material	Length
BACK LEGS	2	100 × 75mm (4 × 3in) PAR softwood	1035mm (41in)
FRONT LEGS	2	75 × 75mm (3 × 3in) PAR softwood	430mm (17in)*
SIDE FRAME RAILS	4	75 × 50mm (3 × 2in) PAR softwood	480mm (19in)
FRONT RAIL	1	As above	1790mm (70$\frac{1}{2}$in)
LOWER BACK RAIL	1	140 × 32mm (5$\frac{1}{2}$ × 1$\frac{1}{4}$in) PAR softwood	1790mm (70$\frac{1}{2}$in)
UPPER BACK RAIL	1	75 × 50mm (3 × 2in) PAR softwood	1880mm (74in)*
BACK SLATS	32	38 × 25mm (1$\frac{1}{2}$ × 1in) PAR softwood	Distance between back rails
SEAT BOARDS	4	140 × 32mm (5$\frac{1}{2}$ × 1$\frac{1}{4}$in) PAR softwood	1865mm (73$\frac{1}{2}$in)
DOWELS (seat to lower back rail)	5	From 12mm ($\frac{1}{2}$in) hardwood dowelling	Approx. 95mm (3$\frac{3}{4}$in)
DOWELS (to join seat boards and fit back slats)	As required	From 8mm ($\frac{5}{16}$in) hardwood dowelling	Approx. 40mm (1$\frac{1}{2}$in)
SHRINKAGE PLATES	5	Zinc-plated steel	

Also required: metal hammer-in glides for legs

* Overlength and then cut to size after fixing – see text

TOOLS

WORKBENCH (fixed or portable)

MARKING KNIFE

STEEL MEASURING TAPE

STEEL RULE

TRY SQUARE

PANEL SAW (or circular power saw)

TENON SAW (or power jigsaw)

CHISELS

MARKING GAUGE

MORTISE GAUGE

POWER DRILL

DOWEL or CENTREPOINT DRILL BIT – 8mm ($\frac{5}{16}$in)

FLAT BIT – 12mm ($\frac{1}{2}$in)

DOWELLING JIG

ONE PAIR OF SASH CRAMPS (or webbing cramp)

SMOOTHING PLANE (hand or power)

POWER ROUTER and ROUNDING OVER BIT

MALLET

ORBITAL SANDER (or hand-sanding block)

GARDEN BENCH ASSEMBLY

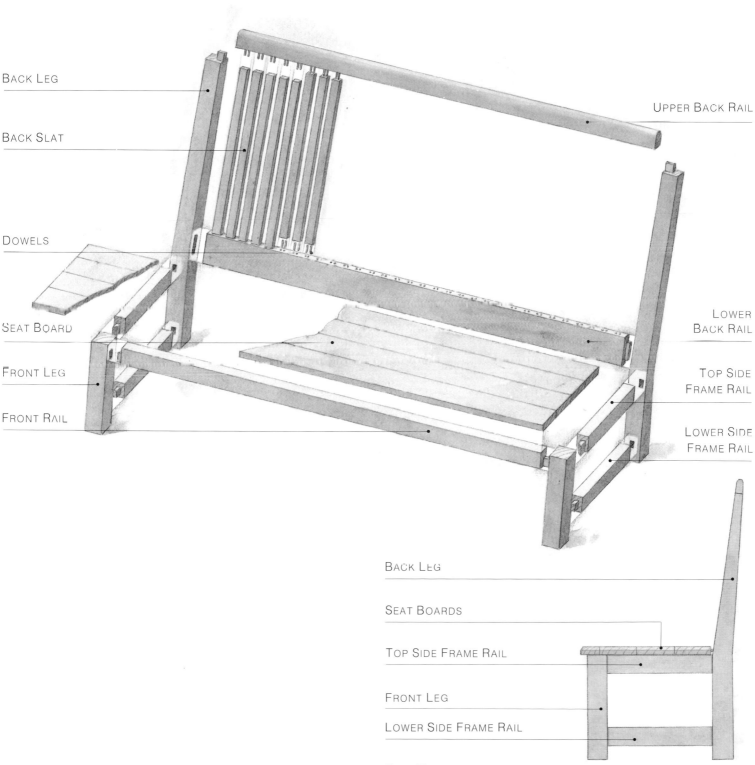

BACK LEG

BACK SLAT

DOWELS

SEAT BOARD

FRONT LEG

FRONT RAIL

UPPER BACK RAIL

LOWER BACK RAIL

TOP SIDE FRAME RAIL

LOWER SIDE FRAME RAIL

BACK LEG

SEAT BOARDS

TOP SIDE FRAME RAIL

FRONT LEG

LOWER SIDE FRAME RAIL

SIDE ELEVATION

GARDEN BENCH

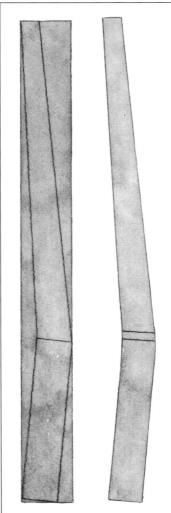

1 **Shaping the Back Legs**
Lay front leg at an angle on back leg and mark its position. Measure 35mm (1⅜in) in from the back at the top and join marks with top of front leg marks. Cut out round marked lines, curving the shape at the back. Mark off seat thickness parallel with top of front leg position.

SEAT SIDE FRAMES

SHAPING THE FRONT LEGS

Cut the front legs overlength – at least 430mm (17in) long in total – and measure 400mm (15¾in) up from the bottom to mark off the finished length. Square a line round the leg on all faces (*see* **Techniques, page 236**). Put the front legs aside for the time being.

SHAPING THE BACK LEGS

The back legs are shaped from 100 × 75mm (4 × 3in) timber. Mark out the legs by laying one of the front legs on the wider face of one of the back legs, sloping at an angle but touching at the bottom and side edges (fig 1). Remember that the front leg is overlength at the top, so align with the finished leg line. Mark round the shape of the front leg onto the back leg.

At the top of the back leg, measure 35mm (1⅜in) from the back face on both sides and join these two points to the top points of the marked front leg position, giving the shape for the back leg (fig 1).

With one back leg marked, cut out round the marked lines, with straight lines at the front face of the leg, but rounding off the angle at the back of the leg to produce a gentle curve. Plane the face edges at the front straight and square to the sides as the joints are measured from this edge.

Use the cut-out back leg to mark the other one and cut it out. When both legs are cut, mark off the seat thickness, parallel with the top of the front leg position, using a seat board and a try square.

MARKING UP THE MORTISES AND TENONS

Take one of the front legs and line one of the side rails (wide face against the leg) to the top marked line (fig 2), taking into account the excess length at the top. Mark off the position of the bottom of the rail onto the leg. Working from this line, mark off the length of the mortise 50mm (2in) up. Square the lines round to the two inside faces (*see* **Techniques, page 236**).

For the bottom joint, measure 60mm (2⅜in) up from the bottom of the leg on the back face, then another 50mm (2in) up for the top of the mortise. Transfer all of these lines to the back of the other front leg using a try square. Square the lines of the top mortise round to the inside face of the second front leg.

Using a try square, transfer the length and position of the mortises from the front legs onto the front face of the back legs.

Take a 19mm (¾in) chisel and set a mortise gauge to this width with the stock set so that the mortise is central to the edge of the side rails (*not* central on the legs).

Mark off the top mortises on the front faces of the back legs, and on the two inside faces of the front legs. Measure from the *outside* edge in each case so that the front and upper side rails will be flush.

On the ends of all four side rails, mark off the tenons (fig 3) and also mark off the tenons on the ends of the front rail.

Re-set the stock on the mortise gauge so that it is central on the legs and mark off the lower mortises centrally on the inside faces of all the legs for the lower side rails.

Measure 50mm (2in) in from each end on one of the side rails, and mark the shoulder of the tenon. Square round all faces. Using a try square, transfer the lines onto all the other side rails. Measure 50mm (2in) in from each end of the front rail and square round as before. To ensure a strong construction, it is important that all the lengths between the shoulders on the side rails are accurately marked. Mark the widths of the top tenon 50mm (2in) from the bottom edges of all the top rails so that the tenons are bare-faced to the lower edge.

The tenons are central on the two *lower* side rails, so measure 10mm (⅜in) up from the lower edge, then 50mm (2in) for the width of the mortise (fig 3).

CUTTING THE JOINTS

Cut the mortises slightly deeper than 50mm (2in) (*see* **Techniques, Mortise and Tenon Joint, page 244**) and then the tenons.

Dry assemble the parts to check the fit. The ends of the tenons on the front rail and the ends of the front tenons of the top side rails will all need to be cut at a 45 degree angle to ensure a tight fit (fig 4).

Cut off the 'horns' (protruding ends) at the tops of the front legs to leave the front legs flush with the upper side rails.

THE BACK

FITTING THE LOWER BACK RAIL

Take a chisel about 12mm (½in) wide and set a mortise gauge to exactly this width. Set the stock so the tenon will be offset to the back on the lower back rail, making a bare-faced tenon joint (fig 1, page 162). Mark the mortise on the inside faces of the back legs, working from

the front faces. Mark the bare-faced tenons on the lower back rail.

Align the lower back rail with the mark for the seat at the front so that it is square to the top front face of the back leg (fig 1, page 162). Mark off the position of the rail, and mark a 15mm (⅝in) shoulder at the top and bottom.

On the lower back rail, mark 50mm (2in) in from the ends and 15mm (⅝in) in from the edges for the shoulders. Before cutting the tenons, check that the length between the shoulders is the same as the front rail. Cut the tenons and then chisel the mortises to a depth of 50mm (2in).

FITTING THE UPPER BACK RAIL

Mark 50mm (2in) down from the top of the back leg and square round using a try square. Transfer these lines to the other leg. With the mortise gauge still set to 12mm (½in) set the stock so that it is central at this shoulder line, working from the front face (fig 2, page 162). Now mark off the tenon on both legs.

② Front Leg Mortises
Mark rail positions on leg. Mortises are central to edge of front and top side rails, central on lower side rail

③ Front and Side Rail Tenons
Top **Cut bare-faced tenons for front and top side rails.** *Bottom* **Tenon is central on lower side rail.**

④ Dry Assembly of Front Legs to Front and Side Rails
Left **Position of cut mortises on front leg.** *Inset* **Plan view shows front rail and upper side rail flush with outside edges of front leg.** *Right* **Ends of tenons are angled on front and upper side rails.**

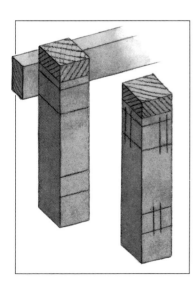

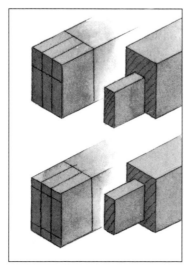

GARDEN BENCH

The upper rail should be cut over-length by 50mm (2in), but use the lower rail to mark the exact length between the shoulders and square round the upper rail at each end. From these lines mark 50mm (2in) to the outside (towards the ends).

With the mortise gauge still set for the width of the tenon, mark the mortises on the bottom edge of the rail, working from the front face (fig 2). Mark the width of each tenon to 50mm (2in) from the inside face of the legs so that the tenons are bare-faced.

Cut the mortises to 50mm (2in) deep, and cut the tenons. Dry assemble the back legs to the upper and lower rails to check the fit and cut off the 'horns' (protruding ends) flush with the outer face of the legs.

SHAPING THE UPPER RAIL

The upper rail has to be shaped at the back to follow the taper of the back legs (fig 3). Strike a line up each back leg to continue the taper onto the rail and then join up these lines by marking a line along the top edge of the upper rail.

Remove the rail and cut off the waste with a power plane or by using a hand saw. This is a long rip cut and will need care. Finish the taper by planing the surface of the upper rail smooth.

FITTING THE BACK SLATS

The width and spacing of the back slats is a matter of preference. We used 38 × 25mm (1½ × 1in) slats, spaced about 19mm (¾in) apart.

The easiest way to fit the slats is to use two dowels top and bottom, positioned by means of a dowelling jig. We used 8mm ($\frac{5}{16}$in) dowels, 40mm (1½in) long. For an even stronger fixing you can use mortise and tenon joints top and bottom, but without a mortising machine it would be a very time-consuming task to make all the necessary joints.

Measure on the back leg the distance from the top of the lower rail to the underside of the upper rail, and cut the slats to this length if you will be fixing them using dowels. Cut the slats about 19mm (¾in) longer at each end if you intend to use mortise and tenon joints.

DETAIL OF THE GARDEN BENCH
For decorative effect, the outside edges of the legs, frame rails, seat boards and so on are chamferred before final assembly.

① Fitting Lower Back Rail to Back Leg
Lower back rail fits square and flush with slope of front face of back leg and will align with back edge of seat boards. Mark mortises on inside faces of back legs and cut bare-faced tenons on lower back rail.

② Fitting Upper Back Rail to Back Leg
Mark mortise on ends of upper back rail (remember it is overlength) and cut out. Mark rail position on top of back legs and cut bare-faced tenons on legs. Cut excess from ends of rail to fit flush with back legs.

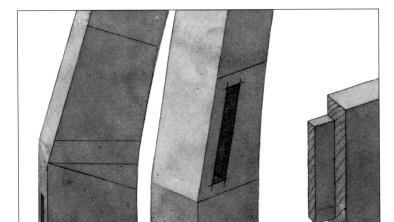

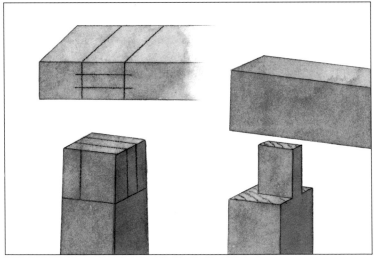

Mark up the ends of the slats for the two dowel holes (fig 4) and, using a dowelling jig, drill the ends of the slats to a depth of 22mm ($\frac{7}{8}$in) using an 8mm ($\frac{5}{16}$in) dowel (centre-point) drill bit.

Mark a centre line along the top edge of the lower rail and the bottom edge of the upper rail for the centre line of the dowel holes.

Work out the positions of the slats along one of these, adjusting as necessary to give an even spacing between the slats. Mark the centres of the dowel hole positions all the way along.

Cramp the two rails together and transfer the dowel centre marks to the other rail. Drill the dowel holes to a depth of 22mm ($\frac{7}{8}$in).

ASSEMBLING THE FRAME

Dry assemble the whole bench. Chamfer the edges of the front and back legs, the lower side rails, the undersides of the upper side rails, the edge of the lower back rail and the underside of the front rail using a router with a chamfering bit or a power plane.

Sand all the components to smooth the faces and edges, and to clean off any pencil marks. Glue up the end frames using a gap-filling waterproof glue such as Cascamite, cramping it tightly until the glue has thoroughly dried.

At this point, an adjustment has to be made to the height of the back legs to allow the seat to angle back slightly to assist rainwater drainage. This is done by standing the end frame on a flat surface, such as the workbench, and packing the front edge of the front leg by 15mm ($\frac{5}{8}$in) using a scrap piece of timber (fig 5).

Using an offcut of the same thickness, scribe the back leg and the side and back of the front leg to the correct angle. Cut off the bottoms of the legs to these lines. Repeat for the other end frame. Glue the front rail and the lower back rail into the end frames, then glue all the dowels and slats into the lower back rail. Apply glue to the tops of the slats and to the dowels and seat-back tenons, then tap the upper back rail into place. You will need someone to help you with this.

THE SEAT

CONSTRUCTION

The seat is a solid piece formed by dowelling together a number of narrow lengths of timber. Use a dowelling jig and join to the frame with 8mm ($\frac{5}{16}$in) dowels, 40mm ($1\frac{1}{2}$in) long, spaced about 150–225mm (6–9in) apart.

After dowelling, glue the lengths together using a gap-filling waterproof wood adhesive, such as Cascamite, and hold the assembly together with sash cramps or folding wedges against a fixed batten nailed to a worktop.

When the glue has dried, sand the surface flush and position the seat on the seat bench frame, leaving a 4mm ($\frac{1}{8}$in) wide gap at the back for drainage. Mark round so that there is a 19mm ($\frac{3}{4}$in) overhang at each end and at the front, then trim the seat to this line.

Cut a 12mm ($\frac{1}{2}$in) chamfer on the top edges at the front and sides using a router with a rounding over bit or a power plane.

FIXING

Fix the seat down using zinc-plated shrinkage plates – two at each end and three along the front – and screw into the seat rails and underside of the seat.

To keep the seat rigid so it will not bow in the middle, drill through the back rail into the seat in five places using a 12mm ($\frac{1}{2}$in) flat drill bit. Drill about 50mm (2in) into the seat. Cut five lengths of 12mm ($\frac{1}{2}$in) dowel about 95mm ($3\frac{3}{4}$in) long. Use a tenon saw or the point of a nail to cut two grooves 2–4mm ($\frac{1}{16}-\frac{1}{8}$in) deep along the dowel lengths to allow glue and air to escape as the dowels are driven into position.

Apply waterproof adhesive to the holes and hammer the dowels into position using the mallet. After the glue has set, saw off the protruding ends flush with the seat rail.

Chamfer the bottom edges of the legs so the wood will not split if the bench is dragged on the ground. To prevent the legs rotting, fix large, metal hammer-in glides to the bottoms of the legs.

3 Shaping Upper Back Rail
Mark sides and back of back rail to follow taper of back face of back leg. Remove waste and plane smooth.

4 Fitting the Back Slats
Mark slat and dowel positions on rails. Fit slats between back rails using two dowels each end.

5 Angling the Legs
Top Stand bench frame on a flat surface and pack front leg with scrap timber. Scribe legs as necessary.

6 Cross-section of Seat
Bottom Seat boards are butted up and joined using dowels. Longer dowels fix seat to lower back rail.

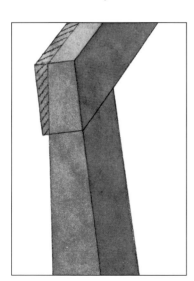

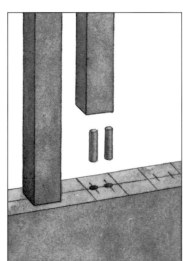

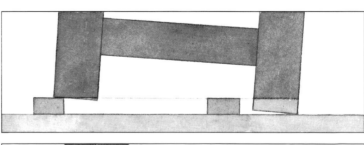

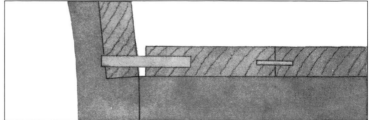

OCTAGONAL TREE SEAT

Even in the smallest garden, a tree seat makes an inviting point of interest. Any type of seating really makes a garden look furnished, but a seat which encircles a tree is particularly appealing. Children enjoy playing on, under and around the shady platform and seem to gain endless amusement sitting on opposite sides from each other or their parents.

Although this seat looks complicated, it is actually fairly simple to make.

Nevertheless, it is a time-consuming project. Because the back leans inwards, cutting the back slats could have been quite a difficult proposition. To prevent unnecessary complication, a gap has been left between the slats to accommodate any discrepancies that may occur.

Other design simplifications were made. There is a simple bold structure for the frame underneath rather than complicated mortise-and-tenon joints.

Softwood is an easy timber to work with and contributes a great deal to the ease with which a structure like this can be made. But softwood does need to be protected in some way, by treating with preservative, and then by applying a final finish of wood stain or, as in this case, paint. Depending on where in your garden the seat is positioned, you might like to choose a brighter colour: a strong blue would be very effective.

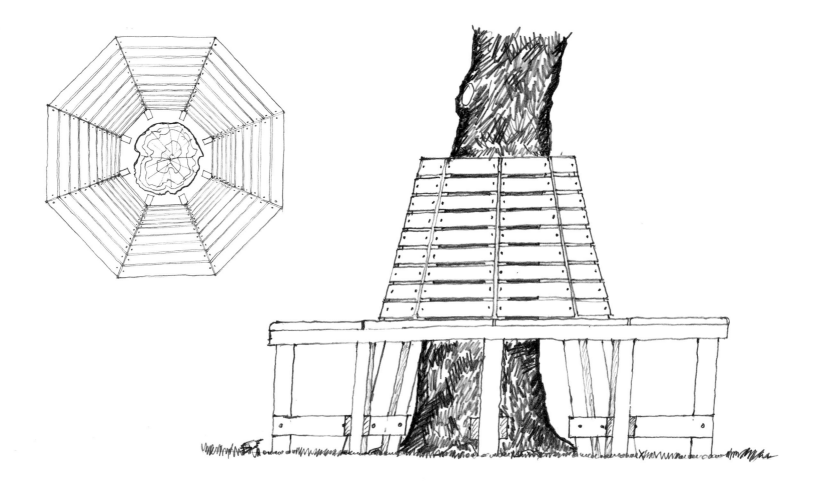

OCTAGONAL TREE SEAT

TOOLS

WORKBENCH (fixed or portable)

STEEL MEASURING TAPE

STEEL RULE

TRY SQUARE (or combination square)

SLIDING BEVEL

PROTRACTOR

CIRCULAR POWER SAW – preferably bench-mounted (or panel saw)

TENON SAW

POWER DRILL

DRILL BIT – approximately 3mm ($\frac{1}{8}$in) diameter

COUNTERSINK BIT

SCREWDRIVER

CLAW HAMMER

NAIL PUNCH

PINCERS

SMOOTHING PLANE (hand or power)

MATERIALS

Part	Quantity	Material	Length
BACK LEGS	8	75 × 50mm (3 × 2in) PAR softwood	1050mm (42in)
FRONT LEGS	8	As above	500mm (20in)
SEAT FRAME RAILS	32	75 × 25mm (3 × 1in) PAR softwood	530mm (21in)
SEAT SLATS	48	As above	As required
APRON BOARDS	8	As above	As required
BACK SLATS	72	50 × 16mm (2 × $\frac{5}{8}$in) PAR softwood	As required
APRON FIXING BATTENS	8	25 × 25mm (1 × 1in) PAR softwood	150mm (6in) shorter than apron boards

Also required: waterproof woodworking adhesive; 38mm (1$\frac{1}{2}$in) No 8 zinc-plated countersunk wood screws

The size of this eight-sided tree seat is governed by the size of the tree you wish to surround. Remember, you must leave room for the trunk to expand as the tree grows! Some trees grow faster than others: we built our seat around a small walnut tree, which is a slow-growing species, but even so we allowed an internal diameter of 600mm (24in) at the very top of the back support. Quite large tree specimens are available from good garden centres, so it could be worth planting a small 'standard' tree (that is, one with a long trunk) just as the focal point around which to build this seat.

The basic construction consists of eight separate frames on which the seat and backrest slats are fixed. The frames are of a pre-determined size, but the length of the slats is varied according to the internal diameter of the seat.

The seat is made in two sections, dry assembled to each other, so the two halves can be easily unscrewed to fix around the tree.

SEAT FRAMES

Cut the components of the seat frames to length.

Chamfer the front face of each back leg at an angle of 22$\frac{1}{2}$ degrees from the centre line of one of the 75mm (3in) faces (fig 1). It is best to do this using a circular saw canted over at the correct angle – use a sliding bevel aligned on a protractor to set this. Finish off using a hand or power plane for a smooth finish.

1 Chamfering the Back Leg
Draw a line down middle of front face of each back leg. Chamfer at a 22$\frac{1}{2}$ degree angle from this line.

2 Making the Spacing Template
Cut a spacing template from a scrap piece of board to the dimensions shown below. The template is used for accurate positioning of the front and back legs and the seat frame rails to make up the seat frames.

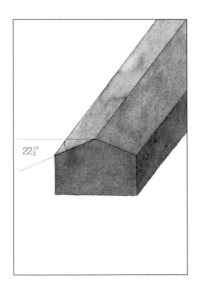

22$\frac{1}{2}$°

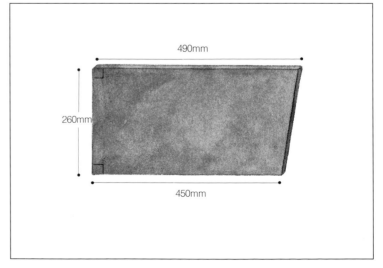

490mm

260mm

450mm

OCTAGONAL TREE SEAT ASSEMBLY

BACK SLAT

BACK LEG

SEAT SLAT

SEAT FRAME

APRON BOARD

SEAT FRAME RAIL

FRONT LEG

SEAT FRAME RAIL

Octagonal Tree Seat

Using a scrap of hardboard or chipboard to the shape and dimensions shown (fig 2, page 166), make up a template for fixing the seat frame rails on to the front and back legs to make up the seat frames.

Temporarily nail a batten to your workbench to give a flat surface to rest the feet of the legs against. Lay the front and back legs of one frame on the bench with two seat frame rails on top and the spacing template between them (fig 1). The back leg must be angled to align with the back of the template and the front leg should be exactly flush with the front edge of the template. The bottom of the legs should be resting against the batten nailed to the workbench.

The bottom seat frame rail is positioned so that it overlaps the front leg by 12mm ($\frac{1}{2}$in), while the top frame rail should be flush with the front and top of the front leg.

If a suitable flat workbench is not

② Finished Construction of the Seat Frames
Top **Glue and screw seat frame rails to legs, then trim overlap at the back so it is parallel with slope of back leg and protrudes 12mm ($\frac{1}{2}$in).** *Bottom* **Finished frame shows frame rails screwed in position to front and back legs.**

DETAIL OF SEAT LEGS

Gravel-filled holes around the front and back legs of the seat frames make levelling easier and keep the legs off water-logged ground, reducing the risk of the wood rotting.

① Making Up the Seat Frames
Lay the front and back legs of one frame on a flat surface so they are flush with template. Top frame rail rests on template and is flush with the top and front of front rail; bottom frame rail overlaps front leg by 12mm ($\frac{1}{2}$in).

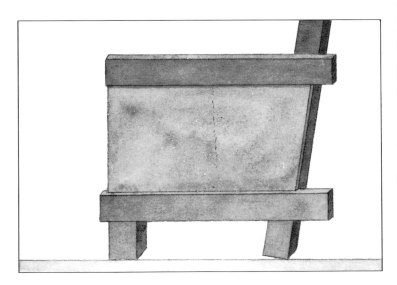

available for this setting out, the pieces can be laid out on a flat floor, with the legs resting against an adjacent wall, so that the wall aligns the base of the legs.

Glue the top of the seat frame rail in place using a waterproof woodworking adhesive (such as Cascamite), then drill pilot holes and screw it to the front and back legs using two screws at each end. Glue and screw the bottom seat frame rail to the legs in the same way.

Turn the frame over and position the other two seat frame rails in the same way, top and bottom. It is very important that these rails are exactly square to the ones on the other side so that the rails will be flush across the top where the seat slats will be fixed (fig 2).

To complete the construction of the frames, the seat frame rails are trimmed off in line with the back leg, but leaving a 12mm ($\frac{1}{2}$in) overlap (fig 2). Strike a line at this position, and then trim off using a panel saw or circular saw.

Repeat the construction for the remaining seven frames.

SEAT SLATS

The seat slats are cut from 75 × 25mm (3 × 1in) PAR (planed all round) softwood. The dimensions of the seat frames are predetermined, so that the number of slats required will not vary, no matter how large the finished seat. What you will have to calculate yourself, however, is the length of each slat. This will depend upon the internal diameter of the seat, itself dependent on size of the tree trunk around which you assemble the project.

To measure up for the seat section, stand the eight frames around the tree roughly in position and spaced at the required distance from the tree, allowing for growth and depending on how large you want the diameter of the tree seat.

MAKING THE SEAT SLATS

When you are satisfied with the spacing of the seat frames, measure the distance between the centres of the back legs at seat height and calculate the average ('x' in fig 3).

This will be the length of the inside edge of the innermost seat slats (ours are 380mm [15in] long).

Mark length 'x' on to the back edge of a piece of the slat timber and draw 112$\frac{1}{2}$ degree angles off at either end using a sliding bevel. You can then use this slat to help draw up a full-size plan of a seat section (fig 4) which will enable you to cut the remaining five seat slats to the correct length.

To make the full-size plan, mark off the back measurement using the innermost slat as a guide for the angles. Extend the angled lines outwards, using the sliding bevel to double check that the angle is 112$\frac{1}{2}$ degrees. Returning to the seat frame, measure the distance from the centre of the back leg to the front of the frame ('y' in fig 3). On a full-size plan, mark the length 'y' on the angled lines, and add 20mm ($\frac{3}{4}$in) to allow for the approximate thickness of the apron board at the front of the seat. Join up the two marks 'y plus 20mm ($\frac{3}{4}$in)' at the front of the plan, parallel with the back line, to give the front edge of the seat.

You can now work out the necessary spacing for the slats. Place the innermost slat in position on the full-size plan and roughly cut five more slats, making sure that they are overlength. Bunch the slats together against the innermost slat, measure the remaining distance to the front line of the seat, and divide by five to give the amount of space to be left between each slat. If you want to increase the spacing, at this stage plane the edge of the innermost slat to reduce its width.

Using one of the slats and a spacing batten or spacing blocks cut to the width of the calculated space, draw out all six slats in position on the full-size plan. You will then be able to measure off the plan for the exact lengths of all the slats in each section of the seat.

Cut out all the slats for one seat section, but cut 2mm (about $\frac{1}{16}$in) inside each marked line in order to create a deliberate gap between the ends of the slats. You can use the slats cut for the first seat frame as templates for cutting the seat slats for the other sections.

3 Measuring up for the Seat Slats
Measure distance between centres of back legs at seat height ('x') to calculate length of innermost slat. Measure distance between centre of back leg and front of frame ('y') to calculate spacing between slats.

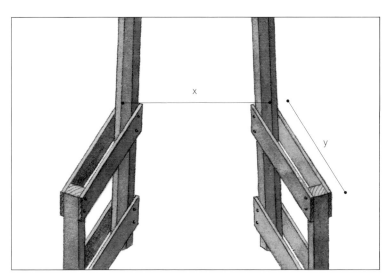

4 Drawing up Full-size Plan of Seat Section
Mark length 'x' and draw lines 'y plus 20mm ($\frac{3}{4}$in)' either end at 112$\frac{1}{2}$ degree angle. Bunch six slats on plan, measure remaining distance to front and divide by five to calculate spacing. Cut spacers, then mark slat positions.

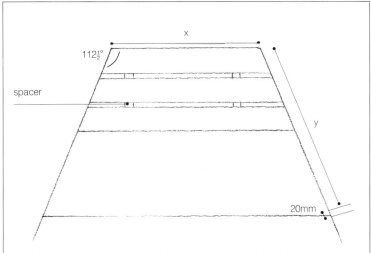

OCTAGONAL TREE SEAT

FIXING THE SEAT SLATS

Fix the innermost slats first. Place the first slat across the back of two seat frames, spaced 2mm (about $\frac{1}{16}$in) in from the centre of the back legs, then glue and screw the slat to the top seat frame rails with one screw at each end (fig 1).

Take another seat frame and innermost slat, and space in the same way. Glue and screw in place as before.

Continue in this way for two groups of three sections each. It is very important that you only dry assemble two sections opposite one another, as you will need to remove the slats on two opposite sides of the structure in order to fix the seat frames around the tree.

To fix the subsequent slats, line up the next shortest slat with the innermost slat (fig 2). With the spacing batten (or blocks) between the slats, align one end of the new slat with a batten held against one end of the previously fixed slat. Glue and screw into the top seat frame rail at each end.

Continue with this second size slat all the way round, remembering only to dry assemble where you did before. Carry on in this fashion, one row at a time, assembling without glue those slats in the two sections that are dry assembled.

Before the frontmost slats are fitted, the apron boards must be assembled (fig 3). Cut a piece of 75 x 25mm (3 x 1in) timber to the longest length of the frontmost slat and bevel back the edges at each end so they are in line with the angles of the seat slat. Cut a 25 x 25mm (1 x 1in) fixing batten about 150mm (6in) shorter than the apron board and glue and screw it centrally in place to join the apron board to the frontmost slat. The front edge of the slat must be flush with the front face of the apron board. Repeat the process to make the other apron boards.

Round off the front edges of the frontmost slats to give a smooth finish. Glue and screw into place at the front edges of the frames, remembering not to glue the dry assembled sections.

THE BACK SLATS

The back of each seat section is comprised of nine slats, cut from 50 x 16mm (2 x $\frac{5}{8}$in) PAR (planed all round) softwood. However, because the back legs are angled, the slats are not all the same length; instead, they get shorter as they reach the top.

Decide on the spacing of the back slats, and use scrap pieces of timber of the required thickness as spacing blocks. Lay the spacing blocks at seat level so that you start with a space, then lay the first slat, left overlength for the time being, in position. Mark off the ends in line with the centres of the back legs (fig 4). Set a sliding bevel to this angle, and cut the back slat to the marked length. Use the sliding bevel to mark off the correct angle and cut the first slats for the remaining back sections to length. Glue and screw the first back slats in place to the front of the back legs of all the seat sections, but leave the slats dry assembled in the same sections as you did before on the seat slats.

Use the spacing blocks to position the next length of slat (fig 4), mark off the ends as before, and cut to length. Repeat for the other seven slats in the row around the seat, and fix in place as before.

Continue in this way, row by row, until the seat back is completed (nine rows in our case). If the back legs protrude above the top slats they can be cut flush with the top of the slats for a neat appearance.

Dismantle the dry joints so that the seat is in two 'halves' (actually, two three-eighths).

ASSEMBLY

Take the two 'halves' of the seat to the tree and partially re-assemble it without glue so you can mark on the ground where the legs are positioned. Dismantle the seat again.

At the leg positions, dig holes for each of the 16 legs, 150mm (6in) in diameter and 150mm (6in) deep, and fill them with gravel. The gravel provides good drainage, reducing the risk of the legs rotting, and allows you to level the seat easily.

① Fixing the Innermost Seat Slats
Use plan as guide but cut slats about 2mm ($\frac{1}{16}$in) short both ends. Space slat about 2mm ($\frac{1}{16}$in) in from centre of back legs, then fix between two top frame rails. Work round frames, but *dry assemble* slats on two facing sections.

② Fixing Subsequent Slats to the Frame
Align next shortest slat with innermost slat: put the spacers or spacing battens in position, align ends of slat with innermost slat, and fix to frame rails. Continue round frame, then repeat for next size slats.

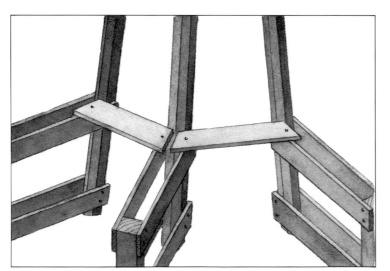

FINISHING

Before painting, it is important to treat the seat with a good-quality wood preservative which can be painted when dry – most clear and green grade preservatives fall into this category. We applied two coats, allowing each to dry thoroughly, and stood the legs in dishes of preservative for a couple of days.

Once the wood preservative is thoroughly dry (allow at least a week), the seat can be painted. We used a microporous paint which needs no primer (apart from preservative) and is intended for outdoor woodwork. The seat can be treated with a water-repellent preservative stain if a 'wood' finish is preferred.

After finishing with paint or wood stain, the seat can be finally assembled around the tree. Make sure the seat is well-bedded in the gravel and stands level on the ground. You can glue all joints at final assembly, or leave two sections of slats 'dry' to allow easy removal of the seat should the need arise.

③   Making the Apron Board
Top Use fixing batten to attach apron board to frontmost slat.
Bottom Front edge rounded over.

④   Spacing and Fixing the Back Slats
Back slats are initially overlength. Use spacing batten or spacing blocks to position back slat, and mark off ends of slat to line up with centres of back legs. Cut slats to length, then reposition and glue and screw in place.

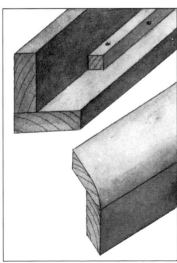

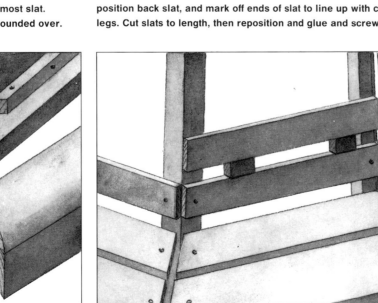

HEXAGONAL ARBOR

An arbor makes a distinctive feature in any garden, displaying climbing plants to great advantage and exposing them to optimum conditions of light and air. Arbors are often all-metal structures, but this simple but elegant framework makes use of ordinary copper tubing and plain wooden rustic posts, readily available from most DIY outlets. The construction process is fairly quick and easy to do.

The three sections of copper tubing (which have been rubbed with plumbers' flux to give them a green colour) are cut to precisely the same length and bent into shape using a curved piece of blockboard or chipboard as a former. Holes are drilled about 100mm (6in) apart along the tubes. Thin green plastic-covered wires are threaded through the holes to make a support for the plants.

As is the case with all posts that need to go into the ground, it is much easier to use spiked steel supports with sockets. The metal spikes are readily driven into the ground and the end of the post can be dropped into the shoe and held in place.

The uprights and cross rails must be treated with a preservative and the resulting dark brown makes a pleasing contrast with the greenish copper.

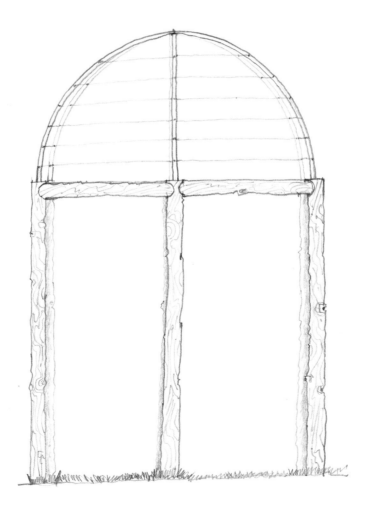

Hexagonal Arbor

This arbor is made from six preservative-treated rustic poles set into the ground at equal intervals and joined by cross rails, with a dome above made from copper tubing. If you brush the tubing with plumbers' flux, a green patina will result. Garden wire is fed around the tubing as a support for climbing plants.

Timber Frame

The height of the frame can be varied slightly. However, the poles should not be less than about 2m (6ft 6in) above ground, otherwise some people may hit their heads on the cross rails; and, for stability, the poles should not be much higher above ground than 2.5m (8ft).

Preparing the Site

Choose a flat site and, using pegs and string lines, mark out the hexagonal shape (fig 1) for the positions. The posts are spaced at 1000mm (39in) centres, with 2m (6ft 6in) between any two opposite posts. It is essential that the post positions are accurately marked.

Dig 600mm (24in) deep holes for the posts. This can be done using a narrow spade or, if available, a post hole borer which is driven into the ground and then removed to deposit excavated earth. Fill the bottom 150mm (6in) of each hole with hardcore to ensure good drainage and prevent the post bottoms rotting.

Making the Framework

Make up six L-shapes comprising a post and a cross rail as follows.

Position two posts in neighbouring holes and wedge them vertically. Measure the internal distance between them and add 50mm (2in) to allow for shaping the ends of the cross rails. Remove the posts.

Use a jigsaw to make a curved cut in the ends of the cross rails so that they fit against the sides of the posts. Alternatively, use a hand saw to cut out V-shapes in the cross rails.

At the top of each post, draw 60 degree angles as a guide to aligning the cross rails (fig 2, bottom). Continue the lines to the opposite sides of the post as a guide for the dowel fixing positions. Cut the dowelling into 150mm (6in) lengths.

Lay one post on a flat piece of ground. Position a cross rail against the post and drill through the post and into the rail to accept the dowel (fig 3). At least 50mm (2in) of dowel should enter the rail. Fit the dowel using waterproof wood adhesive. Repeat to make five more L-shapes.

Erecting the Frame

Position two posts in their holes and align the cross rail that falls between them with both posts. Use a straight-edge and a spirit level to align the posts – if necessary, add or take away a little of the hardcore in the base of the hole. Drill through the 'free' post into the end of the cross rail to align with the angles marked on the top. Join the 'free' post to the cross rail with a dowel as you did before (fig 3).

Continue to join up the L-shaped sections in the same way, checking that the tops of the posts are all at the same height, and then saw off any protruding dowel ends flush with the posts.

Materials

Part	Quantity	Material	Length
POSTS	6	75–100mm (3–4in) diameter treated rustic poles	2.4m (7ft 8in)
CROSS RAILS	6	50–75mm (2–3in) diameter treated rustic poles	As required
DOME BARS	3	22mm ($\frac{7}{8}$in) diameter copper tubing	As required

Also required: approximately 2m (6ft 6in) of 12mm ($\frac{1}{2}$in) diameter hardwood dowelling

Tools

WORKBENCH (fixed or portable)

SPADE or POST HOLE BORER

PANEL SAW

SPIRIT LEVEL

STEEL RULE

POWER JIGSAW

POWER DRILL

HAMMER

SCREWDRIVER

PLIERS

HACKSAW

CRAMPS

SHOVEL

1 Drawing up a Ground Plan
Posts are spaced 1000mm (39in): mark centre and strike off 1000mm (39in) lines at 60 degree angles.

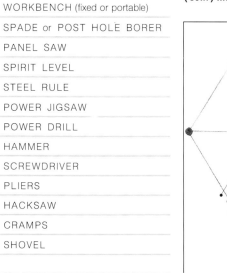

1000mm 60°

1000mm

2 Shaping the Cross Rails
Angle ends of cross rails to fit around posts. Use jigsaw for smooth curve or make V-cuts with hand saw.

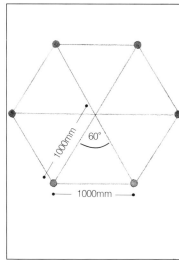

3 Fixing the Cross Rails
Drill holes through posts into cross rails. Insert dowels to fix in place. Angled screw holds dowel in place.

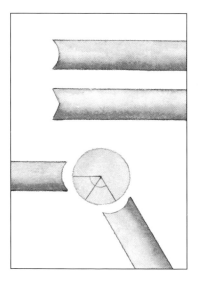
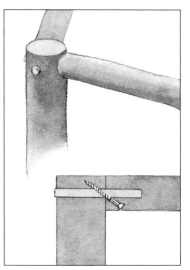

To secure the joints, use a 75mm (3in) screw inserted diagonally through each cross rail (fig 3).

Finally, tie a length of garden wire around the top of the posts, holding it in place on each post using 38mm (1½in) staples. To make the wire taut, twist the two ends together using pliers.

THE DOME

Draw a semi-circle on a large sheet of plywood or chipboard (fig 4) using a pencil and a piece of string to act as a compass. This will describe the section of the dome. When this is done, mark off at 150mm (6in) centres for the positions of holes through which training wires will later be threaded.

Use a piece of 19mm (¾in) chipboard or plywood to make a former for bending the tube to the correct shape. Trace the curve on to the former and cut it out using a jigsaw.

BENDING THE TUBE

Cut the copper tubing to length using a hacksaw. Our tubes were 3.14m (10ft 4in) long. Since the copper will need to be bent a little tighter than the arc, bring it down about 38mm (1½in) at each end.

Cramp the former to a workbench or table and start to bend the piece of tube around it. You will need someone to help you with this: each person should exert a little pressure until the tubing is bent to follow the shape of the former. If you find that the ends lose their shape then you can use a 22mm (⅞in) internal pipe bending spring.

Lay the bent tube on the original dome profile and mark off the 150mm (6in) spacings on to the tube. Drill 3mm (⅛in) diameter holes through the tubing at these marks.

Bend the other two tubes to the shape of the former and then drill the holes as before. Always mark off the spacings on the tubing against the original dome profile.

ASSEMBLING THE DOME

Mark the middle point of each tube, then hammer it flat so that you can drill a 6mm (¼in) diameter hole through each piece (fig 5). Bolt the three pieces together.

Next, drill a 25mm (1in) diameter hole, 50mm (2in) deep in the centre of the top of each post.

The dome can now be lifted on to the top of the posts and the tube ends located in the holes (fig 6). There is sufficient movement in the structure to enable the dome to be positioned.

Thread garden wire through each row of holes, tying each length securely in place.

To fix the dome to the rustic poles, drill straight through the tube horizontally above each post and slip a 50mm (2in) nail through.

Finally make up a dryish concrete mix of five parts sand to one part cement and pour it into each hole along with some small pieces of stone. Tamp it down, then shape it into a convex collar so that rain water will drain away.

④ Dome Section and Former
Mark off 150mm (6in) spacings on semi-circle. Transfer section of curve to plywood to make former.

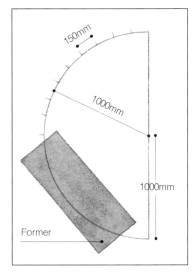

⑤ Fixing the Dome
Flatten out tops of the pieces of tubing, drill a 6mm (¼in) diameter hole through them and bolt together.

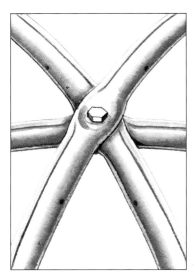

⑥ Fixing Dome to Posts
Drill a hole centrally in the top of each post. Slot dome into post and drive nail through tubing.

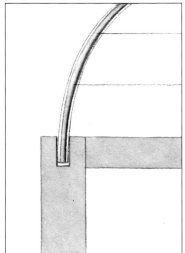

HEXAGONAL ARBOR ASSEMBLY

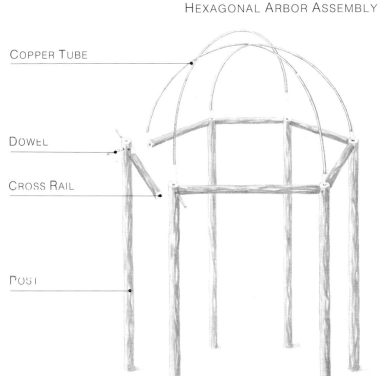

COPPER TUBE

DOWEL

CROSS RAIL

POST

WALK-THROUGH PERGOLA

In a small garden, a pergola, or framework for climbing plants, makes an architectural addition which gives focus to the entire layout, especially when centrally positioned. In a larger garden, a pergola can be extended further to create a proper walkway, a semi-enclosed space to contrast with the open areas of lawn and flowerbed. This particular design can be adapted to vary the length as required, but would not really be effective if made any shorter than three units long.

The structure and the dimensions of the pergola are based around standard trellis panels, which are much cheaper than any you could make for the purpose.

The easiest way to assemble the structure is to construct the top frame first, adding the struts to make the pyramid roof afterwards. Then the position of the posts, or uprights, can be marked out on the ground where you want the pergola to go and metal shoes or spiked steel supports driven in.

The final stage is to cover the outside of the structure with trellis. When viewed from the side, the trellis wall appears to be continuous, but, because the trellis is fixed only to alternate bays, you will get glimpses of the garden as you walk through. As a plain, undressed structure with no covering of plants the pergola has its own attractions, especially when painted a strong positive colour. To support climbing plants over the roof, simply staple wire around the pyramids.

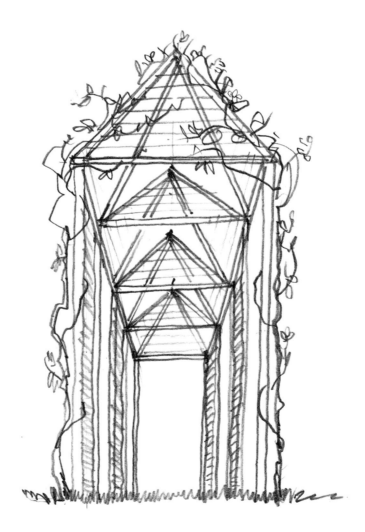

WALK-THROUGH PERGOLA

The light and airy framework of this pergola can be built over a garden path to form a covered walkway of colourful and sweetly scented climbing plants trained over the easy-to-make, but distinctive, trellis and wire-covered framework. Good plants to use include clematis, especially the small-flowered species such as *C montana* and *C armandii*, climbing hydrangea (*H petiolaris*), sweet-scented plants such as jasmine and honeysuckle, and wisteria. The many varieties of ivy are quickly established, although they can be difficult to contain; instead, you could try ornamental grape vines, the leaves of which turn to spectacular colours in autumn.

The 'roof' is a series of simple pyramids on a timber framework which is fixed on top of fence posts held upright by hammer-in steel fence post supports. Training wires for climbing plants are stapled around the pyramids, and trellis panels are fixed at the sides between the post supports.

Trellis panels usually come in 1830mm (72in) widths, and in heights of 600mm (24in), 900mm (36in) and 1220mm (48in). For this project, the panels are turned to give a height of 1830mm (72in) and a width of 1220mm (48in).

The size of the trellis panels also determines the dimensions of the pergola – ours is 1220mm (48in) wide, and the posts are spaced 1220mm (48in) apart. It is best to keep these measurements the same so that the 'base' to each pyramid is a square, ensuring that the struts are in proportion to the main frame. The height of the posts is 2m (6ft 6in) which means that the trellising is raised off the ground by 150mm (6in). We have only fixed trellising to alternate bays, but this is simply for effect. Our pergola is four bays long, but this is variable and you can have more or fewer bays, according to your requirements.

All timber used is sawn and preservative-treated softwood, as used for fencing.

PYRAMID ROOF STRUCTURE
The series of pyramids that form the 'roof' of the pergola add visual interest and extra height to the design. Training wires are stapled around the struts, enabling plants to grow and thrive and to form a 'living ceiling'.

MATERIALS

Note: All timber is sawn and preservative-treated softwood

Part	Quantity	Material	Length
LONG RAILS	2	75 × 50mm (3 × 2in)	5.25m (17ft 3in)
CROSS RAILS	5	As above	1200mm (48in)
PYRAMID STRUTS	16	75 × 25mm (3 × 1in)	1350mm (53in)*
POSTS	10	75 × 75mm (3 × 3in)	2m (6ft 6in)
TRELLIS PANELS	8		1830mm (72in) high × 1200mm (48in)
HAMMER-IN POST SUPPORTS	10		
TRAINING WIRE	1 large coil		
SCREWS		Zinc-plated steel	50mm (2in) No 8
STAPLES		Galvanized fencing type	19mm ($\frac{3}{4}$in)

* Approximate length only – measure and cut on site for accuracy

TOOLS

WORKBENCH (fixed or portable)

STEEL MEASURING TAPE

STEEL RULE

TRY SQUARE

COMBINATION SQUARE – for marking 45 degree angles

PANEL SAW (or circular power saw)

TENON SAW

MARKING GAUGE

POWER DRILL

DRILL BIT – approximately 3mm ($\frac{1}{8}$in) diameter to drill pilot holes for screws

SLEDGE HAMMER

CARPENTER'S HAMMER

CHISEL – about 25mm (1in)

MALLET

WALK-THROUGH PERGOLA ASSEMBLY

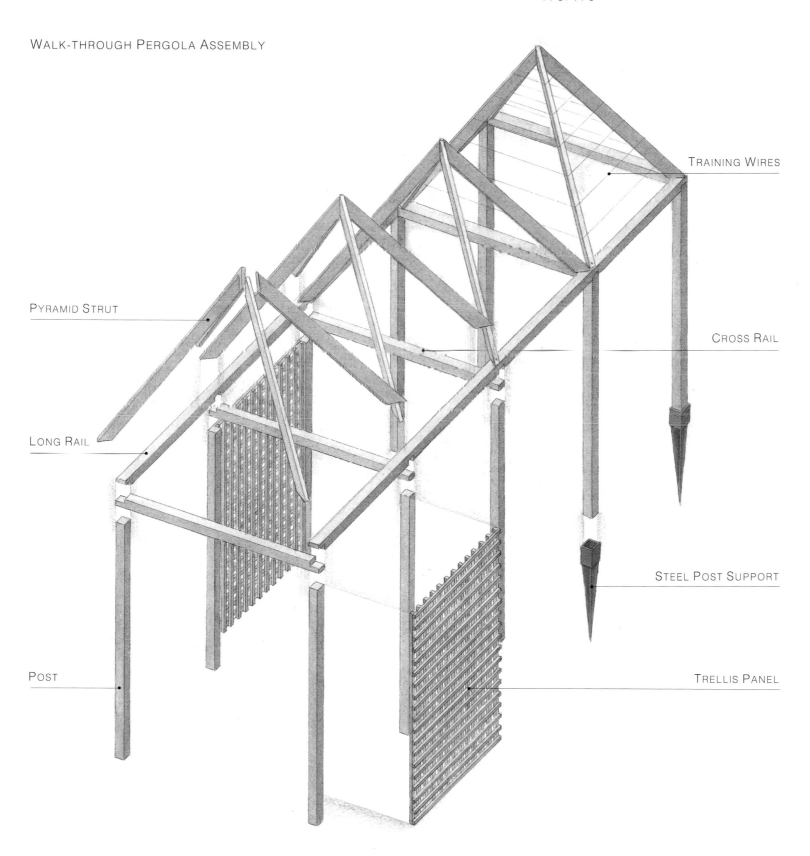

TRAINING WIRES

PYRAMID STRUT

CROSS RAIL

LONG RAIL

STEEL POST SUPPORT

POST

TRELLIS PANEL

WALK-THROUGH PERGOLA

TOP FRAME

Start by making the top frame on which the 'roof' of pyramids is fixed and which will eventually be supported on the vertical posts. The top long rails are made from 75 × 50mm (3 × 2in) sawn and preservative-treated timber, ideally in one full length (that is, if you are making the pergola to the proportions shown in the photograph, the length of four trellis panels plus the five posts of 75mm [3in] width). If it is impossible to buy timber the length required, two shorter lengths can be joined end to end with a simple lap joint or halving joint (see **Techniques, Wood Joints, page 242**).

Cut the cross rails to the width required, in our case 1370mm (54in) (the spacing between two posts plus the thickness of the posts).

Mark out the positions of the posts on the long rails to suit the width of the trellis panels, in our case at *internal* intervals of 1220mm (48in). Cut halving joints at the appropriate places on the long rails and at the ends of the cross rails, so that they form corner halving joints on the cross rails at either end (fig 1) and T-halving joints on the intermediate rails (see **Techniques, page 242**). Form the joints so that the long rails are on top.

Screw the joints together through the cross rails from the underside.

'PYRAMID' ROOF SECTIONS

To work out the exact length of the pyramid struts, measure the diagonal of the base across the frame. Mark this length on a flat floor and strike equal length lines at 45 degrees to this line at either end to give the point of the apex of the pyramid. This gives the lengths of the timber required for the structure forming the pyramid – the measurement should more or less correspond to the length of the cross rails.

Cut the required number of struts slightly overlength and then mitre them all at 45 degrees at both ends in opposite directions and to the correct length required.

To assemble, hold two of the struts in a vice so the mitred faces of one end meet. Screw through from each side using 50mm (2in) No 8 zinc-plated woodscrews (fig 2).

Hold this frame upright in a workbench and lay a third strut against the joint and pilot drill through at 45 degrees into the other frame (fig 3). Repeat for the fourth pyramid strut (fig 4).

Make up the required number of pyramid structures. These are delicate, so handle them carefully.

Place each pyramid on top of the frame already made and fix down into it with a single screw at each corner (fig 5). Once fixed, this is a very strong structure. Repeat for all of the pyramids.

Staple training wires at 150mm (6in) intervals up the pyramids.

FIXING THE POSTS AND FINAL ASSEMBLY

Carry the top structure to its final position and use it to mark on the ground the positions of the fence posts. The posts are spaced at internal intervals of 1220mm (48in) so that they coincide with the cross rail positions.

The easiest way to fix the posts is with steel post supports. These supports are simply hammered into the ground and the posts slot into sockets at the tops of the supports.

Stretch a string line along the line of the posts. This string line will help you to line up the supports and will also give some idea of levels. Push the tip of the support into the ground and use a spirit level to check that it is upright. To drive the support into the ground, a heavy hammer, such as a sledge hammer, will be required. Insert a short length of 75 × 75mm (3 × 3in) timber post into the socket to protect the support from hammer blows, or use a proprietary metal-capped driving tool which should have a tommy-bar handle allowing you to steady the socket and prevent it from twisting as it is hammered in place.

Drive the support into the ground with firm, slow blows of the hammer. At regular intervals, insert a post into the socket and use a spirit level on

---

① Joining Top Frame Rails
Frame rails form corner halving joints at ends and T-halving joints (not shown) at intermediate points.

② Joining First Two Struts
Mitre ends of struts at 45 degrees and butt cut faces together. *Inset* Fix with screws at oblique angles.

③ Adding Remaining Struts
Hold frame in a workbench. Screw through from sides of third strut to face of joint; repeat for fourth strut.

④ Apex of Finished Pyramid
Finished joints neatly form pyramid apex. *Inset* Angled screws fix third and fourth struts to first two struts.

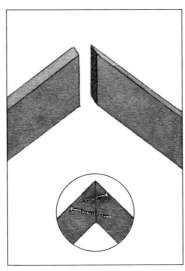

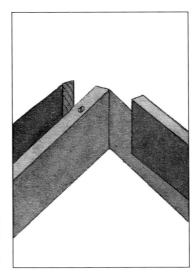

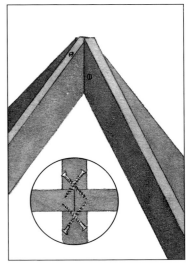

two adjacent faces to check that the spike is going in vertically. Adjustments can be made by pulling or twisting the sockets as necessary.

When the supports have been inserted the posts can be fitted. In some designs of post supports, two bolts have to be tightened to cramp the posts in position, while in others the posts are held with large screws. Double-check that the posts are upright and use a length of straight timber and a spirit level to check that the tops of the posts are level. On flat or slightly sloping ground this will be easy to achieve, but on steeply sloping ground it may be acceptable if the tops of the posts follow the slope of the ground. Use a length of string or a long batten to level the post tops which can be trimmed to an even height, if necessary, using a hand saw.

The next stage is to fix the trellising between the posts (we only fixed it to alternate bays of the pergola). Place bricks or blocks on the ground to support the trellis panels about 150mm (6in) from the ground. We used metal clips to hold the panels of trellis in place and the clips are first nailed to the posts so that they are vertical and inset by the same amount – about 25mm (1in). The panels are then lifted into place and a check is made that the horizontal rails of the trellis panels are level. The panels are then fixed to the clips using zinc-plated screws (see **Techniques, page 251**).

If required, the trellis panels can be fixed directly to the posts. Position and level them as above, then drill through the side frames of the panels so that 75mm (3in) long galvanized fencing nails can be driven through the panels, without splitting them, and into the posts. Three fixings will be required on each side of a 1830mm (72in) high trellis panel.

You will need some help to lift the pyramid roof onto the posts. Adjust the roof so that the vertical posts coincide with the corner and cross rail joints, then nail the frame to the tops of the posts using two 100mm (4in) nails skew nailed through the top frame and into each post (see **Techniques, page 241**).

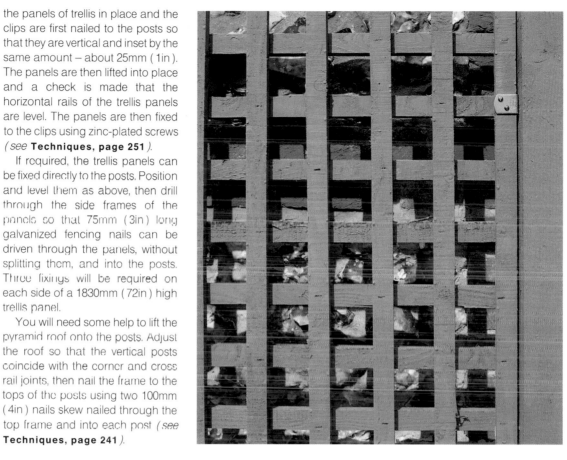

5 **Fixing Pyramids to Frame**
Screw the pyramids to the top frame using a screw through each corner and into the frame rails.

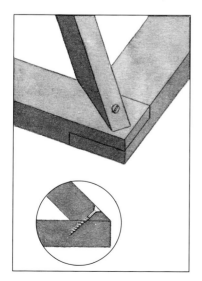

SUMMER HOUSE

Most people could well do with the extra space that a summer house provides. And although this is the perfect place for storing tools, bulbs and seeds, or potting up and a variety of other garden chores, you need not necessarily put it to horticultural use. A DIY workshop, an artist's studio, a guest annexe, the ultimate play house – it is easy to think of a host of functions for this kind of structure to fulfil, although the use it is put to can mean that you will have to seek planning permission before you start building. It could prove invaluable as a home office or study, offering an important psychological separation of home and work for those who work at home. And it is substantial enough to serve as a pavilion on a village cricket green.

The house may appear a daunting prospect for all but the most ardent DIY enthusiast; but the skills you require are well within the average range of ability and there is no need for the kind of refinement demanded by furniture-making. There is no sophisticated jointing and there are few techniques which should not already be familiar. The cost of materials, all readily available, are roughly the same as a family holiday, which makes it fairly reasonable, unless you put a high price on your own time and labour. The major commitment is time. Working alone during the evenings and weekends, it should take about three months. Full-time, with one or two willing assistants, it might only take a couple of weeks.

As far as the design is concerned, there were a number of influences. The idea to use corrugated iron (actually profiled steel) for the roof came from the houses of the Australian outback. The shape of the roof was suggested by the roofline of the traditional cricket pavilion. In different colour combinations, the house acquires quite different aspects: green and white for a cricket pavilion; pale pastels for a seaside look; vibrant blues, greens and pinks to suggest the Caribbean.

The project is a major undertaking. We would recommend that you attempt most of the other projects in the book before tackling this one. But if the demands are high, so are the rewards. What could be more satisfying – or useful – than building your own garden house?

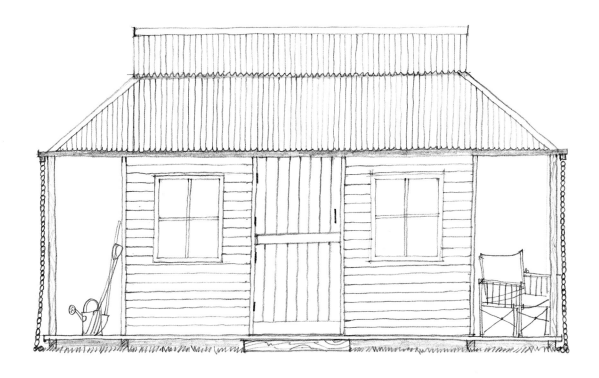

Summer House

A summer house, somewhere in a secluded part of the garden, is a delightful retreat to be savoured when you want to relax away from the bustle of the house. This design captures all the magic, charm and intrigue required from a garden hideaway and just invites you to explore inside. The size of the room is approximately 3.6 × 2.4m (12 × 8ft) which is a comfortable size to furnish with wicker chairs yet remain cosy and intimate. The extended roof covering over the veranda gives the impression of greater size while providing a 1000mm (39in) deep protected area on showery days when you want to sit outside. The size of the base is partly dictated by the area that can be built upon without the need of planning permission. However, check with your local authority, since the use to which you put the building will also affect the need for permission.

The red-and-blue colour scheme chosen here not only accentuates the design and materials but is fun, too. By changing the colour combinations you can substantially alter the finished look of the building; a few suggestions for alternative colours are illustrated on page 197.

The basic structure rests on a level base of concrete slabs which in turn support timber joists. The veranda is treated slatted wood, while the interior floor is exterior-grade plywood finished, in this case, with floor paint, although you could equally use carpets, tiles or boards. It would be perfectly possible to extend the walls to take in the veranda area if you require more indoor floor space. The interior walls are also clad with plywood to give the structure rigidity – between this and the outdoor boarding is a layer of insulation. The level ceiling is covered in tongued-and-grooved

boarding and is also insulated. You could leave the roof structure exposed if you wanted, although you would lose a lot of heat in cold weather as a result. If you require heating, a paraffin heater or a fan heater are the best options.

The chains leading down from the guttering at the four corners of the building act in the same way as the drainpipes, conducting water down to the ground, where four soakaways are dug: a feature of traditional Japanese houses.

The illustrations below and opposite give an overall impression of the construction of the front, back and side walls and of the roof. However, in addition to the project text and illustrations, you may also need to refer to the sections on Materials and Techniques (pages 232–35 and 236–53) when further guidance is needed on individual stages of the construction.

TOOLS

PORTABLE WORKBENCH

STEEL MEASURING TAPE

STEEL RULE

TRY SQUARE or COMBINATION SQUARE

ADJUSTABLE SLIDING BEVEL

PANEL SAW (or circular saw)

POWER DRILL

DRILL BIT – 12mm ($\frac{1}{2}$in) and 3.2mm ($\frac{1}{8}$in)

SPANNER

HAMMER

NAIL PUNCH

PINCERS

CHISEL

MALLET

TIN SNIPS

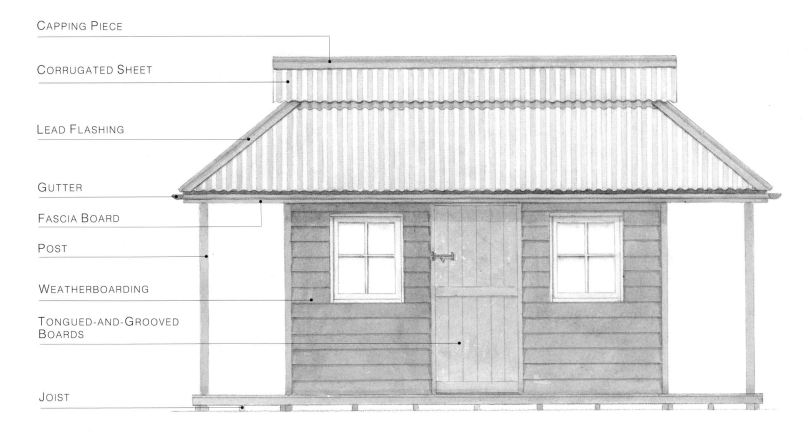

CAPPING PIECE

CORRUGATED SHEET

LEAD FLASHING

GUTTER

FASCIA BOARD

POST

WEATHERBOARDING

TONGUED-AND-GROOVED BOARDS

JOIST

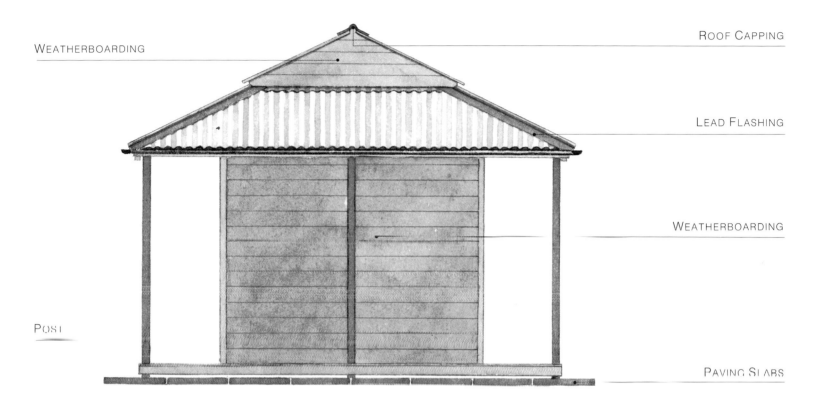

Weatherboarding

Roof Capping

Lead Flashing

Weatherboarding

Post

Paving Slabs

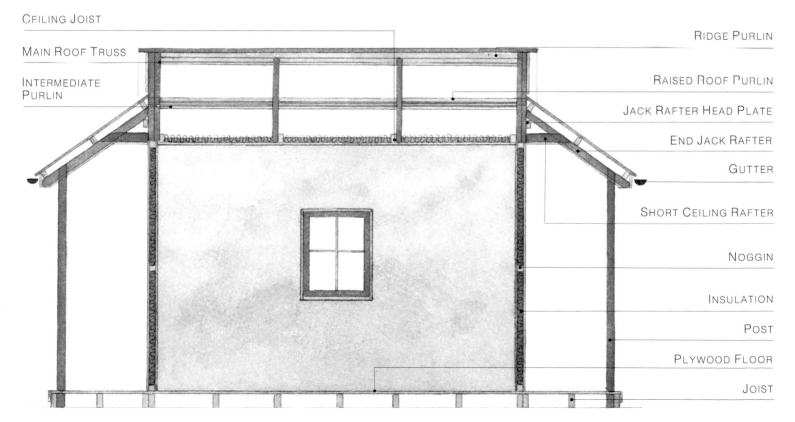

Ceiling Joist

Main Roof Truss

Intermediate
Purlin

Ridge Purlin

Raised Roof Purlin

Jack Rafter Head Plate

End Jack Rafter

Gutter

Short Ceiling Rafter

Noggin

Insulation

Post

Plywood Floor

Joist

Summer House: Foundation and Base

FACING BOARD

POST

WBP PLYWOOD FLOOR

TRIMMER

JOIST

PAVING SLAB (600 × 600 × 38mm)

HALF SLAB (600 × 300 × 38mm)

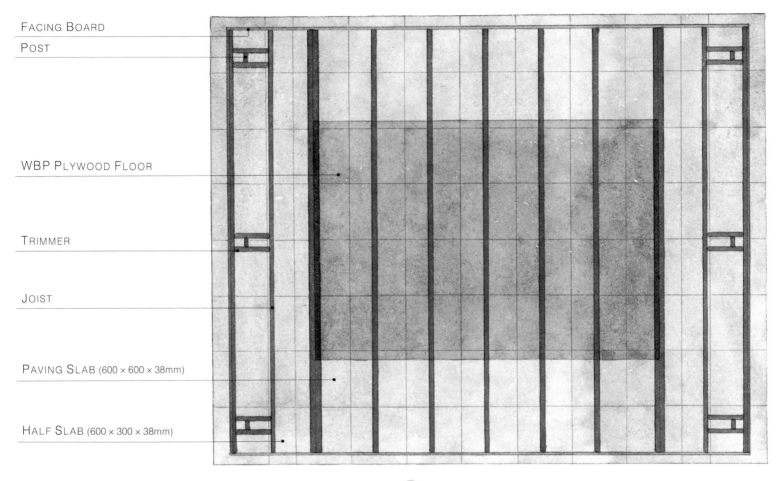

BASE ASSEMBLY

1 Setting Out Position of Base

**Use pegs and stringline to set out base outline. Two sizes of slabs are used –
600 × 600mm (24 × 24in) and 600 × 300mm (24 × 12in) – to ensure joists are
supported centrally while leaving a narrow border around house perimeter.**

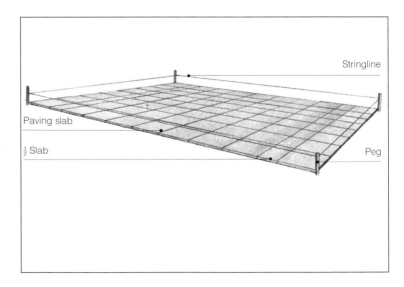

Stringline

Paving slab

½ Slab

Peg

FOUNDATION AND BASE

Set out the site to be covered by the complete base using four corner pegs and a string line (fig 1). Choose a sheltered part of the garden: this will minimize the risk of structural damage in storms and high winds. The summer house is not anchored to the ground, so you must site it with care.

Avoid sloping terrain as this would need a lot of excavation work for a level base to be laid.

The base can be laid using either paving slabs or concrete. If you choose slabs, then you will need 72 slabs measuring 600 × 600 × 38mm (24 × 24 × 1½in). You will also need 10 half-size slabs (600 × 300mm [24 × 12in]). These are required so that a narrow border remains around the walls while the joists rest centrally on the slabs (Foundation and Base illustration, opposite).

The slabs should be laid on a 1:5 mix of cement to sharp sand. You need to build in a slope of 1 in 60 from front to back to ensure that rainwater drains away and does not lie alongside the joists and cause them to rot away.

Alternatively, if you use concrete you will have to dig out about 125mm (5in) of soil and lay a foundation of well-compacted hardcore covered with a 50mm (2in) layer of concrete mixed from one part cement to five parts ballast.

You will have to set up a form-work (wooden frame) of timbers to retain the concrete, again having first pegged out the site. The form work timbers should be held in place using stakes driven into the ground. Old floorboards, or similar, are ideal as formwork. Do not forget to build in a slight fall in the formwork from front to back.

When the base is completed you can lay out the joists. Use 100 × 50mm (4 × 2in) sawn timber for the floor joists, making sure that it has been thoroughly treated with preservative. Ideally, pressure-impregnated timber should be used. There are 13 joists in all, with a double row being used to support the end walls. The outer joists support the veranda floor at each end.

Each joist should be laid on a strip of bituminous felt to serve as a damp-proof membrane and to prevent moisture seeping up through the base. Since the base has a slight fall built into it from front to back, you will need to lay small packing pieces about every 600mm (24in) under each joist to bring it level. This is important since you want to have a level floor.

Next, lay the summer house floor (fig 3). This is 19mm (¾in) WRP (weather- and boil-proof) grade plywood and the area is nominally 3.6 × 2.4m (12 × 8ft). The sheets should be fixed to the joists using 38mm (1½in) No 8 screws at 400mm (16in) centres around the edge. Fix the middle sheet first and then a sheet either side, cut to fit as needed. Next lay 50 × 19mm (2 × ¾in) packing strips of plywood on which the front and back walls will sit.

The end joists, which will support the veranda floor, can be removed temporarily since they will be a hazard during construction.

② Setting Out and Levelling Floor Joists

Timber joists are laid down at 600mm (24in) centres. A double row is needed to support the end walls. Since the slabs are laid to a slight fall, packing pieces are needed below the joists to level them.

③ Laying the Plywood Floor

The floor is formed from 19mm (¾in) thick WBP plywood screwed to the floor joists using 38mm No 8 screws. Lay the middle panel first and then one other panel on each side.

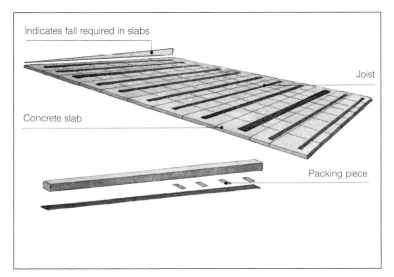

Indicates fall required in slabs

Joist

Concrete slab

Packing piece

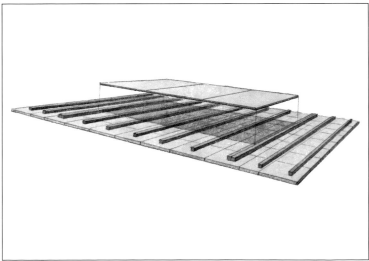

SUMMER HOUSE: WALL ASSEMBLY

WALLS

The inner faces of the walls are made from 12mm ($\frac{1}{2}$in) WBP plywood. Cut out the pieces needed for each of the four walls. The window openings, front and back, are about 700 × 600mm ($27\frac{1}{2}$ × $23\frac{1}{2}$in) and the doorway is about 2000 × 810mm (78 × 32in). If you intend to buy the door ready-made then tailor the door opening to the required size – remember to allow for the dimensions of the door frame reveal.

Taking each wall by turn, lay out the 50 × 50mm (2 × 2in) studding at the centres shown (fig 1). Note also that the short horizontal noggins are intentionally slightly misaligned in order to stagger the screw fixings in the panels.

Lay the plywood panels on the studding with the inside surface uppermost – these will form the internal walls of the house (fig 2). Use 38mm ($1\frac{1}{2}$in) No 8 screws to fix the panels to the studs at 400mm (16in) intervals. Countersink and fill all of the screw heads.

The door and window openings are all framed with 50 × 25mm (2 × 1in) trimmers skew nailed to the studs using 50mm (2in) nails (*see* **Techniques, page 241**).

The walls are joined together using 125mm (5in) long 12mm ($\frac{1}{2}$in) diameter bolts. If you position all four walls (fig 3) using a helper and temporary supporting struts, you can drill bolt holes at the corners through adjoining vertical studs. Cramp each corner before drilling the holes and fixing the bolts, leaving a little 'play' at this stage for final adjustment of the four walls. Four bolts are needed at each corner at the approximate positions indicated (fig 1, centre). The order of assembly is to offer up the front wall to one end wall and bolt together; then bolt the back wall to the other end wall; finally, bolt the two remaining corners together.

When all the walls have been joined and are square, the sole plates of each wall (fig 2, top) can be nailed to the joists using 100mm (4in) nails at approximately 400m (16in) centres.

① Assembling Framework for each Wall
The illustrations show the arrangement of the 50 × 50mm (2 × 2in) studding for each of the four walls. *Top* **Front frame with allowance for the door and windows.** *Centre* **Rear frame with a window opening.** *Bottom* **Solid end walls.**

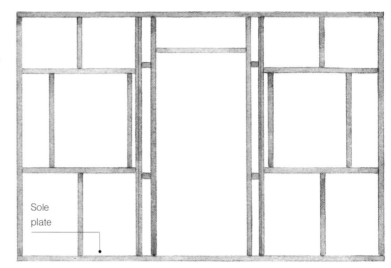

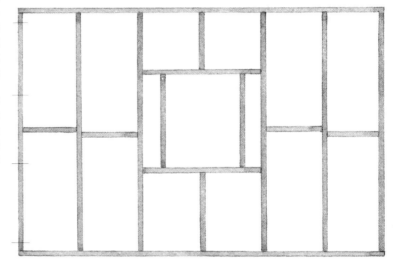

Sole plate

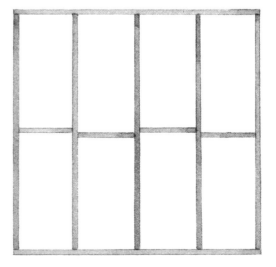

WALL FRAME ASSEMBLY

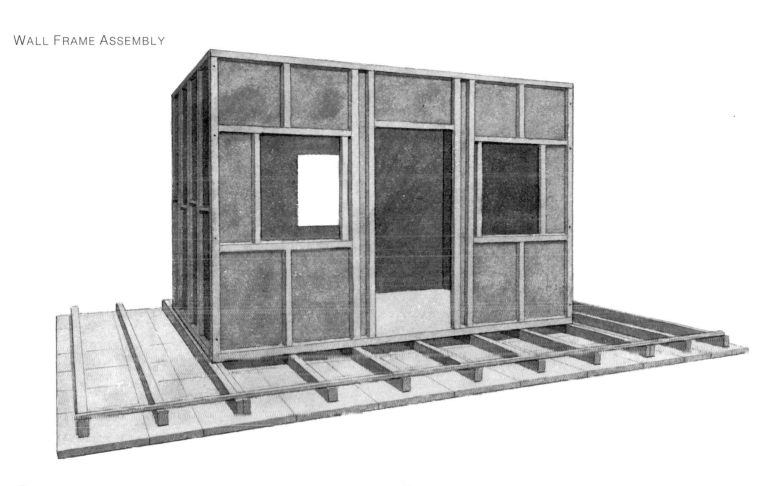

② Adding Inner Walls to Frames
The inner walls are formed from 12mm ($\frac{1}{2}$in) thick plywood. The front wall is made from five pieces with cut-outs for the windows in the side sections. The sheets are fixed to the frame using 38mm No 8 screws.

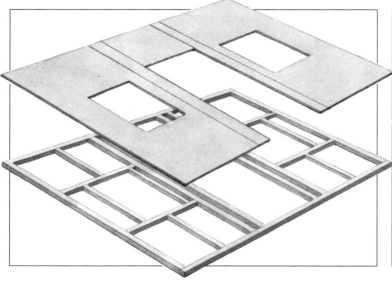

③ Joining the Four Frames Together
Each studding framework is joined together using 125mm (5in) long bolts. Using a helper, supporting struts and cramps, keep the frames aligned at the corners. Drill holes for four bolts at each corner and bolt together.

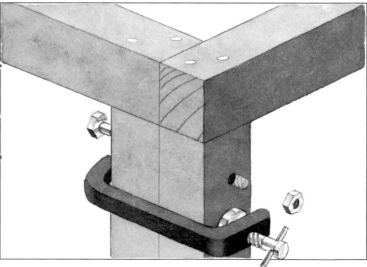

Summer House: Roof Assembly

Layout of Roof Timbers

Wall Plate Purlin

Main Roof Truss

Intermediate Purlin

Short Ceiling Joist

Ridge Purlin

Purlin

Raised Roof Purlin

End Jack Rafter

Ceiling Joist

Hip Board

Eaves Purlin

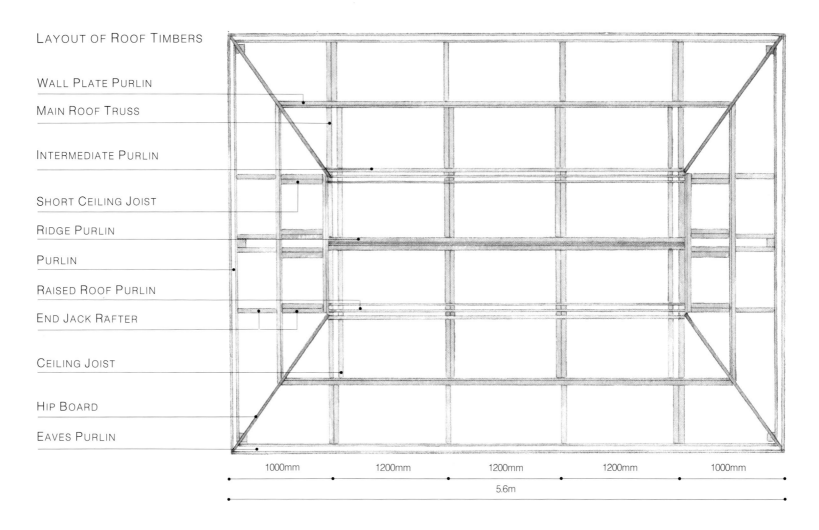

1000mm 1200mm 1200mm 1200mm 1000mm

5.6m

Section across Length of Roof

Main Roof Truss

Jack Rafter Head Plate

Short Ceiling Rafter

Post

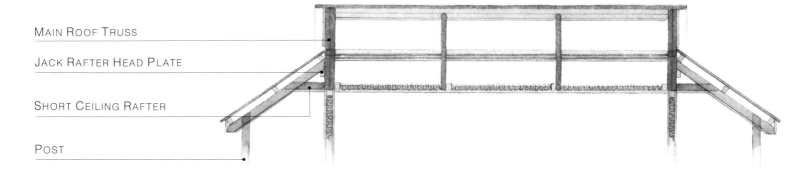

ROOF

The striking, veranda-covering roof of this summer house is a fundamental part of its design. It consists of a pitched roof clad with sheets of corrugated steel and with a 'hip' at either end projecting out to cover the sides of the veranda. It is quite complicated, so it is strongly recommended that you spend a little while studying the plans, and then tackle the construction one step at a time as described here. The positions of the rafters and purlins will become much clearer as you start to fix the pieces together.

MAIN TRUSSES

Start by making the four main roof trusses. Each truss, a triangular-shaped frame mitred at the top, is made from two 75 × 50mm (3 × 2in) angled rafters each about 2.6m (8ft 8in) long (allowing for them being overlength), reinforced with a triangular plywood gusset at the top, and braced with a ceiling joist at the appropriate level.

The rafters are cut at an angle at the top, butted together and held at the correct angle by being nailed to a 12mm (½in) thick triangular plywood gusset. Each triangular plywood gusset is pitched at 26 degrees, and this controls the angle of all the rafters. The rafters are prevented from spreading by the ceiling joists which are bolted to them towards the bases of the rafters.

All the main trusses are the same, except that the two end trusses have double rafters, formed by bolting pairs of rafters together using 12mm (½in) coach bolts with steel timber connectors on the bolts sandwiched between the two timbers. Similar sized bolts and steel timber connectors are used to bolt the ceiling joists to the rafters.

Ensure that the four main trusses are cut and nailed at the same angle: nail up the first truss on a flat surface, and use this truss as a template for nailing subsequent trusses.

Make all the rafters about 200mm (8in) overlength; they can then be cut to the correct length after fixing. Nail the top firrings in place.

FIXING MAIN TRUSSES

Lift the main trusses on to the walls, spacing them approximately 1200mm (48in) apart. Do not forget to position the double rafter trusses at each end. Make sure that all the trusses are square and vertical, and then nail them down to the head plates of the front and back walls, using 150mm (6in) round head nails which should be skew nailed into the head plates (*see* **Techniques, page 241**).

Temporarily hold the trusses in place so that they are vertical: nail long battens diagonally across the rafters to act as bracing (fig 1, below). Position the battens carefully so that there is enough room to fix the purlins at the ridge, wall plate and eaves levels.

FIXING PURLINS

Cut and fix the ridge purlins (horizontal timbers) in place. These are the same overall length as the front and back wall structure and are fixed to the firrings on either side of the apexes of the main trusses.

Cut the eaves purlins (positioned at the front and back to support the outermost edges of the pitched roof covering) 2.5m (8ft 2in) overlength to give an overhang of 1250mm (49in) at each end (fig 2). Fix in place by nailing into rafters.

Next cut the front and back wall plate purlins (the ones above the eaves purlins), approximately 650mm (25½in) overlength at each end to allow for trimming later. Nail in place on the rafters (fig 3). Remove the diagonal bracing and cut and fix the two intermediate purlins (one each side) midway between the ridge and wall plate purlins. These butt up against the ends of the firring pieces, which should now be cut to length. The intermediate purlins are about 300mm (12in) overlength each end for cutting back at an angle later.

MAKING THE RAISED ROOF SECTION

The firrings act as packing over the rafters. Fit a second purlin close to the lower end of the firring pieces to form the raised roof section.

1 Construction of Main Roof Trusses

Each truss is formed by nailing it to a pre-cut 12mm (½in) thick plywood gusset pitched at 26 degrees, and then braced by a ceiling joist. End trusses have double rafters. After positioning, rafters are braced by the purlins.

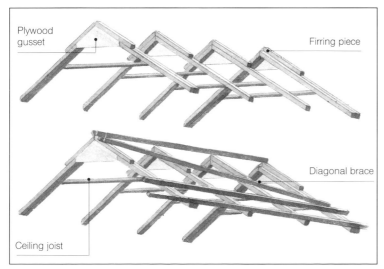

- Plywood gusset
- Firring piece
- Diagonal brace
- Ceiling joist

2 Fixing the Purlins to the Roof Trusses

With trusses spaced along the head plates on the walls, and held upright by temporary diagonal braces, cut and nail the ridge purlins in place. Note that eaves, wall plate and intermediate purlins are left temporarily overlength.

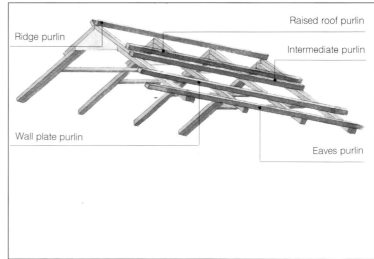

- Ridge purlin
- Raised roof purlin
- Intermediate purlin
- Wall plate purlin
- Eaves purlin

SUMMER HOUSE: HIP ROOF ASSEMBLY

SETTING OUT HIP ROOF AT EACH END

Measure 1000mm (39in) along the top outer edge of the eaves purlin, measuring from the outer face of the outside truss. Tack a line from this point (string will do) to where the end lean-to roof meets the end truss. This should form a roof pitch at the ends of about 36 degrees. Make up a triangle of plywood or scrap battening to this angle and use it to check the roof pitch during all stages of construction (fig 2).

Tie another string line from the top of the first eaves purlin (1000mm [39in] from the face of the end truss) to the top of the corresponding eaves purlin on the opposite side (1000mm [39in] out from the end truss). From this point, take another string line up to where the end lean-to roof meets the end truss. With these string lines in place, 1000mm (39in) out from the end truss, the general arrangement of the roof hips and pitch down to eaves level on the lean-to roofs at each end of the building will become apparent.

Cut the end jack rafters (four at each end) overlength, and also the short ceiling joists for the ends (again, four at each corner). Both are cut from 75 × 50mm (3 × 2in) sawn timber (fig 6).

Cut the jack rafter head plates (which support the jack rafters against the end trusses). Nail or bolt these to the end trusses as shown (fig 3), and after fixing trim the ends of the head plates to the slope of the main roof rafters.

Use an adjustable sliding bevel to set the angle required for the ends of the jack rafters where they butt against the end trusses, and trim the ends of the jack rafters to this angle. On the underside of each rafter cut a birdsmouth (notch) so that the rafter will sit neatly on the head plate. The eaves ends are left overlength for the time being.

Nail the four jack rafters and the four short ceiling joists in place at each end. Check that the top of the rafters are aligned and slope in line with the previously fixed string guidelines. Make sure that the undersides of the short ceiling joists

are horizontal and are in line with the undersides of the ceiling joists at the front and back of the building.

Note that in the centre of the ends there are two rafters fixed 75mm (3in) apart (fig 4). Later these will be bolted to the central veranda support post.

Cut the 150 × 25mm (6 × 1in) hip boards (rafters) overlength and hold them as close to their final position as possible so that the correct angles can be marked on the ends of the front and rear purlins which rest against the hip boards and which are now cut to length. Again, an adjustable sliding bevel is used to mark these angled cuts, which are angled in two directions to ensure that the ends of the purlins fit tightly against the hip boards when these are fixed in place.

At the top, the hip board is notched to fit over the jack rafter head plate (fig 3), and the end of the hip board is angled so that the hip board fits tightly against the main end truss. This angle needs careful marking with an adjustable sliding bevel to ensure an accurate

fit, particularly of the support notch at the top end. The top surface of each hip board should be lined up with the top of the purlins.

The hip boards can now be fitted and held in place by nailing to the ends of the front and rear purlins.

Next, cut and fasten by nailing the three 75 × 50mm (3 × 2in) purlins on the lean-to roofs at the ends of the building. They must be cut to length and angled so that they butt tightly against the hip boards at the ends, and align at the corner hips with the front and back purlins.

Cut and fit the 75 × 75mm (3 × 3in) veranda support posts in the middle of the end sections to fit between the concrete base and the twin central jack rafters. The base of each post should sit on a small piece of lead, which seals the end grain very effectively. Using timber connector plates and 12mm ($\frac{1}{2}$in) diameter coach bolts, drill and bolt to the floor joists at the base and between the twin jack rafters at the top. Leave overlength for the time being, and later trim flush, angled with the tops of the purlins.

---

1 **Cross-section of the Width Showing the Raised Roof Section**
Note how the firring pieces lift the ridge and raised roof purlins to create the raised roof section. Also look at the eaves area and note how the truss ends are trimmed vertically, level with the front top edge of the eaves purlin, to give a plumb fixing for the fascia board to which the gutters are fixed.

2 **Trimming the Rafter Ends**
Sliding bevel marks rafter ends (shown without eaves purlin). Use a template to check roof pitch.

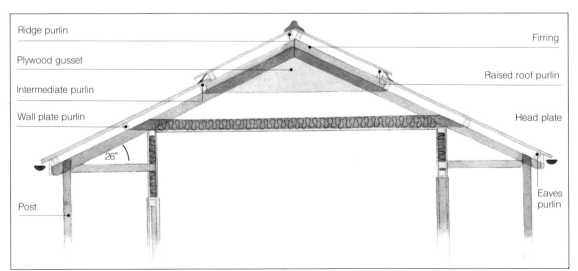

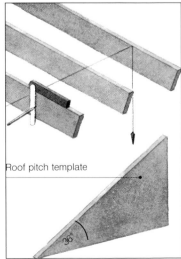

HIP ROOF ASSEMBLY

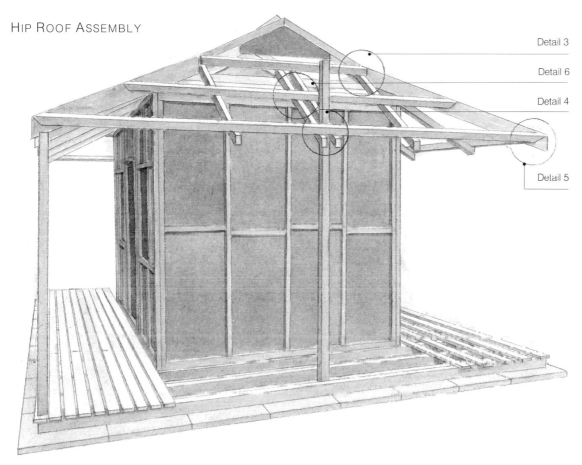

Detail 3

Detail 6

Detail 4

Detail 5

The 75 × 75mm (3 × 3in) corner veranda support posts fit between the concrete base and the top sides of the hip boards. Allow 25–30mm (1–1¼in) clearance from the eaves purlins. The undersides of the hip boards are notched to take posts, and the top ends of the posts are cut out with matching notches which allow them to be bolted to the hip boards (fig 5). Cut the post tops to the same angles as the roof pitches and to the level of the purlins.

FITTING FASCIA BOARDS

Use a sliding bevel to mark the rafter ends with a vertical line where they will be trimmed. When the fascia boards are fixed on to the rafter ends they will be upright, allowing gutters to be fitted. Trim the rafters in line with the top of the eaves purlin. The bottoms of the rafter ends are trimmed level with the bottom of the fascia boards, either before or after the fascias are fixed. Also trim the ends of the hip boards to take the fascia boards.

Cut the fascia boards from 150 × 25mm (6 × 1in) sawn timber.

---

3 Hip Board/Head Plate Join
Notch hip board to fit over jack rafter head plate. Angle board end to fit against truss. Purlins fit against hip.

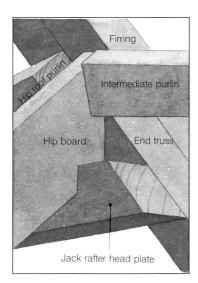

4 Intermediate Veranda Support Post
Posts bolt between central jack rafters. Saw tops level with purlins.

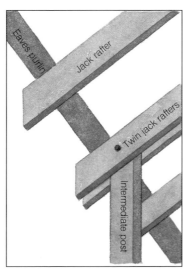

5 Corner Post/Hip Board Join
Notch hip boards for corner posts, which are slotted to fit over hips. Bolt and trim tops to roof slope.

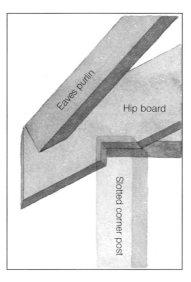

6 Jack Rafters/Ceiling Joists
Underside view of the jack rafters nailed to short ceiling joists. Tops of rafters must align.

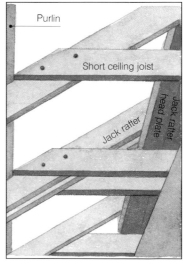

Summer House: Roof and Detailing

Fitting Corrugated Metal Roof

You can buy corrugated metal sheets cut to any size. Fix the lower sections first by nailing through the peaks of the corrugations into the purlins and screwing through the valleys using special self-sealing screws. Make sure that adjacent sheets overlap by at least two corrugations on each side of the panels.

Fix a lead flashing along the lower purlin of the raised roof sections and press the lead down on to the lower roof sheets using a roller. Apply a similar strip of flashing from the main end trusses on to the end lean-to roof sheets (fig 1). Nail 12mm ($\frac{1}{2}$in) feather-edge boards to the end trusses to form gable ends (*see* **Techniques, page 251**).

Finally, fix the raised-roof corrugated sheets, screwing and nailing (as above) into the firring pieces. Adjacent sheets must overlap at least two corrugations on both sides of each panel. Fit and fasten metal capping pieces to the ridge and hips of the hip roof sections.

① Lower Roof Flashing
Lay lead flashing along the lower raised roof purlin; roll the flashing on to the lower roof sheets.

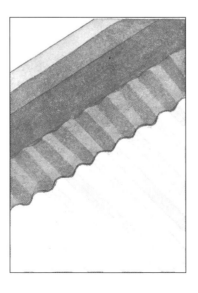

Detailing

With the main walls constructed and the roof in place, the final detailing jobs can be completed.

Between the wall studs on all four walls, fit 50mm (2in) thick Rockwool wall batts for insulation (fig 4). The material is semi-rigid and, if necessary, can be held in place by tapping panel pins into the studs in much the same way that glass is held in a window frame.

The window and door frame reveals are then cut to length from 125 × 25mm (5 × 1in) PAR (planed all round) softwood and temporarily screwed in place (figs 2 and 3). Make up the window frames from 50 × 50mm (2 × 2in) timber screwed together, and then nail through the outsides of the frames to fix the glazing 'bars (these are stocked by timber merchants). Screw the frames into the reveals.

The weatherboarding can now be nailed in place on each wall, starting at the base and working upwards (fig 4). Cut the boarding to fit neatly around the window and door frames (*see* **Techniques, page 251**).

Cut and nail in place the 150 × 25mm (6 × 1in) fascia boards to the eaves and the 50 × 50mm (2 × 2in) rafter ties.

Closing battens are needed at the four corners of the summer house to close off the end grain of the weatherboards. The battens should be cut to length and fixed temporarily in place.

Having checked everything over you can now start to decorate. Remove the closing battens while the weatherboards are treated with exterior grade preservative, stain or paint, then paint the battens in a contrasting colour before nailing them back in place.

The door and window frames can now be painted, along with the roof and fascia board.

Now fix the guttering, giving it a slight fall towards each corner, where a small hole should be cut. Fix a chain through each outlet and run it down to the ground to channel rain water into a soakaway. Alternatively, you could fit a combined stopend and downpipe outlet at each corner of the guttering; however, this will mean that you will not be able to run the chains down to the ground at the exact corners of the summer house – to the detriment of the overall design.

It the external joists were temporarily removed while the project was being built then relay them now on a strip of bituminous felt and fix them to the veranda support posts as described earlier (page 192).

The 'duckboard' floor of the veranda is now formed by screwing 75 × 25mm (3 × 1in) slats to the joists leaving 19mm ($\frac{3}{4}$in) spaces between them. Use 50mm (2in) long No 8 screws.

The window can now be glazed using 3mm ($\frac{1}{8}$in) glass held in place with glazing bars pinned to the frame. It is important that the glazing bars are fixed square to each other so that the glass will slot comfortably in place. Check each 'window' for square by measuring the diagonals, which should be equal. When ordering the glass, buy it 2–3mm (about $\frac{1}{8}$in) smaller than the window opening, both in width and height, to allow for normal expansion.

If you prefer, you can buy a ready-made ledged and braced door; alternatively, you can make one using tongued-and-grooved board ing with 100 × 25mm (4 × 1in) timber for the ledges (cross rails) and braces (diagonals). The door can be full-length or a stable door as here. If you choose the latter, you simply make the two smaller doors with a lower ledge for each one. In a full-length door, only one central ledge is needed.

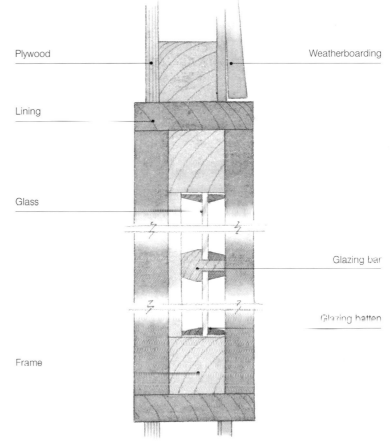

Plywood — Weatherboarding
Lining
Glass
— Glazing bar
— Glazing batten
Frame

2 Fixing the Door Head
Screw door lining to the studwork, with 25 × 12mm (1 × $\frac{1}{2}$in) doorstops nailed to sides and top of frame.

3 Window Frame Assembly
Above The top and bottom sections of the frame are fixed to the 125 × 25mm (5 × 1in) linings.

4 Fixing Weatherboarding
Below Exterior walls are formed from overlapping boards nailed to the studwork; work from bottom up.

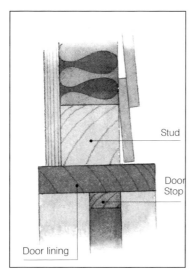

Stud
Door Stop
Door lining

Summer House: Detailing

A ledged and braced door is made by simply nailing the boards to the ledges and braces. It is constructed by laying the top and bottom ledges on a flat surface and then screwing the tongued-and-grooved boards to them (see **Techniques, page 251**). The boards should overlap the ledges by about 25mm (1in) at either end.

The diagonal brace is then fitted by notching it into the ledges and, again, screwing through the door and into the brace. The purpose of the brace is to transmit the weight to the hinges and so prevent the door from sagging. It is important that the braces are fixed the right way round as shown (fig 1).

Use two butt hinges to hang each door. These are fixed to the end grain of the ledges. If you make a framed door then also use butt hinges: two 75mm (3in) sizes for each half of a stable door, or three for a full-length door.

Next, fit the 25 × 12mm (1 × $\frac{1}{2}$in) door stops – two vertical pieces and a horizontal top piece – to the door reveal (fig 2, page 195). These stops must be positioned accurately: hold the door in place and mark the positions of the stops immediately inside its closed position. This ensures that the stops are fitted accurately. Here, they are positioned about 25mm (1in) back from the front of the door reveal.

Complete the interior by cladding the ceiling using tongued-and-grooved boards, not forgetting to insert Rockwool insulating batts between the joists (fig 2), held in place by panel pins as with the walls. The walls can be decorated according to your requirements using exterior paint, varnish stain, or microporous paint.

Finally, at each corner, dig a 300 × 300 × 300mm (12 × 12 × 12in) soakaway hole and fill with shingle or pebbles (fig 3). Bed the ends of the chains into them so that they are held tautly in place.

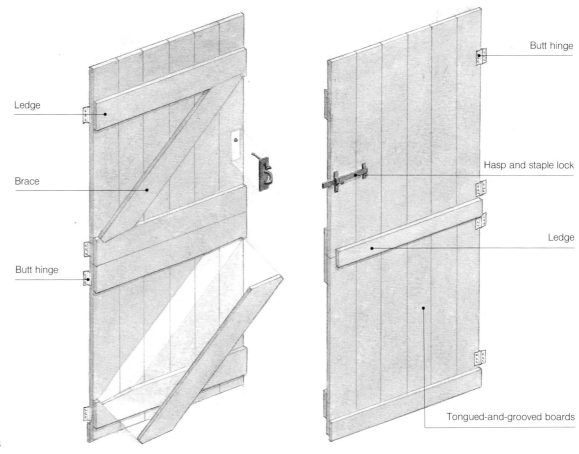

Ledge

Brace

Butt hinge

Butt hinge

Hasp and staple lock

Ledge

Tongued-and-grooved boards

① Door Assembly
Above **The ledged and braced door can either be a stable door (as shown) or a single unit.**

② Insulating the Ceiling
Clad the ceiling with tongued-and-grooved boards, and place insulating batts between the joists.

③ Making the Soakaways
A chain conducts rainwater from the gutters to a soakaway – a hole filled with shingle or pebbles.

DEN ... GAZEBO ... HIDEAWAY ... CHALET ... SHANTY ... BOTHY ... HUNTING BOX ... CROFT ... PAD ... OUTHOUSE .

SHACK ... PLAY HOUSE ... SNUG ... CABIN ... SHED ... BOLT HOLE ... STUDIO ... PAVILION ... LODGE ... RETREAT ...

POTTING SHED ... HUT ... SANCTUARY ... HIDEY-HOLE ... CUBBYHOLE ... HAVEN ... GARDEN ROOM ..

Summer House

A Change of Scenery

In a secluded part of the garden, the summer house can be used as a simple retreat. The interior is large enough to function as a tool room and potting shed (right) or as a cosy study or home office (opposite).

CLIMBING FRAME

Slide, swing, climbing frame, sandpit and make-believe house – this play structure will be the focus of hours of fun outside. A particular advantage of this structure is its adaptability. You can tailor the size of the frame to suit the amount of space at your disposal; you can vary the width or spacing of the bars; or go on to create a Meccano-like warren of interconnecting structures following the same basic theme. There is one proviso: the poles should not be required to span a greater distance than about 1.5m (5ft), otherwise they might crack.

Construction depends on a simple system of upright posts and poles. The poles are slotted through holes drilled in the posts and secured by screws at the side; probably the most difficult part of the making is ensuring that the holes are drilled accurately. The sandbox consists of overlapping boards at the sides; the 'roof', made of sheets of exterior-grade plywood, has the double purpose of helping to keep the sand dry in rainy weather and giving a suggestion of a play house. The slide platform and slide are also simple to make.

A key safety consideration is ensuring that the entire structure is anchored securely to the ground. There are various ways of achieving this, but one of the most straightforward is to use a post-hole borer to remove the earth and then to concrete the posts firmly in place. Round over the concrete to encourage rainwater to drain away from the posts. And because the frame will be left outdoors in all weathers, it is important to buy pressure-treated wood (treated pine is ideal) and to coat it thoroughly with preservative to prolong its life.

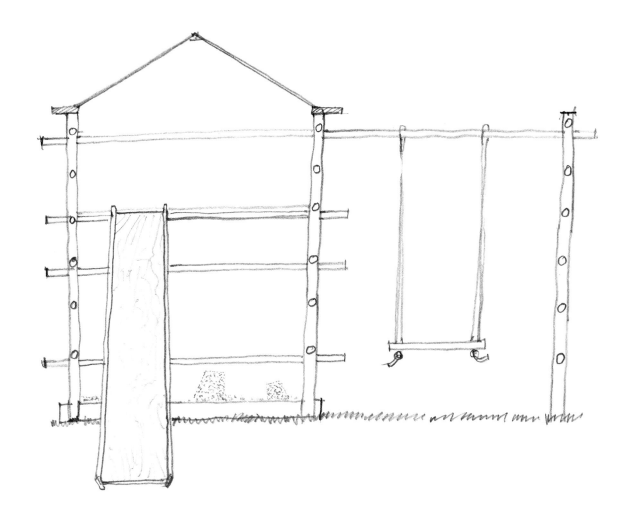

CLIMBING FRAME ASSEMBLY

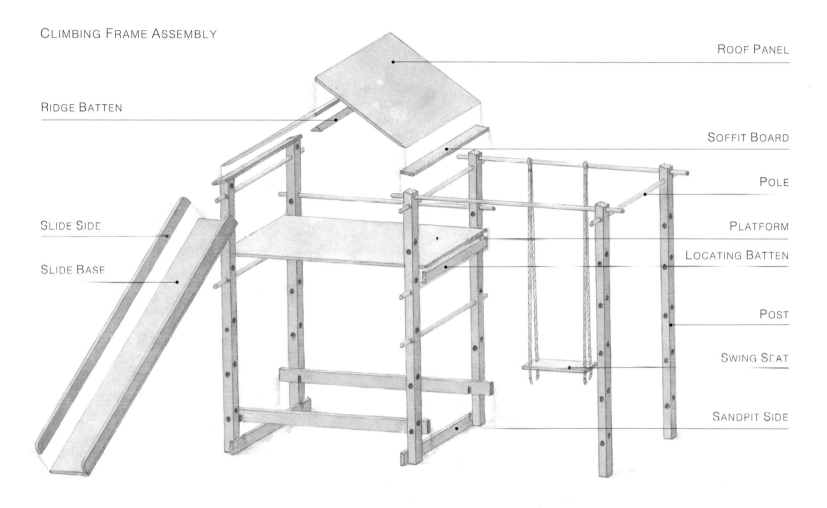

RIDGE BATTEN

SLIDE SIDE

SLIDE BASE

ROOF PANEL

SOFFIT BOARD

POLE

PLATFORM

LOCATING BATTEN

POST

SWING SEAT

SANDPIT SIDE

The design of this climbing frame encompasses something for children aged between about two and seven, so that more than one child in a family can play on it at the same time. For the very young there is a sandpit; the slide will keep older children occupied; and the 'house' created by the roof and platform above the sandpit will provide the perfect backdrop for hours of imaginative outdoor play.

The climbing frame *must* be made from pressure-treated timber and is finished with three or four coats of good-quality, exterior-grade clear varnish. The unpainted finish allows the structure to blend

sympathetically with the garden. Before starting work, steep the ends of the posts that will be below ground in good-quality wood preservative for 24 hours.

This climbing frame is intended for use solely in a garden, since it must be concreted into the ground for stability. It should be sited on a flat area of lawn free of obstacles or hazards; if the lawn is liable to dry out and become very hard in the summer, you should dig a pit around the bottom of the frame and fill it with wood chips or another impact-absorbent material sold specifically for use in playgrounds to reduce the risk of injury.

The framework consists of six posts with holes drilled at intervals down their length through which horizontal poles, 35mm (1¼in) in diameter, are slotted to form bars. The number of poles used is optional and their arrangement can be varied quickly and easily since each pole is held in place to the posts with 'locking' screws. These screws can be taken out at any time to release a pole. When poles are repositioned, it is essential always to replace the screws and tighten them. It is not necessary to use poles in every hole – gaps can be left according to the sizes and needs of the children using the frame.

The play platform, constructed from solid 18mm (¾in) plywood is secured to its platform with locating battens and turnbuckles.

The removable slide is located on to a supporting pole with two turnbuckles. It can then be taken down and stored when not required for long periods of time.

The swing should be suspended from the highest pole, with poles at the front and back of the swing omitted to allow unhindered movement. The height of the seat above the ground is determined by the age of the children for which it is intended and, subsequently, by the lengths of rope used.

CLIMBING FRAME

TOOLS

TRY SQUARE

STEEL RULE

SLIDING BEVEL

POWER DRILL and drill bits

FLAT BIT or EXPANSIVE BIT

COUNTERSINK BIT

DRILL STAND

POWER PLANE (for chamfering)

POST-HOLE BORER or
NARROW SPADE

SPIRIT LEVEL

SMOOTHING PLANE (hand or
power)

ROUTER and ROUNDING-OVER
BIT

POWER FINISHING SANDER (or
hand-sanding block)

CONSTRUCTION

The construction of the frame is straightforward, the most arduous part being the digging of the holes for the six supporting posts. This can be done using a narrow spade, but a post-hole borer – a large, corkscrew-like tool obtainable from a hire shop – makes the task much easier. It is twisted back and forth to make the hole and lifted out to deposit the waste earth.

CUTTING THE POSTS TO LENGTH

Cut the six posts to length: 2.45– 2.6m (7ft 6in–8ft) long, according to how high you intend the frame to be above ground. Remember that at least 750mm (30in) of each post should be sunk into the ground and concreted in place.

MARKING THE POSTS

Using a try square, draw a line on all four faces of each post, 750mm (30in) up from the bottom, to mark the earth-level once the posts are erected. On one face of the post, mark hole positions at 300mm (12in) intervals above the earth-level mark (fig 1). Make sure that each mark is centrally positioned.

On an adjacent face, mark the first hole 240mm (9½in) up from the earth-level mark. Then work up the post, marking off hole positions at 300mm (12in) intervals as before. This will ensure that the climbing bars are staggered on adjacent sides of the climbing frame (fig 2).

Mark the five remaining posts in the same way.

MAKING THE HOLES

Drill the holes through the posts using a 36mm (1⅜in) drill or an expansive bit. To ensure that each hole is at the centre of the post and is square to the verticals, use a drill stand or use a try square as a visual guide when drilling.

The holes for the locking screws are made in the faces of the posts adjacent to the pole holes. Each screw hole must align with the centre of each pole hole. Drill a countersunk clearance hole for a 37mm (1½in) No 10 woodscrew until the clearance hole meets the larger pole hole. Make sure all the locking screw holes are on what will be the inside faces of the posts.

ASSEMBLING THE FRAME

Cut 21 poles, 35mm (1¼in) in diameter and 1510mm (59⅝in) long; chamfer or round over the ends.

Assemble the posts and poles on site. At this stage, insert poles through the holes in the posts evenly all round the structure, even if you intend to omit or redistribute some later. Ensure that the locking screw holes are on the inside faces of the posts and position the poles so that they protrude by 75mm (3in) at each end of the posts.

With all the posts in position, insert the locking screws, driving each one half way through the poles to make the assembly rigid.

Mark out the six post positions accurately on the ground. Remove the frame and dig post holes about 100mm (4in) in diameter, using either a narrow spade or a post-hole borer. The holes should be 150mm

MATERIALS

Part	Quantity	Material	Length
POST	6	75 × 75mm (3 × 3in) PAR softwood	As required
POLE	21	35mm (1¼in) diameter dowelling	1510mm (59⅝in)
SOFFIT BOARD	2	100 × 25mm (4 × 1in) PAR softwood	1560mm (61½in)
ROOF PANEL	2	12mm (½in) WBP plywood	1560 × 800mm (61½ × 31½in)
RIDGE BATTEN	1	75 × 50mm (3 × 2in) PAR softwood	1560mm (61½in)
SLIDE BASE	1	12mm (½in) WBP plywood	2250 × 400mm (88½ × 15¾in)
SLIDE SIDE	2	75 × 25mm (3 × 1in) PAR softwood	2250mm (88½in)
PLATFORM	1	19mm (¾in) WBP plywood	1360 × 760mm (53½ × 30in)
LOCATING BATTEN	4	50 × 25mm (2 × 1in) PAR softwood	Cut to fit
TURNBUCKLE	6	Offcut of 12mm (½in) plywood	As required
SANDPIT SIDE	4	73 × 25mm (3 × 1in) PAR softwood	1400mm (55⅛in)
SWING SEAT	1	150 × 25mm (6 × 1in) PAR softwood	500mm (19¾in)

Also required: 25mm (1in) diameter rope, string and tape for swing; concrete for anchoring posts; 42 37mm (1½in)
No 10 woodscrews for 'locking' poles to posts

① Drilling the Posts
Mark ground level on each post and then mark off pole hole positions at intervals indicated.

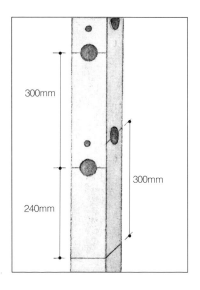

300mm

240mm

300mm

(6in) deeper than the length of post to be buried, so in this case they will need to be 900mm (36in) deep. Place a 150mm (6in) layer of well-compacted hardcore in the bottom of each hole for drainage, and to prevent the posts rotting.

Lift the framework into the holes. Check the assembly is level and plumb and that the marked lines are all at ground level. If necessary, remove the framework and adjust the hardcore as required.

Make up the concrete, using a mix of sand, aggregate and cement in the ratio 1:5:1. Wear gloves to avoid the risk of burns. Pour the ingredients on to the mixing area, and turn it over with a shovel until it is a uniform grey colour. Make a hole in the top of the pile and add a little water at a time.

Turn over the mix until the water is absorbed, then add more water and mix again to produce pliable concrete that is not too wet or sloppy.

Tip some of the concrete into a hole, add a few pieces of broken brick and tamp them down with a stick so that there are no air pockets

around the post. Fill the remaining 300mm (12in) of each hole with concrete, rounding it into a collar around the bases of the posts so that rainwater flows away.

Allow the concrete to set, then arrange the poles as required, inserting all the locking screws.

Saw all the post tops to a chamfer of 10 degrees, using a sliding bevel to mark off the angle accurately (fig 2). The two pairs of posts that will support the roof are chamfered in opposite directions to allow for the pitch of the roof (see **Climbing Frame Assembly, page 201**). The two uncovered end posts are also chamfered to drain rainwater.

FIXING THE ROOF

Cut the two soffit boards to size. Along the underside of each, cut a 6 × 6mm ($\frac{1}{4}$ × $\frac{1}{4}$in) drip groove, 10mm ($\frac{3}{8}$in) in from the edge. Screw each one down into the tops of the posts where the roof will be.

Plane the top edge of each roof panel to an angle of 53 degrees and plane the bottom edge to an angle of 37 degrees (fig 3). Use a sliding

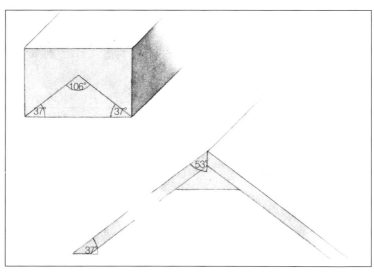

② Assembling the Poles

Round over the ends of the poles and feed them through the holes in the posts so that they protrude by a maximum of 75mm (3in) at each end. Note top of post is chamfered at 10 degrees.

③ Making the Roof

Above Angle ridge batten as marked so that it will fit in apex of roof. *Below* Angle apex end of roof panel at 53 degrees and other end at 37 degrees. Glue and screw roof panels to ridge batten at apex.

CLIMBING FRAME

bevel to mark the angles. Mark out and cut the ridge batten to corresponding angles (fig 3, page 203).

Fix the two roof panels at the apex by gluing and screwing down into the ridge batten. Use 25mm (1in) No 8 woodscrews at approximately 300mm (12in) centres.

Place the assembled roof on to the soffits, check for alignment, then secure it by screwing upwards through the soffits into the roof panel edges. Use 37mm (1½in) No 8 screws at approximately 300mm (12in) centres (fig 1).

SLIDE

Fix the sides to the base with waterproof, exterior adhesive and screw up through the base into the sides. Ensure that the edges are flush and use 37mm (1½in) No 8 countersunk screws at 400mm (16in) centres.

Round over all the edges and the corners of the sides at both ends.

The slide is anchored to the pole using battens and notched turnbuckles (fig 2). Cut two 50 × 25mm (2 × 1in) battens to the width of the

slide. Screw the battens to the slide base, one at the top and the second about 38mm (1½in) down from the bottom of the first, so that the battens snugly enclose the pole of the climbing frame to which the slide will be attached.

Insert two screws into the lower batten, with about 38mm (1½in) of the threaded shank protruding. Saw off the screwheads and smooth the jagged points of the sawn ends.

Make two turnbuckles from 12mm (½in) plywood, cutting a small notch towards the bottom of one side so that they can be locked in place around the screws using a butterfly nut on each. Screw the turnbuckles to the top batten as shown (fig 2), as tightly as possible, but remembering that they must pivot. This method of anchoring gives a safe, secure fastening, but allows the slide to be removed and packed away if required.

Fill the screw holes in the base. Sand it and the sides thoroughly to ensure there are no splinters, then apply several coats of exterior-grade varnish to all surfaces.

When anchoring the slide for use, it must not be any higher than the fourth pole up, otherwise the gradient will be too great. Place an impact-absorbent gym mat at the base, with the back edge held in place underneath the slide.

PLATFORM

The platform can be positioned across any opposite pairs of bars. If the slide is in use, then the platform must be positioned across bars corresponding to the slide level to provide a means of entrance.

Cut the 18mm (¾in) plywood to size. Glue and screw a 50 × 25mm (2 × 1in) locating batten to each of the shorter sides of the platform panel, flush with the edges. Use three 37mm (1½in) No 8 countersunk screws on each side. Sand the platform to remove splinters.

Cut out four turnbuckles, about 70 × 20mm (2¾ × ¾in) from 12mm (½in) plywood. Round over the ends and screw up into the underside of the locating battens, so that the turnbuckles pivot on the screws (fig 3). Varnish all surfaces.

(fig 3, page 203).

SANDPIT

Remove the turf from the area of the sandpit and simply lay down concrete paving slabs. Butt the edges closely together. If the lawn is uneven, level it with sand. Lay a sheet of thick polythene on top of the slabs so that no vegetation or insects creep into the sand.

Cut the sides of the sandpit to protrude 25mm (1in) beyond the posts at each end. Position each side piece against the inside face of two posts and mark off on the side where it meets the inner corner of the posts. Cut cross-halving joints on the longer side of these marks (fig 4). Round over the top edges. Screw the sides to the posts using two 37mm (1½in) No 8 countersunk screws at each end (fig 5).

If you want a greater depth of sand in the pit, either use wider boards or excavate the lawn to the required depth and use boards of sufficient width to rise 75mm (3in) above ground level. Fill the pit with special fine-grade sand available from toy centres.

---

1 Fitting the Soffit Board
Screw soffit board down into top of post; then screw through board up into bottom edge of roof panel.

2 Fitting the Slide
Screw battens to the underside of the slide base so they enclose the pole. Screw turnbuckles to the top batten so that they pivot across to enclose sawn-off screws in lower batten and are held in place using butterfly nuts.

3 Fitting the Platform
Glue and screw battens to edges of short side of platform. Add turnbuckles to hold platform in place.

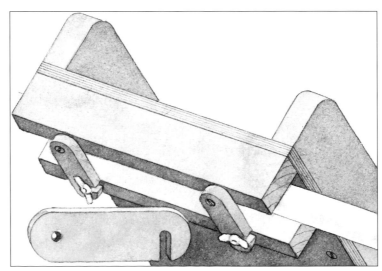

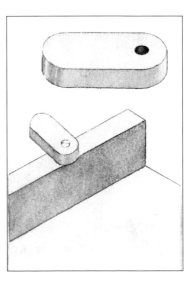

4 Making the Sandpit Sides
Mark the inside post corners on the sandpit sides and cut cross-halving joints to join the sides.

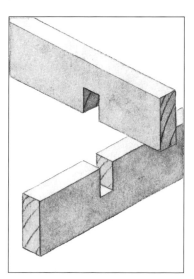

5 Fitting the Sandpit Sides
Screw the sandpit sides to the inside faces of the posts so that they protrude 25mm (1in).

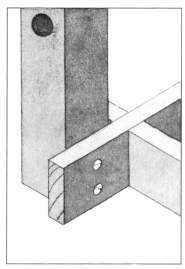

6 Adding a Swing
Feed rope through holes in swing seat and knot tightly beneath. Make loop at top for pole to feed through.

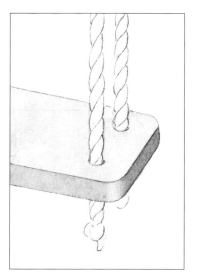

SWING

Drill two holes at either end to take 25mm (1in) diameter rope. Round off the corners and sand the seat smooth. Thread the rope through each pair of holes and tightly knot each end. Wind string at the top to form a loop and knot it firmly.

Feed one end of the pole through the post at the highest position, through the rope loops, and through the opposite post. Centre the swing between the posts, mark the rope positions, and remove the pole. Cut shallow V-shapes in the top of the pole at the rope positions, then feed it back in place. Insert the locking screws, position the ropes in the grooves and screw or nail them in place. Varnish the seat.

If you prefer, you could suspend a tyre from the rope instead.

COLD FRAME

If you cannot afford a greenhouse, a cold frame is the next best thing. Most important for raising seedlings or growing early vegetables, it can also be used to provide salad ingredients such as lamb's lettuce, broquette or treviso all through the winter: a year-round usage which makes it an invaluable addition to any garden. If you do have a greenhouse, a cold frame can be used to harden off bedding plants raised in the greenhouse and as a place for overwintering tender biennials.

The design of this cold frame varies little from the traditional version which is such a common garden sight. Extremely versatile and very simple to make, the wooden base is treated with exterior-grade preservative, contrasting with the crisp, white painted 'light' or glazed lid. An important feature of the design is the ability to remove the entire light so that there is free access to the area of ground covered by the cold frame, enabling it to be dug over and planted easily.

Cold frames should be sited in south-facing positions where they will receive maximum sunlight, but, because they are usually portable, the position can be varied from year to year. If there is a danger of scorching at the height of summer, the glass may need to be coated with white 'obscuring paint'.

Unlike traditional cloches or glass bell-jars, a cold frame can be made simply and economically to provide a versatile extension of the growing season.

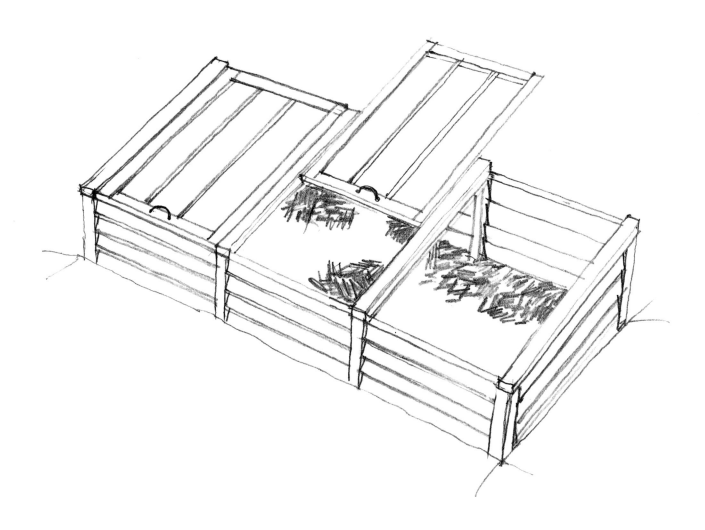

COLD FRAME

TOOLS

WORKBENCH (fixed or portable)

STEEL MEASURING TAPE

STEEL RULE

TRY SQUARE (or combination square)

PANEL SAW (or circular power saw)

TENON SAW

MARKING GAUGE

POWER DRILL

DRILL BIT – approximately 3mm ($\frac{1}{8}$in) diameter

COUNTERSINK BIT

SCREWDRIVER

CLAW HAMMER

NAIL PUNCH

PINCERS

CHISEL – about 25mm (1in)

MALLET

SASH CRAMPS (or folding wedges)

MATERIALS

Quantities are for the three-bay frame illustrated

Part	Quantity	Material	Length
FRAME STRUCTURE			
BOTTOM RAILS	4	50 × 50mm (2 × 2in) sawn and treated softwood	1220mm (48in)*
FRONT POSTS	4	As above	270mm (10$\frac{1}{2}$in)*
BACK POSTS	4	As above	400mm (16in)*
TOP RAILS	4	As above	1230mm (48$\frac{1}{2}$in)*
TOP SUPPORT BATTENS	6	25 × 25mm (1 × 1in) PAR softwood	1230mm (48$\frac{1}{2}$in)
FRONT FIXING BATTENS	6	As above	330mm (13in)*
BACK FIXING BATTENS	6	As above	460mm (18in)*
FRONT & BACK CLADDING	As required	6 × 19 × 150mm ($\frac{1}{4} \times \frac{3}{4} \times$ 6in) feather-edge boarding	Width of glazing frame plus clearance
END CLADDING	As required	As above	1120mm (44in)
GLAZED LIGHTS			
SIDE RAILS	6	50 × 38mm (2 × 1$\frac{1}{2}$in) PAR softwood	1270mm (50in)
TOP RAILS	3	As above	800mm (31$\frac{1}{2}$in)
BOTTOM RAILS	3	75 × 25mm (3 × 1in) PAR softwood	800mm (31$\frac{1}{2}$in)
CENTRAL GLAZING BARS	3	38 × 25mm (1$\frac{1}{2}$ × 1in) PAR softwood	1270mm (50in)
GLASS SUPPORT BATTENS – LONG	12	25 × 12mm (1 × $\frac{1}{2}$in) PAR softwood	1150mm (46in)*
GLASS SUPPORT BATTENS – SHORT	6	As above	400mm (16in)*
GLASS SHEETS	18	Approx. 425 × 400mm (17 × 16in) clear glass	

Also required: 3 D-handles; metal glass clips; mastic for bedding glass; sprigs for holding glass in place; glazed light supports; hinges (optional)

* Leave overlength and then cut to size after fixing – see text

A cold frame will be appreciated by all keen gardeners, whether their speciality is flowers, fruit or vegetables. The frame will be useful for seedlings, propagation and for growing tender and/or early plants.

Our frame has been developed from the tried and tested standard cold frame that has evolved over the years. The main frame is made from sawn and preservative-treated (tanalized) softwood, put together in a series of inset 'bays' clad with feather-edge boarding fixed between the main frames. This gives the frame a distinctive style and avoids the bland appearance of a conventional cold frame. However, you may prefer to run the cladding along the whole length of the frame, which is quicker and easier.

The size of the frame from front to back and end to end is optional and can be varied as you wish according to what you want to grow. Our frame is a good average size, being 370mm (14$\frac{1}{2}$in) high at the front, 500mm (20in) high at the back and 1220mm (48in) from front to back. The beauty of this design is that you can have a single section, or make a block of two, three or more. We have built a three-section frame, and quantities in the Materials chart are for a frame of this size.

The glazed lights in our design are loose, giving flexibility in use. You have the option of sliding them back a little way for ventilation, farther back to tend for plants within the frame, or they can be lifted at the front and propped open a little way for ventilation. Alternatively, they are easy to slide off, either from the front or the back, allowing them to be removed completely. However, you could glaze the lights with sheets of clear plastic, which is also a safer option if young children play in the garden. In this case, you would fix the lights at the back with hinges; you will need a 75 × 50mm (3 × 2in) timber rail along the back, level with the support battens.

COLD FRAME ASSEMBLY

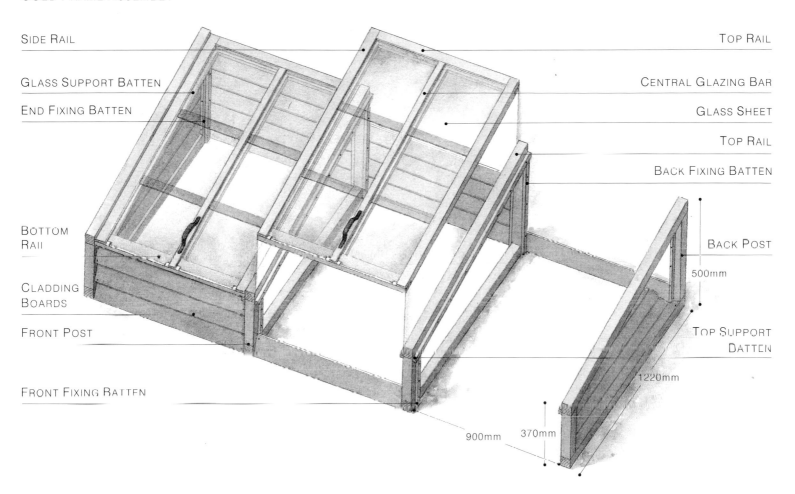

SIDE RAIL

GLASS SUPPORT BATTEN

END FIXING BATTEN

BOTTOM RAIL

CLADDING BOARDS

FRONT POST

FRONT FIXING BATTEN

TOP RAIL

CENTRAL GLAZING BAR

GLASS SHEET

TOP RAIL

BACK FIXING BATTEN

BACK POST

500mm

TOP SUPPORT BATTEN

1220mm

900mm   370mm

FRAME STRUCTURE

MAKING THE DIVIDERS

The ground frame structure is built around four dividers (if you are making a three-bay cold frame), and construction starts with these. Start by cutting out the four components of the dividers – the top and bottom rails, and the front and back posts – from 50 × 50mm (2 × 2in) sawn softwood all at least 50mm (2in) overlength.

Lay the bottom rail down and mark off its final length centrally on one side. Place the front and back posts in position alongside.

Mark off the final heights of the front and back posts, and then lay the top rail alongside these top marks (with the correct post heights on the outer edges of each) so that the correct angles to cut the tops of the posts can be marked. Cut the posts to length.

Nail up the frame by skew nailing through the bottom and top rails into the posts.

Once the frame has been finished, check it for square, then cut off the 'horns' (protruding ends) of the top and bottom rails so they are flush with the posts. Make up the required number of frames – four in our example.

SUPPORT AND FIXING BATTENS

Place an offcut of the 50 × 38mm (2 × 1½in) glazing frame side rail, 2mm ($\frac{1}{16}$in) down from the upper edge of the top rail to position the top support battens. You will need one on each side of the central dividing frames and on the inner sides of the end frames. Nail them in place, then saw the ends flush with the front and back posts.

Unless you are nailing the cladding in continuous lengths to the front and back of the dividing frames, you will need to nail fixing battens to the front and back posts.

Hold the battens in place so that the tops can be marked at the angle of the top support batten. Cut the battens to this angle, then screw them in place so that they are flush with the inside edges of the front and back posts (fig 1, page 212). Saw the ends of the battens flush with the bottom edge of the bottom rail. Fix side battens on both sides of the dividing frames, and on the inner sides of the end frames.

To support the cladding at the ends, measure internal heights of the front and back posts on the end frame. Cut battens to these lengths and fix to the inside edges of the end frames (fig 2, page 212).

Cold Frame

Glazed Lights

Cut out all the components. Each glazed light frame will require two sides, one top rail, one bottom rail and one central glazing bar (fig 3).

Mark out all the joints as shown (fig 3). The sides are jointed to the top rail using corner halving joints (*see* **Techniques, Halving joint, page 242**). The bottom rail is lapped on to the sides so that the bottom rail is on the underside.

The glazing bar is joined to the top rail with a T-halving joint and to the bottom rail with a lap joint on the *opposite* side (the underside) so that it laps on to the bottom rail as shown (fig 3).

Letter all the joints clearly to identify them for assembly, and then cut them all out.

Making up the Glazed Light Frames

Glue all the joints to the top and bottom rails, starting with the central glazing bar. Use a waterproof woodworking adhesive such as Cascamite. Turn the frame over so that it can be screwed together from the underside. Use a try square to make sure that the frame is square, and hold it with cramps to keep the joints tight while drilling two pilot holes and a countersink for each of the three top joints. Screw the top joints together.

Drill and screw the bottom corner joints with three screws each. Measure to check that the central glazing bar is central on the bottom rail, then drill two holes and screw the bar to the bottom rail.

Lay the frame on a flat surface and check it is square by measuring the diagonals. Then nail on a bracing batten to keep the frame square while the glue is drying. Clean off any excess glue with a damp cloth and leave the joints to dry.

Repeat the process for the required number of frames – in this case three.

Glass Support Battens

Cut four lengths of 25 × 12mm (1 × ½in) batten to the internal length of the glazing frame and nail them so that they are flush with the underside of the frame.

Then cut two lengths to the internal widths between the side battens at the top. Nail the battens at the top between the two pairs of side battens, with the lower edge flush with the underside of the frame.

Repeat for the other frames.

Cladding

Although we used feather-edge boarding for cladding the frame, other cladding boards could equally well be used – for example, shiplap, tongued-and-grooved, or V-jointed.

For the sides, cut the cladding to the internal dimensions of the end frames. Fix the cladding, working up from the bottom board, nailing into the fixing battens. When using feather-edge boards, the cladding boards should overlap by about 12mm (½in), and the nails holding the lower edge of each board should pass through the top edge of the board beneath to hold it securely. Use galvanized round head nails. When fixing the end cladding, the top boards must be shaped to the slope of the top rail.

The front and back cladding boards are cut to fit between the dividing frames so that the glazed frames, when fitted, will be a loose fit. You will need to leave enough clearance to allow for the timber to swell when it gets wet. Check that the main dividers are spaced so that there is about 2mm (1/16in) clearance between the dividers and the sides of the glazing frames so that they will slide easily.

Nail the cladding boards to the front and back fixing battens, working up from the bottom boards as before. The upper corners at each end of the top boards will have to be notched out so that the cladding boards will fit tightly around the top support battens.

If you are fixing the front and back cladding in a continuous strip, dispense with the front and back fixing battens, and nail the cladding boards directly to the front and back posts of the dividing frames. If the boards are of insufficient length to

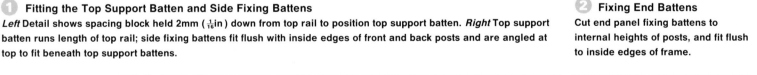

1 **Fitting the Top Support Batten and Side Fixing Battens**
Left Detail shows spacing block held 2mm (1/16in) down from top rail to position top support batten. *Right* Top support batten runs length of top rail; side fixing battens fit flush with inside edges of front and back posts and are angled at top to fit beneath top support battens.

2 **Fixing End Battens**
Cut end panel fixing battens to internal heights of posts, and fit flush to inside edges of frame.

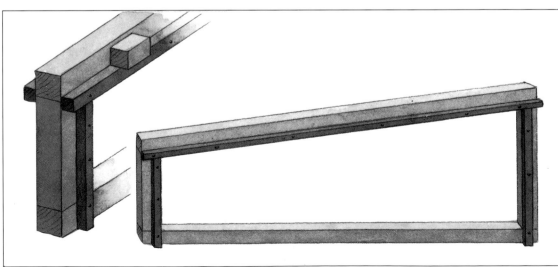

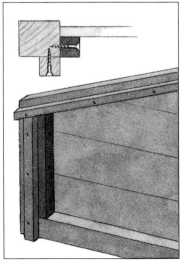

3 Making the Frames for the Glazed Lights

Top Corner halving joints fit side rails to top rail; T-halving joint fits glazing bar to top rail; lap bottom rail to underside of side rails and glazing bar. *Bottom* Glue and screw from underside; bracing batten holds frame square.

clad the frame in continuous strips, shorter lengths of cladding boards can be used: simply butt joint them together so that the joint coincides with the mid-point of a front or back post. Stagger these joints so they do not line up with joints in boards directly above or below.

PRESERVING AND FINISHING OFF

It is most important to treat the whole of the frame assembly with at least two coats of clear or green grade wood preservative. When dry, this can then be painted with a micro-porous or exterior gloss paint, or it can be treated with a water-repellent preservative stain if a natural wood colour is required. You must not use creosote or any wood preserver that is harmful to plants.

FITTING THE GLASS, HANDLES AND HINGES

Have the glass cut to fit the glazed frames. We had ours cut in three sheets on each side, with the bottom sheet feeding first and subsequent sheets overlapping the previously fixed sheet. The bottom sheet is held by small aluminium clips, nailed to the bottom glazing frame rail and

bent back over the edge of the glass to prevent it from slipping out. All the sheets are bedded into mastic on the glazing support battens. The glass sheets are held with small nails, called glazing sprigs, nailed into the side rails so that they are horizontal and hold the glass down. The bottom edges of the overlapping sheets of glass rest against two glazing sprigs which prevent the sheets from sliding down.

As an alternative to glass, the lights can be glazed with clear plastic sheeting, which is cheaper and much safer. Make sure that you buy purpose-made horticultural plastic which will encourage the plants to thrive and will also prevent premature yellowing and cracking of the plastic. Do *not* buy plastic containing an ultra-violet (UV) inhibitor as nothing will be able to grow in the cold frame.

To make it easier to lift the glazed lights for ventilation and access to the plants, screw a D-handle into the bottom end of the glazing bar.

If the glazed lights are left loose, they can be lifted at the front edge and wedged open with a wooden block for ventilation; the lights can also be slid backwards or forwards to gain access to inside the frame.

Alternatively, the glazed lights can be hinged at the back, and this is a particularly good option when the lights are glazed with plastic and are therefore lighter. In this case, cut a 75 × 50mm (3 × 2in) batten to the total length of the frame and bevel the top edge to allow the glazed light to fold back beyond 90 degrees (to rest open against a wall or fence behind the frame). With the batten level with the top support battens, screw it to the back posts. Then screw hinges into the back edges of the glazing frames, and into the top edge of the bevelled batten (*see* **Techniques, Butt hinge, page 248**).

A simple ventilation prop can be made from a 150 × 100 × 50mm (6 × 4 × 2in) timber block with

25mm (1in) steps cut along one edge to allow variable ventilation up to 150mm (6in). Another method is to fix a swing-down prop to hold the glazed light partially open. The prop can be fixed to the underside of the central glazing bar and held out of the way in a spring tool clip when not in use.

If the frame is glazed with plastic lights and hinged at the back, fix hooks and eyes to the front edge of the frame to hold the lights firmly closed in windy conditions.

The frame should be positioned in a sunny place, and can simply be rested on the soil. Alternatively, you could place it on a partially buried row of bricks which will help to keep the timber dry. If the frame is to be permanently sited, it should be placed on a strip of damp-proof course placed on two rows of bricks over a concrete foundation. Fix the frame using expanding wall bolts inserted into the brick foundation through the bottom rails, or you could use metal strips screwed to the foundation and to the inside of the frame structure.

4 Glass Support Battens

Cut side battens to internal lengths of frame and top battens to internal length between side battens.

COMPOST BIN AND PLANTER

The compost bin and planter are very similar in construction, made from rough-sawn boards fixed to posts. The simple nature of the design and lack of precision required in the finishing mean that these two structures offer a good means of practising your DIY skills and gaining the confidence to move on to more elaborate projects.

A compost bin is an invaluable asset for the gardener, providing a supply of rich organic matter which makes all the differ-ence to the way plants grow. At the same time, recycling your garden and kitchen waste is environmentally beneficial and economically sound.

The front posts of the bin are doubled up, making a slot where boards can be dropped into place as the pile builds up, or easily removed as the compost is taken out. It is worth buying 'pressure pre-served' timber – compost is both hot and wet, so the wood needs the maximum degree of protection.

The planter provides a support for young trees, many of which either blow over or suffer from 'windrock', instability of the root structure where growth stops and starts rather than proceeding at an even pace. The cross supports enable the trunk to be fixed firmly in place while the tree becomes established.

The planter is painted with a coat of black tar to preserve the wood. Coach screws are used to bolt the boards to the uprights, giving a smart finishing touch.

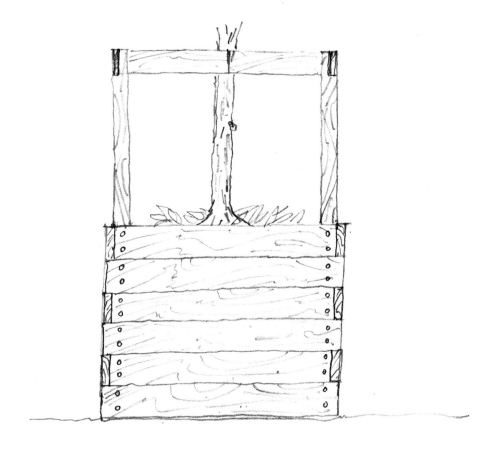

COMPOST BIN

The principle of construction for the compost bin is the same as for the planter (pages 219–221). It is made from fencing-quality sawn and preservative-treated timber which is often sold and cut in imperial as well as metric sizes.

The size of the bin can be varied to suit the site, but it should not be too large, since air will not be able to get to the centre of the heap, hindering the production of good garden compost.

Our bin is about 915mm (36in) square. The height can also be altered according to your own requirements, but you should work in multiples of 150mm (6in) plus an allowance for ventilation gaps between the boards. Our bin is about 990mm (39in) high. Bear in mind that you want a height at which it will be comfortable to tip garden waste into the bin. Also, the heap does not want to be too high or you will not be able to climb onto the heap to tread down the waste material. Opinion varies on the optimum size for the ventilation gaps; we suggest 12–19mm ($\frac{1}{2}$–$\frac{3}{4}$in).

CONSTRUCTION

Cut all of the components to the lengths specified in the Materials chart below. The posts are left long and are cut down to size after the boards have been fixed to allow for the ventilation gaps between the boards. The bin is held together with coach screws, and G-cramps are useful for holding the boards squarely in place while they are being fixed. The coach screw heads are a decorative feature of this compost bin, and it is important that they line up with each other and are the same distance in from the corners.

At the front of the bin, the only fixed board is at the bottom. The other retainer boards slot into the groove between the posts and are built up to the height required. They are therefore easily removed to gain access to the bin contents when the time comes to fork out the rotted compost.

MATERIALS

Note: All timber is sawn and preservative-treated softwood

Part	Quantity	Material	Length
'LONG' BOARDS	9	150 × 25mm (6 × 1in)	915mm (36in)
'MIDDLE' BOARDS	6	As above	890mm (35in)
'SHORT' BOARDS	4	As above	865mm (34in)
RETAINER BOARDS	6*	As above	As above
POSTS	6	50 × 50mm (2 × 2in)	1220mm (48in)
COACH SCREWS	100	Zinc-plated steel	8 × 50mm ($\frac{5}{16}$ × 2in)

* Cut 7 retainer boards if you want the boards at the front to be level with the boards at the side and back

TOOLS

WORKBENCH (fixed or portable)

STEEL MEASURING TAPE

STEEL RULE

TRY SQUARE

PANEL SAW (or circular power saw)

MARKING GAUGE

POWER DRILL

DRILL BIT – approximately 6mm ($\frac{1}{4}$in) diameter to drill pilot holes for coach screws

SPANNER

ONE PAIR OF G-CRAMPS

---

1 Fixing the First Board to the Posts
A 'short' length of board is fixed to the two posts flush and square with the ends to form the bottom row of the back of the bin. Two coach screws at each end hold it in place.

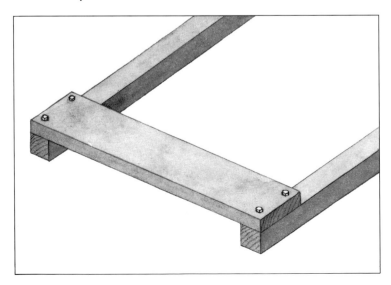

2 Adding the Side Posts and First Retainer Board
A 'long' board at both sides is screwed in place, flush with the ends of the posts. The first retainer board rests against the back of the front posts and is later screwed to the posts from behind.

COMPOST BIN ASSEMBLY

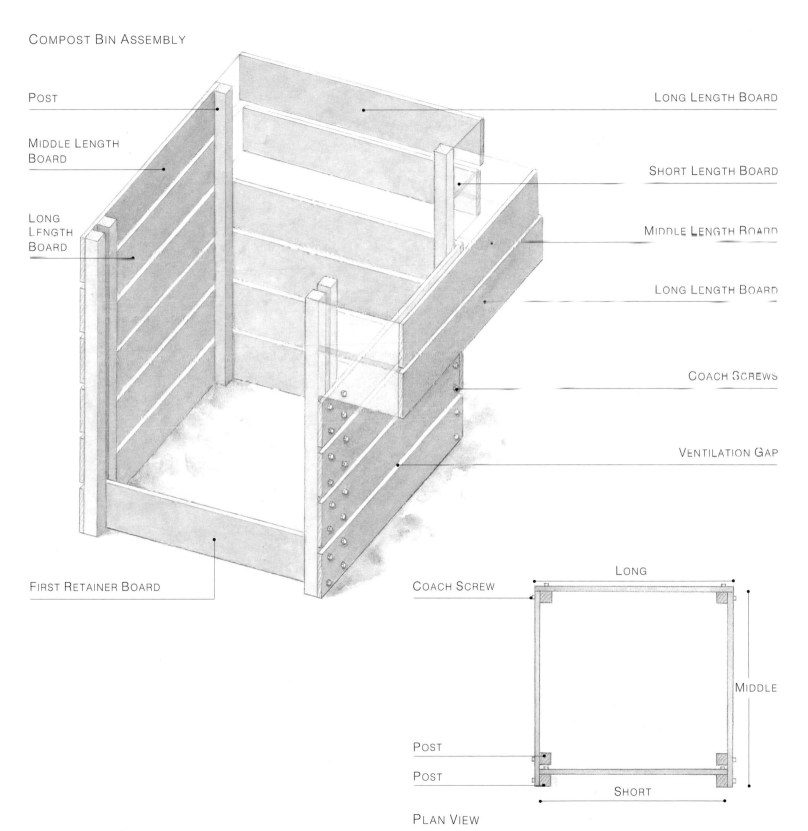

POST

MIDDLE LENGTH BOARD

LONG LENGTH BOARD

FIRST RETAINER BOARD

LONG LENGTH BOARD

SHORT LENGTH BOARD

MIDDLE LENGTH BOARD

LONG LENGTH BOARD

COACH SCREWS

VENTILATION GAP

COACH SCREW

LONG

MIDDLE

POST

POST

SHORT

PLAN VIEW

COMPOST BIN

SQUARING THE FIRST ROW

Start to form the back of the bin by laying two of the posts on a flat surface. Then lay a 'short' length of board across them flush with the bottom ends of the posts, so the outer edges of the posts are 865mm (34in) apart (fig 1, page 216).

Check that the board is square to one of the posts, then cramp it to the post. Drill pilot holes for two coach screws and insert the screws to fix the board to the post.

Use a second board at the other end of the posts to ensure that they are square to the 'short' length of board, then double-check that the post is square to the first board using a try square. Drill pilot holes for the two coach screws to be inserted into the other end of the first board, the same distance in as the coach screws at the other end.

Stand the frame upright and place a 'long' board along the side, flush with the post, and secure it to the post with a G-cramp. Pilot drill and screw it to the post using two coach screws centred on the post.

Repeat for the other side with another 'long' length of board.

Place another post inside this board flush with the end, check that it is square at the top using another 'long' board, and screw into the post through the side board using two coach screws as before.

Take a retainer board and place it on the inside of the front posts (fig 2, page 216).

BUILDING UP THE ROWS OF BOARDS

Place spacing blocks or a spacing batten about 12–19mm ($\frac{1}{2}$–$\frac{3}{4}$in) thick on top of the back board, then lay a 'long' length of board across the top (fig 1). Check that it protrudes an equal distance beyond the outside edges of both the posts, then fix it in place with two coach screws at each end as before. For neatness, make sure that the coach screws line up with those on the board in the row below.

Repeat the process with one 'middle' length board on each side; these should both fit flush with the ends of the back board.

Continue working in this way, one row at a time so that the back boards run alternately with 'short'/'long' lengths, and the sides with 'long'/'middle' lengths to the height required. Ours is six boards high plus spaces.

As you work it is important to check that the structure is square by holding a spare board at the top flush with the posts each time a new board is added.

THE FRONT

With the bottom board at the front, screw through into the back of the front posts using two coach screws at each end.

Place the final two posts in position behind the coach screw heads, leaving at least a 12–19mm ($\frac{1}{2}$–$\frac{3}{4}$in) gap from the front board to create a slot in which the retainers will be a very loose fit. Hold a post in position on the side boards using a G-cramp, then mark a vertical line on the outside of the boards for the coach screw positions (fig 3).

Screw through each board into the post from the outside using two

coach screws per board. Repeat for the post on the other side.

Drop the retainer boards into the slots created by the two posts on each side, building the retainers up to the height required. If you want the retainers to finish level with the boards at the sides and back, rip cut the top one to size.

Finally, cut off the tops of the posts so that they are flush with the top edges of the boards.

Place the bin in an appropriate site away from general view. Almost all types of organic matter can be used for producing compost, although anything too bulky should be avoided because it will slow down the rate at which composting takes place. Similarly, large quantities of leaves also tend to slow the process, and are best kept to decompose separately. Farmyard manure, on the other hand, will accelerate production, and it is a good idea to add a layer of manure or proprietary compost accelerator to your bin every 125–200mm (5–8in). Your compost should be ready after six months or so.

---

1 Building Up the Rows of Boards
Use spacing blocks or a spacing batten to allow for ventilation gaps when fixing subsequent boards to the back and sides. Alternate 'short' and 'long' boards at the back, 'long' and 'middle' boards at the sides.

2 Back Corner Detail
Saw the posts so they are flush with top boards. Note that coach screws line up for a neat appearance.

3 Forming the Front Slot
A second post each side is screwed 38mm (1½in) behind front posts and retainer boards drop in place.

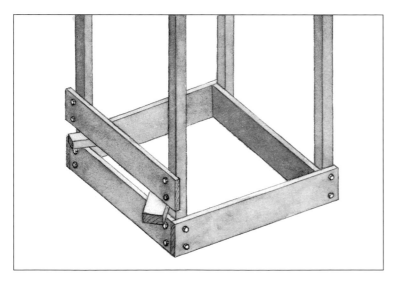

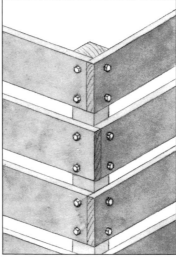

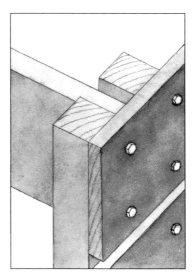

PLANTER

This planter allows you to grow trees, roses, shrubs and other flowers where normally you would not be able to, such as on a paved patio or on a concrete path or driveway. The planter is made from fencing-quality sawn and preservative-treated timber. Much of this is still sold in imperial sizes, although all suppliers will accept orders given in either imperial or metric units. Since the finished planter would be too heavy to lift, there is no need for a floor panel – the planter is placed where required, the planting compost is added and the tree or shrub is planted. There is normally room for other plants around the edge, which will enhance your display.

The size of these planters can be varied according to your specific needs – ours is 760mm (30in) square and 760mm (30in) high, which is a good size for medium-sized trees. For smaller shrubs and flowers you can make smaller planters, and if these are of a size that will still be light enough to move when planted, then it is worth fixing a floor panel in the planter so that you can reposition it at will (see **Making a Floor Panel, page 221**).

The corner posts are extended upwards and are joined at the top by two cross pieces which form a useful tree support. The planter is held together with coach screws, and it is important that these should neatly align with each other.

POSTS – CUTTING THE TOP JOINTS

Cut the corner posts to length, and then use the clean sawn end of the post to mark out the top joint for housing the cross supports. Place the edge of a length of 75 × 25mm (3 × 1in) timber (cut from 150 × 25mm [6 × 1in]) centrally on the post end at a 45 degree angle and mark its position (fig 1).

Place the cross support 3mm ($\frac{1}{8}$in) down from the top of the post, ensure it is at right angles, and mark off the bottom edge. Square round on all four faces, then gauge lines down the sides of the post from those drawn at the top.

Cut down the marked lines on each side of the post with a tenon saw and use a coping saw to remove the centre section.

Repeat for other three posts.

TOOLS

WORKBENCH (fixed or portable)

STEEL MEASURING TAPE

STEEL RULE

TRY SQUARE

COMBINATION SQUARE – for marking 45 degree angles

PANEL SAW (or circular power saw)

TENON SAW (or power jigsaw)

COPING SAW

MARKING GAUGE

POWER DRILL

DRILL BIT – approximately 6mm ($\frac{1}{4}$in) diameter to drill pilot holes for coach screws

SPANNER

ONE PAIR OF G-CRAMPS

HAMMER – if fitting floor panel

MATERIALS

Note: All timber is sawn and preservative-treated softwood

Part	Quantity	Material	Length
'LONG' BOARDS	10	150 × 25mm (6 × 1in)	760mm (30in)
'SHORT' BOARDS	10	As above	710mm (28in)
CORNER POSTS	4	50 × 50mm (2 × 2in)	1350mm (53in)
CROSS SUPPORTS	2	150 × 25mm (6 × 1in) cut to 75 × 25mm (3 × 1in)	1220mm (48in) cut to length as required
COACH SCREWS	80	Zinc-plated steel	8 × 50mm ($\frac{5}{16}$ × 2in)

① Marking Top Joint on Posts
Mark cross support centrally at 45 degrees. Gauge lines down post to marked position and remove centre.

② Fixing the Second Frame to Form Main Construction
Fix 'short' boards flush with the ends of two lots of two posts. Screw 'long' boards to the sides of one frame, then place the second frame inside the 'long' boards so that the ends are square and flush.

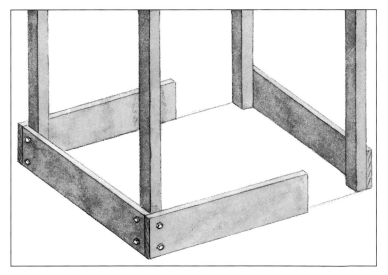

PLANTER

MAIN CONSTRUCTION

Lay two of the corner posts on a flat surface and place a 'short' length of board across them flush with the ends so that the outer edges are 710mm (28in) apart.

Secure the board to the posts by drilling two pilot holes at one end, about 25mm (1in) from the end, and screw in two of the zinc-plated coach screws. For a neat finish try to ensure that each coach screw is the same distance from the edge.

Hold a spare board at the other end to make sure that the post is square, double check using a try square and secure the opposite end of the first board in the same way, drilling the holes the same distance in from the outside edge.

Repeat the process with the other two posts, fixing a 'short' board between them at the base.

Stand one of the frames upright, and place a 'long' length of board along the side flush with the post and secure it in place using a G-cramp. Pilot hole and screw to the corner post with two coach screws centrally on the post. Repeat for the other side of the frame, using a 'long' length of board as before.

Place the other frame inside these 'long' boards, with the corner posts on the inside (fig 2, page 219). Fix the sides to the corner posts with two coach screws at each side.

BUILDING UP THE ROWS OF BOARDS

Take another 'short' length of board and place it on top of the fixed 'long' board so its ends are flush with the posts. Cramp the board to the posts using a pair of G-cramps and fix it in place with two coach screws at each end, aligning them with the screws on the board below.

Take a 'long' length of board and place it on the adjacent side so it overlaps the end of the short board (fig 1). Make sure the end is flush, then screw it into the corner post.

Continue in this way, one row at a time, so that the 'short'/'long' boards run alternately, and ends are visible on each side on alternate rows. Build to five boards high (or whatever height you have decided on). It is most important to check that the structure is square as you work: do this by holding a board at the top flush with the posts each time a board is added.

FIXING THE CROSS SUPPORTS

Measure diagonally across the corner posts at the top of the planter and add 50mm (2in) so that there will be an overhang at each end. Cut two lengths to this measurement from 75 × 25mm (3 × 1in) timber.

At the middle of these two cross supports, cut two cross halving joints (see **Techniques, page 242**) and slot together. Fit the cross supports into the slots in the corner posts and glue them in place (fig 3).

Unless you wish to colour the wood there is no need to apply a special finish, as preservative-treated timber is used for this project.

① Building Up the Sides of the Planter
Build up the rows one at a time, fixing 'short' boards above 'long' boards and vice versa. Always check boards are square with the frame and ends are flush before screwing in place. Align screws with those on the boards below.

② Joining the Cross Supports
Cut cross halving joints in the middle of the two cross supports so that they slot together.

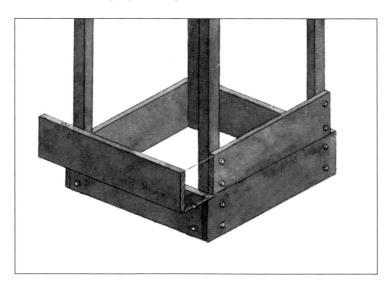

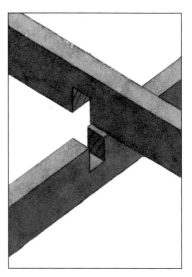

If you do want to change the colour of the wood, apply a water-repellent preservative wood stain of the desired shade. To avoid getting stain onto the coach screw heads, push lengths of plastic or rubber tubing over the heads before staining the planter.

MAKING A FLOOR PANEL

If a floor panel is required, screw 50 × 50mm (2 × 2in) battens to the inside of the planter at the base. Lay 150 × 25mm (6 × 1in) boards across the planter, resting on the battens. Space the boards so that there are narrow gaps about 3mm ($\frac{1}{8}$in) wide between them to allow drainage of excess water. To assist the base in supporting a heavy weight of soil, reinforce it with additional 50 × 50mm (2 × 2in) battens spaced about 225mm (9in) apart under the floor panel and running at right angles to it.

Move the planter to the chosen site before adding the soil and planting the tree or shrub. A layer of small stones at the bottom of the planter will assist drainage.

3 Fixing Supports to Posts
The cross supports fit into the slots cut in top of each post and protrude an equal distance. Glue in place.

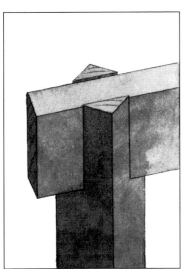

PLANTER ASSEMBLY

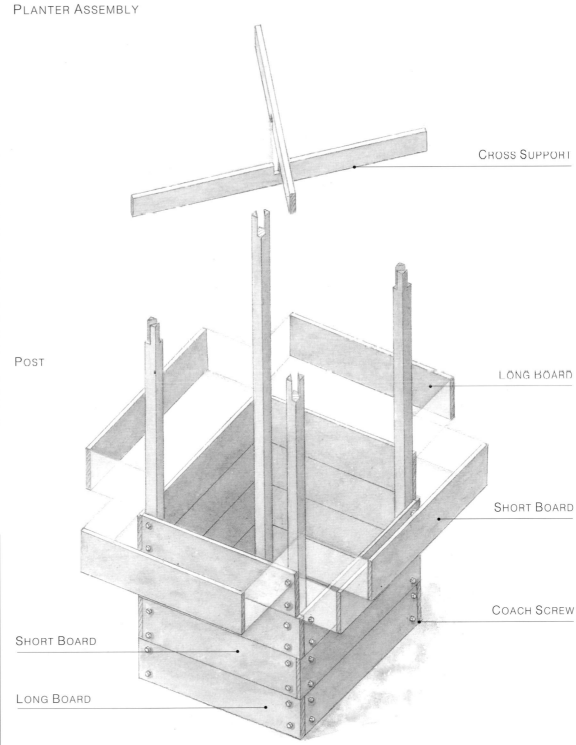

CROSS SUPPORT

POST

LONG BOARD

SHORT BOARD

COACH SCREW

SHORT BOARD

LONG BOARD

JARDINIERE

This elegant, rectilinear jardinière, or plant stand, is inspired by the work of the early twentieth-century designer Josef Hoffmann (1870–1956). He was a Viennese architect, a founder member of the Wiener Werkstätte and a pioneer of functional design. His furniture displays a lack of embellishment and an interest in proportion that was developed further by designers of the Modernist Movement.

Essentially a simple structure, it is made slightly more complicated by the number of right-angled joints. The jardinière incorporates a shallow tray at the top and a shelf at the bottom to hold a collection of plant pots. It is intended for both outdoor and indoor use. The gridded design has been painted a pale 'bone' colour, but other neutral shades would be equally effective.

The idea of grouping elements together to increase their impact is as important in garden design as it is in the design of interiors. Filled with geraniums, the jardinière would brighten up a corner of a patio or seating area, while, positioned near the kitchen door, either outside or in, the stand would also make a convenient home for a collection of herbs grown in containers.

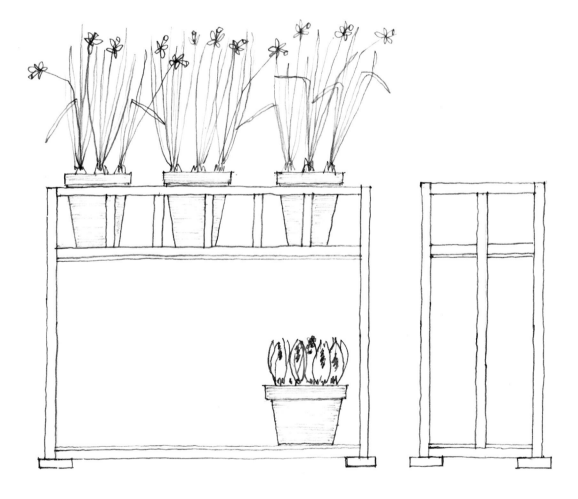

JARDINIERE

This simple stand for plants and flowers looks equally good in the garden or the conservatory. The jardinière shown here is made from PAR (planed all round) softwood and then painted. However, if you want to retain the timber finish, then be sure to make it from good-quality softwood or even hardwood, which can then be treated with a water-repellent preservative stain.

The design of the frame uses a number of wood joints, and for ease of assembly we suggest that these are dowelled together. For a stronger job, the joints could be mortised and tenoned, but unless you have a mortising machine it would be too time-consuming to attempt to construct the frame by this method.

TOOLS

WORKBENCH (fixed or portable)

MARKING KNIFE

STEEL MEASURING TAPE

STEEL RULE

TRY SQUARE

PANEL SAW (or circular power saw)

TENON SAW (or power jigsaw)

CHISEL

MARKING GAUGE

POWER DRILL

TWIST DRILL BIT – 3mm ($\frac{1}{8}$in)

DOWELLING JIG

DOWEL BIT – 10mm ($\frac{3}{8}$in)

MALLET

SCREWDRIVER

POWER SANDER (or hand-sanding block)

MATERIALS

Part	Quantity	Material	Length
CORNER POSTS	4	38 × 38mm (1$\frac{1}{2}$ × 1$\frac{1}{2}$in) PAR softwood	779mm (30$\frac{5}{8}$in)
MIDDLE POSTS	2	As above	711mm (28in)
LONG RAILS	6	As above	847mm (33$\frac{3}{8}$in)
END RAILS	6	As above	237mm (9$\frac{5}{16}$in)
VERTICAL PIECES	10	As above	122mm (4$\frac{3}{4}$in)
SHELVES	2	6mm ($\frac{1}{4}$in) WBP plywood	270 × 880mm (10$\frac{5}{8}$ × 34$\frac{5}{8}$in)
FEET	4	Offcut of hardwood or softwood	90 × 90 × 30mm (3$\frac{1}{2}$ × 3$\frac{1}{2}$ × 1$\frac{1}{8}$in)

Also required: 10mm ($\frac{3}{8}$in) diameter dowelling; 50mm (2in) No 8 zinc-plated screws; panel pins

FRAME CONSTRUCTION

Cut all the components to length, following the Materials chart.

MAKING THE END FRAMES

Cut a halving joint to form the intersection of the middle post with the middle end rail (see **Techniques, page 242**). Mark off on the middle post where the middle end rail will cross it using one of the short vertical pieces as a spacer. The top of the cross halving joint will be this distance down from the top of the middle post.

Mark out and cut the halving joint on the middle post and the middle end rail (fig 1). Repeat for the other end frame.

Strike diagonal lines to mark the centre points for the dowel holes on the ends of all the end rails, on the ends of the middle posts and on the ends of all the short vertical pieces. Using a dowelling jig and a dowel bit (or a drill fitted with a dowel bit and held in a vertical drill stand) drill 10mm ($\frac{3}{8}$in) diameter holes centrally into the marked positions. The hole depths should be slightly over half the lengths of the dowels (ie, 22mm [$\frac{7}{8}$in] deep holes for 40mm [1$\frac{1}{2}$in] long dowels). This gives a small cavity at the end which will accommodate trapped air and glue (see **Techniques, Dowel joints, page 245**).

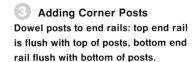

① Fixing Middle End Rail
Mark position of middle end rail on middle post and cut halving joints to fix the two pieces together.

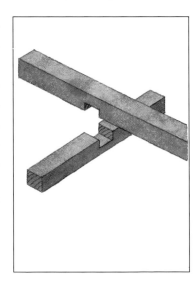

② Top and Bottom End Rails
Mark dowel hole positions centrally on both ends of middle rail. Dowel to top and bottom end rails to fix.

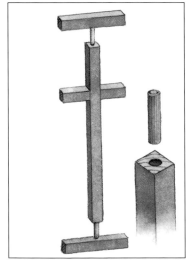

③ Adding Corner Posts
Dowel posts to end rails: top end rail is flush with top of posts, bottom end rail flush with bottom of posts.

JARDINIERE ASSEMBLY

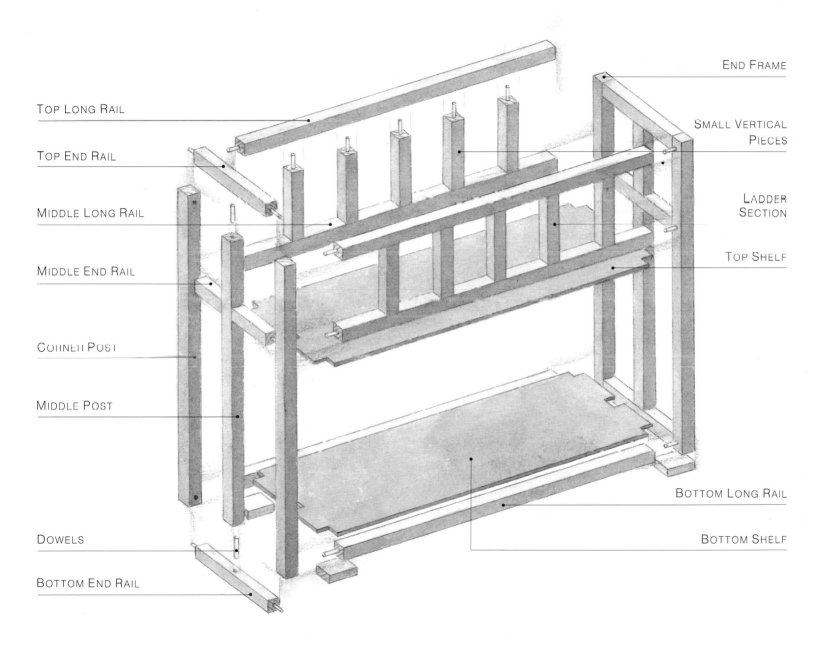

TOP LONG RAIL

TOP END RAIL

MIDDLE LONG RAIL

MIDDLE END RAIL

CORNER POST

MIDDLE POST

DOWELS

BOTTOM END RAIL

END FRAME

SMALL VERTICAL PIECES

LADDER SECTION

TOP SHELF

BOTTOM LONG RAIL

BOTTOM SHELF

JARDINIERE

Mark out the position of the top and bottom end rails on to the inside faces of the corner posts and strike diagonals again to mark the positions of the dowel holes. Drill the holes as before. Also mark out on each corner post the dowel hole positions for the middle rail, which is the same distance down as the length of a short vertical piece plus the 38mm (1½in) depth of the top end rail. Square round on to the other internal face of each corner post to mark the dowel hole positions to take the top, middle and bottom long rails.

Dry assemble the middle post and the middle end rail together to form a cross, and then dowel on the top and bottom end rails, again without glue (fig 2, page 224). Complete the dry assembly of the end frames by adding the corner posts (fig 3, page 224).

FRONT AND BACK FRAMES

To make up the front and back frames, which look like ladders, mark the positions of the short vertical pieces along one long rail, and mark dowel hole centres regularly and centrally along the rail (fig 1). There is an internal spacing of 110mm (4½in) between each short vertical piece, and also between the end-most vertical pieces and each of the corner posts.

Use this rail as a pattern to transfer the marks on to three of the other long rails. Drill all the dowel holes to the required depth and dry assemble the ladder frame sections.

Drill the dowel holes on the inside of the corner posts, using the marks transferred from the front and back ladder frame construction.

Mark the dowel hole positions centrally on the ends of the bottom long rails, then drill the holes in them and in the bottoms of the corner posts as before.

Dowel and dry assemble each ladder frame section, together with the long bottom rails, into the corner posts of the end frames (fig 2).

Make sure that the assembly is square and fits together perfectly, dismantle in reverse order, then re-assemble, this time gluing the joints using waterproof wood adhesive.

SHELVES

The two shelves are cut so that they finish half-way across the thickness of the frame, rather than fitting flush with the outside edges of the frame rails. Notch out the corners and the central part at the ends to fit round the middle and corner posts.

Cut out the bottom shelf to fit on to the bottom rails, and glue and pin it down to the frame (fig 3).

The top shelf is glued and pinned to the underside of the middle rails.

FEET

The feet are fixed underneath each corner and protrude at the sides and ends by the same amount as the 'step' for the bottom shelf (that is, approximately 19mm [¾in]) (fig 4). Any offcut of softwood or hardwood can be used to make them.

Apply waterproof woodworking adhesive, then screw up into the rails using two screws for each foot.

Fill any gaps using an exterior-grade cellulose filler. Finally, paint as required or apply a water-repellent wood preservative stain.

① Adding Vertical Pieces
Vertical pieces are dowelled in place at equal internal spacings between top and middle long rails.

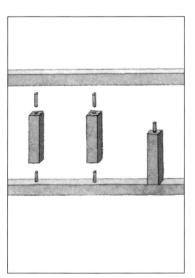

② Frame Assembly
Mark dowel positions on corner posts and ends of top, middle and bottom long rails. Drill and join.

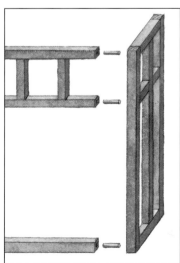

③ Adding Bottom Shelf
Cut shelf to finish half-way across frame rails. Notch ends to fit around posts. Glue and screw in place.

④ Adding the Feet
Cut feet from offcuts of wood. Glue and screw them up into rails so that they protrude by about 19mm (¾in).

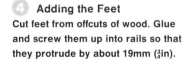
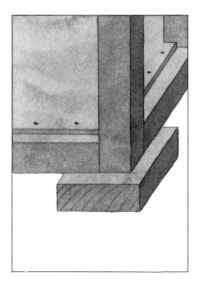

TOOLS

Bench stop and vice A woodwork vice is fitted to the underside of a bench, with the jaws level with the bench top. The jaws are lined and topped with hardwood to protect the work and any tools being used. Some vices also incorporate a small steel peg (a 'dog') that can be raised above the main jaw level. This allows awkward or long pieces of wood to be cramped in position when used with a bench stop which is fixed at the opposite end of the bench.

Sliding bevel (1) This is a type of square used to mark out timber at any required angle. The sliding blade can be locked against the stock by means of a locking lever and the blade can form any angle with the stock.

Marking gauge (2) Essential for setting out woodworking joints, this is used to mark both widths and thicknesses with only a light scratch. The gauge comprises a handle, on which slides a stock bearing a steel marking pin. This movable stock can be locked in any position with a thumb screw so the steel pin is fixed at a precise point.

Mortise gauge (3) Similar to a marking gauge, it has two pins, one fixed, one adjustable, to mark out both sides of a mortise at the same time. Some types have an additional pin fixed below the beam so that the tool can be used as a marking gauge.

Profile gauge This is also called a shape tracer or a scribing gauge. It comprises a row of steel pins or plastic fingers held in a central bar. When pressed against an object, like a skirting board, the pins follow the shape of the object.

Marking knife Used to score a thin line for a saw or chisel to follow, ensuring a precise cut. The flat face of the knife can be run against the blade of a try square or straight-edge.

Metal detector Pinpoints metal objects such as electric cables and water and gas pipes hidden in walls, ceilings and floors. Electronically operated, it buzzes or flashes when metal is found.

Mitre box A simple open-topped wooden box used to guide saws into materials at a fixed 45 or 90 degree angle, to ensure a square cut.

Plumb bob and chalk A plumb line is used to check verticals and mark accurate vertical lines, in chalk, on walls. A plumb bob is simply a pointed weight attached to a long length of string. Before use, the string can be rubbed with a stick of coloured chalk. Hold the string in the required position at the top, wait for the plumb bob to stop swinging, then carefully press the string against the wall at the bottom and then pluck the string to leave a line on the wall. More expensive models of plumb bobs incorporate line winders and powdered chalk containers which automatically dust the line with chalk as it is withdrawn.

Portable workbench A collapsible, portable workbench is vital for woodworking. A large, fixed workbench in a garage or shed is important, but the major advantage of the portable type is that it is lightweight and can be carried to the job, where it provides sturdy support when final adjustments have to be made.

A portable bench is like a giant vice – the worksurface comprises two sections which can be opened wide or closed tightly according to the dimensions of the work and the nature of the task. It can hold large and awkward objects firmly in place while you work.

Scribing block To fit an item neatly against a wall (which is very unlikely to be completely flat), the item has to be 'scribed' flat to the wall using a small block of wood and a pencil (see **Techniques, page 246**). A scribing block is simply an offcut of wood measuring about 25 × 25 × 25mm (1 × 1 × 1in). The block is held against the wall, a

sharp pencil is held against the opposite end of the block, and the block and the pencil are moved in a unit along the wall to mark a line on the item to be fitted. If you cut to this line, the item will then fit tightly against the wall.

Spirit level (9) Used for checking that surfaces are horizontal or vertical. A 100cm (36in) long level is the most useful all-round size. An aluminium or steel level will withstand knocks and it can be either I-girder or box-shaped in section. Ideally, a 250mm (10in) 'torpedo' spirit level is also useful to have, for working in confined spaces such as alcoves and inside cupboards. It may be used with a straight-edge over longer surfaces or to check if two points are aligned.

Steel measuring tape A 3m (3yd) or 5m (5yd) long, lockable tape (metal or plastic) is best, and one with a top window in the casing makes it easier to read measurements.

Steel rule Since the rule is made of steel, the graduations are indelible and very precise. A rule graduated on both sides in metric and imperial is the most useful. The rule also serves as a precise straight-edge for marking cutting lines.

Straight-edge Can be made very simply from a length of 50 × 25mm (2 × 1in) scrap wood. It is used to tell whether a surface is flat and also for checking whether two points are accurately aligned with each other.

Trimming knife A razor-sharp blade which is used to mark extremely accurate cutting lines and for a wide range of trimming jobs. The type with a retractable blade is the safest to use.

Try square (4) An L-shaped precision tool comprising a steel blade and stock (or handle) set at a perfect right-angle to each other on both the inside and outside edges. Used for marking right-angles and for checking a square.

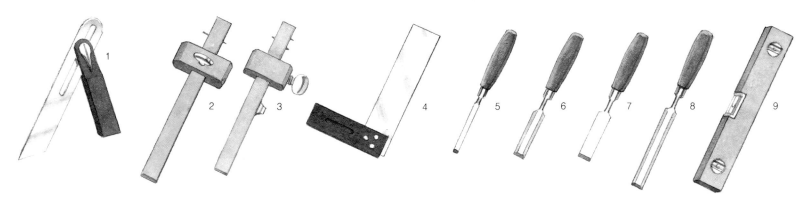

TOOLS FOR SHARPENING AND CUTTING

CHISELS

Used to cut slots in wood or to pare off thin slivers. Some chisels may be used with a mallet when cutting slots. When new, a chisel's cutting edge is ground and must be honed with an oilstone to sharpen it.

Mortise chisel (5) Used with a mallet for cutting deep slots.

Firmer chisel (7) For general DIY use.

Bevel-edge chisel (6) Used for undercutting in confined or cramped spaces such as when making dovetail joints.

Paring chisel (8) Has a long blade for cutting deep joints or long housings.

Cold chisel Generally used for masonry, the cold chisel is a hexagonal-shaped rod made from solid steel. In addition to cutting out old pointing, it can be used to cut metal bars or chop off the heads off rivets.

Oilstone and honing guide The first sharpens and the second maintains the correct angle for sharpening chisel and plane blades. An oilstone is a rectangular block of stone with grit on both sides. Oil is used as a lubricant while the blade is being sharpened on the stone.

The honing guide is an inexpensive tool which makes sharpening easier and more efficient. The blade to be sharpened is inserted at an angle and cramped in place, then the guide is rolled back and forth on the surface of the oilstone.

Dowelling jig A simple dowelling jig cramps on to a piece of work, ensuring that the drill is aligned accurately over the centre of the dowel hole to be drilled. It also guides the drill vertically.

DRILLS

Hand drill (10) For drilling holes for screws or for making large holes, particularly in wood. It will make holes in metal and is useful where there is no power source. A handle attached to a toothed wheel is used to turn the drill in its chuck.

Power drill (11) These range from a simple, single-speed model (which will drill holes only in soft materials) to a multi-speed drill with electric control. Most jobs call for something in between the two, such as a two-speed drill with hammer action. The two speeds enable most hard materials to be drilled and the hammer action means that you can also drill into the hardest walls.

Drill stand Enables a power drill to be used with extreme accuracy when, for example, joining dowelling (see **Techniques, page 245**). The hole will be perpendicular to the surface and its depth can be carefully controlled. The drill is lowered on to the work with a spring-loaded lever which gives good control and accuracy.

DRILL BITS

You will need a selection of drill bits in various sizes and of different types for wood and metal for use with a drill.

Auger bit (17) Has a tapered, square shank that fits into a carpenter's brace. It is used to make deep holes in wood, the usual lengths being up to 250mm (10in). Diameters range from 6mm ($\frac{1}{4}$in) to 38mm (1$\frac{1}{2}$in). The tip has a screw thread to draw the bit into the wood.

Flat bit (16) Is used with an electric drill. It has a point at the end of the shank and its flat shank end allows it to slot into the drill chuck. Diameters are from 12mm ($\frac{1}{2}$in) to 38mm (1$\frac{1}{2}$in). For maximum efficiency the bit must be turned at high speed from about 1000 to 2000 r.p.m. It can be used to drill into cross grain, end grain and also man-made boards.

Countersink bit (15) After a hole is drilled in wood, a countersink bit is used to cut a recess for the screwhead to sit in, so ensuring that it lies below the surface. Different types are available for use with a carpenter's brace and an electric drill.

Head diameters are 9mm ($\frac{3}{8}$in), 12mm ($\frac{1}{2}$in) and 15mm ($\frac{9}{16}$in). Carbon-steel bits are used on wood, but high-speed steel bits can be used for wood, plastic or metal.

Twist drill bit (13) Used with an electric drill for drilling small holes in wood and metal. Carbon-steel drills are for wood, drilling into metal requires a high-speed steel bit.

Dowel bit (12) Used to make dowel holes in wood. The tip has two cutting spurs on the side and a centre point to prevent the bit from wandering off centre. Diameters range from 3mm ($\frac{1}{8}$in) to 12mm ($\frac{1}{2}$in).

Masonry bit (14) Has a specially hardened tungsten-carbide tip for drilling into masonry to the exact size required for a wallplug. Special percussion drill bits are available for use with a hammer drill when boring into concrete.

End-mill/Hinge-sinker bit (18) Primarily used for boring 35mm (1$\frac{3}{8}$in) or 25mm (1in) diameter flat-bottomed holes in cabinet and wardrobe doors to accept the hinge bosses on concealed hinges. End mills are used in electric drills, ideally fitted in drill stands, and should be set to drill no deeper than 12mm ($\frac{1}{2}$in).

Expansive bit If you need to cut a hole of a diameter larger than 38mm (1$\frac{1}{2}$in), you will not be able to use a flat bit. Instead, you can use a hole saw, a jigsaw or an expansive (sometimes called expanding) bit, which is fitted to a hand drill, for the job.

Power router (19) This portable electric tool is used to cut grooves, recesses, and many types of joints in timber, as well as to shape the edge of long timber battens to form decorative mouldings. A whole range of cutting bits in different shapes and sizes is available and when fitted into the router the bits revolve at very high speed (about 25,000 r.p.m.) to cut the wood smoothly and cleanly (20). Although hand routers (which look like small planes) are available, whenever routers are referred to in this book, it is the power router to which the remarks are directed.

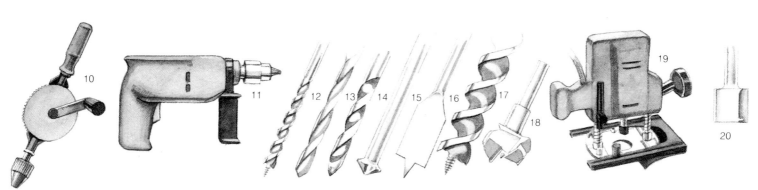

Tools

Saws

Circular saw (1) Invaluable for cutting large pieces of timber or sheets of board. It will also cut grooves and angles. The most popular size has a diameter of 187mm (7¼in). Circular saws can be extremely dangerous and must be used carefully. The piece of work must be held securely and the blade depth set so that it will not cut into anything below the work. The tool should be fitted with an upper and a lower blade guard. Support your work on scrap battens to avoid cutting into workbenches or floors.

Coping saw (2) Used to make curved or circular cuts. It has a narrow blade, which can be swivelled. When cutting, the blade can be angled as necessary so that the frame clears the edge of the work. Drill a hole close to the edge of the piece to be cut out, and thread the coping saw blade through the hole before reconnecting it to the handle and starting to cut.

Dovetail saw (3) Also called a gent's saw, this fine-toothed form of the tenon saw with a stiffened back is ideal for making delicate and precise saw cuts. It is also particularly useful for making dovetail joints.

Hacksaw For cutting metal. A traditional hacksaw has a wooden handle and a solid metal frame. The blade is tensioned by a wing-nut. Modern hacksaws have a tubular frame which is adjustable for different lengths of blade. A 'junior' hacksaw is ideal for sawing small items or for working in confined spaces.

Hole saw This will cut perfectly round holes, but you need to buy a separate blade for each different diameter hole required. The blade clips to a plate which is then cramped to a central twist drill bit and fitted to the chuck of a power drill. Place the twist bit at the centre of the hole required and drill at a slow speed.

Jigsaw (7) Will cut timber and a variety of man-made boards, and is much more versatile than a circular saw, although not as quick or powerful. It also cuts curves, intricate shapes, angles and holes in the middle of panels. The best models offer variable speeds – slow for hard materials and fast for soft. The latest models have either a reciprocating or a pendulum action. In the latter case the blade goes backwards and forwards as well as up and down, which allows for much faster cutting on straight lines. Throw away blades when they become blunt – keep a spare blade or two in reserve.

Padsaw (5) Designed to cut holes and shapes in wood. It has a narrow, tapered blade which will cut keyholes, for example. A hole is first drilled and the saw blade is inserted to make the cut. Padsaws are useful for cutting holes for inset sinks where a power jigsaw is not available

Panel saws (4) Are hand saws used for rough cutting rather than fine carpentry. They have a flexible blade of 510–660mm (20–26in), and are useful for general-purpose cutting of wood and fibre boards.

Tenon saw (6) For cutting the tenon part of a mortise and tenon joint (see **Techniques, page 244**), and also useful for other delicate and accurate work. Its fine teeth can cut across the grain without tearing fibres. The saw has a stiffened back and the blade is about 250–300mm (10–12in) long.

Surforms Available in a range of lengths from approximately 150–250mm (6–10in), these rasps are useful for the initial shaping of wood. However, further fine finishing by hand is needed to obtain a smooth surface. The steel blade has a pattern of alternating small teeth and holes through which waste wood passes, so that the teeth do not get clogged up. When blunt, the blade is simply replaced.

Hand Tools

Abrasive paper see **Sanding block**

Cramps

For securing glued pieces of work while they are setting. There are many types of cramp, but the G-cramp is the most commonly used.

Wooden wedges are sometimes useful for securing an object while it is being glued. You can make two by cutting diagonally through a block of wood (see **Techniques, page 237**).

Sash cramps. These employ a long metal bar, and are indispensable for holding together large frameworks, although you can improvise in some cases by making a rope tourniquet. This consists of a piece of rope which is tied around the object, and a length of stick to twist the rope and so cramp the frame tightly.

Webbing cramp A nylon webbing cramp applies even pressure around frames when they are being assembled. The webbing, like narrow seat-belt type material, is looped around the frame, pulled as tight as possible by hand, and then finally tightened by means of a screw mechanism or ratchet winder. Webbing cramps are cheaper alternatives to sash cramps.

G-cramp (8) Also called a C-cramp or fast-action cramp, it is important for our projects that the jaws of the cramp open at least 200mm (8in). The timber to be held in the cramp is placed between the jaws which are then tightened by turning a thumb-screw, tommy bar or other type of handle. In the case of the fast action cramp, one jaw is free to slide on a bar, and after sliding this jaw up to the workpiece, final tightening is achieved by turning the handle. In all cases, to prevent damage to the piece of work, scraps of wood are placed between it and the jaws of the cramp.

Gimlet Used to make a small pilot hole in wood to take a screw. It is twisted into the wood with a continuous circular movement.

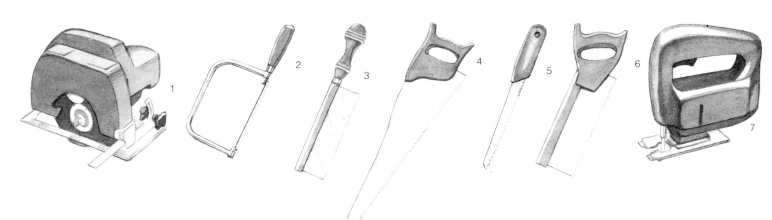

HAMMERS

Cross-pein hammer (10) The pein is the tapered section opposite the flat hammer head, and it is used for starting off small pins and tacks held in the fingers.

Pin hammer A smaller version of the cross-pein; this is useful for light work.

Claw hammer (9) The claw side of the head of the hammer is used to extract nails from a piece of work, quickly and cleanly.

Mallet Most commonly used to strike mortise chisels, although if a chisel has an impact-resistant handle then a hammer may also be used. The tapered wooden head ensures square contact with the object being struck.

Nail and pin punches Used with a hammer to drive nails and pins below the surface so that they are hidden and can then be filled. The pointed end is 'cupped' so that it will fit neatly over a nail or pin head.

Orbital sander Otherwise known as a finishing sander, this gives a fine, smooth surface finish to wood. A gritted sanding sheet is fitted to the sander's base plate. Sheets are graded from coarse to fine, and the grade used depends on the roughness of the surface to be sanded. Orbital sanders produce a great deal of dust, so always wear a mask when using one.

Pincers Used to remove nails and tacks from wood. The bevel-edged jaws grip the nail close to the surface of the wood, and the pincers are rocked back and forth to extract it.

PLANES

Smoothing plane (11) A general-purpose, hand-held plane for smoothing and straightening surfaces and edges. The plane is about 250mm (10in) long and its blade 50–60mm (2–2½in) wide. The wider the blade the better the finish on

wide timber. There is a fine adjustment for depth of cut and a lever for lateral adjustment.

Power plane (14) Finishes timber to precise dimensions. A one-hand model is lightweight and can be used anywhere, whereas the heavier two-hander is more cumbersome and is therefore intended for workbench use. An power plane will also cut bevels and rebates.

Jack plane (13) Longer than a smoothing plane, it is used for straightening long edges and is a good all-purpose plane.

Block plane (12) Held in the palm of the hand, it is easy to use for small work and chamfering edges. Also useful for planing end grain.

Rasp A rasp is a type of coarse file for wood, available with flat or half-round surfaces. It is used to shape wood, often when scribing an edge to fit against a wall.

Sanding block and abrasive paper A sanding block is used with abrasive paper to finish and smooth flat surfaces. The block is made of cork, rubber or softwood and the abrasive paper is wrapped around it. Make sure in doing so that the paper is not wrinkled or you will not achieve a smooth, even finish. Abrasive paper used without a block tends to produce an uneven surface. Sheets of abrasive paper are graded from coarse to fine and are selected according to the roughness of the surface to be sanded. Coarse paper is used for a very rough surface and fine paper for finishing.

Screwdrivers There is no single type of screwdriver that is better than the rest; personal preference is what matters. They come in many shapes and sizes, and the main differences are the type of tip (for slotted or cross-point screws), the length, and the shape of the handle, which varies from straight or fluted to bulb-shaped. Cross-point screwdrivers can be used on most cross-point screws but the 'Supadriv' recess screw requires a purpose-made screwdriver.

Ideally, you should have a range of screwdrivers for dealing with all sizes of screws. Ratchet models, which return the handle to its starting point, are easy to operate since your hand grip does not need to change. The spiral action screwdriver is very effective (though very expensive) and it works like a bicycle pump rather than by turning the handle.

Cordless screwdriver A fairly new tool, it is quite expensive but can save much time and effort. Mainly used for cross-point screws.

SUPPLEMENTARY TOOLS

Metal file Gives a metal edge the required shape and finish. Most files are supplied with a removable handle which can be transferred to a file of a different size. Flat or half-round files (one side flat, the other curved) are good general-purpose tools.

Paintbrushes A set of paintbrushes to be used for painting and varnishing should ideally comprise three sizes – 25mm (1in), 50mm (2in) and 75mm (3in). A better finish is always achieved by matching the size of the brush to the type of surface – a small brush for narrow surfaces, a large brush for wide areas. Cheap brushes are a false economy.

Spanner A spanner is required for tightening coach bolts or screws, and any type that fits the head of the bolt is suitable. If the correct-size open-ended or ring spanner is not available, any type of adjustable spanner may be used.

Mastic applicator gun Also called a caulking gun, this is used to eject a bead of mastic-type waterproofing sealants into gaps where water might penetrate, such as around shower trays or around sink cut-outs in a kitchen worktop. A cartridge of mastic or sealant is held in a frame, and a plunger pushes the mastic out of a nozzle at the end of the cartridge.

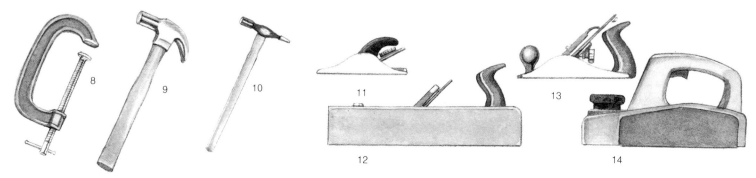

8   9   10   11   12   13   14

MATERIALS

TIMBER

Timber is classified into two groups – softwoods and hardwoods. Softwoods come from evergreen trees and hardwoods from deciduous trees. Check your timber for defects before buying it. Avoid wood which is badly cracked or split, although you need not be concerned about fine, surface cracks since these can be planed, sanded or filled. Do not buy warped wood, as it will be impossible to work with. Check for warping by looking along the length of a board to see if there is any bowing or twisting.

When you get your wood home, condition it for about ten days. As the wood will have been stored in the open air at the yard, it will be 'wet'. Once indoors, it dries, shrinks slightly and will warp unless stored flat on the ground. If you build with wood as soon as you get it home, your structure could run into problems later as the wood dries out. To avoid warping and aid drying, boards should be stacked in a pile, with offcuts of wood placed between each board to allow air to circulate. This will lower the moisture content to about 10 per cent and condition the wood, ready for use.

Softwood Although softwood is usually referred to as 'deal' or 'pine', it comes from many different sources. Softwood is much less expensive than hardwood and is used in general building work. Softwood is sold in a range of standard sizes. After 1.8m (6ft), lengths rise in 300mm (12in) increments up to 6.3m (20ft 8in). Standard thicknesses are from 12mm ($\frac{1}{2}$in) up to 75mm (3in) and widths range from 25mm (1in) to 225mm (9in).

It is important to remember that standard softwood sizes refer to sawn sizes – that is, how it is sawn at a mill. When bought this way, softwood is suitable only for rough constructional work such as floor joists and basic frames. However, the smooth wood used for the projects in this book, for which appearance and accuracy are

important, will need to have been planed. Such wood is referred to as PAR (planed all round), and, since planing takes a little off each face, planed softwood is approximately 5mm ($\frac{3}{16}$in) smaller in width and thickness than its stated size. Standard sizes should, therefore, be thought of as rough guides rather than exact measurements, although it is increasingly common for DIY stores to sell PAR softwood by its actual size rather than its nominal size.

Hardwood Expensive and not as easy to obtain as softwoods, hardwoods often have to be ordered or bought from a specialist timber merchant. Many joinery shops and timber yards will machine hardwood to your exact specification. In home woodwork, hardwood is usually confined to mouldings and beadings, which are used to give exposed sawn edges a neat finish. Today most hardwood mouldings are made from ramin, a pale wood, or from redwood.

BOARDS

Boards Boards are mechanically made from wood and other fibres. They are versatile, relatively inexpensive, and made to uniform quality. They differ from natural wood, in that they are available in large sheets. You need to know the advantages of each type of board before making your choice. All boards are made in sheets of 2440 × 1220mm (8 × 4ft), and most stockists will saw them to the size you require.

Hardboard The best known of all fibreboards. Common thicknesses are 3mm, 5mm and 6mm ($\frac{1}{8}$in, $\frac{3}{16}$in and $\frac{1}{4}$in). As hardboard is weak and has to be supported on a framework, it is essentially a material for panelling. Denser types of hardboard can be used for cladding partitions; softer types for pinboards.

Medium board As it is softer and weaker than hardboard, medium board is often, therefore, used in thicker sheets – usually 12mm ($\frac{1}{2}$in).

MDF (medium-density fibreboard) A good, general-purpose building board. It is highly compressed, does not flake or splinter when cut, and leaves a clean, hard-sawn edge which does not need to be disguised as do other fibreboards. It also takes a very good paint finish, even on its edges. Thicknesses range from around 6mm to 35mm ($\frac{1}{4}$in to 1$\frac{3}{8}$in).

Chipboard Made by binding wood chips together under pressure, it is rigid, dense and fairly heavy. Chipboard is strong when reasonably well supported, but sawing it can leave an unstable edge and can blunt a saw. Ordinary screws do not hold well in chipboard and it is best to use twin thread screws (see **Screws, page 234**). Most grades of chipboard are not moisture-resistant and will swell up when wet. Thicknesses range from 6mm to 40mm ($\frac{1}{4}$in to 1$\frac{1}{2}$in), but 12mm, 19mm and 25mm ($\frac{1}{2}$in, $\frac{3}{4}$in and 1in) are common.

Chipboard is widely available with the faces and edges veneered with natural wood, PVC, melamine, or plastic laminates. The latter are often in coloured finishes and imitation wood-grain effects.

If used for shelving, chipboard must be well supported on closely spaced brackets or bearers. The better-quality laminated boards are far stronger than plain chipboard.

Plywood Made by gluing thin wood veneers together in plies (layers) with the grain in each ply running at right-angles to that of its neighbours. This gives the board strength and helps prevent warping. The most common boards have three, five or seven plies. Plywood is graded for quality, taking into account the amount of knots and surface markings present: A is perfect; B is average; and BB is for rough work only.

MR (moisture-resistant) board is suitable for *internal* jobs where damp conditions prevail, such as in a bathroom. WBP (weather- and boil-proof) board must be used for outdoor jobs. Plywood is available with a range of surface veneers.

MOULDINGS (See page 234)

Square

Rectangular

Scotia

Quadrant

Corner

The usual thicknesses of plywood are 3mm, 6mm, 12mm and 19mm ($\frac{1}{8}$in, $\frac{1}{4}$in, $\frac{1}{2}$in and $\frac{3}{4}$in).

Blockboard Made by sandwiching natural timber strips betweeen wood veneers, the latter usually of Far Eastern redwood or plain birch. Although plain birch is a little more expensive than redwood it is of a much better quality. Other expensive varieties have a double veneer of plywood and an exotic wood. Blockboard is very strong, but can leave an ugly edge when sawn (gaps often appear between the core strips), making edge fixings difficult. Blockboard is graded in the same way as plywood and common thicknesses are 12mm, 19mm and 25mm ($\frac{1}{2}$in, $\frac{3}{4}$in and 1in). It is a very rigid board and is therefore ideal for a long span of shelving.

Laminboard A high-quality blockboard with no gaps between the core strips. It is expensive and is best used only where the quality required justifies the cost.

Tongued-and-grooved boarding Also called match boarding, or matching, this tongued and grooved boarding is widely used for cladding frameworks and walls. The boarding has a tongue on one side and a slot on the other side. The tongue fits into the slot of the adjacent board to form an area of cladding; this expands and contracts according to temperature and humidity without cracks opening up between boards.

Ordinary tongued-and-grooved boarding fits together like floorboards, but tongued-and-grooved boarding for cladding has some form of decoration; this can be a beaded joint, or, more commonly, a chamfered edge, which forms the attractive V-joint of tongued, grooved, and V-jointed (TVG) boarding.

Feather-edge boards These taper from a thick edge across to a thin edge. When fixed in place, the thick edge of one board overlaps the thin edge of the next board.

ADHESIVES AND FILLERS

Adhesives Modern types are strong and efficient. If they fail, it is because the wrong adhesive is being used or the manufacturer's instructions are not followed carefully. For all general indoor woodworking, use a PVA (polyvinyl acetate) woodworker's glue – all glue manufacturers produce their own brand. Use a waterproof PVA in areas where there may be water splashing or condensation. If joints do not meet perfectly, a gap-filling adhesive can be used.

Ceramic tiles require their own special adhesive (of a thick, buttery consistency) which is supplied, ready mixed, in tubs. If tiles are likely to be regularly splashed – around sinks for example – you should use a waterproof tile adhesive. Some brands of adhesive can also double as grouting cement for filling the gaps between tiles.

Fillers If the wood is to be painted over, use a standard cellulose filler – the type used for repairing cracks in walls. This filler dries white and will be evident if used under any other kind of finish. When a clear finish is needed, fill cracks and holes with a proprietary wood filler or stopping. These are thick pastes and come in a range of wood colours. You can even mix them together or add a wood stain if the colour you want is not available. It is best to choose a colour slightly paler than the surrounding wood, since fillers tend to darken when the finish is applied. Some experimentation may be needed, using a waste piece of matching wood.

In fine work, a grain filler is used to stop the final finish sinking into the wood. This is a paste, thinned with white spirit, and then rubbed into the surface. It is supplied in a range of wood shades.

FINISHES

The choice of finish is determined by whether the wood or board is to be hidden, painted or enhanced by a protective clear finish.

Paint A liquid gloss (oil-based) paint is suitable for wood, and is applied after undercoat. Generally, two thin coats of gloss are better than one thick coat. Non-drip gloss is an alternative. It has a jelly-like consistency and does not require an undercoat, although a second coat may be needed for a quality finish. If you intend to spray the paint, you must use a liquid gloss.

Microporous paint This is applied directly to the wood – neither primer nor undercoat is needed. The coating will not flake or blister as the special formulation allows trapped moisture to evaporate. If applied over old gloss paint, it will lose the quality that prevents flaking or blistering.

Preservative Unless timber has been pre-treated with preservative and it is not to receive an alternative decorative finish, you must use a coat of preservative. Modern water-based preservatives are harmless to plant life. They are available in clear, green and a number of natural wood colours. The preservative sinks well into the wood, preventing rot and insect attack.

Varnish Normally applied by brush, varnish can also be sprayed on. It is available as a gloss, satin or matt finish, all clear. Varnish also comes in a range of colours, so that you can change the colour of the wood and protect it simultaneously. The colour does not sink into the wood, so if the surface of the wood becomes scratched or marked then its original colour will show through. For this reason, a wood stain or dye is sometimes used to change the colour of wood. It sinks into the wood, but offers no protection, so a varnish or clear lacquer also needs to be applied.

For outdoor use, you must always use an exterior-grade varnish – this is stated on the container – or a yacht varnish. It is available as a gloss, satin or matt finish, all clear.

Lacquer The best finishing treatment to apply to wood furniture. It is resistant to heat, scratches and solvents, and produces a superb finish.

Half-round

Twice-rounded

Hockey-stick

Reeded

Astragal

MATERIALS: MOULDINGS AND FIXINGS

POLISHES

French polish Refers to a particular polish, but it is also the collective term for all polishes made with shellac and alcohol. French polish is ideal where a light to medium brown tone is required. The finish itself is not highly protective.

Button polish Will give a more golden or orange tone than standard French polish.

White French polish or **transparent polish** Produces a clear finish, allowing the natural colour of the wood to show through. French polishing demands patience if it is to be mastered and many people prefer to apply a clear polyurethane varnish with a conventional wax polish covering it.

CONCRETE

Concrete Made by mixing Portland cement and ballast (a mixture of sand and aggregates) with water. The usual mix for paths, bases and foundations is one part cement to four parts ballast. Although concrete mix is available dry-mixed in bags, it is only economically viable for small jobs. Concrete can be mixed by hand, but it is an arduous task, and it is advisable to hire a small electric mixer.

Precast concrete paving slabs These come in a range of shapes and sizes with 450mm square (18in square) being the most popular, since anything larger is difficult to handle. There is a limited range of colours, and surface finishes are smooth, patterned or textured. Thicknesses are usually 35–40mm (about $1\frac{1}{2}$in).

MOULDINGS

These are used as ornamentation and to cover gaps or fixings in a wooden construction. The term 'moulding' encompasses everything from a simple, thin edging to architraves and skirting boards. A variety of shaped cutters produce many shapes and sizes. In the unlikely event of your being unable to buy the shape you want, you could make your own using a router.

Mouldings are cut from hardwood – usually redwood or ramin. You can buy more exotic hardwood mouldings, mahogany for example, from a specialist timber merchant. These are expensive and you may prefer to stain or varnish a cheaper moulding to obtain the colour you want.

Decorative mouldings are available in standard lengths of 2m or 3m (6ft 6in or 10ft). The following types are among those which are ideal for edging man-made boards and are available in a variety of sizes: half-round; twice-rounded; hockey-stick; reeded; and astragal. Square or rectangular mouldings range from 6×6mm ($\frac{1}{4} \times \frac{1}{4}$in) to 12×38mm ($\frac{1}{2} \times 1\frac{1}{2}$in) in size.

Other types of moulding include scotia and quadrant, which cover gaps between the meeting parts of a structure. Corner mouldings are a plain version of the scotia, and can be used inside or outside a joint.

When buying mouldings, check each one to make sure that the length is straight and free from large or dead knots. Fungal staining is something else to watch for, especially if you intend to use a clear finish. If you need several lengths of mouldings for the same job, check that you get a good match. Have a close look at the edges and colour and grain of each length, as mismatching can leave surface ripples or uneven edges.

FIXINGS

The choice of fixing depends on the size and weight of the materials being fixed.

Battens A general term used to describe a narrow strip of wood used for a variety of purposes. The usual sizes are 25×25mm (1×1in) or 50×25mm (2×1in).

Battens can be screwed to a wall to serve as bearers for shelves or they can be fixed in a framework on a wall, with sheet material or boards mounted over them to form a new 'wall'.

Dowels Used to make framework joints or to join boards edge-to-edge or edge-to-face.

Hardwood dowels are sold in diameters ranging from 6–10mm ($\frac{1}{4}-\frac{3}{8}$in). Generally speaking, dowel lengths should be about one-and-a-half times the thickness of the boards being joined.

Dowels are used with adhesive and, when the joint is complete, it is important to allow any excess adhesive to escape from the joint. Dowels with fluted (finely grooved) sides and chamfered ends will help this process. If you have plain dowels, make fine sawcuts along the length and chamfer the ends yourself.

Nails For general-purpose frame construction.
Round wire nails With large, flat, circular heads, these are used for strong joins where frames will be covered, so that the ugly appearance of the nails does not matter.
Annular ring-shank nails Used where really strong fixings are required.
Round lost head nails or **oval brads** (*oval wire nails*) Used when the finished appearance is important. The heads of these nails are driven in flush with the wood's surface and they are unobtrusive. They should be used when nailing a thin piece of wood to a thicker piece and there is a risk of splitting the wood.
Panel pins For fixing thin panels, these have unobtrusive heads that can be driven in flush with the wood's surface or punched below it.
Hardboard pins Copper-plated and with a square cross-section. They have deep-drive diamond-shaped heads that sink into the surface – ideal for fixing hardboard and other boards to timber in areas subject to condensation, where steel pins could cause black staining.
Masonry nails For fixing timber battens to walls as an alternative to screwing and wallplugging. Where a quick and permanent fixing is required, use the hardened-steel type.

Screws All types of screws are available with conventional slotted heads or cross-point heads.

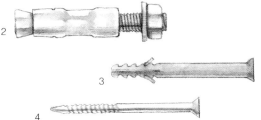

The latter are the best type to use if you are inserting screws with an electric screwdriver.

For most purposes, screws with countersunk heads are ideal as the head lies flush with the surface after insertion. Round-head screws are for fixing metal fittings such as door bolts, which have punched-out rather than countersunk screw holes. Raised-countersunk head screws are used where a neat appearance is important.

Wood screws These have a length of smooth shank just below the head. This produces a strong cramping effect, but there is a possibility of the unthreaded shank splitting the wood.

Twin-thread screws Less likely to split wood than wood screws. Except for larger sizes, they are threaded along their entire length, giving an excellent grip in timber and board. The best types are zinc plated, and so rust-resistant.

Coach screws For heavy-duty fixings when making frameworks requiring a strong construction. The screws have square or hexagonal heads and are turned with a spanner. A washer is used to prevent the head cutting into the timber.

Wallplugs Use a masonry drill bit to drill a hole which matches the size of screw being used (a No 10 bit with a No 10 screw, for example). Insert the plug in the hole, then insert the screw through the object being fixed and into the plug. Tighten the screw for a secure fixing.

Solid wall fixings The method of fixing to a solid brick or block wall is to use a wallplug. Traditional fibre wallplugs have been superseded by plastic versions which will accept a range of screw sizes, typically from No 8 to No 12.

Stud wall fixings To guarantee a secure fixing for stud walls, you should locate the timber uprights which form the framework of the wall and drive screws into them. If you want to attach something heavy and the timber uprights are not in the required position, then you *must* fix horizontal battens to the timber uprights.

Hollow-wall fixings Used on hollow walls, which are constructed from plasterboard partition or lath and plaster and are found in modern and old houses, respectively. There are many types of these fixings including spring toggle, gravity toggle and nylon toggle, and nearly all of them work on the same principle: expanding wings open up to grip the back of the wall, securing the fixing.

Wall anchor bolt Similar to a wallplug, but with its own heavy-duty machine screw, this is used for heavier objects, such as a kitchen unit, where a more robust wall fixing is required. You need to make a much larger hole in the wall, typically 10mm ($\frac{3}{8}$in) in diameter. The anchor sleeve expands as the bolt is tightened.

Expanding wall bolt This comprises a segmented body which expands as the bolt inside it is tightened. The body grips concrete, brick or stone securely. There are various lengths and diameters and there are also versions containing a hook or an eye. Most bolts are zinc-plated, but aluminium bronze versions are available where greater resistance to corrosion is required, especially for outdoor projects.

Corrugated fasteners For strengthening glued joints in frameworks in garden structures. Sizes are 6–22mm ($\frac{1}{4}$–$\frac{7}{8}$in) deep and 22–30mm ($\frac{7}{8}$–$1\frac{1}{4}$in) long.

LATCHES

Magnetic catches These are most useful on smaller doors which are unlikely to distort. There must be perfect contact between the magnet fixed to the cabinet frame and the striker plate which is fixed to the door. The other important factor is the pulling power of the magnet – on small cabinet doors a 'pull' of 2–3kg ($4\frac{1}{2}$–$6\frac{1}{2}$lb) is sufficient to keep the door closed. On wardrobe doors, however, a 5–6kg (11–13lb) 'pull' is needed to keep it shut.

Magnetic push latches are also useful. Push on the door inwards and it springs open just enough to be grasped and fully opened by the fingers.

Mechanical latches Common types are the spring-loaded ball catch and the roller catch. Again, alignment is vital to success, which is why adjustable types are favoured. A mechanical push latch is activated by pressure on the door itself, so a door handle is not necessary.

Peglock catches Particularly suitable for kitchen and bathroom cabinets, where atmospheric conditions can cause doors to distort.

HINGES

The easiest types of hinge to fix are those which do not have to be recessed into the door or frame – flush, decorative flush (for lightweight doors) or cranked (for cupboard doors). For fixing flaps, piano hinges are used. They are sold in 1.8m (6ft) lengths, and are cut to size with a hacksaw. For heavy doors or for a neat finish, butt hinges, which are recessed, are a good alternative.

Adjustable concealed hinges are used for chipboard and MDF doors. A special drill bit is required to cut cylindrical holes in the door, but the hinges are adjustable once fitted.

SLIDING DOOR TRACKS

Doors can either be suspended from above or supported from below. The track for glass or panel doors is made from PVC, and comes in a variety of colours. The door simply slides along the channel in the track.

Top-hung track Small tongued sliders or adjustable wheel hangers fixed to the top edge of the door sit in the track. Small guides keep the bottom edges of the door aligned.

Bottom-roller track The door slides on small rollers located in the track. Guides fitted at the top of the door keep it aligned in the track.

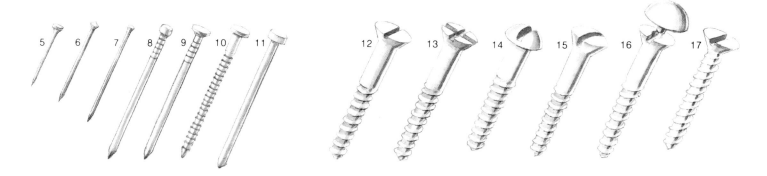

TECHNIQUES: SAWING AND CUTTING

WOOD

Wood is available either sawn or planed. Sawn wood is rough in appearance, but is close in width and thickness to the dimensions you specify when ordering. Planed wood is smoothed on all sides, but planing removes about 5mm ($\frac{3}{16}$in) from both the nominal width and the thickness. Sawn wood is ideal for building frameworks, but choose planed wood where a smooth finish is important. Wood should be straight and relatively knot-free. The surface should also be undamaged.

When building a framework of critical thickness (such as the basic kitchen unit modules on page 30) you may find it difficult to obtain wood of exactly the required thickness. If so, buy wood that is slightly oversized and plane it down.

After building, a fine surface can be obtained by sanding, either by hand with abrasive paper wrapped around a sanding block, or by using an electric orbital sander. In both cases, start with medium-grade abrasive paper and finish with fine; only sand in line with the grain, rather than across it, as this can cause scratching.

Wood finishes If a varnish, wax polish or paint finish is required, it can be applied easily with a brush (or rag). An alternative, often used by professional furniture makers, is to finish woodwork with a quick-drying cellulose lacquer (*see **Materials, page 233**), which can be applied with a paint sprayer. Before spraying, make sure that any holes are filled with stainable wood filler, and stain the surface, if required, before sanding it smooth. The first coat of lacquer is applied as a sealer. Leave it to dry for 30–60 minutes, then rub down the surface with fine abrasive paper. Next, apply a second, finishing, coat of lacquer.

MEASURING AND MARKING SQUARE

Mark cutting lines lightly with a hard pencil first, then use a trimming knife, straight-edge or try square along a rule to create a sharp, splinter-free line.

To mark timber square, use a try square with the stock (handle) pressed against a flat side of the timber, called the face side or face edge. Mark a line along the square, using a knife in preference to a pencil, then use the square to mark lines down the edges from the face mark. Finally square the other face side, checking that the lines join up right round the timber.

Check a try square for accuracy by pressing it against a straight edge. Mark along the blade, then turn the handle over to see if it aligns with the line from the other side.

If you are measuring and marking a number of pieces of the same length, then cramp them together and mark across several of them at the same time.

SPACING BATTEN

This is simply an offcut of wood, about 19mm or 25mm square ($\frac{3}{4}$in or 1in square), which is used to ensure that any slats to be fixed across a frame are spaced an equal distance apart. To ascertain the length to cut the spacing batten, simply bunch all the slats at one end of the frame. Measure to the other end of the frame and divide by the number of spaces (which you can count while you have the slats laid side by side). The resulting measure is the length to cut the spacing batten, which is used to set each slat into its exact position.

BRACING

When making a door or any similar frame, it is vital that it should be square, with corners at perfect right-angles. You can ensure this by using one of two bracing methods.

3-4-5-method Measure three units along one rail, four units down the adjacent rail, then nail a bracing batten accurately to one of the unit marks. Pull into square so that the bracing batten measures five units at the other unit mark, forming the long side of a triangle. Saw off the batten ends flush with the frame, but do not remove the batten until the frame is fitted in place. For large doors such as those on wardrobes, fix two braces on opposing corners.

① Marking Timber to Length and Square All Round
Mark across the face of the timber with a trimming knife held against a try square blade. Move knife round corners and mark sides, and finally mark other side to join up the lines.

② Using Spacing Battens to Space Out Slats Evenly
Bunch the battens together at one end of the frame, then measure to the other end of the frame. Divide this number by the number of spaces required; cut spacing batten to this length.

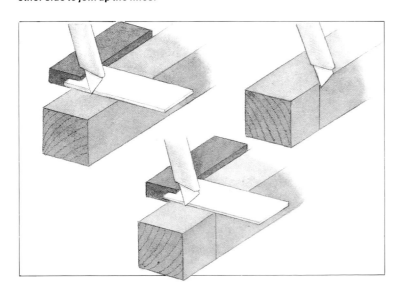

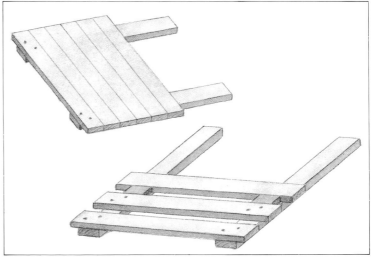

Try square method Nail a batten into one rail, pull into square by using a try square, and then nail the batten into the adjacent rail.

MAKING FOLDING WEDGES

Folding wedges are very useful for cramping large frames on a bench top during assembly. The wedges are always used in pairs, but more than one pair may be used to hold a large framework.

Make each pair of wedges from a piece of timber (hardwood is an ideal material for this) measuring $330 \times 38 \times 38$mm ($13 \times 1\frac{1}{2} \times 1\frac{1}{2}$in). Make the wedges by sawing the timber diagonally into two pieces.

To use the wedges, a wooden batten is first nailed to the bench and the item to be cramped is placed against the batten. Another batten is nailed to the bench, parallel with the first, and about 45mm ($1\frac{3}{4}$in) away from the item. The wedges are now placed between the item and the second batten. Next, the ends of the wedges are knocked inwards with two hammers, thereby cramping the frame.

③ Bracing a Frame Square
Nail a batten across a corner of the frame so that a 3-4-5 shape triangle is formed.

SAWING AND CUTTING

Cross-cutting to length by hand Hold the timber firmly with the cutting line (see **Measuring and Marking Square, page 236**) overhanging the right-hand side of the bench (if you are right-handed). With the saw blade vertical and the teeth on the waste side of the line, draw the handle back to start the cut. To prevent the saw from jumping out of place, hold the thumb joint of the other hand against the side of the saw blade.

Rip cutting by hand With the timber or board supported at about knee height, start the cut as described above, then saw down the waste side of the line, exerting pressure on the down cut only. If the saw blade wanders from the line, cramp the edge of a timber batten exactly above the cutting line on the side to be retained, and saw along it.

Using a portable power saw If the cutting line is only a short distance from a straight edge, adjust

④ Making Folding Wedges
Saw wood diagonally. Nail batten to bench; wedges fit between batten and item being cramped.

the saw's fence so that when it is run along the edge of the timber, the blade will cut on the waste side of the cutting line. If the timber is wide, or the edge is not straight, cramp a batten to the surface so that the saw blade will cut on the waste side of the line when it is run along the batten.

Ensuring a straight cut When cutting panels or boards using a power circular saw or jigsaw, the best way to ensure a straight cut is to cramp a guide batten to the surface of the work, parallel with the cutting line, so that the edge of the saw sole plate can be run along the batten. Obviously, the batten position is carefully adjusted so that the saw blade cuts on the waste side of the cutting line. Depending on which side of the cutting line the batten is cramped, when using a circular saw, it is possible that the motor housing will foul the batten or the G-cramps used to hold it in place. In this case, replace the batten with a wide strip of straight-edged plywood cramped to the work far enough back for the motor to clear the cramps.

⑤ Cross-cutting to Length
Hold the timber firmly. Steady the saw blade with the thumb joint as you start to saw.

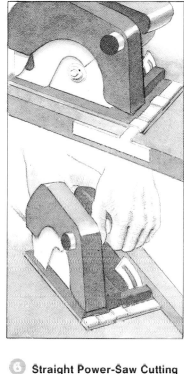

⑥ Straight Power-Saw Cutting
***Top* Use the rip fence of the saw if cutting near the edge of the piece of timber. *Bottom* cutting alongside the batten.**

⑦ Cutting with a Tenon Saw
Start the cut as for a hand saw. As the cut progresses keep the blade horizontal.

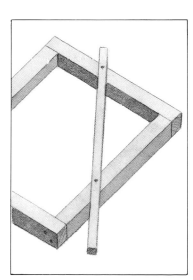

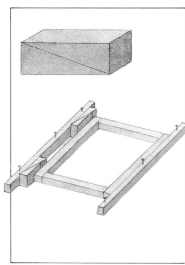

TECHNIQUES: CUTTING AND PLANING

CUTTING A CIRCLE

With a jigsaw Mark the circle on the face of the panel. If you do not have a compass, a good makeshift alternative can be made with a loop of string pivoted on a drawing pin at the centre of the circle. Hold a pencil vertically in the loop at the perimeter to draw the circle.

In order to have a neat, splinter-free edge, carefully score round the cutting line with a trimming knife. By scoring the cutting line it will be easier to follow the line and get a smooth edge.

To start the cut, drill a hole about 10mm ($\frac{3}{8}$in) in diameter just on the inside of the circle. Insert the jigsaw blade through this hole and start the cut from this point, sawing just on the waste side of the cutting line.

With a coping saw Mark out the circle, score the cutting line, and drill a hole just inside the circle as described above. Disconnect the blade from one end of the frame, pass the blade through the hole, and re-connect it to the frame. It will

be best to cramp the piece of work vertically when cutting the circle. The blade can be turned in the frame as necessary to help the frame clear the piece of work, but even so, with a coping saw you will be restricted in exactly how far you are able to reach away from the piece of work. If the circle is some way from the edge, use either a power jigsaw or a hand padsaw to cut it.

With a padsaw A padsaw, also called a keyhole saw, has a stiff, triangular pointed saw blade attached to a simple handle. A very useful padsaw blade is available for fitting in a regular knife handle.

Because this saw has no frame, it is ideal for cutting circles and other apertures, like keyholes, anywhere in a panel.

Preparation of the circle for cutting, such as marking out, scoring, and drilling for the blade, is the same as for the other methods. When cutting with a padsaw, keep the blade vertical and make a series of rapid, short strokes without exerting too much pressure.

CUTTING CURVES

The technique is basically the same as for cutting a circle, except that there will be no need to drill a hole in order to start the cut. You can use a jigsaw, coping saw, or padsaw to make the cut. A coping saw is ideal for making this type of cut because most of the waste can be removed with an ordinary hand saw, you will be cutting close to the edge of the wood, so the saw frame will not get in the way.

CUTTING GROOVES AND HOUSINGS

The easiest way to cut grooves (or housings) is to use a router fitted with a bit set to the depth required for the groove. Use a straight-sided router bit. Ideally, the router bit should be the exact width of the groove or housing, so that it can be cut from one setting. If this is not possible, then use a smaller router bit and cut the groove or housing in two or more goes. Make the first cut along the waste side of the line with a batten clamped in line with the

housing to guide the base of the router. If a deep groove is required, it may be necessary to make a shallow cut first, then a deeper one.

To cut housings by hand, start by marking out the groove with a trimming knife which will ensure a neat finish. Hold the piece of work on a bench and, with a tenon saw, make vertical cuts just inside the marked lines to the depth of the groove. If the groove is wide, make a series of other vertical cuts in the waste wood. Now chisel out the waste, working from each side to the middle. Finally, with the flat side of the chisel downwards, pare the bottom of the housing so that it is perfectly flat.

CUTTING REBATES

A rebate is an L-shaped step in the edge of a piece of timber.

To cut a rebate by hand, use a marking gauge to mark the rebate width across the top face of the piece of work and down both sides. Mark the depth of the rebate across the end and sides.

Hold the timber flat and saw down on the waste side of the marked line

---

1 Straight Rip-cutting
Cramp a straight batten alongside the cutting line and saw beside the batten. A wedge holds the cut open.

2 Using a Power Jigsaw
For a straight cut clamp a batten alongside line. Cut a circle by following line.

3 Cutting Circles by Hand
1 Drill a small hole and cut circle using a padsaw; *2* making cut with a coping saw.

4 Chiselling a Groove
After making saw cuts along marks, chisel out waste from each side. Finally pare base flat.

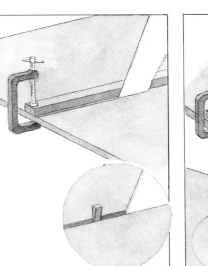
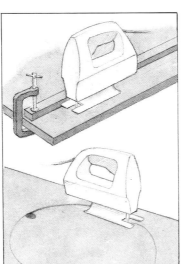
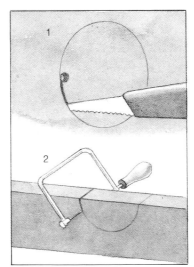

to the depth of the rebate. Then use a chisel to cut out the waste one bit at a time along the end grain.

It is very easy to cut a rebate using a router, and in this case it is not necessary to mark out the rebate unless you want a guide to work to. However, do practise on scrap wood to be sure of setting the router to cut to the correct depth and width.

If using a straight cutter, adjust the guide fence on the router so that the correct width is cut, then plunge and adjust the cutting depth so that the router will cut to the correct depth. When the router is correctly set up, simply hold it flat on the piece of work and move it against the direction of the cutter's rotation.

If you are using a cutter with a guide pin, simply adjust the depth of cut and then run the cutter along the edge of the wood to form the rebate. The cutter will follow irregularities in the wood, so make sure your wood is perfectly straight.

MAKING A V-BLOCK

A V-block is useful for holding circular items steady while they are being worked on. Make the block from a length of 75 × 50mm (3 × 2in) PAR timber – the actual length should be a little longer than the item to be held. The V is made to a depth of about 25mm (1in) in the 75mm (3in) side of the timber. Cut the V using a circular saw with the blade tilted to 45 degrees. Cramp the block firmly and fit the saw with a guide fence to keep the cut straight. Cut up one side and down the other. Practise on scrap wood while adjusting the depth and width of cut to give the correct size V-shape. Alternatively you can use a V-cutter bit in a router but it may take two or three passes to make the V to the full depth and width of the cutter.

PLANING

By hand Make sure that the plane blade is sharp and properly adjusted. Stand to one side of the work with feet slightly apart so you are facing the work and feeling comfortable. Plane from one end of the piece of work to the other, starting the cut with firm pressure on the leading hand, transferring it to both hands, and finally to the rear hand as the cut is almost complete. Holding the plane at a slight angle to the direction of the grain can sometimes improve the cutting action.

With a power plane Remove ties or loose clothing; overalls are ideal. Wear goggles and a dust mask. Check the work is cramped in place. Start the plane and turn the adjuster knob to set the depth to cut. Start with a shallow cut and increase the cutting depth if necessary.

Stand comfortably to one side of the work and, holding the plane with two hands, set it into the work at one end and pass it over the surface to the other end. Push the plane forwards steadily; not too fast or you will get a wavy surface finish. When you have completed the work, switch off and make sure that the blades stop spinning before resting the plane down with the cutting depth set at zero.

DRILLING

To ensure that screwheads lie level with the surface of plywood, chipboard and hardwood use a countersink drill bit.

To minimize the risk of splitting timber, drill pilot and clearance holes for screws. For small screws, pilot holes can be made with a gimlet.

The clearance hole in the timber should be fractionally smaller in diameter than the screw shank.

The pilot hole in the timber to receive the screw should be about half the diameter of the clearance hole. The depth of the pilot hole should be slightly less than the length of the screw.

Drilling vertical holes To ensure vertical holes mount the drill in a stand. If this is not possible, stand a try square on edge so that its stock is resting on the work alongside the drilling position, and the blade is pointing up in the air. Use this as a siting guide and line up the drill as close as possible with the square to ensure the drill is vertical. It is also helpful if an assistant can stand back and sight along the drill and square from two sides to ensure the drill is straight.

⑤ Making a V-block
Cut out a V in a block of 75 × 50mm (3 × 2in) timber using a circular power saw tilted to cut at 45 degrees.

⑥ Drilling Vertical Holes
With a drill stand, not only will the drill bit be held vertical, but depth is controlled.

⑦ Freehand Drilling Guide
When drilling it can be helpful to stand a try square alongside the drill to ensure accuracy.

⑧ Drilling Depth Guide
There are various guides to control drilling depths, such as rings for bits, and sticky tape.

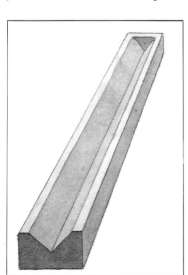

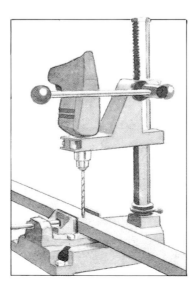

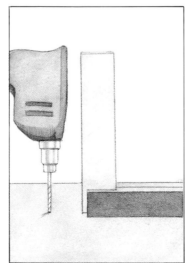

TECHNIQUES: WALL FIXINGS

SCREWING

When screwing one piece of wood to another ensure that half of the screw penetrates through the bottom piece of wood. Its thickness should not exceed one-tenth of the width of the wood into which it has to be inserted. Keep screws at a distance of five times their shank diameter from the side edge of the wood, and ten times the shank diameter from its end.

NAILING

The correct length of nail to use is two-and-a-half to three times the thickness of the timber being fixed. However, check that the nail will not pierce right through two pieces being fixed. Wherever possible nail through the thinner piece of wood into the thicker piece.

Nails grip best if driven in at an angle ('skew nailing'). A row of nails should be driven in at opposing angles to each other. Framework joints are usually held in by skew nailing. Cramp or nail a block of wood temporarily against one side of the vertical piece to stop it sliding as the first nail is started.

To prevent wood from splitting, particularly if nailing near an edge, blunt the points of the nails by hitting them with a hammer before driving them home. Blunt nails will cut through timber fibres neatly, while pointed nails are more likely to push the fibres apart like a wedge, leading to splitting.

WALL FIXINGS

Solid wall The normal fixing for a solid wall is a woodscrew and plastic or fibre wallplug. Before drilling the fixing hole, check with a metal detector that there are no pipes or cables hidden behind the surface. Drill the holes for the wallplug with a masonry drill bit in an electric drill. The wallplug packing will indicate the drill size to use. Switch to hammer action if the wall is hard. The screw should be long enough to go through the fitting and into the wall by about 25mm (1in) if the masonry is exposed, and by about 35mm (1⅜in) if fixing into a plastered wall.

If the wall crumbles when you drill into it, mix up a cement-based plugging compound (available from DIY stores). Turn back the screw by about half a turn before the compound sets (in about five minutes). When it is hard (in about one hour) the screw can be removed and a heavy fixing can be made.

If your drill sinks easily into the wall once it has penetrated the plaster layer, and a light grey dust is produced from the hole, you are fixing into lightweight building blocks. In this case, special winged wallplugs should be used for soft blocks.

To make a quick, light-to-medium weight fixing in a solid wall, a masonry nail can be used. Choose a length that will penetrate the material to be fixed, and pierce an exposed masonry wall by 15mm (⅝in) and a plastered wall by about 25mm (1in). Wear goggles in case the hardened nail snaps when you strike it, and hammer it gently through the material to be fixed and into the wall.

Lath and plaster For a strong fixing, screw directly into the main vertical studding timbers to which the laths are nailed. You can find these studs with a metal detector (see **Stud wall,** below).

For a lightweight fixing you can screw into the wood laths. These can be located by probing with a pointed implement such as a gimlet. Then insert a twin-thread woodscrew. For medium-to-heavyweight fixings into lath and plaster, drill between the laths and use a cavity-wall fixing suitable for lath and plaster, such as a spring toggle, gravity toggle or nylon toggle.

Stud wall For a strong fixing into a plasterboard-covered stud wall, make a screw fixing directly into the vertical timber studs. You can find these by tapping the wall to check where it sounds most dense, and then probing these areas with a pointed implement until a firm background is found. Alternatively, you can make a small hole in the wall, and push a stiff wire into it horizontally until an obstruction is felt, which will be the stud. Withdraw the wire and hold it on the surface of the wall

---

① Drilling Holes for Screws in Timber
Drill a clearance hole in the thinner piece. Countersink this hole, then drill a pilot hole to slightly less than screw length. *Inset* To counterbore, drill to the diameter of the screw head, to required depth then as above.

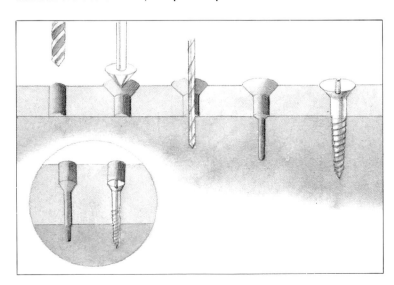

② Techniques for Joining Wood by Nailing
Nail should be two-and-a-half to three times the thickness of the timber being fixed. Assemble frames on bench by nailing against batten. *Inset* Blunt nail points to avoid splitting timber.

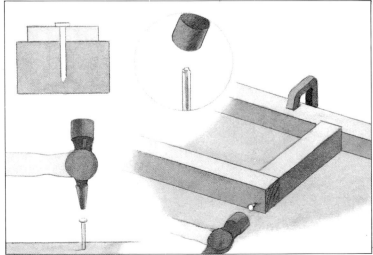

so that the edge of the stud can be marked. By drilling about 25mm (1in) to the farther side of this mark, the centre of the stud will be found and a screw can be inserted.

To avoid making holes in the surface of a wall, a metal detector can be used. Move it over the wall to locate a pattern of nail fixings and mark this on the surface. Vertical rows of nails indicate a stud. Alternatively, use one of the newer electronic stud and joist detectors. This is moved over the surface to detect a change in density between the different construction materials. A change indicates a stud.

If a fixing cannot be made into a stud, a lighter fixing can be made into plasterboard by using a fitting designed for that material. Follow the manufacturer's instructions for the size of hole required, which can be made in plasterboard with an ordinary twist drill bit.

Cavity wall Cavity walls comprise a solid inner leaf of bricks or building blocks surfaced with plaster and separated from the outer leaf of bricks or stone blocks by a cavity about 50mm (2in) wide.

When tapped, a cavity wall sounds solid. For fixings, treat it as a solid wall (see page 240).

BEVELLED BATTENS

These provide a very secure method of holding heavy objects on to a wall. The battens are formed by sawing a strip of wood lengthways with the saw blade set at 45 degrees. This results in two interlocking pieces of wood. One piece, with the sloping face pointing upwards and the narrower face facing the wall, is screwed to the wall. The other piece, with the sloping face pointing downwards and the narrower side facing the item to be hung, is screwed to the item to be fixed. When the item is lifted into place, the battens interlock for a very secure fixing.

For security, the battens should be formed by sawing a 100 × 25mm (4 × 1in) strip of timber lengthways. Screw fixings, applied to the wall and into the item to be hung, should be at about 200mm (8in) intervals. Use No 10 woodscrews, 38mm (1½in) long, into the item to be hung, and 65mm (2½in) long into the wall. Wallplugs will also be required.

FIXING RIGHT-ANGLE BRACKETS

These are right-angle steel strips pre-drilled for screw fixing and are useful for fixing timber frames to walls and ceilings, as long as brackets are positioned out of sight (see **Fixing down worktops, page 36**).

Decide where you want the bracket, hold it in place on the frame and use a pencil to mark the centre of one screw fixing position. Drill a pilot hole and fix the bracket with one screw. Repeat for the other brackets. Position the frame and check that it is vertical. Mark centre points of the bracket fixing holes on the wall or ceiling. Remove the frame and use a masonry drill to make plug holes at the required positions. Press plugs into holes. Before replacing the frame and screwing brackets in place, check that brackets are still accurately positioned on the frame. Drill pilot holes for remaining screw fixings, and insert screws.

③ Skew Nailing for Strength
Assemble frames by skew nailing (driving nails at an angle). The joint will not then pull apart.

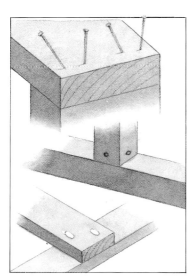

④ Using a Nail Punch
For a neat finish, use a nail punch to drive nail heads below the surface, then fill indentation.

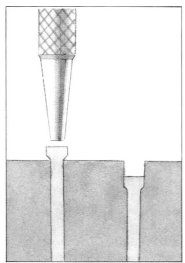

⑤ Using Bevelled Battens
For a secure fixing on a wall use bevelled battens made by sawing a batten lengthwise at 45 degrees.

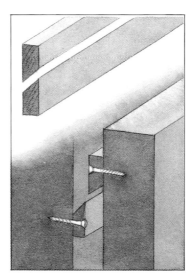

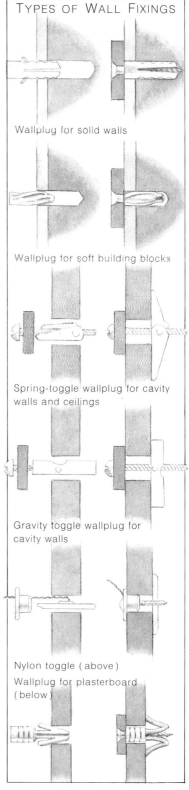

TYPES OF WALL FIXINGS

Wallplug for solid walls

Wallplug for soft building blocks

Spring-toggle wallplug for cavity walls and ceilings

Gravity toggle wallplug for cavity walls

Nylon toggle (above)

Wallplug for plasterboard (below)

TECHNIQUES: WOOD JOINTS

WOOD JOINTS

Butt joint This is the simplest frame joint of all. The ends of the timbers to be joined must be cut square so that they butt together neatly. Corner and T joints can be formed, which are glued and nailed for strength. Corrugated fasteners can also be used to hold these joints, especially where the sides of the frames will be covered to hide the fasteners. When T joints are being formed from inside a frame, they can be skew nailed.

Corner joint These are simple 'knock down' fittings fixed with screws; they are used to fix boards together at right-angles. They are described as 'knock down' because some are in two parts for easy disassembly, and even the simple fittings can be unscrewed. They do not look very attractive, but are useful where they will be hidden – by a fascia, for example.

Mitre joint Popular for making picture frames, but suitable for other

right-angled corner joints. Cut the joints at 45 degrees using a mitre box as a guide. A simple mitre joint is glued and pinned, but a stronger joint can be made using dowels, or by making oblique saw cuts into which wood veneers are glued.

Halving joint Also known as a half-lap joint this may be used to join wood of similar thickness at corners or to T or X joints. The joint is formed by cutting each piece to half its thickness. Use a try square to mark the width of the cut-outs and a marking gauge set to half the thickness of the wood to mark their depth. Be sure to cross-hatch the waste wood with a pencil so that the correct side is removed. To form a corner half-lap, saw down as for making a tenon joint (page 244). To form a 'T' or 'X' half-lap, saw down on each side of the 'T' cut-out to the depth of the central gauge line, then chisel out the waste.

Housing joint Used mainly for shelving, this is basically a slot into which a shelf fits. The 'through'

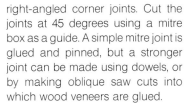

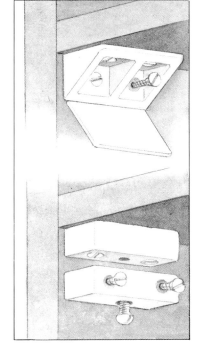

② Corner Fitting Joints
Ideal for joining woods and boards at right angles. *Top* **A one-piece fitting;** *Bottom* **A two-part type. Both are easily fitted using screws.**

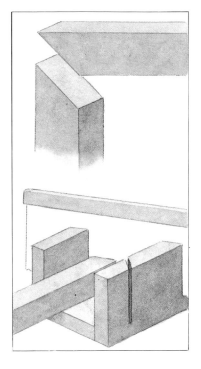

⑤ Cutting Mitre Joints
Mitres make right-angle corner joints. Using a mitre box as a guide for ensuring a 45 degree angle cut out the joint with a tenon saw.

① Simple Butt Joints
Top **Corner and** *Bottom* **T joints can be formed by skew nailing or by using corrugated fasteners.**

③ Types of Halving Joints
Top **A corner halving joint.** *Bottom left* **A T-halving joint.** *Bottom right* **A cross halving joint.**

④ Forming a Halving Joint in Timber Battens
Mark width of the cut-out. Mark half the thickness of the wood with a marking gauge. Cross hatch area to be removed. Saw down sides with a tenon saw, then chisel out the waste.

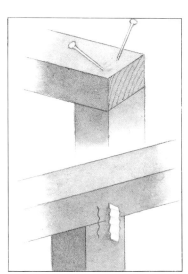

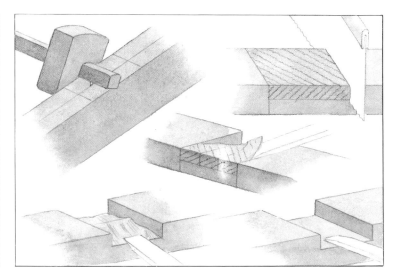

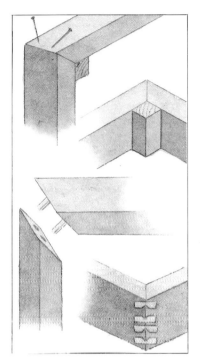

⑥ Forming Mitre Joints
Top Glue and pin together a simple mitre joint. *Bottom* Reinforce the joint with a corner block, dowels or wood veneer.

⑧ Types of Housing Joints
Top A through housing joint. *Middle* Through housing joints on the side of a central support. *Bottom* A corner housing joint.

⑦ Stages in Forming a Through Housing Joint
Mark width of the housing according to thickness of wood being joined. Use a trimming knife. Mark depth with marking gauge. Cut down sides with tenon saw. Chisel out the waste, working from both sides to the middle.

housing joint goes to the full width of the shelf, while a 'stopped' housing joint is taken only part of the way across the board. Chisel the waste away from each side. In the case of a stopped housing, chisel the waste from the stopped end first. If you have a router, it is easier to cut a housing joint by running the router across the board against a batten which is cramped at right-angles to the board.

A rebate joint is similar to a housing joint at the top of a board, and can be cut in a similar way.

BARE-FACED HOUSING JOINT

This type of housing joint, used at the corners of a frame, is a much stronger joint than the common butt joint or lapped joint because the tongue of one piece is held in a housing cut in the other piece. The joint will be held firm with good woodworking adhesive and by nailing or screwing down through the top into the upright. However, because of the short grain on the outside of the groove, this piece is left overlong while the joint is made, and then the 'horn' (the excess timber) is cut off neatly, flush with the side of the joint. The tongue should be no thicker than half the width of the timber being joined.

Carefully mark out the joint with a trimming knife, a try square and a marking gauge. The depth of the housing should be about one-third to a half the thickness of the upright. Cut the sides of the housing to the required depth using a tenon saw held vertical, or a carefully set circular saw. Cramping a batten alongside the housing will help to keep the cut straight. Remove the waste with a chisel, working from both sides to the middle, and holding the chisel with the flat side downwards. Alternatively, cut the housing with a router (*see* **Cutting grooves and housings, page 238**)

Mark out the vertical piece so that the tongue will fit exactly in the housing. Use a marking gauge to mark out the tongue. Cut the rebate with a router or with a tenon saw to form the tongue (*see* **Cutting grooves and housings, page 238**).

⑨ Stages in Making a Bare-faced Housing joint
Leave a 'horn' of surplus timber to support the short grain which will be on outside of the groove. Mark width of piece being joined. Mark and cut housing as before. Saw off horn.

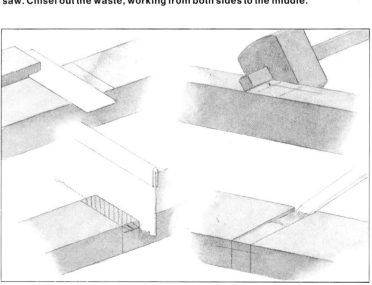

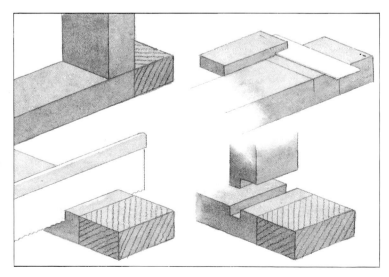

Techniques: Wood Joints

Mortise and tenon joint A mortise and tenon joint can be marked out with a mortise gauge. Mark out the tenon (the tongue) so that it is one-third of the thickness of the piece of wood. The mortise (the slot) is marked at the same width in the other piece. The length of the mortise should match the width of the tenon being fitted. Drill out most of the waste with a series of holes using a bit slightly smaller than the mortise width. Working from the centre, chop out the mortise with a chisel to the depth required. If making a through joint (in which the end of the tenon is visible), turn the wood over and complete the mortise from the other side.

Hold the tenon piece upright, but sloping away from yourself, secure in a vice, and use a tenon saw carefully to cut down to the shoulder. Then swivel the wood around to point the other way, and saw down to the other side of the shoulder. Next, position the wood vertically and cut down to the shoulder. Finally, place the wood flat and saw across the shoulder to remove the

② Marking and Cutting a Mortise and Tenon Joint
Mark the length of the mortise slot to match the size of the rail being joined. Set the mortise gauge to the width of the chisel being used to cut out the mortise slot. (Chisel should be about one-third the width of wood being joined.) Use the mortise gauge to mark the mortise, and also the tenon, on the rail. Drill out the mortise and complete the cut with a chisel. Use a tenon saw to cut out the tenon.

③ Making a Haunched Mortise and Tenon Joint
Leave rail over-long. Mark out as before but allow for shoulder at top. Cut mortise slot, then saw down sides of shoulder which is completed with a chisel. Cut tenon as shown.

① Mortise and Tenon Joints
Top A common or stopped mortise and tenon joint. *Bottom* Through mortise and tenon joint.

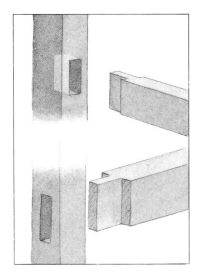

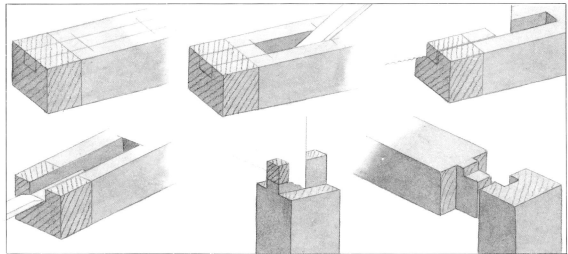

waste. Repeat for the waste on the other side of the tongue. Check that the two pieces fit well before gluing and assembling the joint. For added strength and a better appearance, cut small additional shoulders at each end of the tenon.

Haunched mortise and tenon joint For joints at the corner of a large frame, a square haunch or shoulder can be left in the tenon to increase its effective width and considerably strengthen the joint.

The joint is marked out with a try square, marking knife, and marking gauge as for an ordinary mortise and tenon, but allowance is made for a square shoulder at the top.

To prevent the small amount of cross-grain timber above the mortise from being pushed out when the mortise slot is cut, the rail is left over-long at this stage to create a 'horn' which is cut off after the joint has been made and assembled.

Bare-faced mortise and tenon joint If the tongue of a tenon joint is offset to one side, this produces a

bare-faced tenon as shown in the diagram. This produces a strong joint where narrow rails, such as the trellis rails in the Japanese wardrobe doors (page 92), meet the thicker frame rails. The mortise slots in the frame rails can be cut farther back from the front edge for extra strength, and the bare-faced tenons of the trellis rails allow the front faces of these rails to lie flush with the front face of the door.

A bare-faced tenon is cut in the same way as a halving joint.

Dowel joint Dowels are a strong, simple means of joining wood.

Use pre-cut grooved dowels with bevelled ends (*see* **Materials, page 234**). These range from 6mm ($\frac{1}{4}$in) diameter by 25mm (1in) long to 10mm ($\frac{3}{8}$in) by 50mm (2in). The dowel length should be about one-and-a-half times the thickness of the wood being jointed. If you need to use dowelling of a larger diameter (as used in the cupboard door frames in the kitchen) cut your own from lengths of dowel. Cut grooves down the length of dowel to allow

glue and air to escape, and chamfer the ends. When making your own dowels, their length can be twice the thickness of the wood.

On both pieces of wood, use a marking gauge to find the centre line, and mark with a pencil. Drill the dowel holes to half the dowel length with the drill held in a drill stand, or aligned with a try square stood on end. Drill the dowel holes in one of the pieces to be joined, insert centre points in the holes, then bring the two pieces of the joint together so they are aligned. The centre points will mark where the dowel holes should be in the second piece of wood. Drill the holes to half the dowel length, plus a little extra for glue. Where dowels are used for location rather than strength, such as for joining worktops, set the dowels three-quarters into one edge and a quarter into the other.

Put adhesive in the hole and tap dowels into the holes in the first piece with a mallet. Apply adhesive to both parts of the joint; bring the pieces together and cramp them in position until the adhesive has set.

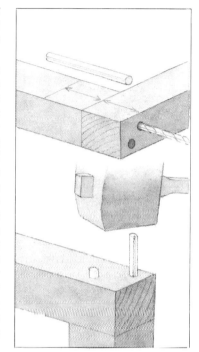

⑦ Making a Dowelled Frame
If edge of frame will not be seen, drill holes for dowels after making frame. Hammer dowels home; cut ends flush after glue dries.

④ Making a Bare-Faced Mortise and Tenon Joint
Tenon is offset to one side. Mark and cut as shown here.

⑤ Types of Dowel Joint
Dowels can join panels edge to edge and join frames at corners. They can be hidden or have ends exposed.

⑥ Dowels to Join Panels
Right Mark dowel positions. Drill holes, insert centre points. Mark second piece.

⑧ Using a Dowelling Jig
If dowels are to be hidden, a dowelling jig makes it easy to drill holes that align in both pieces.

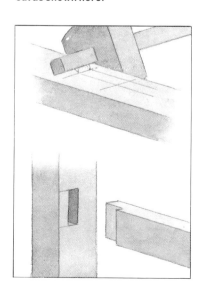

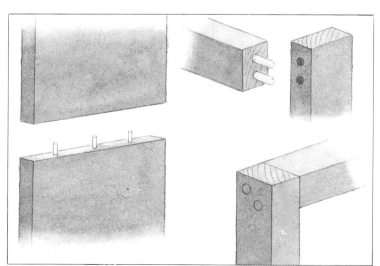

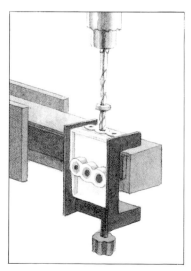

Scribing and Levelling

Scribing long lengths When you are fitting a worktop, horizontal panel, shelf, or vertical panel to a wall, you are likely to find that it will not touch the wall at every point since it is extremely unlikely that the wall will be flat and square. To avoid such gaps, it is necessary to scribe the item to the wall.

Hold the item in place and as close to its final position as possible. If it is a worktop, make sure that it is level and at right-angles to whatever is next to it. If it is an upright, make sure that the front edge is held vertical. Where the gap is at its widest, pull the panel forward so that the gap is 25mm (1in). Take a block of wood 25mm (1in) long and place it on the panel, against the wall, at one end. Hold a pencil against the other end of the block, and draw the pencil and block along the wall so that the pencil makes a line, which reproduces the contours of the wall.

With an electric jigsaw or a padsaw, cut along the line. Where the line is too close to the edge to saw, shape the panel to the line using a shaping tool, such as a Surform or a wood rasp. Press the panel against the wall and check that it fits neatly all the way along.

Scribing in alcoves It is more difficult to scribe in an alcove because a horizontal panel will usually fit neatly only *after* it has been scribed to a wall.

Using a large wooden square (you can make one from timber battens following the 3-4-5 principle of producing a right-angled triangle, see page 236), find out if one, or both, of the side walls are square and flat. If they are, you can carefully measure between them at the required height of the worktop. Then saw off the ends of the worktop to this length and position it, before finally scribing it to the rear wall as described above.

If the side walls of the alcove are not square, you can mark out the worktop using a cardboard template (*see* **Using templates**) of each side wall and part of the rear wall which you then scribe to fit.

Using a profile gauge This device (*see* **Tools, page 228**) is used for reproducing a complicated shape and is useful if you have to fit, for example, a worktop around something such as a decorative timber moulding. It comprises a row of movable pins or narrow plastic strips held in place by a central bar. When pressed against a shape, the pins follow the outline of the shape. The profile gauge is then held on the item to be fitted and the shape transferred to it by drawing around the profile gauge with a pencil. After use, realign the pins.

Using templates When cutting around an awkward-shaped object, such as a pipe, it is a good idea to make a template of the obstruction. Make the template from cardboard or thick paper. Cut and fold the template to make it as accurate as you can. When you are satisfied that you have a good fit, place the template on the item to be fitted, and mark around it to produce a cutting line. Alternatively, glue the template in position and cut around it.

Levelling battens When fixing battens to a wall with masonry nails, first lay the battens on the floor and drive the nails almost all the way through them. On the wall, use a spirit level to position the batten horizontally and draw a pencil line along the top edge of the batten. Hold the batten in position and drive one of the end masonry nails part of the way into the wall. Check that the top of the batten aligns with the guide line, then rest the spirit level on the batten and, with the bubble central, drive the nail at the other end of the batten into the wall. Check again that the batten is level before driving in all the nails.

If fixing the batten with screws, drill clearance holes in the batten as above and, with a pointed tool, mark the wall through a screw hole at one end of the batten. Drill and plug the wall at this point (*see* **Wall fixings, page 240**) then screw the batten to the wall. Level the batten as above, mark the other screw positions, then remove the batten and drill and plug the wall in preparation. Finally, screw the wall batten in to place.

1 **Scribing Long Lengths to Fit Against a Wall**
Where gap is widest pull panel forward so gap is 25mm (1in). Hold pencil against 25mm (1in) wide block; move block and pencil along wall to draw cutting line. Cut along this line.

2 **Fixing Levelling Battens to a Wall**
If fixing with masonry nails drive these into battens first. Hold batten in place and mark wall. Holding batten on marked line, insert nail at end. Recheck level; drive in other nails.

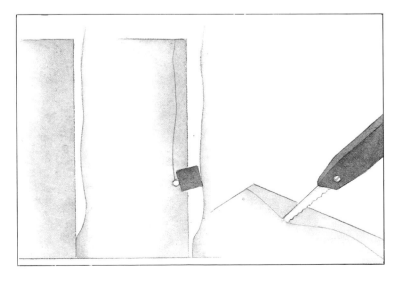

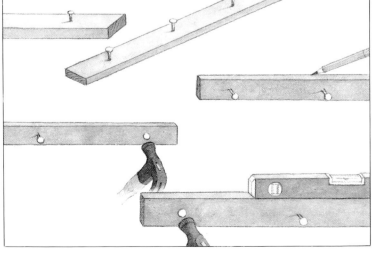

Levelling kitchen units Floors are rarely level, so that when installing kitchen units you must work from the highest spot in the room. Assemble the units and temporarily place them in position. Take a long, straight wooden batten and place this on the top of the units. Place a spirit level on the horizontal batten, to find the highest unit. Work from this unit and bring all the other units up to this level by placing pieces of plywood or hardboard underneath them. After this is done, the worktops can be installed, and the inset sink fitted and connected.

Alternatively, if you have yet to construct the units, you can build each one to the exact height required to compensate for differences in floor level. This levelling technique is very useful for old properties where floors are invariably uneven. First, lay straight battens around the floor where the units will be positioned one batten at the front edge and one at the back. Work from the high point and pack up the battens so that they are level. Mark on them the positions of the units and at each point measure the gap to the floor. Increase the height of each unit by this amount.

Finding verticals Use a plumb line to mark a vertical line on a wall. Tap a nail into the wall where you want the vertical to be, and tie the plumb line to it. When the line is steady, hold a scrap of wood on the wall so it just touches the string and mark the wall at this point. Repeat the procedure at a couple of other places. Alternatively, rub the plumb line with chalk. When it stops swinging, press it against the wall, then pluck the string to leave a vertical chalk line on the wall.

HANGING DOORS

Hinged cupboard or wardrobe doors There are two ways to fit hinged doors; they can be inset to fit between side frames, or they can be lay-on where the doors cover the side frames.

Inset doors look attractive, but they are harder to fit than lay-on doors because they must be very accurately made to achieve a uniform gap all round the opening. Lay-on doors cover the frame and hide any uneven gaps. Also, the concealed hinges that are normally used to hang a lay-on door are adjustable, making it easy to alter the door so that it slides smoothly.

Sliding cupboard and wardrobe doors Small doors slide in double U-channel tracks made from timber or plastic. Shallow U-channel track is fitted along the bottom front edge of the opening and a deeper track is fitted at the top, to the underside of the front edge. The grooves in the track should match the door thickness and it is important to fit the top track exactly vertically above the bottom track. Make sliding doors so that they overlap each other by about 45–50mm ($1\frac{3}{4}$–2in). Their height should be the distance from the top of the groove in the top track to the bottom of the groove in the bottom track, plus 6mm ($\frac{1}{4}$in). After assembly of the unit, the door can be fitted by lifting it up and into the top track, and then slotting it into the bottom track for a neat fit.

Heavier doors must be hung using a top- or bottom-track roller system. Fitting is usually straightforward if you follow the manufacturer's instructions. Even if the track has been fixed so that it is not exactly horizontal, there is usually a way of adjusting the doors so that they move and close smoothly.

FITTING HINGES

Inset doors Flush hinges are the easiest to fit. They are simply screwed to the edge of the door and the frame, and require no recessing. However, they cannot be adjusted after fitting. The inner flap of the hinge is screwed to the edge of the door, while the outer flap is screwed to the inner face of the frame.

Fix the hinges at equal distances from the top and bottom of the door. With a tall or very heavy door, fit a third hinge centrally between the other two. Mark the hinge positions on the edge of the door with the hinge knuckle (joint) in line with the door front. Drill pilot holes and screw on the inner flap. Hold the door in place or rest it on something to

3 Using a Profile Gauge
To reproduce complicated shapes, press the gauge against object; use it as a pattern.

4 A Method of Levelling Kitchen Units
Temporarily position the units or the partition frames. Place spirit level on a straight batten to find the highest unit. Pack plywood or hardwood pieces under other units to bring them to this level.

5 Fitting Sliding Door Track
Heavy doors are best hung on bottom track. Track screws to floor and rollers are inset in door bottoms.

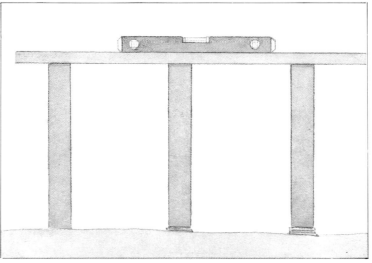

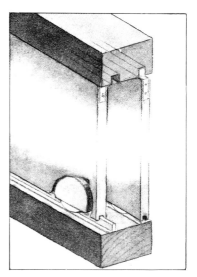

raise it to the correct height, making sure that it is accurately aligned top and bottom, and mark the positions of the hinges on the frame. Remove the door and extend these lines using a try square. Hold the door against the frame so it is in an open position, and screw the outer hinge flaps in place, so that they match up with the guide lines.

Butt hinges are conventional flapped hinges and are available in steel (commonly) or in brass, which is better for high-quality work. They are fitted in the same way as flush hinges, except that the hinge flaps have to be recessed into the timber using a chisel or router.

Mark out the hinge positions as for flush hinges, making sure that the hinges are not positioned so that the fixing screws will go into the end grain of cross members and be likely to pull out.

The length of the hinges is marked out first, using a marking knife, then the width of the hinge and the thickness of the flap are marked using a marking gauge. With a chisel held vertical, and a mallet, cut

down around the waste side of the recess, then make a series of vertical cuts across the full width of the recess. Remove the waste by careful chiselling, then finally pare the bottom of the recess flat using the chisel held flat side downwards.

If you are careful, you can remove the bulk of the waste from a hinge recess using a straight bit in a router. The bit is set to cut to the depth of the recess, and afterwards the corners can be finished off using a chisel.

Lay-on doors Modern, adjustable concealed hinges are the most commonly used. There are many types available, and they come with full fitting instructions. Some types are face-fixed and simply screw in place on the inside face of the door, but usually a special end mill hinge-sinker bit is used to drill a wide, flat-bottomed hole for the hinge body in the rear surface of the door. Next, the base plate is screwed to the side frame. Finally, the hinge is attached to the base plate and the adjusting screws are turned until the door fits perfectly in place.

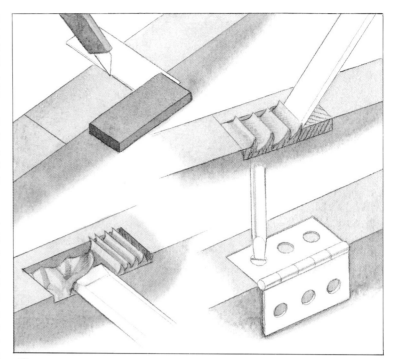

 **The Stages in Fitting a Butt Hinge**
Using a try square and a trimming knife, mark out the length of hinge. With a marking gauge mark width and thickness of hinge flap. With chisel vertical, cut round outline of hinge. Make series of cuts across width of recess. Pare out the waste then check that the flap lies flush. Once this is done, screw the butt hinge in place.

1 Fitting a Flush Hinge
Flush hinges are very easy to fit. Screw the outer flap to the frame and the inner flap to the door.

2 Fitting a Butt Hinge
Butt hinges must be recessed into the door and frame so that hinge flaps are flush with surface.

4 Fitting Face-Fixed Concealed Hinges
This hinge is simply screwed to the inside face of the door and frame.

5 Fitting Recessed Concealed Hinges
Blind hole is drilled for hinge body. The base plate arm is adjustable.

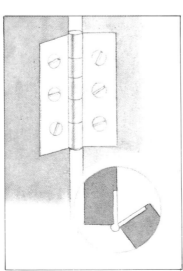

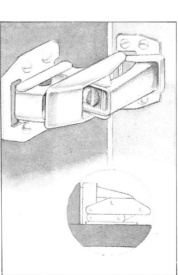

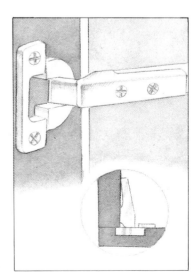

FITTING CATCHES

Many types of concealed hinges have built-in closers, so catches are not required. With conventional hinges, magnetic catches are popular. The magnet is fitted to the side of the cabinet and the catch plate is then positioned on the magnet. The door is closed on to the catch and pressed hard so that the catch plate marks the door. The door is opened and the catch plate is then simply screwed to the door.

Ball catches are very neat devices. On the central edge of the door a hole is drilled to accept the body of the ball catch, which is pressed into place. The door is closed and the ball marks the edge of the cupboard. The door is opened and the striker plate carefully positioned to coincide with the centre of the ball. If you are recessing the striker plate, its outline should be drawn around, using a trimming knife. The striker plate is then recessed into the cabinet so that it lies flush with the surface enabling the catch to operate smoothly.

FITTING DOOR LIFT MECHANISMS

Actual fitting instructions vary with the type of mechanism, but basically all screw inside the cupboard on the side of the carcass, close to the top. Two lift mechanisms are required per door, and they are designed to hold the door open.

Door lift mechanisms reduce the chance of a heavy door falling and trapping a child's head or limbs; you could use them to support the flap-down doors in the Storage House (page 102) or to hold open the hinged table top in the Painting Table (page 148). The mechanism is screwed to the side face of the frame just below the top of the wardrobe, and just inside the front edge. It is held with three screws. The lift-up flap is screwed to the opening part of the mechanism with two screws, the top screw being fixed the thickness of the wardrobe top plus 28mm (1$\frac{1}{8}$in), down from the top edge of the door flap to be sure that the flap opens without disturbing the wardrobe front or the ceiling.

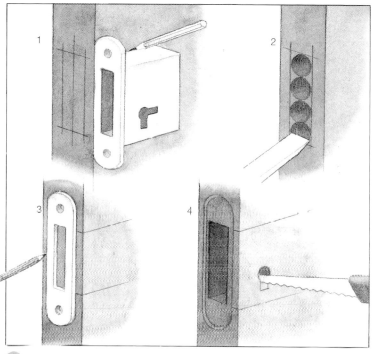

Fitting a Cabinet Mortise Lock to a Cupboard Door
1 Mark the centre line on the door edge and measure and mark the width and thickness of the lock on door edge and outside face. *2* Use a dowel bit to clear out the mortise and clear out the slot with a chisel. *3* Push the lock into the mortise slot and mark around the cover plate. *4* Cut recess for plate; form keyhole using padsaw.

6 Magnetic Cupboard Catch
A magnetic catch is screwed to the inside face of a cabinet and the catch plate is screwed to the frame.

7 Fitting a Ball Catch
Drill door edge centrally for ball catch body which is pressed in place. Striker plate fixes to frame.

9 Fitting Top-Hinged Door Lift Mechanism
Two types of door lift mechanisms are shown below. On the left is a combined hinge and stay which allows the door to be raised and remain in an open position. Also shown is a conventional stay.

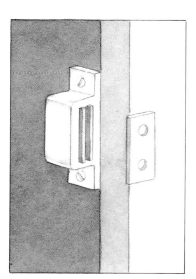

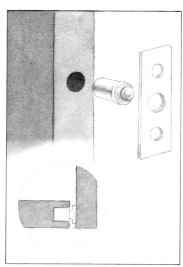

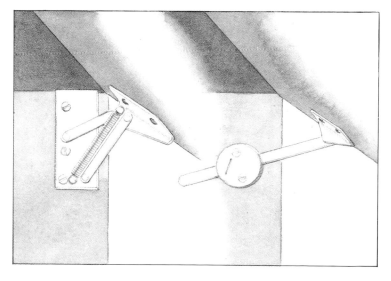

FITTING LOCKS

The neatest lock is a cabinet mortise lock. To fit, mark the centre line in the edge of the door and measure and mark the width and thickness of the lock body. Using a dowel drill bit of the same thickness as the lock body, drill out a series of overlapping holes to remove the bulk of the waste, and clear out the slot with a chisel. Push the lock into the mortise slot, mark around the cover plate and cut a recess. Measure the lock for the keyhole position, mark this on the front face of the door, drill the hole and saw a slot for the key. Close the door, turn out the lock bolt to mark the cabinet side, and fit the lock keep-plate there.

A straight cupboard lock, as used on the Tool Cupboard (page 10), is very easy to fit. It simply screws to the back of the door after the keyhole has been cut out with a padsaw.

Start by making a thick paper template of the outline of the lock with a cut-out for the keyhole accurately positioned. Hold the template on the face of the door and mark the keyhole. Drill a hole at the top to the correct size, and below this drill a line of smaller holes which can be enlarged into a slot for the keyhole using a padsaw.

Hold the lock in place behind the door, and fit the key to position the lock accurately. Mark and drill the fixing lock positions. Screw the lock in place. A brass keyhole escutcheon fitting may be supplied, and this is simply tapped into place into the keyhole flush with the face of the cabinet front.

In the case of the Tool Cupboard project it will be necessary to cut away part of the door side rail to allow the lock to fit flush with the edge of the door. To do this, hold the lock against the edge of the door and on the inside, mark the outline of the lock. Drill through the side rail, within this outline, and carefully chisel away the waste so that the lock fits snugly when it is slipped into place behind the door front.

Once the lock has been fitted, the door should be closed and the key operated so that the lock bolt marks the edge of the other door. With a chisel, cut a rebate in this position for the lock bolt, and then cover the recess with a striking plate (also supplied with the lock). This is held in position, and its outline is marked with a knife. A shallow recess is then cut with a chisel so that the plate can be placed flush with the surface.

A cut cupboard lock, or drawer lock, is harder to fit because a recess has to be cut behind the cupboard or drawer front. A double recess is required – one for the lock mechanism, and the other for the back plate which is also recessed into the edge of the door or drawer for a neat fit and a smooth finish.

Hold the lock in position and mark the outline of the back plate on to the back and the edge of the door. Also mark where the mechanism rebate is required. First cut out the mechanism rebate using a chisel, then make the shallower rebate for the back plate. When the lock fits accurately, cut out the keyhole, then screw the lock in position. Fit the keyhole escutcheon and the striking plate as described above and finally check the lock.

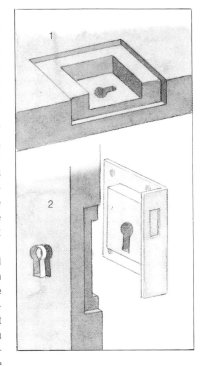

③ Fitting Cut Cupboard Lock
1 First chisel out the recess for the mechanism, then make a shallower rebate for the lock backplate. *2* When lock fits neatly, cut out keyhole.

① Fitting a Surface-Mounted Cupboard Door Lock
Make a template of lock outline. *1* Hold template on the door at lock position. *2* Drill hole and saw a slot. *3* Position the lock with the key in place. *4* Screw lock to door.

② Fitting a Cupboard Lock on a Framed Door
1 Hold the lock in position behind the frame and mark its outline. *2* Drill within the outline and chisel out waste. *3* Slide the lock through the aperture and fit as on left.

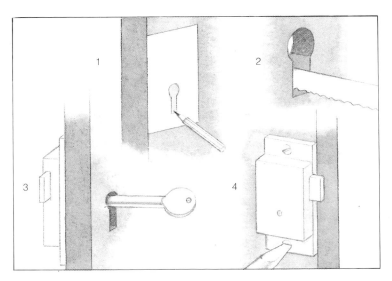

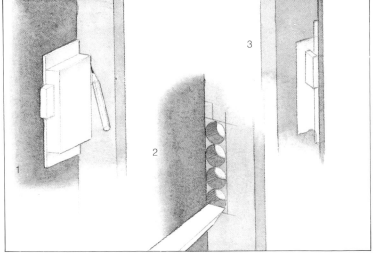

Fixing cladding Always fix cladding boards from the bottom upwards. Use a spirit level to check that the first board is horizontal – if it is not exactly level, the boards above will start to run out of true.

Nail through the centre of the first board into each of the vertical support battens behind, using 25mm (1in) galvanized round head nails. If boards have to be joined to span the full width of the structure, then butt the edges closely and ensure that joints are always made against a vertical support batten.

If you are fixing feather-edge boards, it is important that they overlap uniformly and you will need to use a spacing block cut from a spare piece of wood. If the boards are 112mm ($4\frac{1}{2}$in) wide and the spacer is 100mm (4in) wide then, by aligning the spacer with the bottom edge of the previously fixed board and resting the overlapping board on top, you will get a consistent overlap of 12mm ($\frac{1}{2}$in). Nail through the lower edge of each board, into the top edge of the board it overlaps and through into the batten.

Tongued-and-grooved boards are fixed by driving the nail at an angle through the tongue and tapping the head below the surface. The groove of the next board slides over the tongue to conceal the nail.

Shiplap cladding is fixed in the same way except that the boards do not interlock, but simply overlap.

Fixing trellis Trellis should be fixed about 150mm (6in) clear of the ground so that it will not rot at the base. Stand the trellis on blocks of the correct height while it is being secured to timber uprights or a wall. Use a spirit level to check that the horizontal rails are true, then drill holes into the side uprights of the trellis through which galvanized nails are inserted and then driven into the posts behind. If you nail directly into the trellis there is a chance the wood will split. Three fixings either side of an 1800mm (72in) high trellis panel will suffice. Alternatively, use purpose-made clips screwed to support posts. The trellis panel slots into clips and are then screwed in place.

When fixing to a wall, use 25mm (1in) thick wood blocks behind each fixing point to keep the trellis clear. Pre-drill the holes and use about 75mm (3in) long No 8 or 10 zinc-plated screws and wallplugs.

Fixing posts and poles On concrete paths and paving slabs laid on mortar you can use a steel base as a fixing point for posts. The base is a square plate with a projecting cup into which the post is located. The base is bolted in place.

Metal post spikes are driven into the earth. Again, the post fits into a square cup and is cramped in place. As the post is above ground it is far less susceptible to rotting at the base.

Posts and poles can be fixed directly into soil. In firm soil and where shorter posts are used, then well-compacted hardcore is usually adequate support. In loose soil and for longer posts and poles, a combination of stones and concrete should be used. For a post 1800mm (72in) high, at least 600mm (24in) should be buried below ground.

④ Fixing Cladding
Top Nail tongue, then slot groove of next board over. *Bottom* Use spacing block for feather-edge boards.

⑤ Fixing Posts
Left and top right Post spikes fix posts in place. *Bottom right* Post hole borer digs hole in which to fix post.

⑥ Fixing Trellis Panels
Panel clips are screwed to vertical support posts. Trellis panels slot into clips and are screwed in place.

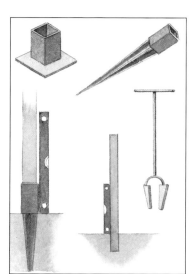

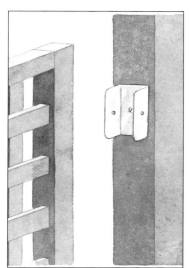

TECHNIQUES: TILING

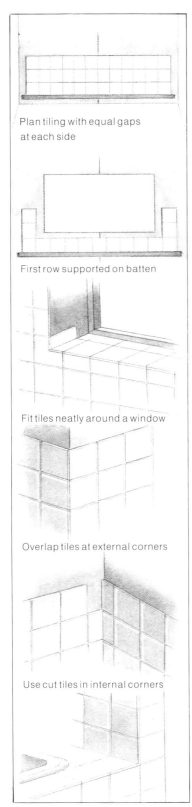

Plan tiling with equal gaps at each side

First row supported on batten

Fit tiles neatly around a window

Overlap tiles at external corners

Use cut tiles in internal corners

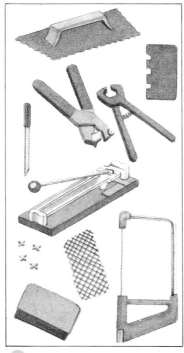

Tools for Tiling
Top to bottom **Adhesive spreaders – metal and plastic; scoring tool; cutting pliers; tile nippers; heavy-duty cutter; spacers; file; saw; grout spreader.**

Planning When tiling, accurate setting out is essential. The tiles must be applied absolutely level and, after tiling, no cut edges should show. Only factory-glazed edges, or half-round edge tiles which are made to be seen, should be visible. With the modular frames of the basic kitchen units (see page 30) note that the frame width is designed so that the front face tiles exactly cover the ends of the frames and the edges of the tiles fixed to each side of the frames. Tiles on the side panels are arranged so that cut tiles are right at the back of the units. Similarly, if any tiles have to be reduced in height, these cut tiles should be at floor-level where they will be less noticeable.

When tiling a plain wall, centralize the tiles on it, using cut tiles of equal width in each corner. If the wall has a prominent window, arrange the tiles to give it a neat border. In both cases, adjust the height of the tiles by having cut tiles at floor or skirting-board level. Plan your tiling scheme so that part-tiled walls and low vertical surfaces, such as the side of a bath, have whole tiles on the top

row. You may have to compromise on the best overall arrangement for the room. To deal with window reveals (recesses), have glazed edges visible around the front of the reveal, and have cut tiles butting up to the window frame.

Setting out Start by making a gauging rod. This is simply a length of straight timber, about 38×12mm ($1\frac{1}{2} \times \frac{1}{2}$in), on which pencil lines are drawn to indicate tile widths, including spacers. To mark the lines, lay out a row of tiles along the gauging rod, with spacers between them – unless tiles incorporating spacers are being used. Draw a line across the gauging rod to coincide with the centre of each joint. If rectangular tiles are used, a second gauging rod is needed for tile heights.

Use the gauging rod(s) to set out accurately the tile positions. When you are satisfied with the arrangement, fix a perfectly straight batten of timber (about 38×12mm [$1\frac{1}{2} \times \frac{1}{2}$in]) horizontally across the full width of the area to be tiled to support the first row of complete tiles. Next, fix vertical battens at each side to support the

Making a Gauging Rod
Lay out a correctly spaced row of tiles and on a batten accurately mark tile widths including spacers.

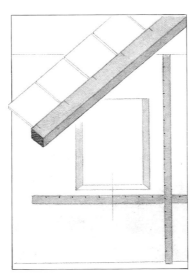

Setting out the Wall
Centralize tiles on a dominant feature like a window, and fix batten one tile height above floor.

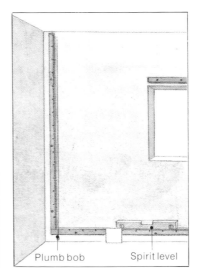

Plumb bob   Spirit level

Starting to Fix Tiles
Also fix vertical battens at each side. Spread adhesive in corner and press tiles firmly into place.

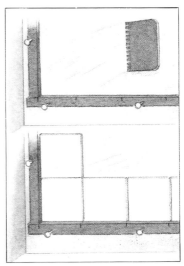

last row of complete tiles at the sides and to keep the tiling square. Use the gauging rods to mark off on the wall battens the exact tile widths and heights, as this will help you to keep the tiling square. If you are tiling a plastered wall, temporarily fix the tiling battens with partly driven-in masonry nails. If tiling on wood or plywood, use ordinary wire nails.

TILING TOOLS

Adhesive spreader A simple evenly notched plastic tool which spreads a bed of tile adhesive.

Tile cutter There are various types of tile cutters available. Some resemble a pencil and have a tungsten-carbide tip which is drawn across the tile to score the surface where the break is required. A better type is a cutter resembling a pair of pincers. This has a cutting wheel to score a cut line, as well as jaws between which the tile is placed before the cutter handles are squeezed, pincer-like, to make the cut. A heavy-duty cutter for thick, large tiles consists of a jig with a cutting-lever arm.

Tile saw Consists of a tungsten-carbide rod-saw blade fitted into a frame. It will cut tiles to any shape: L-shaped, curved, etc. The tile to be sawn is cramped in a vice.

Tile spacers Nowadays it is common for tiles to be supplied with plain edges, rather than with built-in spacer lugs moulded on the edges of the tiles. Spacer lug tiles are simply butted together and are automatically evenly spaced as they are positioned. However, with plain-edge tiles it is important to place spacers between the tiles as they are positioned. This creates even gaps between the tiles for grouting.

Tile nippers A pincer like device for removing narrow strips which are too small to be handled by a conventional cutter. It will also cut shaped tiles.

Tile file Useful for cleaning up sharp and uneven edges of a cut tile.

Grout spreader Flexible rubber blade for spreading grout.

Sponge Used for cleaning away adhesive and grout from the surface of a fixed tile.

Tiling process Start in a bottom corner and spread adhesive over about 1 square metre (1 square yard). Rake it out evenly using the notched spreader which is usually supplied with the adhesive. Working from a corner, press the tiles into the adhesive with a slight twisting motion. If tiles without spacers are used, hold them evenly apart with plastic wall-tile spacers. These can either be pressed well into the joints and left in place, or they can protrude from the surface, in which case they can be pulled out after an hour or so and re-used elsewhere. At this stage, fit whole tiles only. Tiles that have to be cut to fit around obstacles can be fitted later.

Cutting edge tiles Wait for 12 hours after the main area of tiling has been completed, before removing the setting-out battens. Tiles can then be cut to fill the gaps around the perimeter. Measure the space into which the tile is to fit, remembering to allow for the spacers between tiles. Use a tile cutter to cut a straight line across the surface of the tile. Use the notched spreader to apply adhesive direct to the back of the tile, and press it into place. If necessary, smooth rough edges with tile file.

Cutting around difficult shapes To cut around a pipe, snap the tile along the centre line of the pipe, then score the pipe's outline on the surface. For a neat finish, saw around the pipe outline using a tungsten-carbide rod-saw held in a conventional hacksaw frame. Alternatively, nip away the pipe cut-out by snapping off small pieces of the tile, using tile nippers or a pair of pincers. Tiles to be fitted around basins and window openings can also be scored along the cutting line and then nipped. Alternatively, the cut out can be sawn to avoid breakages if the part to be cut out runs close to the edge of the tile.

Finishing off Once the tiles are firm they should be grouted with a waterproof grout applied with a rubber spreader. When the grout is just beginning to set, use a small rounded stick to press the grout into the joint lines, then wipe off the excess grout with a damp sponge. When the grouting has dried, polish the surface with a dry duster.

---

5 Cutting Tiles to Size
Score along glazed side, then break tile along line using a cutting tool. Saw awkward shapes.

6 Cutting Around Pipes
Mark position of hole on face of tile. Snap tile along centre line. Score outline, then nip out waste.

7 Grouting Tiles to Finish
Use rubber blade squeegee to press grout into joints. As grout sets press rounded stick along joints.

8 Drilling a Hole in Tiles
Stick masking tape on drill point. Use masonry drill bit. Switch to hammer action when tile drilled through.

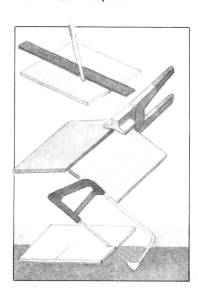

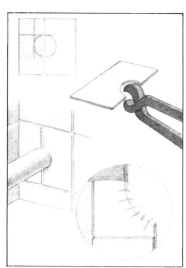

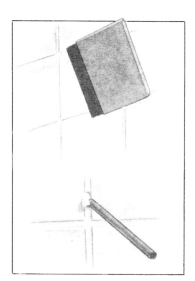

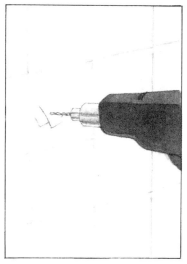

SAFETY

Hundreds of thousands of accidents occur in the home every year. Many of these are the result either of adults undertaking do-it-yourself tasks or of children playing in unsafe environments. Before making any of the projects in this book, always observe the following recommendations.

ADULT SAFETY

Never rush a woodworking or other kind of home improvement job: make sure that you know exactly what skills, tools and materials you will need *before* you start work. This means reading the project instructions, cross-referring to any techniques you are unfamilar with, and, if necessary, practising first on a piece of scrap wood. Check that you have the right tools, and that they are in good working order. If, for any reason, you are borrowing or hiring a tool, read the instructions carefully before you use it, and, again, practise first on a piece of scrap wood.

A clean, tidy work area will enable you to work more quickly and in greater safety: remove waste and clutter at regular intervals. Take special care when using power tools, and always unplug them from the mains electricity when they are not in use. Keep children away from your work area, and warn them that your tools and materials are not toys to be played with. The rule of never leaving tools lying around is a fundamental one to observe if there are children in the house. Try to keep your work area well-ventilated, especially when you are using paint, varnish or solvents.

Wear sensible clothing. Remember that clothes are likely to get torn or dirty. Choose something old, but also consider how you can best protect yourself. Depending on the job, you may need: goggles or safety glasses to protect your eyes; a mask to protect against dust or fumes; gloves to protect your hands when handling, for example, glass; and stout footwear for a firm footing. Overalls are often the safest and most comfortable choice of general clothing.

Paint, turps, varnish and many preservatives are toxic, so treat them with care. Any item being built for use in a child's room or to be played with by a child should be decorated using non-toxic paint and varnish – this is particularly important for the Crib project (pages 120–5). The lead content in these products is now limited by law (for this reason never use up paint that might have been lying around for years), but paints and varnishes labelled 'non-toxic' must not contain any heavy metals at all.

MATERIALS

Cheap materials are a false economy. When choosing your materials, always buy the best you can afford. It is not only much more difficult to make the projects in this book if the faces do not meet properly, it is also more difficult to mark and cut out joints accurately, and more time-consuming, since you will have to plane down all the faces to remove splinters etc.

CHILD SAFETY

Many children sustain serious injuries simply by falling over toys left lying around the house: storage solutions such as the Storage House (pages 102–7) add a play element to tidying up, encouraging children to be as tidy as possible. Other accidents occur when children play with toys or items of furniture that have not been designed or made with children in mind. Make sure that a child is old enough to play with any given toy, and try to reduce the risk of accidents by throwing away any toys that are broken.

CONSTRUCTION

Corners and edges should be smoothed and rounded over wherever applicable: the edges of the panels and boxes in the Storage House must be kept flat and square for them to shut properly, whereas the exposed edges of the Rocking Chair (pages 126–131) can all be rounded over without the design being compromised. Screw heads should always be countersunk, and nail heads punched below the surface to reduce the risk of cuts or injury: use filler to cover the holes and, when it is dry, sand smooth with the surface.

Hinged items always present the risk of entrapment, usually of hands and fingers, feet and toes, but sometimes of a child's head; the latter usually occurs when very young children are holding on to a box with a hinged lid and are reaching inside. To minimize the risk, always make the space between the two hinged panels or surfaces either less than 5mm ($\frac{1}{4}$in) or greater than 12mm ($\frac{1}{2}$in). If you are hingeing a lid (a toy box, for example), bear in mind that a child may sustain additional injuries from the force and weight of the falling lid – in extreme circumstances, this has resulted in child fatalities. For this reason, always fit a support that will hold the lid open. Children have also been known to become trapped inside toy boxes, so it is an excellent idea to drill a couple of adequate ventilation holes in the sides.

FURNITURE

Bear in mind that robust, active children climb up and over all manner of surfaces not really intended for such treatment. Even the most vigilant parent or guardian will be unable to provide wholly uninterrupted supervision, so you should take care to anticipate hazards and reduce the risk of injury.

Children will use shelves, tables, chairs and open drawers in chests of drawers as steps to climb up. In children's rooms, especially, try to keep as much furniture as possible low down, and always use angle brackets or wallplugs to anchor large pieces of furniture to the wall so that there is no chance of them tipping over and causing injury. Bear in mind the weight of the headboard in the Bed with Truckle Drawer project (pages 108–19), since a child's fingers could get trapped. If you build the Wall of Display Shelving (pages 76–81), make sure young children don't see it as an indoor climbing frame – both they and the objects on display will be much safer if you keep them apart.

The Crib project has been built to carefully calculated dimensions for a new-born baby. If you want to make a larger crib for an older child, it is essential that you first investigate safety recommendations concerning spacing of slats, stability, and the risks of strangulation.

TOYS

The younger the child, the more careful you must be about choosing toys: what is safe for a seven-year-old may well be hazardous for a child of eighteen months. A number of the projects in this book involve movement, and these have all been designed and tested for strength and stability. For this reason you should not attempt to modify the designs without first consulting safety legislation concerning toys: up-to-date copies of all safety recommendations can be found at most large reference libraries.

With common sense, many of the potential hazards such as sharp points or edges can be eliminated. Beware of small, detachable parts, which children might swallow or choke on, and pay particular attention to the size and construction of rattles. Inspect labels to check the lead content of any paints you might want to use to decorate toys: the level of lead is now strictly controlled, but paint sold for use on metal furniture still has a relatively high lead content and should therefore never be used to paint toys.

Index

ACKNOWLEDGMENTS

The photographs in this book were specially taken for Conran Octopus by:

Richard Foster, art direction by Claire Lloyd: pages 2, 4 (centre), 6, 102–107, 120–153, 200–207; Hugh Johnson, styled by Claire Lloyd: pages 1, 4 (left and right), 7, 8, 10–35, 48–56, 58–65, 66 left, 67–72, 75 above, 76–81, 83–89, 92–101, 110–111; Simon Lee, styled by Claire Lloyd: pages 36–47, 57, 66 right, 73, 75 below, 82, 90–91, 108, 115, 117; Nadia Mackenzie: 5, 154, 156–199, 208–227.

The publisher would like to thank the following for their assistance:
Bridget Bodoano and the Conran Shop; David Jenkins and the Royal Society for the Prevention of Accidents; Alan Rayner and the staff of Servis Filmsetting Limited; Sean Sutcliffe, Wendy Jones and all at Benchmark Woodworking Limited.

Special thanks to Sean Sutcliffe of Benchmark Woodworking Limited, who built all of the projects; to Paul Bryant for his original artworks and to Sir Terence Conran for his project sketches.

Props in the photographs were lent by the following people, retailers and manufacturers: Alvin Ross/Alfie's Antiques Market; Aston-Matthews Ltd; Authentics; The Conran Shop; Decorative Living; Divertimenti; Eximious Ltd; Franke (UK) Ltd; Gallery of Antique Costume and Textiles; General Plumbing Supplies; Judy Greenwood Antiques; CP Hart Ltd; Heal & Sons Ltd; Ideal Standard Ltd; INC Office Equipment; Paul Jones; The Kitchen Range; London Architectural Salvage Company; Stephen Long Antiques; Meaker & Son; David Mellor Design Ltd; Mothercare UK Ltd; Neff (UK) Ltd; WH Newson and Sons Ltd; The Nursery; Papers and Paint Ltd; Philips Major Appliances Ltd; The Puffin Children's Bookshop; Gail Rose; The Singing Tree; The Tintin Shop; Sam Walker.